Maximizing the Policy Relevance of Research for School Improvement

A Volume in Leadership for School Improvement Series

Series Editor

Pamela S. Angelle
The University of Tennessee

Leadership for School Improvement Series

Pamela S. Angelle, Series Editor

Maximizing the Policy Relevance of Research for School Improvement (2021)
edited by Angela Urick, David DeMatthews, and Timothy G. Ford

Leadership for School Improvement: Reflection and Renewal (2019)
edited by Cherie B. Gaines

Maximizing the Policy Relevance of Research for School Improvement

editors

Angela Urick
Baylor University

David DeMatthews
University of Texas at Austin

Timothy G. Ford
University of Oklahoma

INFORMATION AGE PUBLISHING, INC.
Charlotte, NC • www.infoagepub.com

Library of Congress Cataloging-in-Publication Data

CIP record for this book is available from the Library of Congress
http://www.loc.gov

ISBNs: 978-1-64802-247-0 (Paperback)

978-1-64802-248-7 (Hardcover)

978-1-64802-249-4 (ebook)

Copyright © 2021 Information Age Publishing Inc.

All rights reserved. No part of this publication may be reproduced, stored in a retrieval system, or transmitted, in any form or by any means, electronic, mechanical, photocopying, microfilming, recording or otherwise, without written permission from the publisher.

Printed in the United States of America

CONTENTS

ACKNOWLEDGMENTS

The American Educational Research Association's Leadership for School Improvement Special Interest Group (SIG) has provided us with the support, guidance, and inspiration for this edited volume. We are truly thankful for their dedication to the field and support for this project. In particular, we would like to acknowledge Pam Angelle, the series editor, for her committed efforts, supports, and patience throughout this project. We would also like to acknowledge our colleagues who read, reviewed, and provided constructive feedback on this edited volume, including Curtis Brewer, *University of Texas at San Antonio*, Jayson Richardson, *University of Kentucky*, Virginia Snodgrass Rangel, *University of Houston*, Meredith Wronowski, *University of Dayton*, Don Peurach, *University of Michigan*, Arnold Shober, *Lawrence University*, Daniel Hamlin, *University of Oklahoma*, Elizabeth Farley-Ripple, *University of Delaware*, Joseph Ferrare, *University of Kentucky*, Verónica Vélez, *Western Washington University*, Timothy Drake, *North Carolina State University*, Katherine Cumings Mansfield, *University of North Carolina at Greensboro*, Daniella Hall, *Clemson University*, Debbie Kim, *Northwestern University*, Rachel White, *Old Dominion University*, and Liz Hollingworth, *University of Iowa*.

Maximizing the Policy Relevance of Research for School Improvement, pp. vii–vii
Copyright © 2021 by Information Age Publishing
All rights of reproduction in any form reserved.

CHAPTER 1

INTRODUCTION

Angela Urick
Baylor University

David DeMatthews
University of Texas at Austin

Timothy G. Ford
University of Oklahoma

OVERVIEW

Researchers in the field of educational leadership and policy have spent an enormous amount of time and resources investigating a wide range of elements associated with school improvement. They bring an array of methodological approaches and disciplinary insight to many of the pressing problems that confront schools as well as many of the promising avenues that contribute to school improvement. As a result of the committed efforts of educational researchers, the field has developed professional standards for school and district leaders, leadership and implementation frameworks, and a wide array of theories that policymakers, nonprofit organizations, district leaders, practitioners, and faculty can utilize to improve schools. The state of public education has been vastly improved partly through how research has been applied to policy and practice.

Maximizing the Policy Relevance of Research for School Improvement, pp. 1–12
Copyright © 2021 by Information Age Publishing
All rights of reproduction in any form reserved.

Despite significant improvements in schools, educational inequities and chronic underperformance persist in many contexts and for many marginalized student groups while schools and districts continue to confront a broad array of challenges. Policymakers, district leaders, and nonprofit organizations have directed their attention and resources to addressing a broad range of issues that impact school improvement, such as teacher retention, principal turnover, school choice regulations, professional and organizational learning, student attendance, achievement/opportunity gaps, racial disproportionality in special education, school-to-prison pipelines, bilingual education programming, and the implementation of high-stakes accountability policies. Many of these challenges do not have easy answers. Instead, these challenges are elusive, context-specific, and continuously-evolving in the ever-changing cultural, political, and economic systems that surround schools and policymaking.

Educational researchers working in diverse contexts investigate many of the challenges confronting schools as well as the policies, programs, and approaches that lead to school improvement. In some cases, policymakers have utilized educational research to inform policy. For example, research on effective schools and their leaders in the 1970s (Edmonds & Frederikson, 1978) provided critical insights into effective leadership practices. By the 1980s, this body of research facilitated new school improvement practices and, in some instances, changed the way principals were evaluated (Hallinger & Murphy, 1985). At the same time, starting in the late 1970s, federal programs focused on educational change emerged (Berman & McLaughlin, 1978). This movement culminated in The Comprehensive School Reform Demonstration Program (Title I, Part F; Rowan et al., 2009), which spurred the development of a substantial number of school improvement models—some of which are still being used today. More recently, researchers focused on creating socially just and inclusive schools have provided key insights into effective leadership practices for marginalized students (Theoharis, 2007). Both effective schools research and research focused on inclusion and social justice now permeate professional standards for principal preparation and practice. The U.S. Department of Education and many state education agencies now offer guidance and resource investments based on empirical research to further advance leadership research and preparation.

Researchers have also offered warnings to policymakers and have pointed out significant problems with current and proposed legislation. However, policymakers have not always headed researcher warnings or critically considered existing research. For example, researchers have sounded the alarm about school finance and provided empirical evidence that "money matters" in public education despite the fact that many states maintain inequitable systems of school finance (Baker, 2018). Currently many states are dealing with increasing teacher and leader shortages and the cumulative impacts of high turnover (Darling-Hammond & Podolsky, 2019; Grissom & Bartanen, 2019)—despite the fact that, for decades, researchers have been sounding alarms about the impending "unintended consequences" of overly-punitive zero-tolerance discipline policies (Skiba & Knesting, 2001) as well as high-stakes accountability policies (Nichols & Berliner, 2007). Today, many schools continue to wrestle with these unintended consequences, such as school-to-prison pipelines, cheating scandals, and teaching to the test.

Unfortunately, federal, state, and local policymakers do not sufficiently utilize educational research to inform their decisions. Perhaps, they have their own political agendas and preconceptions. Perhaps it appears that traditional forms of educational research published in academic journals and behind paywalls appear to be more about promoting faculty careers than they are to informing policy decisions. While we do not agree with this perspective outright, we recognize that researchers must come to terms with the fact that traditional forms of scholarship (e.g., academic journals, academic books) are frequently underutilized, ignored, or inaccessible by certain audiences. We believe the field of educational leadership and policy must reconsider elements of research training and current practice and be more responsive in their approaches to design, implementation, research translation, and communication.

Maximizing the Policy Relevance of Research for School Improvement provides a comprehensive examination of the policymaking process, research designs to maximize policy relevance, and multiple ways to disseminate research to policymakers and other audiences. This book's contributors include nationally and internationally recognized educational researchers from across the United States and Canada. The book was initially conceived based on the editors' belief that educational research must play a more significant role in policy development at federal, state, local levels. As faculty in educational leadership and policy programs, we, as the editors, have each individually worked to translate our research in ways that improve schools. We have worked with university research centers, partnered with school districts, and sought ways to utilize our research and expertise to shape policy and improve schools. Our own research has provided insights into effective styles of principal leadership within struggling schools (Urick & Bowers, 2014; Urick et al., 2018), how effective principals create inclusive schools for students with disabilities (DeMatthews et al., 2020), and the role of districts in school leader development and success (Ford et al., 2020). Each of us care deeply about our research areas and have a strong desire to see our research be utilized in policymaking.

We have also recognized that the tenure and promotion system at many universities and professional associations for educational research do not necessarily incentivize research that informs policy. Yet, as we have engaged with our colleagues, we have recognized that most faculty and graduate students have a sincere desire to improve schools and a sincere hope that policymakers utilize their research. Through these experiences, we have come to recognize that researchers have a critical role to play in informing policymakers, but that engaging in the policy arena is a two-way street. Policymakers should rely upon research to inform their decisions, but as educational researchers we must also be knowledgeable about policymaking processes and develop and communicate research in ways that are relevant and accessible to policymakers. Thus, the book was developed and organized as a guide to how educational researchers can maximize the policy relevance of their scholarship. We hope that *Maximizing the Policy Relevance of Research for School Improvement* is not just a guide for researchers and graduate students, but also prompts continued discussions and efforts to ensure educational research is utilized in policymaking.

SIGNIFICANCE OF THIS BOOK

Education policy and policymaking is shaped through the activities of a complex network of educators, educational leaders, researchers, community members, as well as government and nongovernment officials and organizations. Educational researchers are a critical player in this complex network and their investigations of various educational phenomena can answer questions relevant to the design and implementation of education policy for school improvement. Educational research, however, often has limited influence in larger policy conversations and decisions (Orland, 2009), and this is due to many factors. Educational researchers can provide an evidence-based starting place for discussions about school improvement with the complex network of stakeholders engaged in policy development and implementation, but they must be more intentionally and systematically thoughtful about the connections of their work to policy and policy making. Furthermore, researchers can increase the relevance of their work for policy through the careful design and framing of research in collaboration with end-users, and an awareness of its implications. In so doing, researchers can spur the interest and dissemination of their findings to wider audiences. This book offers resources for education researchers, faculty, and advanced graduate students interested in maximizing the relevance of their research on policy for school improvement. In achieving this purpose, the book is organized into three sections: (1) A primer for education policymaking in the United States; (2) Designing research to maximize its policy relevance; and (3) Engaging users of research to communicate its relevance to policymakers.

TARGET AUDIENCE

This book is primarily for education researchers, faculty, and advanced graduate students seeking to improve the visibility and impact of their research on school improvement, particularly in the realm of educational policy and policy making. While this book is a volume in the book series for the American Educational Research Association Special Interest Group, *Leadership for School Improvement*, the importance and usefulness of the topics covered span education research more broadly. Further, the content of this book serves as a comprehensive guide for how education researchers, in general, can better situate their work to influence policy. The book is intended to be utilized by university scholars, graduate students in research or policy courses, postdoctoral fellows, as well as research associates or directors in various organizations relevant to education such as research consulting groups, nonprofits which serve education causes, teacher unions, state agencies or state-level educator organizations/associations, and think tanks. Emerging or established researchers in any of these organizations who want to increase the relevance, significance, and dissemination of their work into education policy will hopefully find this book useful.

WHAT IS COVERED IN EACH CHAPTER?

Educational researchers who seek to maximize the relevance of their research can more effectively do so when they understand the education policy process. Section I, A Primer on Education Policy Making, provides foundational knowledge of the educational policy process. Section I focuses on federal and state policymaking processes, dynamics, and networks, which can help researchers develop a research agenda that can be effectively communicated and translated to policymakers. In Chapter 2, Feldman and Davis provide a detailed account of policy development and implementation at the federal level. They outline a general timeline and process of policy movement which offer multiple vantage points for researcher involvement. Researchers can engage in the Congressional work surrounding bills, appropriations, implementation, and oversight. The authors explain formal procedures as well as political dynamics which converge during policy making and enactment. While this chapter is an overview of federal legislative processes, it is also an introduction to U.S. government which is similar to state level policy making processes.

In Chapter 3, Wisman and Ingle begin by introducing the U.S. education policy context surrounding state level policy. They describe a "new politics of education," detailed by the last 40 years of reform in policy on choice, standards, testing, and accountability. The chapter highlights how different actors have informed particular policy stages. The authors describe policy actors' activities as well as the story lines used to further interests in Common Core State Standards, high-stakes accountability, and charter school legislation. Research or intellectual/creative activity is its own structure which can inform multiple phases of the policy process. The chapter provides recommendations for state level policy researchers, which include extending theories and frameworks guiding studies and seeking a deeper understanding of the interconnections across policies. Of note, this chapter supplies readers with a general understanding of policy frameworks which outline who and what to study.

Educational researchers often develop their scholarly agendas based on their disciplinary training and interest. Historically, research training has not provided significant attention to how research design can influence the policy relevance of research. Section II, Designing Research to Maximize Education Policy Relevance, provides an overview of qualitative, quantitative, and mixed-methods design as well as additional insights into innovative research approaches. In Chapter 4, Woodward, Quinn, Lilly, and Youngs describe the benefits and limitations of research designs for relevance in policy and practice. While experimental designs have been preferred by mainstream education research outlets for the last few decades, such designs are often unable to detail the "how" and "why" which can directly describe needs of actors as a basis for practical changes using local context. The authors explain how experiments, qualitative research, mixed methods, and improvement science designs can contribute policy-relevant findings using example studies which follow high-impact criteria. The chapter provides a review of strengths and weaknesses of each design and how researchers can plan a study and larger research agenda that delivers meaningful findings with information and evidence translatable to policy and practice.

In Chapter 5, Reyes and Scott describe the "how" and "why" of conducting experimental, quasi-experimental, and survey design research to inform education policy. They use a post-positivist perspective to provide readers with a set of assumptions and criteria to follow when applying each design. Because these designs are often used to evaluate programs which stemmed from legislation or policy, the authors discuss their limitations and the surrounding ethical issues which provide the reader with information on how to translate their findings into practice.

In addressing the potential of qualitative research for informing school improvement efforts at both the national and international levels, Potterton and Malin, in Chapter 6, first consider the marginalization of qualitative methods in educational policy research, asserting that too-narrow a focus on "what works" research has served to privilege quantitative research over other methods. Instead, they argue for a renewed recognition of the complementary nature of quantitative and qualitative methods in helping to answer important policy questions, citing the charter school literature as one particular space where qualitative work is being effectively used to fill in the gaps in understandings of this phenomenon left unaddressed by "what works" research. They also cite several seminal qualitative studies in the field of education they feel have had lasting impact on the field and still hold potential policy relevance today. It is through the discussion of these seminal works, as well as a discussion of the potential of knowledge mobilization that Potterton and Malin make the case for how qualitative research can reclaim a space in key education policy debates. They conclude by providing the field with specific examples of these spaces for further investigation within specific areas of policy and school improvement research.

In Chapter 7, Hewitt and Mansfield explain why and how mixed methods approaches can be policy relevant. Mixed methods designs integrate two forms of data which together create a third perspective of understanding for greater depth, context, and leverage. The authors describe the application of six mixed methods designs: convergent parallel, sequential explanatory, exploratory sequential, embedded, transformative, and multiphase. They distinguish between applications or examples which research *on* policy compared to research *for* policy. This distinction makes the reader aware of how to design mixed methods research with a clear policy-relevant purpose. The way in which different mixed designs can address a purpose guides how we engage with policy makers and practitioners, train future researchers, and prioritize the integration of data.

In Chapter 8, Lenhoff, Singer, and Pogodzinski detail the ways in which researchers can use improvement science to evaluate their own policy relevance in research on teams with multiple types of partners (e.g., schools, intermediary organizations, policymakers, or government officials). These authors review literature on research use, improvement science, and research partnerships to examine how they have applied these approaches with their own partnerships in Detroit. They reflect on this research using feedback data collected from their partners. Through this discussion and analysis, they describe how they identified improvement within their research designs, communication, and dissemination. The authors help the reader to understand the nuances of working with external partners toward policy improvement compared to instructional improvement. They provide clear suggestions on the application of improvement science to inform the planning and execution of research, how to facilitate feedback data collection, and the ways in which we might evaluate our impact on policymaking.

In Chapter 9, Wang describes the theoretical background and application of social network analysis in education policy. She provides an understanding of types of networks to study as well as select theories used to explain the connections between actors. Based on this foundational knowledge, she then supplies the reader with methodological approaches using graph theory and defining levels of analysis (i.e., network, node, and dyadic). Wang highlights the value of pairing social network analysis (SNA) with other quantitative or qualitative approaches to further understand related outcomes. She closes with a call to researchers to extend theory based on the use of SNA in education policy and to apply new statistical analyses which appropriately handle interdependent data.

In Chapter 10, Houston, Brewer, and Wronowski encourage the application of critical frameworks to education policy research by outlining the importance of critiquing systems of power and promoting the need for justice. These authors present the main arguments for the use of critical theory, key theorists and how critical theory can be applied to policy research. Next, the application of these approaches within educational policy are described through example studies. With these studies, they provide some suggestions for how to use critical frameworks given particular research methodologies. Finally, the authors conclude by discussing the current realities surrounding policy-relevant research with a critical approach as well as the dangers of ignoring it. Readers are challenged to reflect on their own scholarship with this understanding of how critical theories can transform policy and practice.

In Chapter 11, Cobb explores the ways in which researchers can situate their implications as policy relevant. He explains how researchers might "drop the mic" by purposefully bridging the gaps between research-to-practice and research-to-policy. Cobb provides background about how to position findings for use on the four "Ps," policy, program, procedure, and practice. The chapter also provides background about the categories of research use, instrumental, conceptual, and symbolic, in order to attend to the what and how of implications. He extends these discussions into how this framing is dependent on the selection of research methods and communication with the intended user. Further, planning these approaches from the beginning of a study allows researchers to offer direct implications to a target audience through an appropriate dissemination outlet. Readers are encouraged to identify areas of need from proposed collective research agendas within the field, and to think about reform from the "inside out."

Educational researchers can become experts on state and federal policymaking and strategically develop their research agendas to maximize the policy relevance of their scholarship. Unfortunately, such actions do not guarantee that research findings will widely be disseminated or read by policymakers. Other audiences can impact policymakers, such as the general public, grassroots advocacy organizations, and community organizations. Section III, Engaging Users of Research to Communicate its Relevance, focuses on how educational researchers can translate their research to broader audiences to inform the public, policymakers, and other critical stakeholders. In Chapter 12, Price guides readers through six stages of actively involving policymakers in the research process. This chapter suggests activities, check points, and workshops to build a collaboration with policymakers and key partners across these stages. These six stages include: form a collaboration, assess needs, design the study, share data, discuss results, and establish a feedback loop. Readers are provided with tools and examples to understand how to progress communication to establish a trusting and transparent relationship as well as to support organizational learning and absorptive capacity. The chapter provides insights into how researchers can translate the bounds of study design, data, results, and limitations to partners. and policymakers are able to provide critique and context to researchers to strengthen the implications gained from study results. This bidirectional relationship is mutually beneficial and maximizes the usefulness of research.

In Chapter 13, MacGregor and Cooper describe the current landscape of research-practice-partnerships and their brokering functions. They detail the nature of operating partnerships with an international environmental scan of existing relationships and use these networks to explain brokering activities: linkages, awareness, accessibility, policy influence, engagement, organizational development, implementation support and capacity building. Finally, readers are provided with effective, concrete strategies to improve evidence-use, such as secondments, statements of needs, and asset maps, among others.

In Chapter 14, Biddle and Mitra explain community advocacy with the case of "Communicating School Redesign," which is the implementation of Act 77, a Vermont state policy. This case is an example of how policy can be enacted with public values. Researchers, community groups, and intermediary organizations collaboratively created structures to empower the inclusion of local voices, and active, shared participation, in the shaping of flexible pathways for high school completion. Up for Learning, an intermediary organization providing technical support, promoted the development of youth-adult partnerships across the state to lead school reform efforts for this state policy. The authors share examples of how youth-adult partnerships within different school contexts facilitated community organization efforts to understand how to implement this policy through wide, inclusive dialogue and several other locally-based communication techniques and structures. This case highlights the importance of student-led change processes for conversations around difficult issues, such as equity, and for a focus on the local context and needs.

In Chapter 15, DeMatthews, Reddick, and James explain the value and purpose of writing editorials as a researcher, and particularly as university faculty members. Editorials provide an outlet for scholars to engage in public discourse on important and timely issues. These editorials can help to shape public opinion and translate the work of researchers in accessible language and action. The authors share their backgrounds in education along with their personal experiences writing editorials. They give an overview of general approaches to editorials, word counts, collaborations, outlets, and key tips to consider, such as timeliness, knowing the audience, and getting feedback.

In Chapter 16, Ravitch, Vasquez Heilig, and Brewer discuss the importance of blogging and why they blog. Ravitch, a prolific blogger, posts multiple times a day and understands her purpose as political to push the world in a certain direction. Vasquez Heilig, an occasional blogger, began a blog after receiving tenure because of university administrators' warnings about adversaries to public stances on equity and education policy. He now has a far-reaching blog, with occasional posts, which has had breaking news, provided rapid scholarship, and counternarratives. Brewer, a sporadic blogger, had his first publication of his master's thesis as a blog post. He understands his scholarly work as a commitment to both publishing in peer-reviewed journals and publishing in public platforms. These authors discuss blogging as an extension of traditional academic work and as grounded in academic data. Blogs are a medium for knowledge mobilization in public discourse.

In their concluding commentary, Farley-Ripple, Tilley, Shewchuk, and Sheridan discuss strategies for researchers to gain relevance by framing research-practice-policy gaps with five issues, products, problems, methods, relationships, and structures. While these gaps exist because of a difference in researcher and practitioner cultures and a lack of bidirectional process, the authors provide suggestions to researchers on how to begin to overcome each challenge. For example, researchers can adapt the format of products to connect with practitioner contexts and allow for easy interpretation, and researchers can better understand the needs of practitioners before identifying problems of study, methods and resulting implications. Specific recommendations are provided for each gap along with data on researcher and practitioner perspectives on research approaches and use. Overall, the authors suggest collective action by researchers to redefine how we plan studies, train others, engage practitioners and build systems around our progress, such as tenure expectations, to attend to gaps in relevance.

A CALL TO ACTION

Making research relevant is urgent in an era of information overload, misinformation, and constant connectivity over social media and online media outlets. Traditional norms based on university faculty expectations for tenure and promotion as well as the slow pacing of research products (i.e., academic articles and books) has not prepared the field to address timely challenges faced by practitioners and policy makers. This problem or disconnect between the culture of roles—the problem of the "ivory tower" as it were—has left many researchers, and their findings, out of important decision-making discussions. If scholars want to influence change in education, we must carefully position ourselves and our work as an influential voice in these discussions since we do not hold formal positions of authority or make critical policy decisions at the federal, state, or local levels. Kalil (2017) describes researchers who generate new ideas, identify, and evaluate policy options, support public decision making, ensure implementation, and monitor effectiveness as *policy entrepreneurs*. These policy entrepreneurs are able to extend resources and authority beyond their control because they have an agenda, make it easy for others to help, follow up and through, find and recruit allies, and plan with the end in mind. As researchers, by purposefully framing our work and engaging in relationships with key partners, we can learn how to situate ourselves as a vital training resource and knowledge contributor to resolve our field's most pressing issues. We hope that this book inspires and guides your journey to relevance, as it has ours.

REFERENCES

Baker, B. D. (2018). *Educational inequality and school finance: Why money matters for America's students.* Harvard Education Press.

Berman, P., & McLaughlin, M. W. (1978). *Federal programs supporting educational change: Implementing and sustaining innovations* (Vol. VIII). RAND.

Darling-Hammond, L., & Podolsky, A. (2019). Breaking the cycle of teacher shortages: What kind of policies can make a difference? *Educational Policy Analysis Archives, 27*, 1–34.

DeMatthews, D. E., Serafini, A., & Watson, T. S. (2020). Leading inclusive schools: Principal perceptions, practices, and challenges to meaningful change. *Educational Administration Quarterly.* https://doi.org/10.1177/0013161X20913897

Edmonds, R., & Frederikson, J. (1978). *Search for effective schools: The identification and analysis of city schools that are instructional effective for poor children.* Center for Urban Studies.

Ford, T. G., Lavigne, A. L., Fiegener, A. M., & Si, S. (2020). Understanding district support for leader development and success in the accountability era: A review of the literature using social-cognitive theories of motivation. *Review of Educational Research, 90*(2), 264–307. https://doi.org/10.3102/0034654319899723

Grissom, J., & Bartanen, B. (2019). Principal effectiveness and principal turnover. *Education Finance and Policy, 14*(3), 355–382.

Hallinger, P., & Murphy, J. (1985). Assessing the instructional management behavior of principals. *Elementary School Journal, 86*(2), 217–247.

Kahlil, T. (2017). Policy entrepreneurship in the White House: Getting things done in large organizations. *Innovations.* https://www.mitpressjournals.org/doi/pdf/10.1162/inov_a_00253

Nichols, S., & Berliner, D. (2007). *Collateral damage: How high-stakes testing corrupts America's schools.* Harvard Education Press.

Orland, M. (2009). Separate orbits: The distinctive worlds of educational research and policymaking. In G. Sykes, B. Schneider, & D. N. Plank (with T. G. Ford) (Eds.), *Handbook of education policy research* (pp. 129-144). Routledge.

Rowan, B., Correnti, R., Miller, R. J., & Camburn, E. (2009). School improvement by design: Lessons from a study of comprehensive school reform programs. In G. Sykes, B. Schneider, & D. N. Plank (with T. G. Ford) (Eds.), *Handbook of educational policy research* (pp. 637–651). Routledge.

Skiba, R. J., & Knesting, K. (2001). Zero tolerance, zero evidence: An analysis of school disciplinary practice. *New Directions for Youth Development, 92,* 17–43.

Theoharis, G. (2007). Social justice educational leaders and resistance: Toward a theory of social justice leadership. *Educational Administration Quarterly, 43*(2), 221–258.

Urick, A., & Bowers, A. J. (2014). What are the different types of principals across the United States? A latent class analysis of principal perception of leadership. *Educational Administration Quarterly, 50*(1), 96–134.

Urick, A., Wilson, A. S., Ford, T. G., Frick, W. C., & Wronowski, M. L. (2018). Testing a framework of math progress indicators for ESSA: How opportunity to learn and instructional leadership matter. *Educational Administration Quarterly, 54*(3), 396–438.

SECTION I

A PRIMER ON EDUCATION POLICYMAKING IN THE UNITED STATES

CHAPTER 2

THE FEDERAL EDUCATION POLICY PROCESS

Rachel Carly Feldman
NORC at the University of Chicago

Kendrick B. Davis
The Campaign for College Opportunity

INTRODUCTION

On December 17, 2018, Senator Lamar Alexander (R-TN) announced he would not seek reelection in 2020. As chairman of the Senate Health, Education, Labor, and Pensions (HELP) Committee and a long-time education reformer, his announcement led to speculation that a comprehensive reauthorization of the Higher Education Act of 1965 (HEA) might occur.

Reauthorization of the HEA had not taken place since 2008, and with more and more Americans enrolling in postsecondary education, and more of them taking on significant debt loads, the legislation was due for updating. Of considerable interest was the nexus between student debt and accountability of institutions of higher education. Indeed, since becoming eligible to receive federal student aid, the for-profit sector had swelled. Questionable lending practices, sudden closures, and poor student outcomes led to calls for increased oversight of the sector. To encourage reform of the

Maximizing the Policy Relevance of Research for School Improvement, pp. 15–42
Copyright © 2021 by Information Age Publishing
All rights of reproduction in any form reserved.

industry, the Obama Department of Education implemented "gainful employment" regulations to measure student outcomes and hold institutions accountable to them ("Program Integrity," 2014). Regulations that were revoked by the Trump Department of Education ("Program Integrity," 2019). This regulatory back-and-forth, and others like it, suggested the need for lawmakers to determine the path forward—something which could occur with HEA reauthorization.

While there had been movement towards a comprehensive reauthorization in 2017, it had fizzled out by the end of the 115th Congress. Talks about reauthorization had stalled in both the House and Senate, albeit for different reasons. House Education and Workforce Committee Chairwoman Virginia Foxx (R-NC-5) introduced the Promoting Real Opportunity, Success, and Prosperity through Education Reform or PROSPER Act (H.R. 4508, 115 Cong.), her comprehensive HEA reform, which, while making it through committee (on a partisan vote) and onto the floor of the House, never received a full vote. In the Senate, no such comprehensive reform was put forth. So, the 115th Congress came and went without reauthorization.

The education community held no illusions that the 116th Congress would be any different. With the House of Representatives now controlled by Democrats, the Republican PROSPER Act would never move forward, and the new chairman of the Education and Labor Committee,[1] Bobby Scott (D-VA-3), would promote his own comprehensive bill. With the Senate still in the Republican majority, an HEA reauthorization would require a bipartisan bill in order to pass both chambers. Given the lack of movement when Republicans controlled both chambers, optimism waned, and members of Congress and their staffs resigned themselves to another Congress with little comprehensive movement.

Then Alexander announced his retirement, including HEA reauthorization in his intended legacy. Overnight, the conversation changed. Perhaps a bipartisan bill could be created? Bills slowly being prepped for reintroduction had their timelines pushed forward. Staffers indicated to outside interest groups that some of their priorities might move. Excitement built. Why the change in speculation? As the chair of the HELP Committee and with a lengthy history of supporting education both as the governor of Tennessee and as U.S. Secretary of Education, only Alexander had the authority to ensure an HEA reauthorization bill made it out of committee. With bipartisan support, Senate Majority Leader Mitch McConnell (R-KY) would likely bring the bill to the floor for a vote. Why the rush to reintroduce existing bills impacting sections of HEA? If Alexander wanted HEA to be his crowning achievement, then negotiations would have to occur sometime in the summer of 2019, and any member wishing to have their priorities included would need to introduce their bills beforehand.

This story illustrates both the standard operating procedures and political realities that influence the federal policy process. As Congressional priorities change, bills that have languished in Congress may become viable for passage. In this chapter, we outline the federal policy process—from ideation to implementation—concentrating on potential sites of engagement for education researchers. First, we briefly discuss the parameters of the federal role in education policy as distinct from the role states play. Then, we describe the federal legislative process beginning with bill development through its potential passage into law. Next, we give an overview of how the budgeting, appropriating, and legislating processes influence policy implementation. Then, we discuss how executive agency regulations and policies further shape the enactment of law and lastly, we provide an overview of Congress's oversight responsibilities.

THE LIMITED FEDERAL ROLE IN EDUCATION POLICY

Policies affecting the education of children primarily occur outside of the federal government. Partly because the Tenth Amendment of the Constitution designates to the states powers not explicitly assigned to the federal government, the jurisdiction of the federal government in education is limited. While variation occurs across education sectors, with an increased federal role in higher education and early childhood, most education policy is determined at the state and local levels. State legislatures have continually addressed issues of importance to their states without federal guidance, such as deciding curriculum and teacher certification standards locally. States practice a range of oversight models from prescriptive to permissive in determining how local education agencies can select curricula. For example, while the federal government encouraged their adoption, states independently developed and adopted the Common Core State Standards to provide "consistent, real-world learning goals" for all U.S. students (Common Core State Standards Initiative, 2019).

Education funding is also concentrated at the state and local level. Less than 10% of K–12 funding is provided by the federal government (Leachman et al., 2017). And while in higher education the federal-state division of responsibility is more equally split, each sector typically funds different aspects, with the federal government primarily providing financial assistance to individual students and funding research grants, and states directing funds toward the general operating budget of public institutions.

At the federal level, three comprehensive acts—the Elementary and Secondary Education Act of 1965 (ESEA), HEA, and Individuals with Disabilities Education Act of 1965 (IDEA)—contain a significant portion of the policies influencing the education landscape. Part of President Johnson's

War on Poverty and relying upon the 14th Amendment's call to provide "equal protection of the laws," these acts were devised to increase equitable access to education and educational resources. Title I of ESEA provided economic support directly to low-income K–12 schools and school districts. To this day, Title I remains a major source of funding for those school districts. HEA continues to distribute grants and loans to students who could not otherwise pay for higher education, and IDEA—along with the Rehabilitation Act of 1972—requires schools to provide the necessary resources so that students with disabilities can learn in the least restrictive environment possible. As we discuss the federal legislative process, it is useful to remember the narrow scope of influence under which the federal government operates.

THE FEDERAL LEGISLATIVE PROCESS

The U.S. Constitution solely grants Congress the power to legislate solely. To do so, both chambers of Congress must reach consensus. This is an ever-present challenge. Congress is often constrained in their policymaking "by the president's agenda, by the economy," and by the means necessary to find the votes for passage (Loomis & Schiller, 2018, p. 11). For passage to occur, both policy and politics must align.

Simply, passing a law requires affirmation from both chambers of Congress and the president's signature. A law encapsulates multiple priorities pieced together from members' legislative vision, advocacy organizations' agendas, and research findings all filtered through the requisite staff members, who identify the purpose, craft the policy mechanisms, and determine authorization amounts. Such a process can take months, years, or just days depending upon the political cycle, staffers' competing priorities, members' urgency, and constituents and advocacy group investment. While some aspects of the process must occur linearly, with each stage building upon the next through to passage, input from various stakeholders continues to shape and reshape the bill throughout the legislative process. At every stage, inaction born of myriad barriers is possible, probable, and can thwart the bill's forward momentum. This chapter describes a model process. In reality, steps rarely transpire in the order and manner described. While bill introduction may begin the formal legislative process, this typically occurs after considerable efforts on bill development and socialization.

Bill Introduction

Bill introduction starts the formal legislative process. Each chamber requires bills to be introduced by physically walking hard copies of the legislative text to the clerk. In the House, members manually place their bills into the hopper, the wooden box situated at the clerk's desk. The Senate requires handing the bill to the clerk sitting just outside the Senate chamber.

Upon introduction, every bill receives an identification number (S. for Senate and H.R. for House of Representatives, based on bill origination) in chronological order based on receipt (with some exceptions, such as the numbers 1–10 being typically reserved by the majority party's leadership for their policy priorities). These numbers restart every two years when the slate of bills is cleaned for the new Congressional session. Once a bill receives a bill number, it becomes part of the Congressional Record: the public daily log of the proceedings of both the House and Senate. Upon receipt, the parliamentarian[2] reviews the topic and content and then refers it to the appropriate committees.

Committee Referral

Each bill is referred to a committee of jurisdiction. Since bill content may cross committee jurisdictions, assignment occurs based upon the primary bill topic. Therefore, staff may strategize bill text to privilege committees on which their boss sits or draft bills in such a way to secure referral to a specific committee. Such practice enables members to shepherd their bills through their committees. Because thousands of bills are introduced in every Congress, the committee system ensures bills receive consideration from a subset of legislators (and their staffs), who, by being on committee have developed topical expertise in the laws under their jurisdiction (Black, 2006).

Committee structures vary by chamber and committee. In the Senate, only one committee receives a bill referral even if the content crosses committee jurisdictions, whereas in the House, a bill can be apportioned across several committees. On one hand, these committees act as gatekeepers over the bill; the committee chair, as a senior member of the majority party, determines which bills the committee will consider. Most never reach consideration. On the other hand, bills can be considered without a committee ever having input, if the majority leader bypasses the committee and opts to introduce a bill by unanimous consent directly to the floor.

Making it "out of committee" becomes the first major hurdle an introduced bill must achieve. This is no small feat. Without a committee advocate (ideally in the majority party) who can encourage the chairperson to put it through markup—a process where changes and furtherance of a bill are considered—the proposed legislation will stall indefinitely.

Committee Work: Hearings and Markup

Upon committee introduction, the chairman determines if the bill will advance. As the leader of the committee, the chairman sets the legislative agenda and can wield their power by opting to hold hearings, selecting which bills to mark up, and slow-walking any introduced legislation they would rather not see pass (Oleszek, 2001). By controlling the timing, duration, and witness lists of hearings, the chairman shapes the public perception of the bill (Oleszek, 2001).

Hearings. Hearings represent the public-facing, fact-finding work of the committee (Oleszek, 2001). They reveal the priorities of the chair, who selects hearing topics, while simultaneously calling attention to the issue under discussion and offering an opportunity for both sides to frame the debate (Heitshusen, 2018; Oleszek, 2001).

By the time the hearing occurs, the script has already been set. Staffers have vetted the witnesses, reviewed their written statements, and determined the public message their boss wishes to relay. These staffers, who report to either the chair or ranking member (the most senior member of the minority party) craft this message and coordinate across personal offices. The relationship between the ranking member, the chair, and their respective staffs, as well as the degree of partisanism of the topic, all influence hearing procedure.

Witness lists comprise experts, federal officials with jurisdiction over the proposed legislation, representatives from organizations with vested interest in the proposed legislation, and private citizens whose testimony could sway the public and committee opinion (Oleszek, 2001). Potential participants in the hearing are sought out for the way their testimony can influence bill passage, whether it be because of their expertise, fame, or personal experience (Black, 2006; Oleszek, 2001). They may be selected in a bipartisan or partisan manner and identified based on their topical relevance and position.

The witnesses submit written statements for the public record and present oral remarks at the hearing. Following oral remarks—which typically overlap their written remarks—members of the committee query the witnesses relying upon prepared, and sometimes ad-hoc, questions.

Markup. If a hearing represents the public display of information gathering, then the markup process represents the behind-the-scenes bill negotiations. Rarely does a bill pass through committee without requiring changes. In the case of reauthorization of HEA, a multitude of bills that address various aspects of the law have been introduced. If HEA goes to markup, many of these additional bills will be included into the draft. Thus, rather than independently requiring a vote for each addendum to HEA, the reauthorization will subsume these bills during the markup. With many of these bills addressing the same issues, committee members must negotiate between their competing priorities.

Should a bill be selected for consideration, it undergoes markup—the formal committee procedure through which the bill's merits are evaluated and delivery to the floor is determined. Because disagreement within the committee could harm the chances for later bill passage, the chairman carefully negotiates to create the broadest support for the bill (Oleszek, 2001). As Oleszek (2001), an expert on Congressional procedure, clarifies, "The markup, then, is where committee members redraft portions of the bill, attempt to insert new provisions and delete others, bargain over final language, and generally determine the final committee product." (p. 97). This final product is the committee report which accompanies the edited bill to the floor. This report details both the voted-upon bill text, the rationale behind the legislative text, and any disagreements. Because it describes Congressional rationale for each policy decision, the report becomes useful should an agency question legislative prerogative.

For example, Virginia Foxx, then-chair of the House Education and Workforce Committee, authorized a markup of her HEA reauthorization bill, the PROSPER Act less than two weeks after its introduction. Passing along party lines (23–17), the final committee report included a dissent from the committee Democrats, whose words were designed to influence their House colleagues by suggesting that Republicans wanted to make college less affordable while Democrats were the party championing students over profit. Given the power that committees wield in the House and the fact that both chambers were under Republican control in the 115th Congress, the PROSPER Act should have received some movement. And it did. Rather than stalling after introduction like the Aim Higher Act—the Democratic HEA response introduced by then-Ranking Member Bobby Scott (D-VA-3)—the PROSPER Act moved out of committee and was placed on one of the House calendars for future voting by the entire elected body.

Earning a Place on the Calendar: Floor Introduction and Voting

Since few bills make it out of committee markup, those that do have been groomed for a floor vote. To receive floor consideration, a marked-up bill is placed on the calendar in the order it was received. While calendar placement brings a bill closer to passage, such placement does not guarantee a vote. Each chamber operates its own calendar or calendars according to internal rules. Bills, already labeled with an H.R. or S. number, receive an additional calendar number. However, location on the calendar does not correlate with floor introduction. The majority leader determines which bills will be taken from the calendar and brought to the floor. Thus, the power of being in the majority includes the power to determine what legislation moves onto the floor calendar (Oleszek, 2001).

Numerous influences determine what gets brought to the floor and when. While appearing on the calendar enables a bill to be called for a vote, it does not suggest that action will occur. In the House, any member can advance a vote on legislation, provided the Speaker recognizes the member, thus enabling them to speak (Oleszek, 2001). In the Senate, only the majority leader advances legislation.

Bills can be passed via voice vote or by roll call depending upon the importance of monitoring the vote count, as a voice vote does not require individual identification in the public record. In the Senate, bills generally pass a 60-vote, supermajority threshold "cloture" vote, which forces a vote on the bill in question after a set amount of additional debate time. Thus, while bills only need a simple majority to pass the Senate, they must overcome the higher threshold of cloture first to avoid a potential filibuster. If neither party holds 60 or more seats, then bills rarely pass into law without bipartisan support. The rise of cloture as a gatekeeper is a relatively recent phenomenon and—like all parliamentary procedures—is a rule of agreement, not law.

In the House, a simple majority of 218 yeas (typically recorded since House members cast their votes electronically) is necessary to pass a bill. Given their procedural differences, voting in the House requires working with the Rules Committee to structure a rules package that will enable the legislation to be brought to the floor without significant delays. The Senate requires no such practice.

By the time voting occurs, most members have indicated their voting inclination. For political reasons, some members may need to vote against their party in order to align themselves with their constituents. In such cases, the members will likely have negotiated such behavior with their party leaders ahead of the vote.

In Necessity of Bicameral Passage: The Conference Committee

Rarely do both the House and Senate pass identical bills. Because the president will only sign one bill, both chambers must agree on identical bill language for it to become law. Should both the House and Senate pass different versions of the same bill, one chamber can take up the version from the other chamber and agree to those changes. Alternately, the two chambers could dispatch committee members to form a conference committee to negotiate between the two versions. The produced conference report becomes the negotiated product that reflects compromises made by both chambers and acts as a stand-in for the existing bill versions. This committee report is what the president signs or vetoes.

On to the President

Enacting law requires the signature of the president. Within 10 days of receipt, the president must sign or veto the pending legislation. While Congress does have the power to override a presidential veto, the necessity of two-thirds majority suggests such practice is rare (Heitshusen, 2018). Given this high bar, Congress typically attempts to pass legislation they believe the president will sign. Policies, procedures, and customs govern how bills are treated once they formally enter the legislative process, but it is helpful to consider the development process that occurs outside the formal proceedings in the House and Senate chambers between members.

Developing a Bill

Before a bill can be introduced, the legislation must be developed. Drafting and proposing legislation involves continuous dialogue across multiple stakeholders. Like a researcher's body of work, members and their staff work to create a set of unified themes which guide the office's legislative priorities. These priorities, alongside constituent interest, shape the types of bills members and their staffers pursue. Staff may act as gatekeepers to ideas, determining which to prioritize to their boss and only pursuing those they believe add value for both the public and their boss's priorities. Within this framework, staff members identify policy levers via their network of information resources including think tanks, advocacy organizations, the media, research, government reports, and local stakeholders.

Bill development is an iterative process. While staffers may begin the process, the language of a draft bill can just as likely originate with an advocacy group. Proposals may come either at the request of a staff member or from a group with a policy agenda. The involvement of multiple stakeholders often develops simultaneously. Drafting bill text occurs alongside gathering bill support. Staff vet the ideas with other members' offices and invested advocacy groups.

Through this information gathering process and their own experience and through discussions with the Congressional Research Service (CRS) and other bipartisan legislative support offices, staff identify the issue to be solved and craft legislation designed to address those goals. Without a policy mechanism, problems that need federal support lay fallow.

Developing a bill, like other aspects of the process, requires strategy. Bills intended for passage seek bipartisan support so that they may receive committee and floor consideration. However, not all bills are written for passage; some are messaging bills that reveal or reiterate a member's policy position. Introduced bills are entered into the Congressional Record to become public record. Irrespective of passage, submitting a bill into the record signals members' legislative priorities. Sponsorships and cosponsorships are the mechanism through which members can point to their support networks and accomplishments.

Lining Up Bill Support

Bill passage hinges on the support it receives from the affected parties, involved organizations, other member offices, and sometimes, the public (although at times it makes sense to not publicize a bill to the media). At any point in the process, from idea through introduction, staff may check in with trusted organizations, individuals, and committee staffers to gauge support for the bill.

Organizations play multiple roles in a potential bill's passage. First, they indicate the bill meets the needs of their constituents by writing letters of support. Second, organizations may directly lobby members, primarily through their staff, soliciting support for a policy or program. These fluid negotiations can occur across months, even years, as bills are introduced and reintroduced in subsequent sessions of Congress. Depending upon congressional staff members' relationships with organizations, bills may be drafted to align with organizational priorities.

Member offices consider the effects of the legislation on their regional or state constituents, including local chapters of the groups who would be affected by the bill, when determining whether to cosponsor it.

When Bills Stall

Most bills never make it beyond introduction. Only 4% of introduced bills are ever placed on the legislative calendar. Even fewer receive a vote. At every stage of the legislative process, bills fail to advance. Some introduced bills become amendments and receive passage by riding the coattails of moving legislation. Others undergo reintroduction every Congress with little movement. As previously mentioned, not all introduced bills are designed to become law. Some bills relay a set of values, address constituent concerns, or push topical conversations in a partisan direction. Known as marker bills, these messaging bills become a matter of public record even as they fail to modify law. Just as the currency in academe is publishing, bill introduction is a metric of member productivity in Congress. Rarely bipartisan, marker bills mostly fail to move beyond committee referral. However, a significant portion of their power comes from their ability to shift and drive policy conversations.

Many organizations "grade" congressional members on their performance on the organizations' priorities. These report cards communicate a member's actions and provide a metric for constituents to judge their elected officials based on issues of personal value. These grades are important for senators as they face their constituents in reelection. These criteria vary by organization, but typically include a member's voting record, their bill sponsorship and cosponsorship record, and other criteria the organization deems of value to their members. For example, the National Education Association (2019) ranks members on the accessibility and communication of their in-state and DC offices, while the National Association for the Advancement of Colored People (2018) identifies specific pieces of legislation and gauges how often the members align with those priorities.

APPROPRIATING FUNDS

The "power of the purse" is granted to Congress in Article I of the Constitution. Only Congress can alter tax code, increase revenue, and determine spending priorities (Oleszek, 2001). Yet within this power, the Constitution neglects to outline a process through which this should occur. The Congressional Budget and Impoundment Control Act of 1974 (CBA) imparted such procedural regularity by organizing and operationalizing a calendar of budgetary events for discretionary spending. First, the president's budget formulation must be delivered to Congress by the first Monday of February (31 U.S.C. 1105(a)). Specifically, the executive branch compiles each federal agency's budget requests and packages them within the presidential priorities. Second, Congress sets its own topline budget numbers in consultation with the president's budget and appropriates funds within those caps. Third, federal agencies carry out programs based on Congress's fiscal determinations.

While appropriations bills distribute discretionary funds across governmental entities, almost three-quarters of the federal budget consists of mandatory spending. Public debt, entitlements like Social Security and Medicare, and many defense contracts are all mandatory "uncontrollables" that require funding irrespective of the appropriations process (Oleszek, 2001, p. 42). That is, Congress only appropriates one-third of the federal budget. The appropriations levels that Congress sets determine budgets for all federal agencies, including the Department of Education. The budget includes enough programmatic detail to communicate values and intent, while leaving agencies discretion in how they allocate funds within programs.

Building a Budget

Funding the government involves two steps from Congress. In the first, the Budget Committee generates an annual budget resolution that sets the 302(a) and 302(b) numbers. The former number sets the value for the overall discretionary spending and the latter number distributes that total across the agencies. These values are not law and serve to give the Appropriations Committee a budgetary upper bound. The Appropriations Committee distributes funds across programs within the agencies after receiving assignment of these topline numbers (Saturno et al., 2016; 31 U.S.C. §1301(a), 2006). However, Congress can appropriate funds without enacting a budget.

Passed by both chambers of Congress, but not signed by the president, the budget resolution is not a law. Because of this, the presidential budget has no influence over the budget resolution (Committee for a Responsible Federal Budget [CRFB], 2016). However, because the president retains veto power over all bills passed by Congress, including appropriations bills, it behooves Congress to make some concessions to the presidential budget.

Congress's legislative priorities determine how chambers opt to appropriate the discretionary funds. While laws may contain language authorizing a level of funding necessary for program delivery, those numbers serve only as guideposts for appropriators who, when considering the entire compendium of agency programs, may appropriate a different amount of funds than originally legislated. Frequently the appropriated number is below the authorization level, leaving a law underfunded.

There are 12 appropriations bills addressing different executive agencies, and each receives a 302b allocation. For example, the Labor, Health and Human Services, Education (L-HHS-E) subcommittee appropriates funds for the Departments of Education, Labor, and Health and Human Services. The other appropriations bills are: Agriculture, Rural Development, Food and Drug Administration; Commerce, Justice, Sciences; Defense; Energy and Water Development; Financial Services and General Government; Homeland Security; Interior, Environment; Legislative Branch; Military Construction, Veterans Affairs; State, Foreign Operations; and Transportation, Housing and Urban Development. At times Congress has opted to pass omnibus budget bills which collapse some or all the 12 into larger compendium bills, thus reducing the number of bills to be voted on. (This can sometimes backfire because the entire bill could be rejected over disagreement on a single section. However, by the time an omnibus package has been negotiated, ideally so too have the votes necessary for its passage.)

The passage of the appropriations bills enables agencies to draw funds from Treasury. For example, in 2018 the Department of Education was appropriated $81,164,807,000, with $71.45 million in discretionary funding (primarily for student loans).

Traditionally the House originates appropriations bills, sending the passed bills on to the Senate where that body may amend them. The bills are negotiated until both chambers agree, at which time they are then sent to the president for signing. Recently, adherence to this process has broken down and both chambers have independently passed authorization bills that must be reconciled.

Annual Cycle of Appropriations

The release of the presidential budget in February begins the appropriations process (Table 2.1). Congress sets its own Congressional budget with a deadline of April 15. With the federal fiscal year running from October 1 through September 30, Congress aims to pass the appropriations bills in July or September. As originally framed, the 1974 Congressional Budget Act required the adoption of two budget resolutions each year. The House and Senate were scheduled to complete action on a budget resolution setting advisory targets by May 15 of each year. By September 15, just before the beginning of the fiscal year on October 1, the two chambers should have adopted a budget resolution setting binding limits (Saturno et al., 2016).

Once distribution of the 302b assignments occurs, then the Appropriations Committees in both the House and Senate take up their respective assignments. Formally, each appropriations subcommittee may hold hearings where agency heads and others, as requested, come before their requisite subcommittee and lobby for funding priorities. In both written and oral testimony, agency heads detail their needs and the importance of those needs. Ideally, the House appropriations committee reports the 12 bills to the full House for voting consideration in May or June, with the Senate picking up when the House process concludes (Saturno et al., 2016). Just like with other bills, the appropriations bills passed by the Senate and House must be identical before being sent to the White House for signing. Typically, the two chambers pass non-identical versions that go to a bicameral Conference Committee for reconciliation. The reconciled appropriations bills are then sent onto the president for signing into law.

Table 2.1

Annual Budget Process

October 1	Fiscal year begins
First Monday in February	President delivers budget submission
April 15	Congress submits budget authority to appropriators
May and June	House considers the 12 appropriations bills
June and July	Senate takes up House appropriations bills
Before August recess or prior to October 1	Congress (House and Senate) sends each appropriations bill to the President to become law

In some instances, because Congress is unable to agree on appropriations levels, Congress passes continuing resolutions (CRs) to maintain existing levels of funding. These CRs ensure the government continues to operate while an actual budget deal is negotiated.

When Appropriations Fail: Continuing Resolutions and Partial Shutdowns

Increasingly, appropriations bills fail to pass prior to the start of the fiscal year. These occurrences precipitate withholding of agency funds, thereby potentially stalling grants, subsidies, or other funding upon which constituents rely. To avoid the physical and political repercussions, legislators may pass a CR that maintains current funding levels until a predetermined end point. The Government Accountability Office (GAO) calls a CR a "must pass" piece of legislation because unfunded agencies risk a shutdown (GAO, 1986). Sometimes, however, appropriators cannot even agree on the continuing resolution. Without either an appropriations bill or a CR, agencies must abstain from all activities except those exempted from the discretionary budget process, like the disbursal of student loans.

CRs are an important tool in avoiding full or partial shutdowns. While they enable the government to maintain constant funding, in real dollars this can mean a funding decline as current allotments may not keep pace with inflation.

Policymaking Through Funding Priorities

While some laws require no capital to go into effect, many laws depend upon funds to accomplish their goals. Thus, a program requires both an *authorizing* law to create the policy change and an *appropriating* law to guarantee funds for enactment. Passing laws means little without the necessary funds, therefore, appropriators' use of funds dictates Congress's legislative priorities. Thus, committing sums of money from the Treasury ensures programmatic survival, while withholding funds restricts program implementation.

To make funding determinations, Congressional appropriators consider the presidential budget and member priorities. Members communicate their priorities to the appropriations subcommittees through personal and "Dear Colleague" letters. Personal letters include direct requests from state constituent organizations and highlight the member's agenda. Dear Colleague letters state a funding request for a specified program or suite of programs. They may provide a specific funding amount and include rationale for the request. These letters circulate among congressional offices, with one (or two if it is bipartisan) member's office soliciting support from other offices. Circulated across partisan membership, these letters are delivered to the pertinent subcommittee chair and ranking member and indicate political support for the named program or funding stream. Many times, these letters are drafted at the request of a constituent group, with members leading the same letters every year.

During the spring months that make up the appropriations season, advocacy organizations (including those representing education researchers) and constituents flood Capitol Hill for "fly-in season" to describe for staff how a federal program matters in their lives or the lives of those they help. National organizations tend to coordinate these requests across constituent groups, creating a unified message. Staff track these requests for their boss, although this varies by office.

Typically, appropriators distribute funds for predetermined lengths of time. Such practice enables future legislators to reevaluate program success and continuation. The annual budget process enables them to adjust funding levels based on the previous 12 months. Time-limited funding can be a bargaining tool for the passage of legislation. It also signals priorities. Recently, the White House's 2018 proposed education budget streamlined programs and reduced the Department of Education's budget by $9 billion from 2017 levels. Yet because Congress determines the budget, congressional appropriators chose to fund many programs slated for dismissal (U.S. Department of Education, 2019a).

While the first determinant of policy implementation involves appropriating funds, Congress and federal agencies are responsible for more direct implementation as well.

POLICY IMPLEMENTATION

Perhaps no component of federal policymaking is more relevant to education researchers than its implementation. While Congress may pass laws, negotiations continue even after passage, as agency regulations (or rules) and guidance documents interpret statute and determine implementation practices. How an agency drafts and enforces these documents creates the lived policy experience.

Regulations operationalize legal statute; they have the force and effect of law. Federal agencies (e.g., the National Institutes of Health and Department of Education) and regulatory bodies (e.g., the Food and Drug Administration) draft the regulations to detail how entities will engage with the department, or how entities accepting federal dollars must behave in order to show compliance with existing laws. Because much of the new law modifies or interacts with existing law, regulations detail how practices will change.

As discussed, an overwhelming majority of education policy is designed, implemented, and funded at state and local levels, while the federal government provides regulations and guidance and emphasizes priorities through programs and financial resources (U.S. Department of Education, 2019b).

Regulations, Agency Rulemaking, and Guidance

Congress created executive agencies and grants them the power to regulate to ensure proper implementation of its legal statutes, while freeing itself from direct involvement in the implementation process. Policy implementation is expressed in different forms. Regulation, published in the Federal Register by agencies, contains the specific rules, rights, and obligations citizens must adhere to in all areas of law (Table 2.2). Executive Orders (EOs) are issued when the president wishes to have tighter management of an agency, enforce a national priority, or express a policy priority (Oleszek, 2010).

Agency rulemaking. When a federal agency decides to create, eliminate, or amend a rule (or more generally, a regulation), statute requires them to (1) publish a Notice of Proposed Rulemaking (NPRM) which provides key information, including (a) the department issuing the rule, (b) the proposed rule changes, and (c) the background rationale for the proposed

Table 2.2

Types of Rulemaking and Their Legal Enforceability

Types of Rulemaking	Decision Body	Enforcement	Publication
Statute	Congress	Legally enforceable	Public Law; United States Code
Executive Order	President	Agencies must comply	Federal Register
Regulation	Agency	Legally enforceable	Code of Federal Regulations
Guidance	Agency	Not directly enforceable	Agency

rule change; (2) provide a window of opportunity for the public to submit written comments; and (3) publish the final rule and accompanying statement of basis and purpose not less than 30 days before the rule's effective date (Center for Regulatory Effectiveness [CRE], n.d.). The agency must respond, in writing, to all public comments submitted during the comment period. While they do not need to alter their decree in response to the comments, all comments and their responses must be published in the Federal Register along with the final rule.

Providing public comments is a useful way for education researchers to engage in the federal legislative process. Anyone can submit a response to an NRPM, at which point the agency must respond. Comment periods are open for at least 30 days, often longer, and the electronic submission of comments allows for around-the-clock access to the process. There are no limits to the number of comments a proposed rule may receive, and the general public, including researchers, can recruit others to submit comments aligned with their beliefs and scholarly determinations.

The Administrative Procedures Act of 1946 (APA), particularly section 553, lays out this basic framework for agency rulemaking, including the requirement for public comment. Created during the New Deal's expansion of the federal government, APA was a compromise between the agencies created during that time and those "suspicious of the power given those agencies" (CRE, n.d., p. 5).

Often with the goal of reducing the regulatory burden, presidents have issued EOs that have altered the APA over time (Carey, 2013). President Reagan centralized the review of agency regulations, requiring the Office of Management and Budget's (OMB) Office of Information and Regulatory Affairs (OIRA) to review drafts and final rules before publication in the Federal Register (Carey, 2013). This process greatly increased the workload of OIRA and lengthened the time required to communicate new rules. Next, President Clinton issued EO 12,866 (3 C.F.R. 638) which revoked Reagan's EO and attempted to streamline the regulation process by reducing the number of regulations reviewed by OIRA to those having "economically significant" impact ($100 million annually) and increasing transparency of the rulemaking process (Carey, 2013; Whisner, 2013). The changes cut the number of regulations reviewed by OIRA by approximately three-quarters and reduced the wait time to within a new mandatory 90-day window (Carey, 2019). Each president since 1993 has altered EO 12,866. Most recently, President Trump issued EO 13,771 aimed at deregulation and cost-savings. The "one in, two out" EO requires agencies to offset the costs of any new rules by eliminating equivalent costs associated with at least two previously issued rules (Carey, 2019).

In addition to the general rulemaking process, how agencies create the rules they enforce sometimes occurs internally and sometimes requires input from vested stakeholders. For some of the laws the Department of Education oversees and enforces, it implements a procedure called Negotiated Rulemaking, which requires the department to discuss proposed changes with members of constituent groups and the public prior to issuing a new rule.

Negotiated rulemaking. The Negotiated Rulemaking Act of 1990 sought to bridge what some saw as a divide between federal agencies and impacted interest groups (Carey, 2013). Sometimes referred to as regulatory negotiation or "neg-reg" (for negotiated rulemaking) the process aims to reduce the potential friction (and potential lawsuits) between federal agencies and affected groups by including more stakeholders in the federal rulemaking process (Carey, 2013). That is, negotiated rulemaking is the process through which external private entities who will likely be subject to the future regulations collaborate with the agency in forming the regulations.

Requirements for neg-reg vary by agency. The Department of Education is legally required to use the neg-reg process in creating new regulations for Title IV of HEA but may opt to use the process at other times. Determining if such a practice is in the public interest and necessary includes assessing the likelihood that vested interests can come to a unifying agreement upon a rule (see Copeland, 2006 for a full list of requirements).

Just like with generalized rulemaking, an agency must issue a public notice in the Federal Register, although this time they must (1) state their intent to develop a regulation using negotiated rulemaking (which opens the period of public comment, typically between 30 and 60 days); (2) publish both a final issue list, based on received public comment, and request nominations of members of key constituent groups for the neg-reg committees; (3) select committee members; (4) conduct meetings, many of which are open to the public, and; (5) vote on the final proposed rule.

Interestingly, agencies still retain control of the final outcome throughout the negotiated rulemaking process. First, the final product agreed to by the neg-reg committee is non-binding; agencies can choose to use some or none of the committee's input (Carey, 2013). For instance, should the committee—including department members—fail to agree on a final rule, then the department may implement its preferred plan. Second, the agency determines the level of involvement of external organizations. While the agency must collaborate with representatives of the groups that will be most affected by the regulation (U.S. Department of Education, 2019c), the agency has leeway within the policy as to who they select to represent a constituency. For example, when the Department of Education held Negotiated Rulemaking for Higher Education 2018–19 in the winter and spring of 2019, the agency selected representatives of religious institutions to fulfill the role of financial aid administrator on each of the four committees.

A recent example of an NPRM can help to concretize the process and highlight potential participation in the policymaking process. Generally, Title IX of the Education Amendments of 1972 ensures nondiscrimination based on sex in education programs or activities receiving federal financial assistance. A wide-ranging policy, it governs federally-funded activities at public and private schools in both the K–12 and higher education sectors (Valentine, 1997). Obama-era guidance had expanded the scope of Title IX compliance, requiring schools to adopt comprehensive measures to mitigate sexual harassment. The change in administration meant that enforcement of Obama-era guidelines could be in jeopardy.

In fact, in November of 2018, Trump's Education Department, through its Office of Civil Rights (OCR), published an NPRM suggesting changes to Title IX ("Nondiscrimination," 2018, p. 61,462). Stating that current guidance did not "provide appropriate standards for how recipients must respond to incidents of sexual harassment," the Department proposed regulations designed to ensure both the accuser and the accused received due process under the law ("Nondiscrimination," 2018, p. 61,462). Following the publication of the NPRM, the public, including researchers, engaged in a robust exchange of ideas about the proposed changes.

Guidance documents. Unlike regulations, guidance documents do not require formal publication or public comment. Traditional rulemaking, leading to regulations published in the Federal Register, are subject to further review. As Whisner (2013) observed, not undergoing the formal process enables those who are regulated to have access to guidance quickly; however, this practice can severely impact the fairness and transparency of such guidance. Guidance documents have been a popular and effective way of circumventing the traditional rulemaking process, particularly when disagreements exist between the president and Congress, or when the president feels strongly that a change needs to be made and does not wish to work through a consensus process.

Guidance documents may address issues Congress has not addressed or provide more detail on existing law. Because guidance documents are promulgated by the agency, they do not have the force of law but often have the effect of law, as organizations wish to maintain positive relationships with federal agencies. However, their enforcement depends upon the majority political party and may shift with a new administration. For example, given concerning rates of student discipline referrals, particularly for minority students, and the increasing awareness of such discipline practices' correspondence to later incarceration (e.g., Kim et al., 2010), the Departments of Education and Justice under President Obama issued a joint guidance document on K–12 school discipline for educators, school and district leaders, counselors, community advocates, and other relevant stakeholders, marking the first time such guidance was ever given. Since states hold the primary responsibility for the administration of K–12 education, and because such administration can be uneven, the discipline guidance documents proved critical for enabling and empowering schools and districts to fulfill their legal obligation to individual students and the student body without discriminating based on race, color, or national origin (U.S. Department of Education, 2014).

This example highlights an underlying challenge and controversy with the issuance of guidance documents as a way for the executive branch to conduct rulemaking. Legal ambiguity, often enabled by vague definitions of terms like "agency" and "rule" can provide executives the flexibility to accomplish their, perhaps, unpopular goals.

Questions remain as to the extent to which guidance documents are enforceable, but a recent OMB memo provided much-needed clarity. In April 2019, the OMB issued a memorandum providing an expansive definition of a rule as any complete or partial "statement ... designed to implement, interpret, or prescribe law or policy" (Larkin, 2019). The definition of a "rule" now covers guidance documents as well as opinion letters, policy statements, testimony before Congress, staff instructions, and press releases.

Generally, departmental guidance can be challenged to prevent further enforcement action, but there is significant deterrence from doing so. Challenging the department in court can carry high legal costs or jeopardize a productive working relationship. Further, the courts have previously determined that agency interpretation of its own rule holds final sway, therefore the government tends to win most cases where its guidance documents come under scrutiny. Issues of this type will continue to surround agency rulemaking and guidance as agency heads and presidents test the boundaries of their legal authority in service to their policy agendas.

CONGRESSIONAL OVERSIGHT

Congress is responsible for ensuring that the implementation of its laws align with congressional intent. However, Congress also granted executive agencies latitude in interpreting legal statute (Nolan & Glassman, 2016). Because the Constitution vests the executive branch with the power to execute law, because the executive branch has leeway to interpret congressional intent, and because Congress continually passes new laws, congressional oversight is ongoing. Congressional oversight generally derives from the implied powers in the *necessary and proper clause* of the Constitution (Article I, Section 8), which grants Congress the power and responsibility to engage in any practices not specified elsewhere and use the clause to monitor the activities of the executive branch (Oleszek, 2010). If actions within the executive branch are found to be improper or misaligned with Congressional intent, this clause enables Congress to hold the executive branch accountable for any regulations or behaviors deemed against the intent of Congress.

While the Constitution grants implied authority for Congress to review the actions of the executive branch, specific statutes provide a more detailed scope of authority. The Congressional Review Act (CRA) of 1996 mandates that all final rules must be sent to Congress and the GAO prior to taking effect. There, its members can void the rule by passing a joint resolution of disapproval that the president signs (Larkin, 2019). As with any legislation, the president can exercise veto power, and Congress can override the veto should disagreement arise. The CRA empowers Congress to overturn an agency rule before it takes effect and prevent the creation of a similar rule in the future.

Because its use necessitates agreement between Congress and the president, the CRA has been used sparingly. Prior to the Trump presidency and since its enactment in 1996, the CRA had only been used once among the nearly 50,000 rules that have likely come into effect (Beth, 2001). During the 115th Congress when Republicans controlled both chambers of Congress, President Trump, with Congressional support, was able to rescind 16 existing regulations using CRA (Carey, 2019).

The Government Performance and Results Act of 1993 (GPRA or Results Act) also assists Congress in holding agencies accountable. The Act requires agencies to set multiyear performance goals and measure their progress towards those outcomes. The aim of the act is twofold. First, it enables Congress to hold an agency accountable to its articulated goals. Second, it identifies programmatic inefficiencies and agency overlap, ideally resulting in streamlined federal agencies. Although not an exhaustive list, these statutes are two examples of legal avenues for congressional oversight. How Congress performs these duties is discussed next.

Oversight Methods

Congress leverages formal and informal methods of oversight, originating from committees, personal offices, and Congress (either the House of Representatives or the Senate). Legislators employ these methods for programmatic, political, or institutional purposes (Garvey & Oleszek, 2014).

Hearings and investigations. Congressional committees carry out hearings and investigations to monitor agency responsiveness to their legislative priorities and directives. As previously discussed, the majority party chairs all congressional committees and therefore determines the content and scope of the hearings and investigations, including their frequency and witness lists. An oversight hearing may be organized so that congressional members can learn from agency heads or experts in the field about an agency's operations or a set of programs.

Investigations arise from areas of broad public concern or debate, or where there have been allegations of wrongdoing. Ideally, an investigation identifies the root cause of an issue and provides a path for reconciliation. For example, on September 30, 2010, a hearing inquiring into deceptive enrollment practices of for-profit colleges brought these behaviors into the public forum. Senator Harkin, then chair of the HELP Committee, used the hearing to announce forthcoming legislation restricting the for-profit sector in response to the hearing's findings (Lewin, 2010).

Letters of inquiry and public reports. A critical piece of oversight is the ability of Congress to request information from executive agencies and compel witnesses to testify. Members will write letters of inquiry seeking information from the executive branch to better determine what, if any, future oversight actions are warranted and their proper scope. The information provided in response to letters of inquiry can either detail the inner workings of the agency and their priorities, or the agency can stonewall, only repeating what already exists in the public record.

Dear Colleague letters serve as another form of oversight. These letters, sent from one or many congressional offices to an agency, inquire about a specific practice or practices the agency either should or should not be engaging in and typically requests the agency explain their current practices. At times, current agency behavior may invoke Congress to mandate a behavioral change through statute.

For example, in March of 2018, President Trump established the Federal Commission on School Safety, tasked with producing a report of policy recommendations to help prevent future school shooting tragedies. A collaboration between the Departments of Education, Health and Human Services, Justice, and Homeland Security and chaired by Education Secretary Betsy DeVos, the commission was formed in response to the school shooting incident at Marjory Stoneman Douglas High School in Parkland, FL, where a student took 17 lives.

The commissions' work involved interviews and listening sessions in diverse communities across the country and covered topics like preventing school violence, mitigating the effects of school violence, recovering from attacks, and improving school climate. Prior to the final agency report, the media described how school districts wanted to secure their schools by allotting funds from Title IV-A of Every Student Succeeds Act—the new reauthorization of ESEA—to purchase firearms for their teachers. Congressional Democrats wrote a Dear Colleague letter to Secretary DeVos expressing their opposition to this decision and explaining how allowing firearm purchases, while not outside the scope of the language of the new law, was far from the intention of legislators. However, as a Dear Colleague letter, the document could only urge the Secretary DeVos to stop allowing ESEA funds to go toward arming teachers (Scott et al., 2018).

As the implementing agency of ESEA, the Department of Education declined action, interpreting the statute to mean that Congress did not authorize them to decide how a district could or could not use their ESEA funds (DeVos, 2018). An internal agency memorandum of the question illustrates how congressional ambiguity is passed on to agencies (Botel, 2018): the memorandum recognized that the law "neither clearly authorizes nor prohibits the purchase of firearms or firearms training," and that the Secretary has "discretion to interpret the broad language of the statute" as she sees fit (Botel, 2018, p. 4). In her Congressional response letter, DeVos (2018) also drew on past guidance put forth under the Obama administration which expressed a determination that state and local education agencies should have flexibility in identifying allowable uses of Title IV-A funds. In declining action, she cited that her response maintained her legal role by not expanding or restricting state and local actions (DeVos, 2018).

As this example illustrates, the oversight process requires continual interpretation of the law and the precedent of political actors. It has effects, some of which may be to highlight contrasts between parties, even if it does not always alter regulatory course.

CONCLUSION

This chapter has offered a high-level overview of the federal legislative process with two goals in mind. First, to trace policy development and implementation from a legislative idea and the passing of bill language through agency regulation and Congressional oversight. Second, to illustrate the roles of the people involved in the policymaking process and highlight potential sites of engagement for education researchers. From our perspective, the people involved throughout the policymaking process have a marked effect on policy creation, passage, and enactment.

To review, Congress passes laws, and the executive branch—through its agencies—executes those laws. The process of becoming a law varies; however, all bills must be passed by both chambers of Congress and signed by the president. For those laws that require funding, the budget and appropriations process apportions federal dollars across programs. While passing a law may authorize program funds, it is the appropriations process which ensures federal funding for programs. Without dollars appropriated toward execution of the law, a statute may go into effect, yet never be implemented. Laws that are passed and funded become the responsibility of their implementing agency. The agency charged with managing the new laws issues regulations and guidance documentation determining the policy details not enumerated in statute. Such changes include a comment period during which anyone—legislators, advocacy groups, individuals, and researchers—can submit remarks. Such comments become part of the public record. Regulations prepare a law for interface with the public and carry the force of law while guidance offers recommendations and announces executive priorities. Guidance documents do not have the force of law but are useful—as they indicate agency priorities and suggest what agencies will and will not address or enforce—for constituents who must comply with the law. Once a law passes, Congress has the responsibility of providing oversight of the law. As the executive branch implements these laws, Congress may hold hearings, send letters of inquiry to agencies, and pass new laws in response to agency implementation. Researchers can engage in the hearing process by serving as witnesses and by offering written or spoken testimony for the public record.

Some bills may take years to pass. Most will never become law. Some bills are not slated for passage. Known as marker or messaging bills, they identify a legislator's priorities, appease a constituent group, or alter a broader policy discussion. These bills reveal one way through which the legislative process responds to external demands, events, and pressures (Oleszek, 2010). This permeability in the policy process exposes multiple paths where researchers can impact legislation. Ultimately, influencing policy means sustained engagement with the policy process. The goal of this chapter has been to give researchers an entry point into that process.

REFERENCES

Beth, R. S. (2001). *Disapproval of regulations by Congress: Procedure under the Congressional Review Act.* http://www.au.af.mil/au/awc/awcgate/crs/rl31160.pdf

Black, A. E. (2006). *From inspiration to legislation: How an idea becomes a bill.* Pearson Education.

Botel, J. (2018 July 16). *Memorandum re: Determine options for allowable use for school safety measures under Title IV, Part A.* U.S. Department of Education. https://edlabor.house.gov/imo/media/doc/Title%20IV-A%20Guns%20Memo.pdf

Carey, M. (2013). *The federal rulemaking process: An overview* (CRS Report No. RL32240). Congressional Research Service. https://fas.org/sgp/crs/misc/RL32240.pdf

Carey, M. (2019). *Counting regulations: An overview of rulemaking, types of federal regulations, and pages in the Federal Register* (CRS Report No. R43056). Congressional Research Service. https://fas.org/sgp/crs/misc/R43056.pdf

Center for Regulatory Effectiveness [CRE]. (n.d.). *Part I: Overview of federal agency rulemaking. A guide to federal agency rulemaking.* https://www.thecre.com/forum2/wp-content/uploads/2015/09/ABA-Rulemaking.pdf

Committee for a Responsible Federal Budget. (2016). *The better budget process initiative: Strengthening the budget resolution.* CRFB. http://www.crfb.org/sites/default/files/bbpi_strengtheningbudgetresolution_0.pdf

Common Core State Standards Initiative. (2019). *About the process: Development process.* http://corestandards.org

Copeland, C. W. (2006). *Negotiated rulemaking* (CRS Report No. RL32452). Congressional Research Service. Retrieved from https://www.everycrsreport.com/files/20060828_RL32452_d96657f52838d734a0473cf2a2085467fd412f1f.pdf

DeVos, B. (2018, August 31). *Response letter to Chairman Scott.* U.S. Department of Education. Retrieved from https://deutsch29.files.wordpress.com/2018/09/response-to-rep-scott.pdf

Garvey, T., & Oleszek, W. J. (2014). *Congressional oversight and investigations* (CRS No. IF10015). Congressional Research Service.

Government Accountability Office. (1986). *Appropriations: Continuing resolutions and an assessment of automatic funding approaches* (Report No. 534666). https://www.gao.gov/assets/150/144084.pd

Heitshusen, V. (2018). *Introduction to the federal legislative process in the US Congress* (CRS Report No. R42843). https://crsreports.congress.gov

Kim, C. Y., Losen, D. J., & Hewitt, D. T. (2010). *The school-to-prison pipeline: Structuring legal reform.* New York University Press.

Larkin (2019, June 10). OMB's new approach to agency guidance documents. *The Regulatory Review.* https://www.theregreview.org/2019/06/10/larkin-omb-new-approach-agency-guidance-documents/

Leachman, M., Masterson, K., & Figueroa, E. (2017). *A punishing decade for school funding.* Center on Budget and Policy Priorities. https://www.cbpp.org/sites/default/files/atoms/files/11-29-17sfp.pdf

Lewin, T. (2010, October 1). Rifts show at hearing on for-profit colleges. *The New York Times,* p. A15. https://www.nytimes.com/2010/10/01/education/01education.html

Loomis, B. A., & Schiller, W. J. (2018). *The contemporary congress* (7th ed.). Rowman & Littlefield.

National Association for the Advancement of Colored People. (2018). *How Congress voted in 2017: The NAACP civil rights federal legislative report card.* NAACP. http://www.naacp.org/wp-content/uploads/2010/04/2017-Legislative-Report-Card.pdf

National Education Association. (2019). *Legislative report card.* Retrieved February 20, 2019, from http://www.nea.org/home/19413.htm

Nolan, A., & Glassman, M. E. (2016). *The powers of Congress: A brief overview* (CRS Report No. IF10518). Congressional Research Service.

Nondiscrimination on the basis of sex in education programs or activities receiving federal financial assistance, 83 Fed. Reg. 230 (November 29, 2018). https://www.govinfo.gov/content/pkg/FR-2018-11-29/pdf/2018-25314.pdf

Oleszek, W. J. (2001). *Congressional procedures and the policy process* (5th ed.). CQ Press.

Oleszek, W. J. (2010). *Congressional oversight: An overview* (CRS Report No. R41079). Congressional Research Service. Retrieved from https://crsreports.congress.gov

Program integrity: Gainful employment, 34 C.F.R. § 600 and 668 (2014). https://www.govinfo.gov/content/pkg/FR-2014-10-31/pdf/2014-25594.pdf

Program integrity: Gainful employment, 84 Fed. Reg. 126 (2019, July 1) (to be codified at 34 C.F.R. pts. 600 and 668). https://www.govinfo.gov/content/pkg/FR-2019-07-01/pdf/2019-13703.pdf

Saturno, J. V., Lynch, M. S., & Henif Jr., B. (2016). *The Congressional appropriations process: An introduction* (CRS Report No. R42388). Congressional Research Service. https://crsreports.congress.gov

Scott, R. C., Nadler, J., Thompson, B. G., Polis, J., Jackson, J. L., Payne, D. M., Jr., Bonamici, S., Raskin, J., Coleman, B. W., Adams, A. S., Barragan, N. D., Raskin, J., Coleman, B. W., Adams, A. S., Barragan, N. D., Bass, K., Beatty, J., Beyer, D. S., Jr., Blumenauer, E., … Rochester, L. B. (2018, Aug. 28). *Letter to DeVos on guns.* United States House of Representatives. https://edlabor.house.gov/imo/media/doc/2018-08-28%20Letter%20to%20DeVos%20on%20Guns.pdf

United States Congress. (2019, Feb. 8). *Promoting real opportunity, success, and prosperity through education reform act: Report of the Committee on Education and the Workforce to accompany H.R. 4508 together with minority views.* https://www.congress.gov/115/crpt/hrpt816/CRPT-115hrpt816.pdf

U.S. Department of Education. (2014). *Rethinking school discipline: Remarks of the U.S. Secretary of Education Arne Duncan at the release of the Joint DOJ-ED School Discipline Guidance Package.* https://www.ed.gov/news/speeches/rethinking-school-discipline

U.S. Department of Education. (2019a). *Education Department budget history table: FY 1980–FY 2019 President's budget.* https://www2.ed.gov/about/overview/budget/history/index.html

U.S. Department of Education. (2019b). *Law & guidance.* https://www2.ed.gov/policy/landing.jhtml?src=ln

U.S. Department of Education. (2019c). *Negotiated rulemaking process for Title IV regulations: Frequently asked questions.* https://www2.ed.gov/policy/highered/reg/hearulemaking/hea08/neg-reg-faq.html

United States Code. (2006 Edition). Supplement 4, Title 31 Money and finance, The Budget process, Appropriations, General. 31 USC §1301(a). https://www.govinfo.gov/app/details/USCODE-2010-title31/USCODE-2010-title31-subtitleII-chap13-subchapI-sec1301

Valentine, I. (1997). Title IX: a brief history. *Women's Educational Equity Act Resource Center.* http://www2.edc.org/womensequity/pdffiles/t9digest.pdf

Whisner, M. (2013). Some guidance about federal agencies and guidance. *Law Library Journal, 105*(3), 385–394.

RECOMMENDED READINGS

The Policymaking Process

Black, A. E. (2007). *From inspiration to legislation: How an idea becomes a bill.* Pearson Education.

Davis, L. J. (2016). *Enabling acts: The hidden story of how the Americans with Disabilities Act gave the largest U.S. minority its rights.* Beacon Press.

Redman, E. (2001). *The dance of legislation: An insider's account of the workings of the United States Senate.* University of Washington Press. (Original work published 1973)

Congressional Procedure

Oleszek, W. J. (2001). *Congressional procedures and the policy process* (5th ed.). CQ Press.

Riddick, F. M., & Frumin, A. S. (1992). *Riddick's Senate procedure: Precedents and practices* (No. 101). U.S. Government Printing Office.

Locating Legislation

Codes of Federal Regulations. https://www.govinfo.gov/app/collection/cfr

Congress.gov

Congressional Research Service. https://crsreports.congress.gov/

Federal Register. https://www.federalregister.gov/

United States Code. https://www.law.cornell.edu/uscode/text or http://uscode.house.gov/

NOTES

1. The name of the committee switches from the U.S. House Committee on Education and Workforce to the U.S. Education and Labor Committee depending upon the majority party.
2. The parliamentarian is a nonpartisan staff member well-versed in matters of parliamentary procedure.

CHAPTER 3

ACTORS, INTERESTS, AND ACTIONS IN SHAPING STATE EDUCATION POLICY

R. Aaron Wisman
California State University, Bakersfield

W. Kyle Ingle
University of Louisville

The current educational policy landscape across the United States stands in stark contrast to its form 40 years ago. Since the publication of *A Nation at Risk* (National Commission on Excellence in Education [NCEE], 1983), which created a great sense of urgency about academic achievement and possible consequences for U.S. global competitiveness, a "new politics of education" has emerged (DeBray-Pelot & McGuinn, 2009), culminating in the reauthorization of the Elementary and Secondary Education Act of 1965 (ESEA) as the No Child Left Behind Act of 2001 (NCLB) and most recently as the Every Student Succeeds Act of 2015 (ESSA). Ellison and Aloe (2018) described the new politics of education as an "integrated, mutually reinforcing policy paradigm informed by orthodox neoclassical economic theory and neoliberalism" with bipartisan consensus about "choice, standards, testing, and accountability" (p. 2). In tandem, these policies create

Maximizing the Policy Relevance of Research for School Improvement, pp. 43–74
Copyright © 2021 by Information Age Publishing
All rights of reproduction in any form reserved.

a quasi-market for educational services that purportedly provides political power to students and parents by positioning them as rational actors who choose to attend a particular school based on the relative quality of education provided, operationalized to a great extent by aggregated test scores. However, as Petracca (1991) acknowledged, rationality is often treated narrowly as self-interest and, thus, "values, ethics, and ideas on individual motivation are alien to rational choice theories of human nature" (p. 297). Furthermore, Jabbar (2011) described how concepts from behavioral economics (e.g., status quo bias, the paradox of choice, and framing effects) can complicate parent and student decisions about schools.

Nevertheless, the underlying assumption of this new politics of education is that these market forces will spur systemic improvement in educational outcomes and, simultaneously, give political power to parents and communities, in particular for historically underserved and underrepresented groups and communities. This storyline stands in contrast to contemporaneous policies codifying state takeovers of persistently low-achieving school districts, which might be interpreted as limiting political power of historically marginalized parents and communities. Others have critiqued the central logic of the new politics of education as being devoid of an affective dimension (Calaff, 2008; Hallinan, 2008; Protheroe, 2007; Reile et al., 2017), an element of teaching and learning that acknowledges the ethics of care (Noddings, 2010). As Jones and Nichols (2013) noted:

> The standards movement has had an object-focus—the test ... is everything and nothing else matters. Leading policy makers have been driven by a dichotomous logic whereby it is not possible to focus on quantitative and qualitative measures of excellence at the same time.... Because of this, there is a narrow focus on drill and kill and teaching to the test, which has not allowed for the production of healthy relationships between adults, children and their parents/guardians.... Therefore, the movement itself, with all of its good intentions, is counterproductive to building the relationships between kids and adults that is necessary for schools in highly diverse settings to succeed. (pp. 86–87)

The new politics of education, embodied in NCLB and subsequently reinforced by the Obama administration's Race to the Top (RTTT) initiative, sought to stimulate systemic educational improvement by targeting persistently low-achieving (PLA) schools and offered competitive grant funding to state and local education agencies willing to adopt one of four school improvement models: (a) turnaround, in which the principal and no less than 50% of the school staff were replaced; (b) transformation, in which the principal was replaced and intensive professional development was provided to staff for the purpose of instituting comprehensive instructional and community-based reforms; (c) school closure, and (d) restart, a model that included the conversion of a school to be operated by a charter management organization (CMO) or education management organization (EMO). The RTTT initiative demonstrates the interconnectedness of these mutually-reinforcing policies. First, while the lowest performing schools were identified based on a number of factors (such as graduation rates), the identification of PLA status also took aggregated standardized test scores into account. Second, the restart model explicitly supported the expansion of charter schools. The passage of ESSA, however, returned much authority to state and local education agencies in determining how to improve their lowest performing schools. Yet, the policy paradigm that includes standards, assessment, accountability, and choice remains a prominent feature of the education policy landscape across the United States. With the confirmation of Betsy Devos in 2017, the federal government clearly signaled its intention to expand school choice options through charter schools, school voucher programs, and tax credit scholarships.

As noted above, numerous education and policy scholars have, at least in part, attributed the emergence of the new politics of education to *A Nation at Risk* (NCEE, 1983) and subsequent federal education policy (e.g., DeBray-Pelot & McGuinn, 2009; Ingle & Lindle, 2019; Mehta, 2013). Accordingly, a body of literature on the emergence of state-level policies concerning the adoption of standards, assessment, accountability, and school choice has burgeoned in the wake of the shifting education policy landscape (Ball, 2010; DeBray-Pelot & McGuinn, 2009; Ellison & Aloe, 2018). As Mehta (2013) showed, standards, assessment, and accountability policies that now dominate U.S. educational policy emerged between 1980 and 2001 because a new idea-centered paradigm increased the visibility of education policy as an agenda item among a broad span of policymakers with theretofore varying interest in education policy. Republicans and Democrats alike at the state and federal levels called for education reform, albeit for different reasons. These ranged from demands for equity in standards across schools regardless of socioeconomic status, increased oversight for a system perceived as resistant to change and external pressures, and in response to a post-industrial economy in which improved educational outcomes were seen as a means of improving local, state, and national economies. As a result, educators, students, parents, policymakers, and all other stakeholders operate in an educational system characterized by testing, reporting, choice, increased roles of state and federal governments, and decreased local control and teacher influence.

In their essay on the dilemmas of educational reform, Cohen et al. (2018) identify and discuss issues that school systems face in a changing environment in order to propose considerations for researchers seeking to understand these issues. Cohen et al. begin by discussing the development and legacy of U.S. public schools in the late 19th and 20th centuries.

They then examine leading issues that school systems faced in response to educational reforms characterized by standards, assessment, and accountability. Most notable of these is how schools and districts must manage environmental pressures to become more coherent enterprises that focus on tested outcomes while managing the inherited differentiated organizations and environmental pressures which support these enterprises. Cohen et al. identify four activity domains that are defined by these competing pressures. First is how to build consensus on system-wide outcomes despite counter-pressures that support differentiated outcomes. Second is how to build infrastructure to connect standards-based outcome measures with instruction when most existing elements of infrastructure lack them. Third is how to manage pressures to reorganize staff recruitment and training to support improved outcomes. Fourth is how to balance competing environmental pressures for coherent, improved instruction and school outcomes with those of differentiated programs and organization. Cohen et al. note that open and environmentally dependent educational systems are ripe grounds for future research. This requires that researchers attend to the interaction between externalities and the internalities of the organization, comparing how organizational systems define, design, organize, and improve instruction.

This book serves as a resource for education researchers, faculty, and advanced graduate students seeking to maximize the impact of their research in order to improve learning and learning environments across schools, districts, states, and the nation as a whole—and to shape policies that further improve learning and learning environments. The onus is on researchers to design and implement high-quality defendable research that protects the rights, safety, and welfare of subjects involved in the research and yield findings about the phenomena being studied. If policymakers are to make evidence-based decisions about education, researchers must also determine who the relevant policy actors are and how to get research in front of them to inform actions. In this research synthesis, we seek to provide an overview of the actors, actions, and interests studied in the context of this policy paradigm, as well as a framework for understanding the relative positions, roles, and activities of various actors seeking to stimulate state-level policy reform in the new politics of education. We begin by articulating the set of analytical frameworks selected to guide our review. Next, we synthesize three strands of related bodies of literature, discussing actions of actors studied in the literature reviewed on the Common Core State Standards (CCSS) initiative, high-stakes accountability policies, and charter school legislation. We conclude this chapter with a summary of major themes emerging from the literature on educational policy and pose recommendations for policy scholars and actors who seek to study and affect change in education policy in their own states.

ACTORS

Policy actors are individuals and groups who seek to influence the policymaking process in both formal and informal ways. Policy actors can be institutional actors or noninstitutional actors. Examples of the former are members of Congress, state legislators, presidents, governors, state boards of education, chief state education officers/state superintendents, and the courts. Examples of noninstitutional actors include individuals, interest groups, political consultants, lobbyists, and the media. Among these various policy actors emerge what are known as policy entrepreneurs—individuals with a combination of expertise, authoritative position, access to the political process, negotiating skills, and/or persistence in seeking to initiate a dynamic policy change (Kingdon, 2013; Mintrom, 1997). Given the wide array of policy actors and entrepreneurs in the research literature, categorizing, and typing them is useful in understanding the various roles that they play. To that end, Roberts and King (1991) developed a typology, identifying four categories of public entrepreneurs based on their positions in policy systems: political entrepreneurs, or elected officials in government (e.g., governors, legislators); executive entrepreneurs, or individuals who are appointed to leadership positions within the government (e.g., some members of state boards of education, some chief state education officers); bureaucratic entrepreneurs, or individuals who occupy a formal, although not necessarily a leadership position in the government (e.g., state education agency officials or staff); and policy entrepreneurs, or individuals external to the government "who work ... to introduce, translate, and implement innovative ideas into public sector practice" (p. 152). In reviewing literature on state-level policy reform, we extend the use of these typologies beyond the context of school choice policies to organize the literature on the adoption of state education standards and high-stakes accountability policies as well.

WHEN TO TAKE ACTION: THE STAGES MODEL OF PUBLIC POLICYMAKING

There are policy actors; then there are policy actions that take place within a complex and quite often messy policymaking process. Stages models of public policymaking (e.g., Anderson, 2003) developed in order to simplify this complex process. The policymaking process begins with the identification of a public problem for which redress by governments or their agents is sought. This problem joins any number of other problems vying for attention on the agenda of policymakers. When policymakers with the authority to address the public problem discuss it, the policy agenda stage has begun.

In this stage, the public problem joins others, all waiting to be coupled with a policy solution (Kingdon, 2013). The next stage, the policy formulation stage, encompasses the development of possible policy alternatives. The policy formulation stage is followed by the policy adoption stage, wherein a course of action is chosen from among the various policy alternatives. Policy adoption involves bargaining, compromise, and persuasion in support for a proposed policy (Anderson, 2003). If a policy alternative is not selected, the public problem falls to the wayside, or back into a virtual sea of problems that remain unaddressed by policymakers. If a policy alternative is selected, the pre-enactment stage is concluded and the post-enactment stages—implementation and evaluation—begin. The implementation stage is one in which an adopted policy is put into effect. The evaluation stage includes analysis of the impact(s) of an implemented policy (e.g., program outcomes, costs, intended and unintended consequences).

The stages approach to understanding policy has not been without its critics—notably, that this is an oversimplification of what is a very complicated process (Birkland, 2011; Kingdon, 2013). However, policy scholars continue to turn to this heuristic in order to simplify the complexities of policymaking. Ness (2008) noted that:

> While the public policy literature appears to have reached consensus on the limitations of the stages model since no stage can be studied without overlap into other stages, scholars continue to set their frameworks in the context of these five phases. (p. 14)

Adopting the stages of the policy process heuristic, we recognize the following phases: (a) problem identification and agenda setting, (b) formulation, (c) adoption, (d) implementation, and (e) evaluation. We also acknowledge that while these stages are sequential in nature, they are often not discrete or linear. For example, Anderson (2003) noted that the processes of policy formation and adoption often occur simultaneously, such as when two chambers of a state legislature reconcile conflicts and negotiate modifications to a proposed policy. To frame the actions of policy actors in the policy process of studies reviewed herein, we also make use of the activity structures of policy entrepreneurs proposed by Roberts and King (1991). We align these theoretical frameworks and provide examples of the activity structures of Roberts and King in Table 3.1. In other cases of state-level policymaking, we examine how Hajer's (1995) notion of story lines might be used by policy actors and advocacy groups to build and solidify political coalitions across traditionally ideologically disparate groups of constituencies.

Activity Structures of Policy Entrepreneurs

Using naturalistic inquiry, Roberts and King (1991) provide a rich description of various activities of policy entrepreneurs acting to promulgate support for state legislation that allowed for the establishment of school choice legislation, giving parents and students the choice to attend a school outside their traditional school attendance zones. By introducing the novel (at the time) idea of school choice, translating the idea into actual policy, and then working to implement models, these policy entrepreneurs engaged in myriad activities throughout the policy process, which were then typified via a grounded theory approach by Roberts and King (see Table 3.1). Creative or intellectual activities included generating new policy ideas or applying models and ideas from other policy domains, defining a problem, and selecting a policy solution, and disseminating ideas. Strategic category activities comprised the formulation and evolution of political strategy and developing heuristics for action. Mobilization and execution activities encompassed establishing model programs, cultivating bureaucratic insiders and advocates, collaborating with high-profile individuals and elite groups, acquiring support from elected officials, forming, and coordinating supports across lobby groups, and cultivating media attention and support. Finally, administrative and evaluative activities involved the facilitation of program administration and participating in program evaluation.

This categorization of activities corresponds well with Anderson's (2003) phases of the policymaking process (see Table 3.1) and accentuates the progression of the policymaking process as indiscrete and nonlinear, as acknowledged by Anderson. It is important to note that while Roberts and King (1991) frame the actions of policy entrepreneurs (individuals external to formal government structures and entities) exclusively, Anderson's framework provides a more inclusive model of the policymaking process. Throughout our discussion of the literature pertaining to state-level policies regarding standards, assessment, accountability, and choice, we make explicit connections to both Anderson's phases of the policymaking process and the activity structures of Roberts and King in an effort to situate the activities of public entrepreneurs. We hope this will provide the reader with a useful framework in conceptualizing the actions of policy actors in the policymaking process.

Story Lines to Build and Solidify Political Coalitions

Individuals, coalitions, and interest groups from both sides of the political aisle have actively engaged in the new politics of education. Indeed, NCLB garnered bipartisan support from both Democratic and Republican Parties

Table 3.1

Activity Structures and Actions of Policy Entrepreneurs Typified by Roberts and King (1991) and Corresponding Phase of the Policymaking Process of Anderson (2003)

Activity Structure (Roberts & King, 1991)	Corresponding Phase (Anderson, 2003)	Actions of Policy Entrepreneurs (Roberts & King, 1991)
Creative/Intellectual	Problem Identification and Agenda Setting; Formulation	Generation of new policy ideas or applying models and ideas from other policy domains; definition and articulation of a problem and the identification of a policy solution; dissemination of ideas
Strategic	Agenda Setting; Formulation	Formulation of vision and strategy; evolution of political strategy; development of heuristics for action
Mobilization and Execution	Adoption; Implementation	Establishment of demonstration projects; cultivation of bureaucratic insiders and advocates; collaboration with high-profile individuals and elite groups; enlistment of elected officials; formation and coordination of lobby groups; cultivation of media attention and support
Administrative and Evaluative	Implementation; Evaluation	Facilitation of program administration; participation in program evaluation

(Shoffner, 2016). Interestingly, individuals, coalitions, and interest groups from both sides of the political aisle have been critical of NCLB (Ravitch, 2010). As noted above, policies about educational standards, testing and accountability, and school choice are interdependent and mutually reinforcing. Arguments for these policy reforms, if taken together, might be conceptualized as a story line, or "a condensed sort of narrative that connects different discourses and thus provides the basis of 'discourse coalitions'" (Hajer, 2005, p. 448). For example, Henry and Dixson (2016) noted that "charter schools are positioned in popular and policy discourses as the ideal policy prescription to remedy the educational inequalities in urban areas ... [by] forcing schools to compete for [students]" (p. 219) based on school-level achievement outcomes and other accountability measures while providing opportunities for "authentic democracy, cultural relevance, community uplift, and resistance to White dominance" (p. 220). McDonnell and Weatherford (2013b) described the shifting frames in opposition of the CCSS movement, noting the coalescence of a coalition of resistance centered around arguments ranging from local control of education to "the lack of public debate before [CCSS] adoption, [and] the possibility of an increased testing burden" (p. 495). Such story lines within and between the policies around standards, assessment, accountability, and choice are also given attention in our discussion of these interests below.

INTERESTS IN THE COMMON CORE STATE STANDARDS

Historically, U.S. society has been divided about the aims of schooling. There is a long history of local control in education in the United States, and the adoption of a common curriculum has met political opposition and questions of its constitutionality (Coburn et al., 2016; Cohen & Mehta, 2017; Labaree, 2012; McDonnell & Weatherford, 2013b; Tyack & Cuban, 1995). While professional organizations and state-level policymakers worked to produce and adopt explicit, rigorous standards for learning in the 1980s and 1990s, prior to the new politics of education, there was tremendous variation in content guidelines between states (Porter et al., 2011). The CCSS movement represents an unprecedented effort to standardize a common curriculum across states and affect change in instruction (Coburn et al., 2016). While the CCSS initiative was not a federal initiative, it was supported by NCLB and by the U.S. Department of Education (USDOE) via RTTT grant funding (McDonnell & Weatherford, 2013a; Porter et al., 2011). The CCSS movement was led by both the Council of Chief State School Officers (representing both public and bureaucratic entrepreneurs, depending on the state) and the National Governors Association (representing exclusively public entrepreneurs), but drew on the expertise of educators (bureaucratic entrepreneurs) and others. Adoption of the CCSS was widespread and swift. As Jochim and Lavery (2015) noted, within one year of the release of the CCSS, "forty-five states plus the District of Columbia had signed on, with the support of policymakers on both sides of the political aisle and many prominent advocacy organizations" (p. 380). Methods of CCSS state-adoption varied, with the majority of these states adopting the CCSS by action of a state board of education while a smaller proportion of states adopted the CCSS by executive action of the state's chief education officer or legislative direction, review, or approval (Jochim & Lavery, 2015).

There is a great deal of literature on the actions and interests of actors operating external to, but alongside, government agencies and actors (i.e., policy entrepreneurs). Works, such as those by McDonnell and Weatherford

(2013a, 2013b) have articulated actions of numerous individuals and interest groups acting within and between states to support or curtail CCSS adoption from the early phases of policy adoption through implementation and beyond, such as civil rights organizations and parent interest groups, as well as private foundations, institutes, and service providers. Jochim and Lavery (2015) attended to how CCSS policy support and opposition have evolved over time, in particular across the policy implementation phase. Others (e.g., Polikoff et al., 2016) have used cross-sectional polling data to explore how demographics and other factors—such as political party affiliation or beliefs, opinions, and even misconceptions of the CCSS and other policies (e.g., testing and accountability policies)—predict opposition within states.

McDonnell and Weatherford (2013b) investigated the activities of CCSS supporters, based on interviews, research reports, policy briefs, speeches, blog posts, press releases, media accounts, and congressional testimony produced between 2006 and 2011, as well as participant observer notes of weekly conference calls among groups engaged in implementation of the CCSS. The participants in McDonnel and Weatherford's sample included representatives from each of Roberts and King's (1991) typologies of public entrepreneurs and demonstrate activities in alignment to the activity structures of Roberts and King. McDonnell and Weatherford reported how policy entrepreneurs engaged in strategic category activities as well as creative and intellectual activities by discerning signals from shifting policy environments about the viability of CCSS legislation and evolved policy goals in alignment with these shifts. They drew on international comparisons of data from the Programme for International Student Assessment (PISA) and Trends in International Mathematics and Science Study (TIMMS) to build a story line that included the need for the U.S. to adopt focused, rigorous, and coherent national standards to ensure global competitiveness. To add to this story line, policy entrepreneurs would draw from other data sources; one participant recalling, "we picked and chose evidence depending on the audience" (p. 491). For example, these policy entrepreneurs would highlight the evidence that states with the "largest achievement gaps had the lowest standards" (p. 491) when forging coalitions with civil rights groups, but not with groups representing business interests. These policy entrepreneurs also engaged in mobilization and execution activities (Roberts & King, 1991) by enlisting elected officials and collaborating with high-profile individuals and elite groups, as well as community-based groups.

Drawing on theories of political and policy learning to demonstrate the development of heuristics for action in the development of standards, policy actors acknowledged the pitfalls of the standards movement in the past. Such actions provide an example of strategic category activities

(Roberts & King, 1991) of various types of policy entrepreneurs. McDonnell and Weatherford (2013b) documented efforts to organize the standards development process to include both experts (researchers and policy entrepreneurs) and teachers (bureaucratic entrepreneurs), thus ensuring an evidenced-based approach to writing the standards. Furthermore, the strategic involvement of community-based organizations in the decision-making process sought to keep "federal policymakers informed, but out of it [the CCSS initiative]" (p. 491). Grassroots groups representing communities of color were targeted by policy entrepreneurs with advocacy tool kits that included "information on crafting a message, building a coalition, using data, and accessing the media" (p. 492). These activities represent strategic category activities as well as mobilization and execution activities (Roberts & King, 1991). The interests of groups representing policymakers (i.e., political and executive entrepreneurs) were centered on economic competitiveness, while other policy entrepreneurs (such as civil rights groups) chose to mobilize in support of the CCSS because of issues of equity and interests around reducing variation in the quality of standards between states. As we will show, forging a discourse coalition by merging these two story lines is not as seamless in other policies that have been at the forefront of debates under the new politics of education.

Some scholars have critiqued the CCSS movement on the basis that it "is an elite reform that did little to mobilize mass support and thus opened itself to vigorous opposition" (Cohen & Mehta, 2017, p. 680). The story line emerging from the literature on interest groups opposing the CCSS, such as the National Republican Committee and state-level groups such as Hoosiers Against Common Core and the Tennessee Eagle Forum, as well as from more progressive groups such as Parents Across America, is that the CCSS represent a federal intrusion of local control that limits teacher creativity and creates a way to label schools as failing while over-testing students (Cohen & Mehta, 2017; McDonnell and Weatherford, 2013b); an explicit nod to the interdependence of the CCSS movement with assessment and accountability policies. Interestingly, Polikoff et al. (2016) found that in California, some of the strongest predictors of CCSS opposition were disapproval of President Barack Obama, as well as the misconceptions that states were not allowed to add content to the CCSS, that the CCSS limits teacher creativity, and that the CCSS would amount to too much testing. Another explicit connection between the CCSS and assessment and accountability policies, Jochim and Lavery (2015) point to the centrality of policy implementation as an inflection point in which a wave of political opposition to the CCSS began to gain amplitude in several states, identifying five in which legislation had been passed to replace the CCSS. Dozens of others have seen the introduction of legislation to delay or eliminate the adoption of the CCSS less than four years after adoption. The expansion of conflict around the CCSS has been accompanied by the expansion of partisan disagreement and interest of state legislators (political entrepreneurs) to assume control of education standards (Jochim & Lavery, 2015). Cohen and Mehta (2017) suggested that the CCSS might nevertheless succeed as a niche reform in spite of such recent opposition in many states. Polikoff et al. (2016) suggested that policy actors might garner more support for the CCSS if they had more systematic evidence to counter voter misconceptions about the CCSS.

In exploring the use of evidence by policy actors working in support of the CCSS initiative, McDonnell and Weatherford (2013a) identified connections between the typologies of policy actors, the phases of the policy process, and the types of evidence they used. For example, researchers at universities or think tanks might advance their own research to guide the policy process, whereas other policy entrepreneurs acting in intermediary organizations, such as foundations, nonprofits, and interest groups might select evidence supporting the group's mission. While in the phase of problem identification and policy formulation, for instance, a policy entrepreneur might select evidence that allows them to frame the problem such that their policy solution might be seen as preferential (a strategic category activity). On the other hand, when in the policy development phase, public entrepreneurs might draw more heavily from research findings and experiential knowledge gleaned from bureaucratic entrepreneurs to maintain support and quell opposition. When in the policy adoption phase, however, political entrepreneurs may also look to their party leaders or committee chairs in seeking advice on how to vote. Acknowledging the possibility that while policy actors might misuse research to gain political support, as noted by authors such as Majone (1989) and Stone (2012), McDonnell and Weatherford (2013a) assert that the "competitive nature of the political process and the fact that credibility is the policy advocate's most important resource minimizes outright distortion" (p. 3).

INTERESTS IN HIGH-STAKES ACCOUNTABILITY POLICY

Standards, assessment, accountability, and choice policies "seek to raise student achievement by influencing how teachers teach and how students learn" (Coburn et al., 2016, p. 243). The idea is that making achievement scores publicly available provides a lever of public pressure for educators to improve achievement outcomes, including achievement gaps between historically marginalized student groups and their peers. Labaree (2012) noted that policies seeking to fundamentally change teaching and learning, such as high-stakes accountability policies, have historically been difficult to implement (largely because of the decentralized structure of the U.S.

educational systems), giving rise to the isolation of teachers. This notion of policy to fundamentally change the instructional core was echoed by Cohen and Mehta (2017) in their discussion of difficulties in implementing the CCSS. Moreover, Lavigne (2014) found no evidence that high-stakes accountability policies have improved the teacher workforce (as defined by measures that included student achievement test scores and teacher observations) or student achievement outcomes. However, other researchers have found that high-stakes accountability policies influenced instruction and contributed to increases in student achievement (Au, 2007; Mintrop & Sunderman, 2009; Roderick et al., 2002; Valli & Buese, 2007), albeit modestly, but also contributed to the narrowing of the curriculum and attempts to game the system. For example, Grissom et al. (2017) found that teacher performance measures which incorporated students' performance on state assessments were used to place teachers with more positive performance in tested classrooms the following year. This is troubling, given that some teacher performance measures—such as value-added measures—are unreliable (Aaronson et al., 2007; Goldhaber et al., 2013; Lavigne, 2014). Others have argued that, when political support is maintained at the local level, changes in instruction are possible, at least in niche systems that invest heavily in supporting teachers' professional practice (Cohen & Mehta, 2017; Lavigne, 2014).

Scholars, such as Ingle and Lindle (2019), point to the publication of *A Nation at Risk* (NCEE, 1983) as providing an impetus to spread accountability policy across the United States. In 1973, 27 states had some form of accountability legislation, and teacher evaluations were present in only 12 states (Lavigne, 2014). *A Nation at Risk* questioned the quality of the teaching force and teacher preparation programs, recommended higher pay (including bonuses, but that these bonuses not be tied to standardized test scores) and extending the number of contract days for teachers to engage in professional development. Local education agencies (LEAs) were encouraged to collaborate with school administrators and teachers to create ways to distinguish between novice, experienced, and master teachers—as well as ineffective teachers, who should be supported to improve or be terminated. Teacher accountability remained a prominent feature in federal education policies subsequent to *A Nation at Risk* (e.g., America 2000, Goals 2000, NCLB, RTTT, ESSA). During the presidency of George H. W. Bush, for example, a proposed bill known as America 2000 pushed for states to adopt standards, assessment, accountability, and choice policies. However, Congress failed to adopt legislation based on America 2000. Superfine (2005) suggested that the lack of political will to enact America 2000 was due to calls for states to voluntarily adopt national standards and school choice options, perhaps a testament to the historical primacy of political consensus around school accountability policies.

Later, the Clinton Administration would condition Title I funding of ESEA, via legislation known as Goals 2000, on states adopting both rigorous standards as well as assessment and accountability systems. The passage of NCLB established federal law that mandated all states use annual assessments in reading and mathematics (in Grades 3–8 and once again in high school) and triggered local policymakers to mobilize sanctions against low-performing schools (Coburn et al., 2016) through a framework for corrective actions. Interestingly, Poole (2011) showed that the strength of state-level accountability policy was inversely related to school-level accountability, "defined as a school-level system in which collective behaviors and conditions exist that direct the attention and effort of the internal school community to continuous improvement" (p. 261).

As noted above, RTTT sought to improve achievement outcomes by awarding school improvement grants (SIGs) to states and districts that identified the lowest performing schools and placed specific, high-stakes accountability mechanisms on principals and teachers (Koedel et al., 2017; Nichols & Berliner, 2007; National Board on Educational Testing and Public Policy, 2003). Wong (2013) noted that, "These innovative initiatives sought the support from key state and local actors— including governors [public entrepreneurs], state commissioners [executive or public entrepreneurs], mayors [public entrepreneurs], unions [representing bureaucratic entrepreneurs], and networks of diverse providers [policy entrepreneurs], among others" (p. 413). In the first distributions of SIGs, the districts in 44 states that were awarded grant funding overwhelmingly selected the transformation model for their persistently low-achieving schools (77%), while some selected the turnaround model (21%). Relatively fewer schools were selected for restart (5%) and only 3% of schools were closed (Wong, 2013). The fact that only 5% of schools were selected for the restart model possibly suggests weaker political support for school choice relative to accountability policies. Lavigne (2014) pointed out that, as of 2011, "20 states had policies that require teachers to be eligible for dismissal based on evaluation results" (p. 116). In 2015, however, the passage of ESSA would return some autonomy to states and LEAs in deciding how to turn around their lowest performing schools. Nevertheless, as of 2018, 35 states used performance-based models that tied appropriations to educational outcomes (Hillman et al., 2018).

Issues of accountability have inevitably emerged within and across states in the new politics of education. Litigants in cases, such as in *Vergara v. California*, have sought to make it easier to remove ineffective teachers. Mayors have received attention in the literature for getting involved in political conflict around accountability policies, such as Richard Daley of Chicago, who backed his state's chief education officer's decision to allow Chicago Public Schools to continue offering supplemental education services while agreeing to reduce barriers for private vendors of tutoring services in a compromise (mobilization and execution activities) with former U.S. Secretary of Education Margret Spellings (Wong, 2013). Wong (2014) noted that mayors in large urban districts, such as Chicago, Washington DC, and Boston, have gained significant control over school districts via the power to appoint members of local boards of education and/or the superintendent. Some SEAs (such as in Tennessee) and their chief state school officers (in Kentucky for example) have publicly criticized street-level bureaucrats in their role as policy administrators and evaluators—such as principals and other teacher evaluators—for being unwilling or unable to identify the lowest performing teachers (Lavigne, 2014). In other states, quasi-governmental organizations, such as Louisiana's Recovery School District (RSD), Tennessee's Achievement District, and the Education Achievement Authority (EAA) in Michigan, have emerged as implementers of accountability policies.

In addition to policy actors inside formal government structures, the actions of policy entrepreneurs have gained attention in the research literature on high-stakes accountability policies. The National Association for the Advancement of Colored People (NAACP) Legal Defense and Education Fund (2011), for example, proclaimed ESEA as a civil rights law and supported calls for increased federal accountability for the performance of student groups, while state and local governments, represented by groups such as the National Governors Association, the National Conference of State Legislatures, Council of State Governments, National Association of Counties, and National School Boards Association, wanted greater flexibility in accountability policy (Wong, 2013). Such activity demonstrates the actions of policy entrepreneurs as strategic category influencers (Roberts & King, 1991) by evolving political strategy. Philanthropic groups, such as the Gates Foundation, funded research to create instruments and measures to better measure teacher efficacy (i.e., the Measures of Effective Teaching Project), but Lavigne (2014) has noted a lack of willingness among states to fully fund systems that would provide reliable measures of teacher efficacy. In this way, policy entrepreneurs engaged in mobilization and execution activities (Roberts & King, 1991) by establishing demonstration projects. Policy entrepreneurs also engaged in administrative and evaluative activities (Roberts & King, 1991) as evidenced by program evaluations.

Several key points have emerged from the literature on the use of research in high-stakes accountability policy. While researchers might not fit neatly into any one category of public entrepreneurs proposed by Roberts and King (1991), they certainly have active roles in the policymaking process. Researchers not only play an important role in the evaluation of policies, they identify the implications of their research to inform the need for further analysis, for the identification of policy solutions (creative and intellectual activities), and for the development of heuristics for action or even the evolution of political strategy (strategic category activities). Lavigne (2014) made explicit the paramount importance of ensuring policymakers use the existing research to inform the trajectory of teacher evaluation policies. Other calls (e.g., see Ingle & Lindle, 2019; Wiliam, 2018) continue to highlight the importance of research to gain a better understanding of how to best facilitate teacher improvement. Coburn et al. (2016) argue that accountability policies should not be studied in isolation, but rather researchers should focus on the intersection of these policies with others, in particular with the CCSS. In addition, Poole (2011) noted a paucity of research examining the intersection of student achievement and charter schools. We now turn our attention to the actors and actions in the interests of charter school legislation.

INTERESTS IN CHARTER SCHOOL LEGISLATION

Charters are one relatively contentious example of school choice policies, the third pillar of the new politics of education. Other forms of school choice policies are considered even more contentious, such as school vouchers. The idea behind school choice is that parents and students can choose to attend a school outside of their traditional, neighborhood public school. The Center for Education Research (Center for Educational Research [CER], 2018) defines charter schools as "public schools of choice ... [that] receive enhanced autonomy in exchange for being held strictly accountable for the outcomes they promise to achieve" (p. 4). Shannon and Saatcioglu (2018) noted that:

> In theory, both charter schools and their teachers are granted more autonomy to improve educational performance ... not simply in the form of greater discretion in the classroom, but ... in the form of influence over *all* [emphasis theirs] key official school-wide policies. (p. 1042)

Yet, numerous scholars (Lubienski, 2003; Malloy & Wohlstetter, 2003; Shannon & Saatcioglu, 2018; Tonso & Colombo, 2006) point to the paucity of research supporting the assertion that charter schools provide increased teacher autonomy and input into school policies. The burgeoning body of literature on localized control in charter schools suggests that this pro-charter story line is nuanced. For example, Gawlik (2007) and Torres (2014) found that teachers (representing street-level bureaucrats) in some charter schools perceived a greater sense of autonomy and policy influence than in others. Shannon and Saatcioglu (2018) demonstrated that charter school teachers in their sample perceived less policy influence than teachers in traditional public schools. Others found that teacher autonomy and policy influence are similar across school type (e.g., Hannaway & Woodroffe; 2003; Renzulli et al., 2015).

Nevertheless, this story line is consistent with neoliberal, market-based arguments. Charter schools represent both decentralization and the expansion of a quasi-market of education providers. In this market, choice drives competition between schools such that schools which perform better (i.e., produce higher achievement outcomes) receive more public funding via the students who choose to attend, producing a systemic effect such that all schools gradually improve and equity gaps are reduced as schools which fail to do so are ultimately closed. As we will show, this story line is rich and textured, as policy actors have worked to build consensus among historically disparate groups while counter-story lines of school choice opponents have emerged as well. In addition, this story line is entangled with and reinforced by the story lines of proponents of standards reform and high-stakes accountability policies. The CER (2018) reports that there are nearly 7,000 charter schools in 44 states, enrolling approximately 3 million students. While this represents a small proportion of all K–12 students in the United States, there is a great deal of research on myriad actors and actions centered upon charter school policy since the first state adopted charter school legislation in the 1990s. We begin this section of the chapter by reviewing two research studies on the interstate dynamics and intrastate attributes of states adopting and implementing charter school legislation. We believe those who propose to study or affect policy change acknowledge the potential influence political party dominance can play on the adoption of charter school legislation. Next, we review some literature that articulates the actions of policy actors in other phases of the policy process in an effort to articulate the story line and counter-story line of interested parties. We conclude this section with some implications for researchers in the domain of charter school legislation before a brief discussion concerning the interconnections between these policy domains, as well as a few implications for both policy scholars and actors, before concluding this chapter.

Renzulli and Roscigno (2005) provide an event-history analysis, examining both interstate dynamics and intrastate characteristics in the diffusion of charter school legislation across states and its implementation to draw causal inferences about how these attributes might affect the type of charter school legislation adopted by a state. The authors found that both interstate dynamics (as evidenced by mimetic tendencies, operationalized by the prior adoption of charter legislation in neighboring states) and intrastate attributes played a role in charter legislation adoption. Salient to our analysis on the interests of actors in shaping charter school policy, intrastate attributes—specifically, the relative strength of teachers unions (bureaucratic entrepreneurs) and political party dominance (political entrepreneurs)—played a dominant role in the adoption of either strong charter laws (reducing barriers to charter school founding) or weak charter laws (which are more limiting, in terms of who can open charter schools). Furthermore, the political party affiliation of a state's governor (political entrepreneurs) matters in the implementation of charter school legislation, such that Republican governors predict fewer charter school openings.

Others have investigated variation in state charter legislation with a framework of policy regimes, which "capture dominant and distinct approaches to policy innovations that are informed by common institutional environments among states" (Pelz, 2015, p. 330). In doing so, Pelz (2015) noted political party dominance in state legislative bodies (political entrepreneurs) as a factor in constructing these policy regimes. Comparisons were then made between traditional public and charter school achievement outcomes by policy regime type. First, through a factor analysis, Pelz typified four policy regimes based on intrastate characteristics: independence, support, accountability, and mandate. State charter laws in the independence regime tend to focus on ensuring local control of charter schools. These states tend to have higher charter school enrollments and relatively lower percentages of students in poverty and of minority status with greater support for the Republican Party. States in the support regime have charter laws that tend to promote the spread of charter schools by providing ample funding and have less restrictive policies about who can found a charter school. States in this regime tend to have clusters of charter schools in urban centers, serve higher proportions of minority students, and tend to lean Democratic. States in the accountability regime tend to have laws which focus on ensuring proper oversite of charter schools. Pelz noted that these states might use charter schools to rectify problems with education in urban centers. These states also tend to have charters that serve relatively higher proportions of students in poverty and of minority status. Moreover, states in the accountability regime tend to be heavily Democratic and perform well on the NAEP assessment. Finally, states in the mandate regime tend to have laws that ensure charter schools maintain certain functions of traditional public schools, serve relatively fewer poor and minority students, and tend to lean Republican. Second, Pelz found that the type of policy regime a state adopts is related to charter school performance, "in ways that are consistent with each regime's policy approach" (p. 330). While the works of Pelz and Renzulli and Roscigno (2005) give explicit attention to the apparent interests of political entrepreneurs in shaping charter school policy, other works have focused attention on understanding the actions and interests of other policy actors.

Buras (2011) examined aspects of charter policy formation and implementation in New Orleans since the city's reconstruction following

Hurricane Katrina. Drawing on critical race theory (CRT), Buras framed a "strategic assault on Black communities by education entrepreneurs" (p. 296). This case study analyzed data drawn from interviews, document analysis, field notes, documentaries, and oral histories. Their sample included bureaucratic and political entrepreneurs (teachers unions and members of the state legislature, respectively), the Recovery School District (RSD), a quasi-governmental (bureaucratic) organization acting under the authority of the chief state education officer (an executive entrepreneur in Louisiana), as well as policy entrepreneurs (Cowen Institute, New Schools for New Orleans, teachNOLA, New Leaders for New Schools, Lower 9 School Development Group, etc.). Using these data, Buras mapped the political ecology (that is, the interactions) of these various actors to one another as well as to actors in the federal government. In doing so, Buras demonstrated how these White actors and Black allies engaged in activities throughout the policy process, analyzing how these actions attributed to the exploitation of Black communities. For instance, in framing the policy problem and offering solutions (creative/intellectual activities), political, bureaucratic, and policy entrepreneurs professed charter policy as a solution to mitigate inequities in education and improve public schools. Buras critiqued this story line and framed a counter-story line, positioning these White actors and Black allies as acting in the interests of profit as opposed to the interests of marginalized students and families.

Scott (2009) showed how venture philanthropists (elite policy entrepreneurs) have framed a similar story line on the ability of charter schools to mitigate educational inequities. These policy entrepreneurs have engaged in mobilization and execution activities by establishing demonstration projects and collaborating with high-profile elite groups (such as the Olin Foundation and Bradley Foundation). One such example described how these elite policy entrepreneurs sponsored efforts to "put parents of color out front" (p. 119) in cultivating media attention and support. Other activity structures of venture philanthropists are noted by Scott (2009), such as providing support for administrative activities (by way of funding charter management organizations or helping to develop effective leadership). Others have critiqued the pro-charter story line in a similar way to the critiques offered by Buras (2011). Henry and Dixon (2016), for example, studied the implementation of charter legislation in New Orleans following Hurricane Katrina by critiquing the story line that charters are "the ideal policy prescription to remedy the educational inequalities in urban areas" (p. 219). Identifying the gatekeepers who review charter applications (a collaboration between bureaucratic and policy entrepreneurs), Henry and Dixson found that Black applicants, including street-level bureaucrats (principals) and policy entrepreneurs (former Black educators, business leaders, and lawyers) were "locked out" of the process, framing a counter-narrative about how "the charter school authorization process and thus charter schools in post-Katrina New Orleans reproduce racial inequalities and White dominance" (p. 226).

An additional critique to the pro-choice story line—the nuanced counter-narratives of Black parents—was offered by Ellison and Aloe (2018), suggesting that Black parents perceive opportunities to choose another school as positive, but also sense an information imbalance between Black parents and charter schools and often "feel like it is they who are being chosen by the schools instead of the other way around" (p. 19). Additionally, Ellison and Aloe found that some parents "expressed skepticism over the idea of competition in education" (p. 23), and constructed a composite theme from their analysis that, "parents are running away from public schools and not necessarily toward school choice" (p. 25). This is a phenomenon acknowledged by Vergari (2007), who noted that while some low-income and minority parents in low-performing school districts were not keen on school privatization, they were "interested in charter schools largely on the basis that they promise to bring greater equity to public education" (p. 23). Examining another aspect of the pro-charter story line, Hamlin (2017) asserted that school safety may be a more important factor in parent choices in postindustrial urban areas (such as Detroit) than other indicators of school performance. The construction of these story lines and counter-story lines represent creative and intellectual activities of these and other public entrepreneurs (Roberts & King, 1991). Another story line critical of charter school policies, and school choice policies more broadly, emerges from the body of literature on school desegregation and subsequent re-segregation (e.g., Danns, 2018; Frankenberg, 2017; Kotok et al., 2018; McPherson, 2011; Morantz, 1996). This body of literature also provides an example of how researchers can act to foment policy change by framing arguments in support of or juxtaposed to policy story lines through policy evaluation.

Wilson (2016) described one case, a charter school in Milwaukee serving Somali immigrant students almost exclusively, which was framed as a *counterpublic* (Fraser, 1997). Acknowledging the long history of oppression in the United States, Fraser (1997) argues that there is no universal public sphere, what Habermas (1998) defined as an apolitical public space (such as coffee shops) in which the validity of an argument is measured by its rationale and not by the relative positions of power of those engaged in the argument. As Wilson (2016) stated, "Under conditions of inequality, a unified public sphere reifies existing power structures, privileges dominant groups, and disadvantages the historically subordinate" (p. 922). A counterpublic is a space in which members of a marginalized group might "invent and circulate counter-discourses ... providing a safe space ... and serving as training grounds" (p. 81) for these actors to practice articulating counter-narratives before engaging in a more inclusive, albeit inequitable, public sphere. The educators (bureaucratic entrepreneurs) and policy entrepreneurs described by Wilson (2016), acted in the policy implementation phase through mobilization and execution activities (Roberts & King, 1991) to create a counterpublic space. Such a space can serve as an incubator for continuous development and re-development of story lines and counter-story lines—what Roberts and King (1991) might categorize as creative and intellectual activities.

DeBray et al. (2014) examined the demand for charter research and the use of research by policy entrepreneurs working as either advocates or opponents in charter policy coalitions in New Orleans. While DeBray et al. framed aspects of competing story lines around charter school effectiveness already articulated above, perhaps more salient to the interests of readers of this chapter, DeBray et al. also found that there is little capacity for research in intermediary groups (policy entrepreneurs) across both policy coalitions. DeBray et al. also found that there is little demand for research from state-level policymakers (public entrepreneurs). Moreover, they noted that as charter school effectiveness, relative to traditional public schools, is increasingly questioned, the velocity of charter school implementation is increasing.

As late as 2017, another state (the Commonwealth of Kentucky) adopted charter legislation. In addition to this finding, we acknowledge two themes emerging from the research literature on charter school policy. First, we note that the research on charter school policy has captured the interests and actions of policy actors from all of the typologies acknowledged by Roberts and King (1991). Second, we acknowledge the way that researchers situate policy actors in different ways. Some, for example, explicitly situate two competing coalitions in juxtaposition to one another (e.g., Vergari, 2007; DeBray et al., 2014) while others acknowledge the actions of many individuals and groups (e.g., Renzulli & Roscigno, 2005; Buras, 2011). Others focus on specific typologies of policy actors, such as venture philanthropists (Scott, 2009), or on public entrepreneurs (Cattaneo, 2018). The literature on the interests of policy actors in charter school includes many different types of public entrepreneurs along with rich descriptions of the actions they take and the story lines they shape to affect change in charter school policy.

THE TIES THAT BIND: STANDARDS, ASSESSMENT, ACCOUNTABILITY, AND CHOICE

State education systems within the U.S. are comprised of schools and districts which are loosely-coupled, to a large extent through state statutes and administrative regulations (Labaree, 2012). This structure resists large-scale change in the instructional core occurring in classrooms, which tend to be isolated from one another (Cohen & Mehta, 2017; Labaree, 2012). Yet, the publication of *A Nation at Risk* (NCEE, 1983) was an impetus for widespread political support of accountability in education, in spite of a lack of coherence across states about what was to be taught. As states have adopted accountability systems that, at least partially, incorporated scores on student achievement tests and teacher observations, the U.S. witnessed a rising wave of states adopting a common set of standards (CCSS) in core academic subjects, albeit followed by a subsequent resurgence of political opposition (Jochim & Lavery, 2015; Polikoff et al., 2016). The adoption of common standards and common high-stakes assessments has created a system in which different schools and different types of schools can be compared based upon a common set of criteria. The addition of school choice policies has created a quasi-market for parents and students to choose their educational service providers. The story line of the new politics of education (DeBray-Pelot & McGuinn, 2009) posits that these policies work in tandem to improve systemic inequalities by simultaneously ensuring commonality of curriculum and assessment while further de-centralizing localized authority, providing for diverse types of schools governed in ways not seen in American education prior to the new politics of education (Cookson, 1994). These policy features are somewhat ubiquitous across states, yet there is variation in these policy domains.

The initial proliferation of states adopting the Common Core, followed by the subsequent action of political and policy entrepreneurs in opposition to its implementation, represents an entanglement of competing policy story lines crafted by policy actors from both sides of the political aisle. What remains is a relatively smaller number of states with plans to continue the implementation of the CCSS. Cohen and Mehta (2017) noted that the CCSS movement will likely continue, but as a niche reform, not as the original vision of a common set of standards across the United States. Furthermore, the potential for divergence of state standards may foreshadow some consequences for other policy domains within the new politics of education. For example, if the variation in learning objectives between schools, districts, and states increases again, there may be implications for assessment and accountability policies as different sets of standards require different assessments which would further complicate issues of school choice, where parents and students would be left to base judgements of relative school quality on disparate measures of "achievement."

Some researchers have taken advantage of this variation across states to explore how state education policies might be typified and even related to outcomes of other policies in the new politics of education (Coburn et al., 2016; Poole, 2011). While there is much literature about the actions and interests of policy actors acting to reform standards, accountability, and choice policies within and across states, fewer researchers have studied the ways in which these policy domains might interact. One theme emerging from the literature on these three distinct but interconnected policies is that researchers tend to focus on one of these three policies domains in particular. We join the calls from others (e.g., Coburn et al., 2016; Poole, 2011) to move the research base forward by considering ways to study the interactions of these policies in their specific form both within and between states. Doing so would certainly lead to a greater understanding of how these policies work together, which could better inform public entrepreneurs seeking to improve educational outcomes in their own states. However, we also acknowledge the calls from authors for more systematic research of each of these polices (e.g., Cohen et al., 2018).

Salient to the purpose of this book, we acknowledge the findings of DeBray et al. (2014) who demonstrated that there may be a lack of demand for research from many state and local education policymakers as well as a lack of research capacity among policy entrepreneurs acting as information brokers in intermediary organizations. We believe such a disconnect between the policy literature and policy actors may be due to a failure of educational policy scholars to effectively communicate their research findings to policymakers. Scholars focus on the production of peer-reviewed studies that are not "easily digestible" to politicians or members of the general public. Policymakers, particularly Republicans, may recoil from overtures from educational researchers, suspicious of their motives and political leanings (Hess et al., 2002; Turnage, 2017). Finally, as the field of educational policy, and political science more broadly, is replete with theories seeking to explain the actions and interests of actors, we recommend that future analyses of state-level policies in the new politics of education adopt alternative theoretical and conceptual frameworks than those adopted in the present synthesis. The three forms of New Institutionalism (Hall & Taylor, 1996; Lecours, 2005), for instance, might provide an interesting analysis of the actors, interests, and actions in the new politics of education. While Wang (2016) asserted that "New Institutionalism in organizational analysis has become one of the most widely accepted theoretical approaches in sociology over the past three decades" (p. 348), New Institutionalism did not appear in our search of the literature on the policies reviewed in this chapter. We suggest that application of New Institutionalism as a theoretical approach to policy analysis may yield a rich line of inquiry situated in the new politics of education. Viewed from the perspective of rational choice institutionalism, which emerged from studies of U.S. congressional behavior (Lecours, 2005), scholars might focus their investigation on the impact of our political institutions on individual or collective decisions in the policymaking process. Alternatively, an analysis through the lens of sociological institutionalism might compliment this chapter's focus on policy story lines (Hajer, 2005) by adopting a broader analytical focus on the "symbol systems, cognitive scripts, and moral templates that provide the frames of meaning" (Hall & Taylor, 1996, p. 947) which policy entrepreneurs might draw upon.

A summary of public entrepreneurs (Roberts & King, 1991), whose actions in the policy process were noted in the literature reviewed in this chapter, can be found in Table 3.2. Furthermore, we have organized this sample of policy studies using Anderson's (2003) stages model of the policymaking process. While this certainly does not represent an exhaustive list of scholarly works on the public entrepreneurs central to the study of the new politics of education, we note myriad examples of the types of policy actors who have been studied in this policy context. We believe this categorization may prove useful to policy scholars and actors alike. The distribution of studies across the stages of the policymaking process reviewed herein may provide readers with suggestions about potential gaps to fill in the literature on public entrepreneurs related to the new politics of education. However, some gaps in Table 3.2 might be expected. For example, the lack of literature included on policy entrepreneurs in the policy adoption phase is intuitive, given that policy entrepreneurs are, by definition, actors external to the government. In addition, public entrepreneurs seeking to affect policy change throughout the policymaking process in their own states may benefit from an understanding of what is known about the actors and their actions in fomenting policy change in the context of standards, accountability, and choice. This body of research may serve as a useful guide through the complex process of state-level policymaking. Nevertheless we provide this graphic representation in hopes that the readers of this chapter might be inspired to find new perspectives on the actors and actions in the interests of the new politics of education.

CONCLUSION

In sum, we focus on the *who* of policymaking. Others in this book will focus on the *how* of getting research in front of policymakers in an "easily digestible" form. This chapter frames the actions and interests of actors in the new politics of education using the activity structures and typologies of policy entrepreneurs of Roberts and King (1991), as well as Hajer's (1995) notion of policy story lines, to forge discourse coalitions in the policymaking process. Specifically, we have shown through our review of the literature how the CCSS initiative, high-stakes accountability policies, and charter school legislation are interconnected via a rich and textured story line. Emerging from our review of the educational policy literature

Table 3.2

Public Entrepreneurs Acting in a Given Stage of the Policymaking Process Noted in the Literature Reviewed Herein

Roberts & King's (1991) Typology	Problem Identification & Agenda Setting	Formulation	Adoption	Implementation	Evaluation
Political Entrepreneurs	Governors (Buras, 2011; Cattneo, 2018; McDonnell & Weatherford, 2013a; Wong, 2013) State Legislators (Buras, 2011; Wong, 2013)	Governors (Buras, 2011; Cattaneo, 2018; Ingle & Lindle, 2019; McDonnell & Weatherford, 2013a; Wong, 2013) State Legislators (Buras, 2011; Wong, 2013)	Governors (Buras, 2011; Cattaneo, 2018; Henry & Dixson, 2016; Jochim & Lavery, 2015; McDonnell & Weatherford, 2013a) State Legislators (Jochim & Lavery, 2015)	Governors (McDonnell & Weatherford, 2013b) Orleans Parish School Board (Buras, 2011) Mayors (Vergari, 2007; Wong, 2013)	State Legislators (DeBray et al., 2014; Polikoff, 2016)
Executive Entrepreneurs	Chief State Education Officers (Jochim & Lavery, 2015)	Chief State Education Officers (Buras, 2011; Jochim & Lavery, 2014; Porter et al., 2011) District Superintendents (McDonnell & Weatherford, 2013a) Recovery School District Superintendent (Buras, 2011) Principals (McDonnell & Weatherford, 2013a)	Recovery School District Superintendent (Buras, 2011) Chief State Education Officers (Jochim & Lavery, 2015) State Boards of Education (Jochim & Lavery, 2015)	Recovery School District Superintendent (Buras, 2011) Chicago Public School's Chief Executive Officer (Wong, 2013)	

(Table continued on the next page)

Table 3.2

Public Entrepreneurs Acting in a Given Stage of the Policymaking Process Noted in the Literature Reviewed Herein (Continued)

Roberts & King's (1991) Typology	Problem Identification & Agenda Setting	Formulation	Adoption	Implementation	Evaluation
Bureaucratic Entrepreneurs		State Education Agencies (McDonnell & Weatherford, 2013a) Teachers Unions (McDonnell & Weatherford, 2013a)	Teachers (Shannon & Saatcioglu, 2018) Teachers Unions (Buras, 2011; Giersch, 2014)	Charter Management Organizations (Vergari, 2007) Recovery School District (Buras, 2011) State Education Agencies (Buras, 2011; Henry & Dixson, 2016) Teachers/Principals (Cohen & Mehta, 2017; Lavigne, 2014; Vergari, 2007)	
Policy Entrepreneurs	Bring New Orleans Back Commission (Buras, 2011) Venture Philanthropies (Scott, 2009) NAACP (Wong, 2013)	Bring New Orleans Back Commission (Buras, 2011) Civil Rights Groups (McDonnell & Weatherford, 2013a; Wong, 2013) Venture Philanthropies (Scott, 2009) Intermediary Organizations (DeBray et al., 2014)		Private Institutes and Foundations (Buras, 2011; Henry & Dixson, 2016) Parent Interest Groups (Jochim & Lavery, 2015; McDonnell & Weatherford, 2013b) Private Education Providers (Porter et al., 2011) State-Based Groups (McDonnell & Weatherford, 2013b) Venture Philanthropies (Scott, 2009)	American Institutes for Research (Vergari, 2007) Gates Foundation (Ingle & Lindle, 2019; Lavigne, 2014) Intermediary Organizations (DeBray et al., 2014) Urban South Grassroots Research Collective (Buras, 2011) Venture Philanthropies (Scott, 2009)

centered on these policy domains is the juxtaposition of a common story line (Hajer, 1995), grounded in the new politics of education (DeBray-Pelot & McGuinn, 2009), with a counter-story line (e.g., Buras, 2011; DeBray et al., 2014; Ellison & Aloe, 2018). In particular, these counter-story lines emerge from criticism or a lack of evidence to support the idea that these policies will work together to eliminate achievement gaps between historically marginalized groups and others, with some exceptions. Yet, much is left to be known about how these policy domains interact. We also provide readers with what we hope is a deeper understanding of the interconnections of these policies as a dominant features emerging in the past 40 years on the U.S. educational landscape. Finally, we hope that the implications provided herein for policy scholars and actors seeking to study or foment change in state-level education policy prove to be practical.

REFERENCES

Aaronson, D., Barrow, L., & Sander, W. (2007). Teachers and student achievement in the Chicago public high schools. *Journal of Labor Economics, 25*(1), 95–135.

Anderson, J. E. (2003). *Public policymaking* (5th ed.). Houghton Mifflin.

Au, W. (2007). High-stakes testing and curricular control: A qualitative metasynthesis. *Educational Researcher, 36*(5), 258–267.

Ball, S. J. (2010). New states, new governance and new education policy. In M. W. Apple, S. J. Ball, & L. A. Ganding (Eds.), *The Routledge international handbook of the sociology of education* (pp. 155–166). Routledge.

Birkland, T. A. (2011). *An introduction to the policy process: Theories concepts, and models of public policy making* (3rd ed.). Routledge.

Buras, K. L. (2011). Race, charter schools, and conscious capitalism: On the spatial politics of whiteness as property (and the unconscionable assault on Black New Orleans). *Harvard Educational Review, 81*(2), 296–331. https://doi.org/10.17763/haer.81.2.6l42343qqw360j03

Calaff, K. P. (2008). Supportive schooling: Practices that support culturally and linguistically diverse students' preparation for college. *NASSP Bulletin, 92*(2), 95–110.

Cattaneo, K. H. (2018). Applying policy theories to charter school legislation in New York: Rational actor model, stage heuristics, and multiple streams. *Educational Policy Analysis and Strategic Research, 13*(2), 6–24.

Center for Educational Research. (2018). *National charter school law rankings and scorecard 2018: The essential guide for policymakers and advocates*.

Coburn, C. E., Hill, H. C., & Spillane, J. P. (2016). Alignment and accountability in policy design and implementation: The Common Core State Standards and implementation research. *Educational Researcher, 45*(4), 243–251. https://doi.org/10.3102/0013189X16651080

Cohen, D. K., & Mehta, J. D. (2017). Why reform sometimes succeeds: Understanding the conditions that produce reforms that last. *American Educational Research Journal, 54*(4), 644–690. https://doi.org/10.3102/0002831217700078

Cohen, D., Spillane, J. P., Peurach, D. J. (2018). The dilemmas of educational reform. *Educational Researcher, 47*(3), 204–212.

Cookson, P. (1994). *School choice: The struggle for the soul of American education*. Yale University Press.

Crowley, G. R., & Beaulier, S. A. (2018). Public-sector unions and government policy: Reexamining the effects of political contributions and collective bargaining rights. *Public Finance Reiew, 46*(3), 454–485.

Danns, D. (2018). Policy implications for school desegregation and school choice in Chicago. *Urban Review, 50*, 584–603. https://doi.org/10.1007/s11256-018-0457

DeBray, E., Scott, J., Lubienski, C., & Jabbar, H. (2014). Intermediary organizations in charter school policy coalitions: Evidence from New Orleans. *Educational Policy, 28*(2), 175–206. https://doi.org/10.1177/0895904813514132

DeBray-Pelot, E., & McGuinn, P. (2009). The new politics of education: Analyzing the federal education policy landscape in the post-NCLB era. *Educational Policy, 23*(1), 15–42.

Ellison, S., & Aloe, A. M. (2018). Strategic thinkers and positioned choices: Parental decision making in urban school choice. *Educational Policy*. https://doi.org/10.1177/0895904818755470

Frankenberg, E. (2017). Assessing segregation under a new generation of controlled choice policies. *American Educational Research Journal, 54*(1S), 219S–250S. https://doi.org/10.3102/0002831216634462

Fraser, N. (1997). *Justice interruptus: Critical reflections on the post-socialist condition*. Routledge.

Gawlik, M. A. (2007). Beyond the charter schoolhouse door: Teacher-perceived autonomy. *Education and Urban Society, 39*, 524–553.

Goldhaber, D. D., Goldschmidt, P., & Tseng, F. (2013). Teacher value-added at the high-school level: Different models, different answers? *Education Evaluation and Policy Analysis, 35*(2), 220–236.

Grissom, J. A., Kalogrides, D., & Loeb, S. (0217). Strategic staffing? How performance pressures affect the distribution of teachers within schools and resulting student achievement. *American Educational Research Journal, 54*(6), 1079–1116. https://doi.org/10.3102/0002831217716301

Habermas, J. (1989). *The structural transformation of the public sphere: An inquiry into a category of bourgeois society*. MIT Press.

Hajer, M. A. (1995). *The politics of environmental discourse: Ecological modernization and the policy process*. Clarendon Press.

Hajer, M. A. (2005). Rebuilding ground zero: The politics of performance. *Planning Theory and Practice, 6*(4), 445–464. https://doi.org/10.1080/14649350500349623

Hall, P. A., & Taylor, R. C. R. (1996). Political science and the three new institutionalisms. *Political Studies, 44*, 936–957.

Hallinan, M. T. (2008). Teacher influences on students' attachment to school. *Sociology of Education, 81*, 271–283.

Hamlin, D. (2017). Are charter schools safer in deindustrialized cities with high rates of crime? Testing hypotheses in Detroit. *American Educational Research Journal, 54*(4). https://doi.org/10.3102/0002831217705060

Hannaway, J., & Woodroffe, N. (2003). Policy instruments in education. *Review of Research in Education, 27*, 1–24.

Henry, K. L., & Dixson, A. D. (2016). "Locking the door before we got the keys": Racial realities of the charter school authorization process in post-Katrina New Orleans. *Educational Policy, 30*(1), 218–240. https://doi.org/10.1177/0895904815616485

Hess, F. M., Wurtzel, A., & Rotberg, I. C. (2002). Reform, resistance, … retreat? The predictable politics of accountability in Virginia. *Brookings Papers on Education Policy, 5*, 69–122.

Hillman, N. W., Fryar, A. H., & Crespín-Trujillo, V. (2018). Evaluating the impact of performance funding in Ohio and Tennessee. *American Educational Research Journal, 55*(1), 144–170. https://doi.org/10.3102/0002831217732951

Ingle, W. K., & Lindle, J. C. (2018). A policy and political history of educational supervision. In S. Zepeda & J. Ponticell (Eds.) *Handbook of educational supervision* (pp. 17–44). Wiley-Blackwell.

Jabbar, H. (2011). The behavioral economics of education: New directions for research. *Educational Researcher, 40*(9), 446–453.

Jochim, A., & Lavery, L. (2015). The evolving politics of the Common Core: Policy implementation and conflict expansion. *The Journal of Federalism, 45*(3), 380–404. https://doi.org/10.1093/publius/pjv015

Jones, B. A., & Nichols, E. J. (2013). *Cultural competence in America's schools: Leadership, engagement, and understanding*. Information Age Publishing.

Kingdon, J. W. (2013). *Agendas, alternatives, and public policies* (2nd ed.). Pearson.

Koedel, C., Li, J., Springer, M. G., & Tan, L. (2017). The impact of performance ratings on job satisfaction for public school teachers. *American Educational Research Journal, 54*(2), 241–278. https://doi.org/10.3102/0002831216687531

Kotok, S., Frankenberg, E., Shafft, K. A., Mann, B. A., & Fuller, E. J. (2017). School choice, racial segregation, and poverty concentration: Evidence from Pennsylvania charter school transfers. *Educational Policy, 31*(4), 415–447.

Labaree, D. F. (2012). *Someone has to fail: The zero-sum game of public schooling*. Harvard University Press.

Lavigne, A. L. (2014). Exploring the intended and unintended consequences of high-stakes teacher evaluation on schools, teachers, and students. *Teachers College Record, 116*, 1–29.

Lecours, A. (2005). *New institutionalism: Theory and analysis*. University of Toronto Press.

Lubienski, C. (2003). Innovation in educational markets: Theory and evidence on the impact of competition and choice in charter schools. *American Educational Research Journal, 40*, 395–443.

Majone, G. (1989). *Evidence, argument, and persuasion in the policy process*. Yale University Press.

Malloy, C. L., & Wohlstetter, P. (2003). Working conditions in charter schools: What's the appeal for teachers? *Education and Urban Society, 35*, 219–241.

McDonnell, L. M., & Weatherford, M. S. (2013a). Evidence use and the Common Core State Standards movement: From problem definition to policy adoption. *American Journal of Education, 120*, 1–25. https://doi.org/0195-6744/2013/12001-0001

McDonnell, L. M., & Weatherford, M. S. (2013b). Organized interests and the Common Core. *Educational Researcher, 42*(9), 488–497. https://doi.org/10.3102/0013189X13512676

McPherson, E. (2011). Moving from separate, to equal, to equitable schooling: Revisiting school desegregation policies. *Urban Education, 46*(3), 465–483. https://doi.org/10.1177/0042085910377431

Mehta, J. (2013). How paradigms create politics: The transformation of American educational policy, 1980–2001. *American Educational Research Journal, 50*(2), 285–324.

Mintrom, M. (1997). Policy entrepreneurs and the diffusion of innovation. *American Journal of Political Science, 41*(3), 738–770.

Mintrop, H., & Sunderman, G. L. (2009). Predictable failure of federal sanctions-driven accountability from school improvement—And why we may retain it anyway. *Educational Researcher, 38*(5), 353–364.

Morantz, A. (1996). Money and choice in Kansas City: Major investments with modest returns. In G. Orfield & S. E. Eaton (Eds.), *Dismantling desegregation: The quiet reversal of Brown v. Board of Education* (pp. 241–263). The New Press.

National Commission of Excellence in Education. (1983, April). *A nation at risk*. http://www.ed.gov

NAACP Legal Defense and Education Fund. (2011). *Accountability principles for ESEA reauthorization: A joint statement of civil rights leaders.*

Ness, E. C. (2008). *Merit aid and the politics of education.* Routledge.

Nichols, S., & Berliner, D. C. (2007). *Collateral damage: How high-stakes testing corrupts America's schools.* Harvard Education Press.

Noddings, N. (2011). *Philosophy of education* (3rd ed.). Westview Press.

Pelz, M. L. (2015). State policy regimes and charter school performance. *Journal of School Choice, 9*, 330–353. https://doi.org/10.1080/15582159.2015.1061382

Petracca, M. P. (1991). The rational choice approach to politics: A challenge to democratic theory. *The Review of Politics, 53*(2), 298–319.

Protheroe, N. (2007). Emotional support and student learning. *Principal*, 50–54.

Polikoff, M. S., Hardaway, T., Marsh, J. A., & Plank, D. N. (2016). Who is opposed to Common Core and why? *Educational Researcher, 45*(4), 263–266. https://doi.org/10.3102/0013189X16651087

Poole, S. M. (2011). The relationship between external accountability policy and internal accountability: A cross-state analysis of charter and traditional public schools. *Journal of School Choice, 5*, 261–280. https://doi.org/10.1080/15582159.2011.604225

Porter, A., McMaken, J., Hwang, J., & Yang, R. (2011). Common Core standards: The new U.S. intended curriculum. *Educational Researcher, 40*(3), 103–116. https://doi.org/10.3102/0013189X11405038

Ravitch, D. (2010). *The death and life of the great American school system: How testing and choice are undermining education.* Basic Books.

Reile, K., Mills, M., McGregor, G., Baroutsis, A. (2017). Exploring the affective dimension of teachers' work in alternative school settings. *Teaching Education, 28*(1), 56–71.

Renzulli, L. A., Barr, A. B., & Paino, M. (2015). Innovative education? A test of specialist mimicry or generalist assimilation in trends in charter school specialization over time. *Sociology of Education, 88*, 83–102.

Renzulli, L. A., & Roscigno, V. J. (2005). Charter school policy, implementation, and diffusion across the United States. *Sociology of Education, 78*, 344–366.

Roberts, N. C., & King, P. J. (1991). Policy entrepreneurs: Their activity structure and function in the policy process. *Journal of Public Administration Research and Theory, 1*(2), 147–175.

Roderick, M., Jacob, B. A., & Bryk, A. S. (2002). The impact of high-stakes testing in Chicago on student achievement in promotional gate grades. *Educational Evaluation and Policy Analysis, 24*(4), 333–357.

Scott, J. (2009). The politics of venture philanthropy in charter school policy and advocacy. *Educational Policy, 23*(1), 106–136. https://doi.org/10.1177/0895904808328531

Shannon, E. W., & Saatcioglu, A. (2018). School characteristics and teacher policy influence: Evidence from New York City. *Educational Policy, 32*(7), 1041–1069. https://doi.org/10.1177/0895904816682318

Shoffner, M. (2016). Education reform from the two-sided Congressional coin. *Journal of Law & Education, 45*(2), 269–277.

Stone, D. (2012). *Policy paradox* (3rd ed.). Norton.

Superfine, B. M. (2005). The politics of accountability: The rise and fall of Goals 2000. *American Journal of Education, 112*(1), 10–43.

Tonso, K. L., & Colombo, M. (2006). Parental choice and the decision to decharter an urban, black, middle school. *Journal of School Choice, 1*(1), 85–118.

Torres, A. C. (2014). "Are we architects or construction workers?" Re-examining teacher autonomy and turnover in charter schools. *Education Policy and Analysis Archives, 22*(124), 1–23.

Turnage, C. (2017, July 10). Most Republicans think colleges are bad for the country. Why? *The Chronicle of Higher Education*. https://www.chronicle.com/article/Most-Republicans-Think/240587

Tyack, D. & Cuban, L. (1995). *Tinkering toward utopia: A century of public school reform*. Harvard University Press.

Valli, L., & Buese, D. (2007). The changing roles of teachers in an era of high-stakes accountability. *American Educational Research Journal, 44*(3), 519–558.

Vergari, S. (2007). The politics of charter schools. *Educational Policy, 21*(1), 15–39. https://doi.org/10.1177/0895904806296508

Wang, Y. (2016). Homology and isomorphism: Bordieu in conversation with New Institutionalism. *The British Journal of Sociology, 67*(1), 348–370.

Wiliam, D. (2018). *Creating the schools our children need: Why what we're doing now won't help much (and what we can do instead)*. Learning Sciences International.

Wilson, T. S. (2016). Contesting the public school: Reconsidering charter school as counterpublics. *American Educational Research Journal, 53*(4), 919–952. https://doi.org/10.3102/0002831216658972

Wong, K. K. (2013). Politics and governance: Evolving systems of school accountability. *Educational Policy*, *27*(2), 410–421. https://doi.org/10.1177/0895904813479089

Wong, K. K. (2014). Redesigning urban districts in the USA: Mayoral accountability and the diverse provider model. *Educational Management, Administration, and Leadership*, *39*(4), 486–500. https://doi.org/10.1177/1741143211404952

SECTION II

DESIGNING RESEARCH TO MAXIMIZE EDUCATION POLICY RELEVANCE

CHAPTER 4

CONSIDERATIONS IN THE DESIGN OF HIGH-IMPACT POLICY-RELEVANT RESEARCH

Tyler Woodward, Alexa Quinn, Sarah Lilly, and Peter A. Youngs
University of Virginia

Over the past two decades, there has been an increased emphasis in educational research in the United States on randomized controlled trials, interventions, and other efforts to establish causal relationships between policy initiatives and key outcomes for students, teachers, and schools. This change has been due to several factors including the 2002 National Research Council (NRC) report, *Scientific Research in Education*; the creation of the Institute of Education Sciences (IES) in 2002 within the U.S. Department of Education and its strong focus on experimental research; the formation of the What Works Clearinghouse (WWC) within IES in 2002; the creation of the Society for Research on Educational Effectiveness (SREE) in 2004; and the emphasis in educational policy research journals over the past 15 years on establishing causal inferences through the use of experimental designs.

This heightened focus on randomized controlled trials and interventions is consistent with the notion that high-impact, policy-relevant research is

Maximizing the Policy Relevance of Research for School Improvement, pp. 77–107
Copyright © 2021 by Information Age Publishing
All rights of reproduction in any form reserved.

characterized by (a) the identification of causal relationships between interventions and outcomes; (b) consistent findings across multiple studies; and (c) findings that have clear practical implications for teachers and administrators (NRC, 2002; SREE, 2019). This emphasis on experiments and interventions has led to important scientific advances that have often had a direct influence on educational policy. For example, findings from experimental research on mathematics instruction for students with disabilities (Butler et al., 2003; Fuchs et al., 2003; Fuchs et al., 2008; Tournaki, 2003) and instructional coaching (e.g., Biancarosa et al., 2010; Campbell & Malkus, 2011; Kraft et al., 2018; Pianta et al., 2017) have directly informed policymaking at the state and district levels.

At the same time, the notion that research must be characterized by (a), (b), and (c) in order to be high-impact and policy-relevant is highly contested among researchers, policymakers, and professional educators. In addition, randomized controlled trials in areas such as teacher professional development have produced inconsistent findings and no clear guidance for policy; and experimental studies in areas such as literacy instruction have generated clear, consistent findings that were poorly translated into policy and practice. Further, researchers have sometimes been unable to replicate the findings of prominent experimental studies and scholars have shown that teachers, administrators, and other professional educators often look for resources other than experimental studies to inform their practice and help them make professional decisions.

Given the contested nature of experimental research in education as well as challenges in using such research to inform policy and practice, it is important to consider the policy relevance of this approach and of other research methods and approaches. Thus, this chapter examines the role of rigorous quantitative, qualitative, mixed methods, and improvement science research in guiding educational policy formation and implementation in the United States. We argue that qualitative, mixed methods, and improvement science approaches are likely to be high-impact and policy-relevant when they (a) explain how and why policies and interventions are or are not implemented by education professionals; (b) examine the role of individual actors' beliefs, incentives, and capacity with regard to policy enactment; (c) consider local contextual factors; and/or (d) address ways in which educators' social networks shape research use and policy implementation (McLaughlin, 1987; Penuel et al., 2017; Portes, 2000). We also contend that programs of research in particular areas should feature a range of research methods across multiple studies (Moss & Haertel, 2016).

In this chapter, we argue that it is important for educational researchers, policymakers, and professional educators to acknowledge and understand the ways in which rigorous, high-quality qualitative, mixed methods, and improvement science research can be high-impact and policy relevant.

In the first section, we describe the role of the 2002 NRC report, IES, WWC, SREE, and educational policy research journals in strengthening the emphasis on experimental designs in educational scholarship. The second section considers contributions, limitations, and the contested nature of randomized controlled trials and interventions in informing educational policy. In the next three sections, we provide support for our thesis by discussing what it means for qualitative, mixed methods, and improvement science educational research to be high-impact and policy relevant, providing examples of research in each tradition, and discussing the ways in which these exemplars meet our criteria for being high-impact and policy relevant (see (a) through (d) above). Finally, we conclude by revisiting our central argument and considering implications for researchers, policymakers, and professional educators.

AN INFRASTRUCTURE TO SUPPORT EXPERIMENTAL RESEARCH IN EDUCATION

In the early 2000s, a confluence of factors led many educational researchers in the U.S. to focus much more on randomized controlled trials, interventions, and establishing causal inferences than they had done so previously. One key factor were general questions about the quality and impact of educational research. Several researchers documented persistent concerns about the rigor of educational research, the usefulness of research for professional educators, the role of university schools of education, and the federal role in educational research (Clifford & Guthrie, 1990; Kaestle, 1993; Labaree, 1996) A second important factor was the 2002 publication of a report by a NRC committee. The committee was co-chaired by Richard Shavelson and Lisa Towne and included several educational researchers, a retired district superintendent, a foundation official, and a student testing company representative. In its report, the committee identified principles of scientific quality in education and examined ways in which a federal research agency could foster scientific quality in educational research (NRC, 2002).

This NRC committee argued that high-quality, rigorous educational research is characterized by six principles: (a) it poses significant questions that can be investigated empirically, (b) it links research to theory, (c) it uses methods that enable direct examination of the question(s), (d) it provides a coherent and explicit chain of reasoning, (e) it can be replicated and generalized across studies, and (f) it is openly shared to allow professional scrutiny and critique (NRC, 2002). These principles could be applied in making judgments about the quality of experimental, quantitative nonexperimental, qualitative, and mixed methods research studies. The

NRC committee also put forth design principles for a federal research agency that would be likely to promote high-quality educational research. These principles included (a) maintaining a well-qualified staff; (b) creating a high-level governing board and standing peer review panels; (c) protecting the agency from political interference; (d) supporting research that addresses short-, medium-, and long-term issues that are relevant to policy and practice; (e) ensuring adequate funding; and (f) investing in infrastructure, including supporting the educational research community, promoting data sharing, and maintaining connections with policy and professional educator communities (NRC, 2002).

A third key factor that led to the increased focus on experimental studies was the creation in 2002 of the Institute of Education Sciences (IES) within the U.S. Department of Education. IES replaced the Office of Educational Research and Improvement (OERI) and from the outset it placed a strong emphasis on scientific quality in educational research. In fact, IES has reflected many of the design principles for a federal research agency articulated in the 2002 NRC report. For example, it has been led by several distinguished researchers including Grover Whitehurst (2002–08), John Easton (2009–14), Ruth Curran Nield (2015–17), William Brock (2017–18), and Mark Schneider (2018–present). IES is advised by the National Board for Education Sciences whose members include several leading education scholars and it has employed standing peer review panels to make decisions about grant awards. It has also built a strong infrastructure for research by funding doctoral training programs, setting expectations regarding data sharing, and, as discussed below, working to improve links with policymakers and professional educators.

Since the early 2000s, IES has funded educational research projects through the National Center for Education Research (NCER) and the National Center for Special Education Research (NCSER). Its approach to funding research and supporting the accumulation of scientific knowledge based on research has had a strong, direct effect on the growth of randomized controlled trials and interventions in educational research. In particular, through its goal structure IES has placed a strong priority on research that (a) features experiments, or (b) is likely to build over time to experimental studies. For many years, the five IES goals included Exploration (Goal 1), Development and Innovation (Goal 2), Efficacy and Replication (Goal 3), Effectiveness (Goal 4), and Measurement (Goal 5).

Goal 1 studies examine associations among constructs to establish connections that may form the basis for future interventions or strategies to improve education outcomes. These connections are usually correlational as opposed to causal. Goal 2 studies involve testing interventions or strategies; results from these studies can (a) indicate that the intervention or strategy is promising enough to justify more advanced testing, or (b) lead to additional work to refine the intervention or strategy or the underlying theory. Goal 3 studies allow for testing of an intervention or strategy under ideal circumstances, including with a higher level of support or developer involvement than would be the case under normal circumstances. Results from these studies could lead to additional work to better understand the theory undergirding the results or could indicate that the intervention or strategy is sufficiently promising to warrant more-advanced testing. Goal 3 studies can include initial efficacy evaluations of interventions that have not been rigorously tested before, along with follow-up and retrospective studies.

Goal 4 studies examine the effectiveness of an intervention or strategy under circumstances that would typically prevail in the target context. The importance of "typical" circumstances means that there should not be more substantial developer support than in normal implementation, and there should not be substantial developer involvement in the evaluation of the intervention or strategy. Goal 5 studies focus on developing new assessments, refining existing assessments, and/or validating existing assessments. For Fiscal Year (FY) 2019, IES changed its goal structure so that Goal 3 studies will only focus on Efficacy and Goal 4 studies will focus on Replication and Effectiveness; that is, Goal 4 will now support all replication studies of interventions that show prior evidence of efficacy, including but not limited to effectiveness studies. IES hosts an annual research conference each winter for principal investigators of IES-funded research studies.

In addition to its approach to funding educational research, IES has supported experimental research through the What Works Clearinghouse (WWC), which provides systematic reviews of studies on the effectiveness of educational policies and programs. WWC has published reviews on such topics as literacy, mathematics, science, English learners, children with disabilities, behavior, early childhood, postsecondary, and charter schools. These reviews place a strong value on findings from experimental studies compared to findings from non-experimental studies.

The creation of IES, its goal structure, and WWC have strongly contributed to the increased focus on randomized controlled trials and interventions. These factors have provided strong incentives to researchers to focus on (a) experimental research, and (b) research that is likely to identify interventions or strategies that can be tested in experimental studies. These changes have been complemented by important developments in the broader field. In 2004, a small group of researchers participated in discussions about the idea of establishing a research organization that would focus on applying scientific principles to the study of educational issues. Building on these discussions, Mark Constas, Barbara Foorman, and Larry Hedges submitted a proposal to IES for grant funding to support the initiation of such an organization. IES's decision to fund this grant helped lead to the creation of the SREE in 2005.

From the beginning, SREE's focus has been strongly consistent with the 2002 NRC report and with IES' goal structure. In particular, its mission is to advance "research on policies, programs, and practices that cause educational and related outcomes" (SREE, 2019). SREE serves as a specialist organization in the field of education that concentrates on studying questions of cause-and-effect that can directly inform professional educational practice. It holds an annual conference each spring and publishes the *Journal of Research on Educational Effectiveness.* Through these outlets, it has played a significant role in the growth of experimental research in the U.S. over the past 15 years.

The heightened attention to experimental studies and causal inference can also be seen in the types of scholarship that have been published in the two leading educational policy research journals in the U.S, during the past 10 to 15 years. *Educational Evaluation and Policy Analysis* (EEPA) was created in 1979, is published by the American Educational Research Association (AERA) and has long been considered a leading journal in educational policy research. Under several successive editor teams, and especially over the past decade, EEPA placed a strong emphasis on quantitative research that tests causal relationships or that identifies interventions or strategies that can be tested in future research. *Education Finance and Policy* (EFP) is published by the Association for Education Finance and Policy (AEFP). EFP was initiated in 2006 and quickly became recognized as a high-impact journal. During its short history, it has concentrated primarily on experimental studies and other designs that test causal relationships.

A series of reports published by the NRC between 1999 and 2003 provided a foundation for a much different approach to educational research than the one emphasized by the 2002 NRC Report, IES, and SREE. In 1999, the NRC published *Improving Student Learning: A Strategic Plan for Education Research and Its Utilization,* which featured a proposal for a series of strategic education research partnerships (SERPs). In particular, this report proposed the creation of four large-scale networks involving researchers, professional educators, and policymakers in the areas of learning and instruction, student motivation, transforming schools, and utilization. This proposal explicitly addressed the need to combine aspects of field-initiated and program-driven scholarship in these networks and to support research utilization among professional educators (NRC, 1999).

In 2003, the NRC's SERP committee released a report, *Strategic Education Research Partnership,* that described an organizational structure for advancing the goals first identified in the 1999 NRC report. This structure had three main components: (a) a set of school districts where professional educators and researchers would work together to define questions and engage in research; (b) research and development teams that would provide support to these partnership sites; and (c) a central organization with responsibility for budget, communications, program coherence, and long-term planning (NRC, 2003). This report was complemented by a 2004 NRC report, *Learning and Instruction: A SERP Research Agenda,* which described a potential agenda for the learning and instruction SERP. In particular, this report proposed a series of initiatives in the areas of early reading, reading comprehension, early mathematics, algebra, physics, and science education across grades K–12. The proposed initiatives generally focused on research, development, and testing of curriculum, instruction, and assessment approaches in these areas as well as the types of teacher knowledge required to enact them (NRC, 2004).

The 1999, 2003, and 2004 NRC reports had much less of an immediate influence on educational research in the 2000s compared to the 2002 NRC report, IES, and SREE. At the same time, the proposals featured in these reports have been taken up in more widespread and significant ways during the past 10 years through improvement science approaches including research practice partnerships (RPPs) and networked improvement communities (NICs; Bryk, 2015; Peurach, 2016; Peurach et al., 2018). We discuss RPPs and NICs in the fifth section of this chapter and consider how they have built on the foundational ideas articulated in the 1999, 2003, and 2004 NRC reports.

In summary, several factors combined to generate a much stronger focus on randomized controlled trials and interventions in educational research. The organizational structure of IES and the types of research studies that it has funded are remarkably consistent with the blueprints presented in the 2002 NRC report. In addition, several professional conferences and widely visible journals have served as important vehicles for disseminating results from experimental research. As discussed in the next section, these developments in research have produced notable scientific advances that have directly influenced educational policy. At the same time, experimental research is highly contested and there are limitations to experimental research and the ways in which it informs educational policy. In the next section, we consider both contributions and limitations of randomized controlled trials and interventions.

CONTRIBUTIONS AND LIMITATIONS OF EXPERIMENTAL RESEARCH

The increased emphasis on randomized controlled trials and interventions has led to several key developments that have directly influenced educational policy and practice. For example, there is widespread agreement based on the results of experimental studies regarding the characteristics of effective mathematics instruction for low-performing students and students with disabilities at the elementary and middle school levels. In particular, intervention studies have documented the importance for such students of explicit instruction in mathematics, visual representations, fact fluency practices, and teaching students to distinguish among problem types (Butler et al., 2003; Fuchs et al., 2003; Fuchs et al., 2008; Tournaki, 2003). With regard to instructional coaching, several randomized controlled trials and quasi-experimental studies have provided consistent evidence that coaching has a strong relationship with improvements in teacher effectiveness in reading and mathematics, especially at the early childhood and elementary levels (e.g., Biancarosa et al., 2010; Campbell & Malkus, 2011; Kraft et al., 2018; Pianta et al., 2017). These research findings have influenced both policy and professional practice.

At the same time, experimental research is highly contested for several reasons. For example, well-designed experimental studies sometimes generate findings that are difficult to translate into policy and practice. In the area of literacy instruction, the National Reading Panel (NRP) published a landmark report in 2000 (National Reading Panel & National Institute of Child Health and Human Development, 2000). This report featured a meta-analysis that drew on several experimental and quasi-experimental studies to identify five pillars of effective reading instruction: comprehension, phonemic awareness, phonics instruction, reading fluency, and vocabulary instruction. For each pillar, there was strong and consistent research evidence in support of practice in that area. The Reading First policy, part of the 2001 No Child Left Behind legislation, required school districts to purchase and enact curricula aligned with these five pillars.

An IES-funded study of Reading First found, though, that it did not effectively translate research findings into policy or practice and was thus problematic for a number of reasons (Gamse et al., 2008). First, many curricula that were made available to districts as part of Reading First had never been studied and subsequent research indicated that most did not accurately reflect the instructional practices featured in the studies used in the NRP meta-analysis. In addition, Reading First focused only on reading and did not address other critical aspects of literacy instruction such as writing, conceptual knowledge, or motivation. As a result, instruction that focused only on the five pillars identified by the NRP was incomplete and ineffective. Further, Reading First did not take account of the fact that more variation is typically present among teachers who are using the same literacy curriculum than among curricula themselves (Gamse et al., 2008).

In terms of beginning teacher induction, two large-scale randomized controlled trials found no effect of comprehensive induction on teacher retention or instructional practices in the first or second year of teaching

(Glazerman et al., 2010; Schmidt et al., 2017). Comprehensive induction involves providing release time to accomplished teachers who participate in mentor training and work full-time providing one-on-one support to groups of novice teachers. Each of these studies provided evidence that this type of induction support is causally related to increased teacher effectiveness at the end of the second (Schmidt et al., 2017) or third year of teaching (Glazerman et al., 2010). But the null effects on teacher retention and instructional quality reported in these studies led many states and districts to focus less on or eliminate policies requiring comprehensive induction for beginning teachers.

With regard to teacher professional development (PD), experimental studies have produced inconsistent findings (Hill et al., 2013). Some IES-funded cluster randomized trials reported that PD influenced student achievement (e.g., Connor et al., 2007; Landesman Ramey et al., 2011; Landry et al., 2009; Penuel et al., 2011; Powell & Diamond, 2011). At the same time, several other cluster randomized trials generated null findings or findings that were primarily null (e.g., Buysse et al., 2010; Cabalo et al., 2007; Gersten et al. 2010; Santagata et al., 2011). In addition, two large experimental studies by Michael Garet and colleagues (Garet et al., 2008, 2011) reported no impact of PD in elementary reading or middle school mathematics on achievement gains. Although these findings have been mixed, researchers have worked with the larger corpus of data to identify features of effective PD through analyses of methodologically rigorous studies. Based on a review of 35 studies, Darling-Hammond et al. (2017) posit that effective PD is (a) content-focused; (b) includes active learning consistent with adult learning theory; (c) supports collaboration, typically in job-embedded contexts; (d) uses models and modeling of effective practice; (e) provides coaching and expert support; (f) offers opportunities for feedback and reflection; and (g) is of sustained duration.

In addition to concerns about null or inconsistent findings, researchers in psychology and other disciplines have raised important questions about the replicability of experimental studies. For example, Brian Nosek and a team of researchers replicated 100 studies that had been published in three leading psychology research journals. The research team worked with the authors of the studies to mirror the original datasets and research designs as much as possible. Of the 100 studies, Nosek and colleagues were able to replicate the findings for fewer than 40 of them (Open Science Collaboration, 2015). Their work raised important questions about the pressures that researchers face to identify statistically significant findings in their studies in the absence of strong evidence supporting such findings.

Researchers have responded in several ways to concerns about the contested nature and limitations of experimental studies in shaping educational policy and professional practice. As we illustrate in the next three sections, one response has been to look to qualitative, mixed methods, and improvement science studies to complement the knowledge gained from randomized controlled trials and offer additional ways to understand policy implementation and effects. Research in these traditions typically focuses less on identifying causal relationships and more on explaining how and why particular interventions are or are not implemented and how individuals' characteristics and attributes of their networks shape policy enactment. In addition, some researchers have proposed alternative approaches to conducting research while maintaining a focus on experimental designs. For example, Hill et al. (2013) have argued that PD researchers should carry out randomized clinical trials across multiple sites in which PD program content is held constant while varying the ways in which it is provided; and then examine effects on proximal outcomes associated with student achievement, such as teacher self-efficacy and knowledge. When they identify impacts on proximal outcomes, the next step would be to conduct random assignment studies with measures of instruction and student achievement (Hill et al., 2013).

Further, there is growing interest in requiring researchers to share data publicly when legally feasible to do so, especially data collected as part of federally-funded projects. For example, Nosek cofounded the Center for Open Science, which seeks to promote scholarly practices in which the processes, content, and outcomes of research activities are openly accessible to others (Nosek & Bar-Anan, 2012; Nosek et al., 2012). As part of this effort, Nosek and colleagues have called for changes in the ways in which research is conducted and communicated. In terms of the conduct of research, their recommendations include making data publicly available, sharing research methods and tools, and documenting research practices (Nosek et al., 2012). With regard to communication, they call for open access for the public to all research journal articles, separating the process of publishing articles from that of evaluating them, using review services to disseminate articles to and through particular journals, publishing the results of peer reviews of manuscripts, and moving to open, continuous processes of peer review (Nosek & Bar-Anan, 2012).

In a 2018 article, Nelson et al. asserted that the field of psychology has experienced widespread changes during the past decade, in part as a result of the earlier scholarship by Nosek and others that raised concerns about replicability. In particular, Nelson and colleagues reported that many more researchers in psychology are voluntarily posting their data, replication attempts are being published in leading journals, and researchers are increasing their sample sizes and committing to data collection and analysis plans in advance (Nelson et al., 2018). It is less clear whether such practices have been widely adopted by educational researchers in recent years.

POLICY-RELEVANT QUALITATIVE APPROACHES IN EDUCATION

In this section, we argue that it is vital for educational researchers, policymakers, and professional educators to acknowledge and understand the ways in which rigorous, high-quality qualitative research can be policy relevant and potentially high-impact. As previously mentioned, over the last 20 years experimental research has been increasingly emphasized. However, qualitative approaches in education research are vital for various reasons—one of which being that they can address the gaps that experimental methods are unable to fill.

Rather than generating objective descriptions and determining relationships, qualitative researchers search for meaning in natural settings in order to create rich narratives. These narratives are subjective mainly because they rely heavily on participant perspectives, that is, how people make sense of and interpret their experiences, define specific terms, and conceptualize their lives (McMillan & Wergin, 2010). Large-scale quantitative studies (e.g., randomized controlled trials) that use research methods that aim to generalize to larger populations have had a significant effect on education policy. These quantitative studies, however, can be characterized as having a significant "distance" from study participants (Pyrczak, 2017, p. 137). Qualitative research has been uniquely valuable when examining education policy because of its ability to close that "distance" and provide in-depth analyses of teachers' instructional practices and students' schooling experiences. Further, qualitative approaches can supplement the information acquired from quantitative research studies and provide additional ways to understand policy contexts.

It is also important to consider specific criteria that can help in determining how qualitative research can be policy relevant and high-impact. We argue that qualitative research approaches (along with mixed methods and improvement science) are likely to be high-impact and policy relevant when they (a) explain how and why policies and interventions are or are not implemented by education professionals; (b) examine the role of individual actors' beliefs, incentives, and capacity with regard to policy enactment; (c) consider local contextual factors; and/or (d) address ways in which educators' social networks shape research use and policy implementation (McLaughlin, 1987; Penuel et al., 2017; Portes, 2000). The studies described in this section align with some or all of these criteria and illustrate how qualitative approaches to education research can be policy relevant and high-impact. The first study is particularly relevant because of its emphasis on teachers' beliefs about policy enactment and how specific institutional and contextual factors seemed to influence this enactment.

Anagnostopoulos et al. (2010) investigated the National Board for Professional Teaching Standards (NBPTS) and teachers' work and collegial relationships. Although the authors made it clear that this was a mixed methods study design, the qualitative strand of the study was strongly emphasized. Overall, Anagnostopoulos et al. reported that the qualitative strand consisted of an "interviewed-based, collective case study in four elementary schools, two in each state," that "prioritized qualitative data to explore the meanings that teachers and principals ascribed to NBPTS certification and how it entered into and shaped their collective work" (p. 343). In addition, institutional theory was utilized to better understand how the NBPTS certification process interacted with occupational structures and beliefs.

The authors reported that the NBPTS certification process created tensions among the teachers regarding the meaning and value of financial rewards, distinctions, and extended duties. Further, Anagnostopoulos et al. (2010) indicate that it was fair to question the "balance of dollars, distinction, and duties," as these contextual factors can "alter teachers' collective work" (p. 365). The authors also reported that their study was important for policymakers to consider as it points to the relevance of using NBPTS certification to increase teacher salaries. The authors contend that perhaps creating decent wages for all teachers might be more likely to establish an "effective teaching force than basing wage hikes on NBPTS" (p. 365).

As a result of effectively using institutional theory, Anagnostopoulos et al.'s (2010) study aligns with our policy-relevant criteria—specifically, this study examined the role of teachers' beliefs and collegial relationships regarding the enactment of the NBPTS certification process and considered local contextual and institutional factors that influenced the enactment of policy. This study is an example of how the policy of NBPTS certification can alter institutional contexts to the extent that resentment and tensions obstruct teachers from partaking in the certification process. Another study that has used qualitative approaches to understand state-level policy is that of Booher-Jennings (2005). This study, similar to Anagnostopoulos et al. (2010), is policy relevant because it examined the role of individual actors' beliefs, incentives, and capacity with regard to policy enactment and considered local contextual factors that shaped policy implementation (McLaughlin, 1987; Penuel et al., 2017; Portes, 2000). To illustrate this, we turn to an in-depth explanation of this study.

In a landmark qualitative case study, Booher-Jennings (2005) focused on how one elementary school responded to the demands of the Texas Accountability System. The author interviewed 26 teachers as well as school and district administrators, observed classrooms and teacher meetings, and analyzed documents. The author's use of qualitative methods allowed her to conduct an in-depth analysis that quantitative research methods would not have supported. For example, Booher-Jennings acted as a participant-observer in both third- and fourth-grade classrooms, in teacher meetings with parents, at special school events, and in third-grade tutoring sessions. This added up to a total of 180 hours of participant observations. Lesson plans were also reviewed along with teacher e-mails and memos sent to schoolwide staff, faculty meeting minutes, "strategic planning" documents, and running records that consisted of multiyear academic information about individual students (p. 237). The use of these qualitative methods allowed Booher-Jennings to explain how an elementary school responded to the Texas Accountability System in great detail.

In addition to Booher-Jennings's (2005) use of qualitative methods, she drew on neoinstitutional theory, similar to Anagnostopoulos et al. (2010), to explain how the elementary school in her study mediated the Student Success Initiative (SSI) associated with the Texas Accountability System. Using this theory, Booher-Jennings reported that teachers intended to promote the impression of improved test scores by utilizing a "constellation of educational triage practices" (p. 232). In other words, teachers grouped students into three categories as a response to SSI policy, which required all third-grade students to pass a state reading test to be eligible for fourth grade. These groups included "safe cases," "suitable cases for treatment," and "hopeless cases" (pp. 232–233). These groupings had a substantial influence on how teachers used resources and enacted instructional practices to aim for a higher accountability rating.

Booher-Jennings (2005) reported that teachers regulated resources based on these groups of students, which resulted in the provision of more resources to "accountables," who were students included in the school's overall accountability rating (p. 233). She also found that the "accountables" group was intentionally reduced, as teachers referred students for special education. Teachers also redirected resources away from the students grouped as "hopeless cases" while "bubble kids" (i.e., students on the cusp of passing the state test) received a variety of targeted instructional practices (p. 233). Booher-Jennings's use of neoinstitutional theory enabled her to explain how and why teachers actively treated some students so differently and at the expense of other students because of the new high-stakes testing and accountability policy.

Another important finding of this study was that the institutional environment defined a "good" teacher as one that increased student test scores. This caused teachers to alter their views and made them willing to "triage" specific students to varying degrees. In other words, Booher-Jennings (2005) presented evidence that high-stakes testing and accountability policies seemed to push teachers to alter their instructional practices and modify how they allocated or did not allocate resources to support students. Overall, this study produced noteworthy findings that are policy relevant based on our prescribed criteria.

While these studies meet our criteria for being examples of policy-relevant studies and potentially high-impact, it is important to note that, during the past 20 years, qualitative education research has not been at the center of policy decisions. Rather, randomized controlled trials, interventions, and studies establishing causal relationships have been emphasized. We argue in this chapter, however, that it is vital for educational researchers, policymakers, and professional educators to acknowledge and understand the ways in which rigorous, high-quality qualitative research can be high-impact and policy relevant. Over the past 40 years, studies conducted using qualitative research methods have indeed impacted the education policy landscape. For example, the well-known RAND Change Agent study, conducted from 1973–1978, represented a noticeable transformation in which planned educational change was examined by asking "how" and "why" questions (McLaughlin, 1990).

The Change Agent study consisted of a national study of four different federally-funded programs which were created to establish and maintain "innovative practices in the public schools" (McLaughlin, 1998, p. 71). Overall, qualitative field research was a vital component of the Change Agent study, as it allowed the researchers to understand how the implementation of new policies transpired. Findings from the Change Agent study that altered the education landscape include the fact that implementation perspectives and local choices dictate outcomes; policy outcomes cannot mandate what matters (i.e., local capacity and will); and classrooms, schools, and school districts are not uniform in their existence, but rather consist of immense local variability in curriculum, grading, and student placement policies (McLaughlin, 1990). These findings were established largely because of the qualitative field work strategies. Overall, qualitative approaches to education research can fill in the gaps where teacher perspectives have been left out. The work of Anagnostopoulos et al. (2010), Booher-Jennings (2005), and the Change Agent study are three prime examples that are policy relevant because of their qualitative focus on "how" and "why" questions that remain pertinent to our understanding of education policy.

Limitations and Strengths of Qualitative Research

There are a few limitations of qualitative studies when used for education policy research. First, the qualitative studies discussed in this section cannot be generalized to larger populations because of small sample sizes. Second, qualitative studies can neither establish causal relationships nor identify specific impacts of policies and other education reforms on student outcomes. Qualitative approaches, however, close the "distance" between researchers and study participants and make it possible for researchers to produce in-depth analyses (Pyrczak, 2017, p. 137). In the studies described in this section, the researchers were able to ask specific "how" and "why" questions that demanded the use of a variety of methods (e.g., interviews, document analysis, classroom and participant observations) to generate in-depth analyses of teachers' practices and beliefs about policy enactment. Further, in these studies, researchers used theoretical frameworks (e.g., institutional theory) to determine how institutional structures seemed to influence teachers' perspectives about particular policies. Yin (2017) has described the use of theory and conceptual frameworks as "the main vehicle" for generalizing the findings of qualitative research (p. 42). Lastly, another strength of qualitative approaches is that they can complement knowledge derived from quantitative research. This will be discussed next in this chapter's section on mixed methods research.

POLICY-RELEVANT MIXED METHODS APPROACHES IN EDUCATION

Another avenue toward high-impact research is the design of investigations that use a variety of methods to study interventions and policy initiatives. Often referred to as "mixed methods," this approach to research involves drawing on multiple traditions of inquiry in order to best answer questions or develop policy. Accordingly, mixed methods research is associated with the pragmatic paradigm: seeking practical solutions to problems and taking an explicitly value-oriented approach to research (Johnson & Onwuegbuzie, 2004). A pragmatic approach to research has strong alignment with informing and implementing high-impact policy, which is outcome-oriented by definition.

Traditionally, "mixed methods" has been defined as research that integrates qualitative and quantitative data in order to answer research questions that cannot be addressed using either approach alone (Creswell & Plano Clark, 2018). However, we echo the call of Moss and Haertel (2016) to instead encourage methodological pluralism: rather than be limited by qualitative/quantitative dichotomies, policy-relevant research should draw flexibly on different methods for different purposes. We argue that purposes such as triangulation, complementarity, and development of new measures are ways that mixed methods can contribute to policy relevance by explaining both the how and why, examining the role of individual actors, and considering contextual factors.

Evidence of the value of mixed methods for policy-relevant research can be observed in the research techniques used by the RAND Corporation. RAND, a nonprofit, nonpartisan organization, uses research to develop solutions to public policy challenges. While RAND researchers certainly employ "gold standard" experimental designs described previously, these quantitative methods are often combined with other methods for a variety of purposes. A recent example is the National Summer Learning Project (NSLP) funded by The Wallace Foundation. The NSLP was a five-year study that evaluated the effectiveness of large-scale, voluntary, district-run summer learning programs serving low-income elementary students (McCombs et al., 2014). The study included approximately 5,600 students in five urban school districts—Boston; Dallas; Duval County, Florida; Pittsburgh; and Rochester, New York—and followed them from third to seventh grade.

The RAND researchers used a randomized controlled trial to assess the effects of summer program participation on measures of student achievement and social and emotional skills over the short and long term. They found strong evidence that voluntary summer learning programs can produce short-term gains in mathematics and that after two consecutive summers, students with high attendance (i.e., 20 or more days per summer) outperformed their peers in both mathematics and ELA and displayed stronger social emotional competencies (Augustine et al., 2016).

These findings were valuable, but they were made actionable through the RAND researchers' efforts to study program implementation. In addition to outcome measures, they collected extensive data about the summer programs and classroom instruction to help examine how implementation seems to be related to program effects. The researchers conducted about 900 interviews with district leaders, program leaders, school leaders, coaches, and teachers that informed recommendations they made about planning, curriculum, and enrichment activities. They also observed summer sites with successively longer and more comprehensive observation protocols for a total of over 2,000 hours of summer program activities. In addition, the researchers worked with elementary education professors to examine curriculum quality.

In later years of the study, a RAND observer followed each classroom of students for one full day, creating a minute-by-minute time log of the program's mathematics, ELA, and enrichment classes. These observational data were integrated with quantitative data from surveys to create evidence-based recommendations for summer programing. An extensive report based on this study provided guidelines for planning, selecting, and training teachers; recruiting students; ensuring sufficient time on task; coordinating academic curricula and instruction; implementing enrichment activities; creating a positive summer climate; and managing program costs and revenues (Schwartz et al., 2018). An additional report focused on integrating summer programming into core district priorities and operations (Augustine & Thompson, 2017).

The NSLP is illustrative of the policy potential of mixed methods research. The detailed findings about program implementation help make the causal findings replicable. A concrete example of policy relevance is the addition of a $500,000 line item to the Massachusetts Fiscal Year 2019 Budget to support summer learning programs that enact the recommendations outlined in the RAND report (Commonwealth of Massachusetts, 2018).

This example elucidates the value of using a combination of methods to inform policy. In this large-scale study, with multiple published reports that focus on different aspects of the data and findings, researchers were able to triangulate across data sources, shed light on different aspects of the intervention, and gather data to inform future measures of program success. In the sections that follow, we consider these three purposes of mixed methods research—as categorized by Greene (2007) and championed by Moss and Haertel (2016)—with examples from the field of education. We argue that triangulation, complementarity, and development of new measures contribute to policy relevance by allowing researchers to explain the how and why, examine the role of individual actors, and consider contextual factors.

Triangulation

One of the most compelling purposes of mixed methods approaches is triangulation: using data from different sources to corroborate a finding or support an inference. In a powerful example of this, Hill et al. (2011) compared observational measures of teacher quality to quantitative value-added scores. Value-added models use current and historical test scores in an attempt to estimate a teacher's effect on student achievement growth. There is evidence that teacher effects explain variation in student test score gains (Rockoff, 2004). As a result, policymakers have widely adopted this approach; the 2009 federal Race to the Top initiative even encouraged teacher evaluation to include value-added measures as a component. The assumed explanatory factor is quality of teaching, yet minimal observational research has examined this assumption.

Hill and colleagues collected extensive observational, interview, and survey data for 24 middle school mathematics teachers. The small sample allowed for in-depth investigation into teachers' knowledge and practice, sufficient statistical power for the goal of the study, and timely dissemination of information for policy relevance. The researchers also gathered student achievement outcomes to produce value-added scores. In the analysis, they integrated these two data sources to draw conclusions. While the authors found some alignment between value-added scores and other measures of teacher quality, there was also confounding data. They presented case studies to illustrate the differences in classroom instruction between two teachers with similar value-added scores. Following discussion of the findings, the researchers concluded that "value-added scores alone are not sufficient to identify teachers for reward, remediation, or removal" (Hill et al., 2011, p. 826). Instead, they recommended the use of value-added scores in combination with discriminating observation systems. In this way, the study also serves the purpose of "illuminating taken-for-granted perspectives and allowing them to evolve" (Moss & Haertel, 2016, p. 200). This was made possible by the triangulation of data collected using multiple methods.

Complementarity

Another major purpose of mixed methods research is complementarity: using a variety of methods in order to illuminate different aspects of the phenomena of interest (Greene, 2007). A recent example with policy relevance is Giersch's (2018) study of academic tracking and high-stakes testing. Giersch used multilevel modeling with a large longitudinal data set from North Carolina to explore the relationship between academic tracking in high school (measured by proportion of honors classes taken) and college achievement. Results of statistical analyses indicated that tracking is not only associated with gaps in achievement but also affects the usefulness of high-stakes tests for predicting college performance. For all-honors students, high-stakes tests and high school GPA were both significantly correlated with college GPA. For mixed or no-honors students, only high school GPA was a predictor of college GPA.

Giersch explored the "why" through a second phase of the study, conducting semi-structured interviews with classroom teachers to explore possible reasons that test scores would lose predictive validity in the lower track but grades would not. Interview data indicated that even though state standards and exams remained the same for lower-track students, teachers modified their classroom expectations and instructional methods in ways that de-emphasized the content of the exams (Giersch, 2018). The study has several clear implications for policy related to academic tracking and high-stakes testing. The results of multilevel modeling reinforced previous findings that standardized tests are a limited measure of college success and highlighted the role of tracking in reinforcing disparity. The qualitative phase of the study provided a detailed picture of individual actors, highlighting teacher-level concerns and identifying potential explanatory factors, as well as indicating a path forward through combined classes.

Development

Development describes efforts to use the results from one method to help develop or inform another method (Greene, 2007). When gathering data that may be specific to certain lived experiences or contexts, it can be especially valuable to draw from the emic perspective in designing survey items or quantitatively-scored tasks. In a recent example of this type of study, Xie and Li (2018) sought to understand how Chinese parents, teachers, and principals perceived preschool readiness. The study was motivated by an initiative in China that seeks to provide universal early childhood education by 2020, meaning children would enter preschool by age three. Semi-structured interviews were conducted with 24 parents, 11 teachers, and four preschool principals. In a second phase, a survey was conducted with 231 parents. The study design allowed themes from interviews to guide the development of survey items. The surveys were then used to validate the findings from the interviews. The researchers found that the three-construct "conception of preschool readiness" (i.e., ready child, ready family, ready preschool) created based on interviews was validated by the larger survey sample. The researchers also identified three main concerns in terms of preschool readiness that have the potential to inform policy. Thus, this is an example of high-impact, policy-relevant research because it considers local contextual factors.

Future Considerations for Policy-Relevant Mixed Methods Research in Education

One of the challenges in conducting mixed methods research is determining valid ways to combine different types of data (Fetters & Freshwater, 2015). This often involves "quantitizing" or coding and counting qualitative data in order to analyze it quantitively. Several recent advances in mixed methods designs allow for more robust approaches to combining data types. For example, Alexander et al. (2019) recently shared a new approach to group discussion analysis that uses visual replay methodology (VRM), a graphic way to investigate discourse patterns during small group discussion. The researchers began with a video-recorded discussion, went through a coding process, and then conducted an integrated analysis that involved overlaying separately-produced "replay diagrams" that displayed elements such as who was speaking and for how long. VRM thus offers a relatively unobtrusive way to observe human interactions and allows qualitative data to be considered alongside quantitative data. The authors explained that the insights gained from overlaying can be used for specifying variables and for hypothesis development, and provided an example using small group discussions about project experiences, where the diagrams reveal visual communication patterns (Alexander et al., 2019).

Other researchers have also explored ways to increase the validity of quantitative findings. In a 2018 study, van Velzen integrated mixed methods data to explore the complex phenomena of metacognition in high school and college students. Data were collected in the form of paired open- and closed-ended questions, with each question including a qualitative and quantitative component. Data were analyzed separately before being integrated. However, in a new approach labeled "conversion consolidation-investigation," van Velzen (2018) consolidated the mixed data twice, creating two data sets that each quantitized the previously coded open-ended questions differently. The two sets were then compared, indicating strengths and weaknesses of the different approaches. This study encourages educational researchers to consider the variety of ways that qualitative data may be consolidated with quantitative data. Van Velzen's findings highlight the fact that an initial approach may not fully capture the qualitative findings; study conclusions may be strengthened by considering alternative ways of integrating data.

The examples described above illuminate the contributions that can be made with mixed methods approaches to educational research; however, they also indicate potential challenges. Undertaking mixed methods research often requires more resources, both tangible and intangible. It also requires additional advance planning by investigators to design data collection and analytic approaches that complement one another and can be implemented rigorously. Nevertheless, there are clear benefits for policy when these additional steps are taken. We call for a pragmatic approach to research and agree that "embracing the learning opportunities of methodological pluralism will enhance our collective capacity to respond resourcefully to the unknown challenges ahead" (Moss & Haertel, 2016, p. 234). Therefore, we emphasize the importance of considering the various purposes for combining methods when developing high-impact policy-relevant research.

IMPROVEMENT SCIENCE APPROACHES IN EDUCATION

Practitioners currently face pressure to rapidly improve education (Bryk, 2015), and research suggests that their social networks are often a key resource in efforts to change practice (Coburn & Russell, 2008; Frank et al., 2004). At the same time, practitioners' social networks seldom include researchers (Neal et al., 2015). To accelerate improvement through the implementation of research-based initiatives, researchers are currently exploring educational improvement science approaches to focus on the creation of shared knowledge and narrow the research-practice gap (LeMahieu et al., 2017). The notion of strategic educational research partnerships (SERPs) was first introduced two decades ago (NRC, 1999). Improvement science approaches, including research-practice partnerships (RPPs), networked improvement communities (NICs), and design-based implementation research (DBIR), by definition, build upon the aforementioned SERP criteria as practitioners and researchers collaboratively explore possible interventions to address problems of practice (Coburn et al., 2013) and increase the role of research in educational improvement (Coburn & Penuel, 2016) through long-term partnerships.

By partnering researchers with practitioners, RPPs afford practitioners direct access to research. When RPPs include structured NICs and DBIR, the results of these partnerships can be widely shared. Structured NICs consist of deliberately "coordinated, disciplined efforts among a large number of people and places" (Bryk, 2015, p. 473). Through DBIR within an NIC, researchers and practitioners work together to identify a specific problem of practice, test different interventions to consider how approaches may depend on contextual factors, and utilize implementation science to scale their reliable, practice-based interventions. As researchers bring this formalized method of building a shared base of tested interventions to their RPP, practitioners are also able to contribute to, as well as leverage, collective knowledge to address problems at scale instead of working in isolation with access to only the expertise present within their own classroom, school, or district (Bryk, 2015). By working together on a common strategy, the collaborative work of researchers and practitioners to collectively solve problems accelerates about how to improve.

Furthermore, as improvement science approaches bring researchers and practitioners together through these formal partnerships, such approaches often feature networks of collaborators that operate differently from common role relationships in education (Cohen-Vogel, et al., 2018). Thus, traditional roles of practitioners ("doers") and researchers ("knowers") shift as RPP participants work together as "improvers" (Bryk, 2015, p. 475). Similarly, improvement-focused educational research approaches offer opportunities for researchers who may have previously used different methodologies to engage in methodological pluralism and utilize each individual's expertise toward scaled improvement.

Each of these new relationships may become extended partnerships that remain consistent throughout the improvement process. Improvement science approaches call for design, implementation, and scaling processes to be combined in the same education setting (Datnow et al., 2002; Redding et al., 2017). Doing so has the potential to reduce the inconsistent results that typically occur in a conventional school improvement approach in which different settings are used for the intervention's design-and-test stages versus the implementation-at-scale stage. As improvement approaches increase opportunities for these often-isolated stakeholders to work together for extended periods through inter-organizational networks, social networks may then take hold and grow within these partnerships.

As a result, RPPs should "employ intentional strategies to foster partnerships, with carefully designed rules, roles, routines, and protocols that structure interaction" (Coburn & Penuel, 2016, p. 49). However, Russell et al. (2017) recognized that, while progress has been made in some improvement networks, overall progress in educational improvement is neither quick nor consistent, due to a lack of systematic organization. Thus, there is a need to develop frameworks that simultaneously, and separately, support both practitioners and researchers, extend the partnerships in their overlapping social networks, and provide the necessary structures that help sustain RPPs toward making scale improvements possible (Fishman et al., 2013).

In order to initially structure and successfully launch an NIC, Russell and colleagues proposed a framework of necessary strategic actions. These actions include the development of a theory of practice improvement, the creation of organizational norms through which to implement improvement research methods for data collection and analysis, structures to scaffold the learning of how to implement these methods, leadership considerations for the organization and maintenance of the NIC, and careful attention to the development of norms and a culture that are consistent with the NIC's goals. This is particularly important given the possibility of different backgrounds and educational viewpoints among the many roles represented within an NIC (Coburn et al., 2009; Spillane, 1998). Furthermore, the participants must believe that these aims are valuable toward making improvements (Wentworth et al., 2017). Lastly, to achieve long-term improvement at scale, stakeholders must focus on both supporting local ownership on the part of principals and teachers while promoting improvement efforts. If these areas of action are successfully addressed, then educators can learn more quickly and accumulate knowledge that allows for the potential to solve educational challenges on a systemic level (Russell et al., 2017).

Prior research shows that the conditions most conducive to a successful RPP are trust between researchers and practitioners, a defined focus, and reasonable behavioral norms (Coburn & Penuel, 2016). Since these conditions are connected to the social networks that researchers and practitioners build, and particularly in consideration of the shift in RPP participants' roles compared to those in traditional education hierarchies, social network analysis (SNA) may be useful in understanding how to support successful partnerships toward improvement. SNA is a research method used to examine individual or group relationships and interactions that can increase access to desired resources and expertise (Otte & Rousseau, 2002; Hopkins et al., 2018). In the long-term relationships possible in improvement science approaches, the overlapping social networks of researchers and practitioners may increase social network factors of successful reform, including practitioners' access to expertise, the availability of resources that may enable changes in practice, and the deepening of trust through the repeated interactions and proximity made possible when researchers and practitioners work together within the same social networks (Coburn & Russell, 2008).

Research on RPPs may also provide strategies and tools for participants in RPPs to evaluate their own efforts. Wentworth et al. (2017) examined ways in which RPPs may influence the degree to which educators utilize research to make decisions. After developing a survey from experiential case studies of three RPPs, the authors piloted the survey to consider practitioners' perceived impact of participating in an RPP. They concluded that "certain conditions in [RPPs] may be more conducive to the development among educators of behaviors, mindsets, and perceptions associated with evidence-based decision-making" (p. 241). These conditions may then influence long-term outputs (i.e., how practitioners utilize research to change policy or practice or inform the research that researchers engage in) and intermediary outputs (i.e., how practitioners and researchers behave as well as their mindsets when working together in RPPs).

However, prior SNA also identifies possible challenges when researchers and educators are included in the same professional networks. In RPPs, practitioners and researchers may struggle to effectively communicate (Coburn & Penuel, 2016), face incongruence due to turnover (Coburn & Penuel, 2016; Fishman et al., 2013), and feel the need to internalize new professional identities as improvers (Coburn et al., 2008). Educational leaders may struggle to recognize potential benefits of improvement approaches due to mixed feelings toward the validity of research as an improvement framework, an inability to interpret research findings, and even mistrust of the introduction of potentially biased and politically-motivated researchers into their educational system (Penuel et al., 2016).

Toward ensuring the longevity of RPPs, time must be allocated to enable participants to develop the trust necessary for school-wide reform (Tschannen-Moran & Hoy, 2000). This increased time may help offset the additional demands made of RPP participants (Bryk, 2015; Cannata et al., 2017) as increased burnout could occur due to the additional duties within an NIC. For teachers, this may take the form of allowing them to enact iterative intervention testing through consecutive teaching assignments (i.e., teaching the same grade level or curriculum). For tenure-track researchers, this may take the form of reduced pressure to publish during the design and testing stages of improvement iterations (Cannata et al., 2017). It may also be necessary to create new professional roles to coordinate efforts and avoid "communication and coordination issues" (Bryk, 2015, p. 473). These efforts may help ensure the availability of practitioners and researchers to commit to long-term RPPs in order to sustain partnerships toward the development of trust and a willingness to work through challenges (Coburn et al., 2013).

To increase the impact of research on policy, SNA studies of various types of RPPs are critical to understanding successful relationships within educational improvement communities. Future SNA research could potentially inform successful implementations of RPPs by considering the educational settings in which practitioners successfully utilize research and develop strategies to optimize productive collaboration within various types of partnerships.

To increase the relevancy of educational research to policy, research on RPPs is crucial to understanding how improvement science approaches in education are enacted and supporting these approaches toward reducing the research-practice gap, recognizing education as a networked community, and improving education at scale. Since it is critical that individuals are invested and "[develop] the will and agency" (Bryk, 2015, p. 468) necessary for both creating and sustaining RPPs (Coburn et al., 2013), there is a need to identify appropriate research methods and develop theories that simultaneously support practitioners and sustain partnerships. Research and theory should also provide the infrastructure for policies that help sustain improvement communities toward making scale improvements possible (Fishman et al., 2013; Peurach, 2016) while promoting collective, accelerated improvement as an important aspect of the culture of education (Cannata et al., 2017).

CONCLUSION

In this chapter, we have argued that scholars, policymakers, and professional educators should be cognizant of the ways in which rigorous, high-quality qualitative, mixed methods, and improvement science research can be high-impact and policy relevant. For example, qualitative studies by Anagnostopoulos et al. (2010) and Booher-Jennings (2005) explicated ways in which teachers and principals enacted NBPTS assessments and high-stakes testing and accountability policy. In these studies, the authors investigated how educators' beliefs, incentives, and capacity along with aspects of their local contexts led them to implement reforms in ways that differed from policymakers' intentions.

Similarly, mixed methods research by Hill et al. (2011), as well as Giersch (2018), helped explain why two prominent policies—teacher value-added scores and high-stakes testing—may have led to unintended consequences. In each study, the researchers first reported associations among main variables of interest and then drew on qualitative data to further explain these associations. Using mixed methods data, Hill and colleagues provided evidence that teachers with high value-added scores did not necessarily enact high-quality mathematics instruction, while Giersch explained why teachers in lower-track classes altered their instruction to place less emphasis on high-stakes exams.

Improvement science approaches call for educators and researchers to work closely together to engage in research and enact reforms. Such approaches can increase teachers' and principals' access to expertise, promote trust, and lead to changes in practice. By definition, improvement science approaches take account of educators' beliefs, incentives, and capacity with regard to potential reforms as well as local contextual factors. In addition, social network analysis can be used to understand features of successful networks of educators and researchers, identify challenges to sustaining such partnerships, and develop strategies for promoting collaboration.

While randomized controlled trials and interventions have become much more prevalent in educational research during the past 20 years, researchers, policymakers, and professional educators have identified a number of limitations to such approaches. In view of these limitations, it is important to consider the role that qualitative, mixed methods, and improvement science approaches can play in explaining how and why policies and interventions are or are not enacted by teachers and principals and in producing scholarship that is both relevant for policy and consequential for practice.

REFERENCES

Alexander, E., Eppler, M. J., & Bresciani, S. (2019). Visual replay methodology: A mixed methods approach for group discussion analysis. *Journal of Mixed Methods Research, 13*(1), 33–51.

Anagnostopoulos, D., Sykes, G., McCrory, R., Cannata, M., & Frank, K. (2010). Dollars, distinction or duty: The meaning of the National Board for Professional Teaching Standards for teachers' work and collegial relations. *American Journal of Education, 116*(3), 337–369.

Augustine, C. H., McCombs, J. S., Pane, J. F., Schwartz, H. L., Schweig, J., McEachin, A., & Siler-Evans, K. (2016). *Learning from summer: Effects of voluntary summer learning programs on low-income urban youth.* RAND Corporation.

Augustine, C. H., & Thompson, L. E. (2017). *Making summer last: Integrating summer programming into core district priorities and operations.* RAND Corporation.

Biancarosa, G., Bryk, A. S., & Dexter, E. R. (2010). Assessing the value-added effects of literacy collaborative professional development on student learning. *Elementary School Journal, 111*(1), 7–34.

Booher-Jennings, J. (2005). Below the bubble: "Educational Triage" and the Texas Accountability System. *American Educational Research Journal, 42*(2), 231–268.

Bryk, A. S. (2015). 2014 AERA distinguished lecture: Accelerating how we learn to improve. *Educational Researcher, 44*(9), 467–477.

Butler, F. M., Miller, S. P., Crehan, K., Babbitt, B., & Pierce, T. (2003). Fraction instruction for students with mathematics disabilities: Comparing two teaching sequences. *Learning Disabilities Research & Practice, 18*(20), 99–111.

Buysse, V., Castro, D. C., & Peisner-Feinberg, E. (2010). Effects of a professional development program on classroom practices and out- comes for Latino dual language learners. *Early Childhood Research Quarterly, 25*, 194–206.

Cabalo, J. V., Ma, B., & Jaciw, A. (2007). *Comparative effectiveness of professional development and support tools for world language instruction: A report on a randomized experiment in Delaware*. Empirical Education.

Campbell, P. F., & Malkus, N. N. (2011). The impact of elementary mathematics coaches on student achievement. *The Elementary School Journal, 111*(3), 430–454.

Cannata, M., Cohen-Vogel, L., & Sorum, M. (2017). Partnering for improvement: Improvement communities and their role in scale up. *Peabody Journal of Education 92*(5), 569–588.

Clifford, G. J., & Guthrie, J. W. (1990). *Ed school: A brief for professional education*. University of Chicago Press.

Coburn, C. E., Bae, S., & Turner, E. O. (2008). Authority, status, and the dynamics of insider–outsider partnerships at the district level. *Peabody Journal of Education, 83*(3), 364–399.

Coburn, C. E., Honig, M. I., & Stein, M. K. (2009). What's the evidence on districts' use of evidence? In J. D. Bransford, D. J. Stipek, N. J. Vye, L. M. Gomez, & D. Lam (Eds.), *The role of research in educational improvement* (pp. 67–87). Harvard Education Press.

Coburn, C. E., & Penuel, W. R. (2016). Research-practice partnerships in education: Outcomes, dynamics, and open questions. *Educational Researcher, 45*(1), 48–54.

Coburn, C. E., Penuel, W. R., & Geil, K. E. (2013). *Practice partnerships: A strategy for leveraging research for educational improvement in school districts.* William T. Grant Foundation.

Coburn, C. E., & Russell, J. L. (2008). District policy and teachers' social networks. *Educational Evaluation and Policy Analysis, 30*(3), 203–235.

Cohen-Vogel, L., Allen, D., Rutledge, S., Harrison, C., Cannata, M., & Smith, T. M. (2018). Organizing for school improvement: The dilemmas of research-practice partnerships. *Journal of Research on Organization in Education, (2)*1.

Commonwealth of Massachusetts. (2018). Budget Summary FY2019: Education: Education (K–12): 7061–9814—Budget Summary. https://budget.digital.mass.gov/bb/gaa/fy2019/app_19/act_19/h70619814.htm

Connor, C. M., Morrison, F. J., Fishman, B. J., Schatschneider, C., & Underwood, P. (2007). Algorithm-guided individualized reading instruction. *Science Magazine, 315*(5811), 464–465.

Creswell, J. W., & Plano Clark, V. L. (2018). *Designing and conducting mixed methods research* (3rd ed.). SAGE.

Darling-Hammond, L., Hyler, M. E., & Gardner, M. (2017). *Effective teacher professional development.* Learning Policy Institute. https://learningpolicyinstitute.org/sites/default/files/product-files/Effective_Teacher_Professional_Development_REPORT.pdf

Datnow, A., Hubbard, L., & Mehan, H. (2005). *Extending educational reform: From one school to many.* Routledge.

Fetters, M. D., & Freshwater, D. (2015). The 1 + 1 = 3 integration challenge. *Journal of Mixed Methods Research, 9*(2), 115–117.

Fishman, B. J., Penuel, W. R., Allen, A. R., Cheng, B. H., & Sabelli, N. (2013). Design-based implementation research: An emerging model for transforming the relationship of research and practice. *National Society for the Study of Education, 112*(2), 136–156.

Frank, K. A., Zhao, Y., & Borman, K. (2004). Social capital and the diffusion of innovations within organizations: The case of computer technology in schools. *Sociology of Education,* 77(2), 148–171.

Fuchs, L. S., Fuchs, D., Prentice, K., Burch, M., Hamlett, C. L., Owen, R., Hosp, M., & Jancek, D. (2003). Explicitly teaching for transfer: Effects on third-grade students' mathematical problem solving. *Journal of Educational Psychology, 95*(2), 293–305.

Fuchs, L. S., Powell, S. R., Hamlett, C. L., & Fuchs, D. (2008). Remediating computational deficits at third grade: A randomized field trial. *Journal of Research on Educational Effectiveness, 1*(1), 2–32.

Gamse, B. C., Jacob, R. T., Horst, M., Boulay, B., & Unlu, F. (2008). *Reading First Impact Study Final Report* (NCEE 2009-4038). National Center for Education Evaluation and Regional Assistance, Institute of Education Sciences, U.S. Department of Education.

Garet, M. S., Cronen, S., Eaton, M., Kurki, A., Ludwig, M., Jones, W., Uekawa, K., Falk, A., Bloom, H. S., Doolittle, F., Zhu, P., & Sztejnberg, L. (2008). *The impact of two professional development interventions on early reading instruction and achievement* (NCEE 2008-4030). National Center for Education Evaluation and Regional Assistance, Institute of Education Sciences, U.S. Department of Education.

Garet, M. S., Wayne, A. J., Stancavage, F., Taylor, J., Eaton, M., Walters, K., Song, M., Brown, S., Hurlburt, S., Zhu, P., Sepanik, S., & Doolittle, F. (2011). *Middle School Mathematics Professional Development Impact Study: Findings after the second year of implementation* (NCEE 2011-4025). National Center for Education Evaluation and Regional Assistance, Institute of Education Sciences, U.S. Department of Education.

Gersten, R., Dimino, J., Jayanthi, M., Kim, J. S., & Santoro, L. E. (2010). Teacher study group: Impact of the professional development model on reading instruction and student outcomes in first grade classrooms. *American Educational Research Journal, 47*, 694–739.

Giersch, J. (2018). Academic tracking, high-stakes tests, and preparing students for college: How inequality persists within schools. *Educational Policy, 32*(7), 907–935.

Glazerman, S., Isenberg, E., Dolfin, S., Bleeker, M., Johnson, A., Grider, M., Jacobus, M. & Ali, M. (2010). *Impacts of Comprehensive Teacher Induction: Final Results from a Randomized Controlled Study*. U.S. Department of Education, Institute of Education Sciences.

Greene, J. C. (2007). *Mixed methods in social inquiry*. Jossey-Bass.

Hill, H. C., Beisiegel, M., & Jacob, R. (2013). Professional development research: Consensus, crossroads, and challenges. *Educational Researcher, 42*(9), 476–487.

Hill, H. C., Kapitula, L., & Umland, K. (2011). A validity argument approach to evaluating teacher value-added scores. *American Educational Research Journal, 48*(3), 794–831.

Hopkins, M., Wiley, K. E., Penuel, W. R., & Farrell, C. C. (2018). Brokering research in science education policy implementation: The case of a professional association. *Evidence & Policy: A Journal of Research, Debate and Practice, 14*(3), 459–476.

Johnson, R. B., & Onwuegbuzie, A. J. (2004). Mixed methods research: A research paradigm whose time has come. *Educational Researcher, 33*(7), 14–26.

Kaestle, C. F. (1993). Research news and comment: The awful reputation of education research. *Educational Researcher, 22*(1), 23–31.

Kraft, M. A., Blazar, D., & Hogan, D. (2018). The effect of teacher coaching on instruction and achievement: A meta-analysis of the causal evidence. *Review of Educational Research, 88*(4), 547–588.

Labaree, D. F. (1996). The trouble with ed schools. *Journal of Educational Foundations, 10*(3), 27.

Landesman Ramey, S., Ramey, C. T., Crowell, N. A., Grace, C., & Timraz, N. (2011). The dosage of professional development for early childhood professionals: How the amount, density, and duration of professional development may influence its effectiveness. In J. A. Sutterby (Ed.), *Early childhood professional development: Research and practice through the early childhood educator professional development grant* (pp. 11–32). The Emerald Group.

Landry, S. H., Anthony, J. L., Swank, P. R., & Monseque-Bailey, P. (2009). Effectiveness of comprehensive professional development for teachers of at-risk preschoolers. *Journal of Educational Psychology, 101*, 448–465.

LeMahieu, P. G., Grunow, A., Baker, L., Nordstrum, L. E., & Gomez, L. M. (2017). Networked improvement communities: The discipline of improvement science meets the power of networks. *Quality Assurance in Education, 25*(1), 5–25.

McCombs, J. S., Pane, J. F., Augustine, C. H., Schwartz, H. L., Martorell, P., & Zakaras, L. (2014). *Ready for fall? Near-term effects of voluntary summer learning programs on low-income students' learning opportunities and outcomes*. RAND Corporation.

McLaughlin, M. W. (1987). Learning from experience: Lessons from policy implementation. *Educational Evaluation and Policy Analysis*, *9*(2), 171–178.

McLaughlin, M. W. (1990). The RAND Change Agent Study revisited: Macro perspectives and micro realities. *Educational Researcher*, *19*(9), 11–16.

McLaughlin, M. W. (1998). Listening and learning from the field: Tales of policy implementation and situated practice. In A. Hargreaves, A. Lieberman, M. Fullan, & D. W. Hopkins (Ed.), *International handbook of educational change: Part two* (1st ed., pp. 70–84). Kluwer.

McMillan, J. H., & Wergin, J. F. (2010). *Understanding and evaluating educational research* (4th ed.). Pearson.

Moss, P. A., & Haertel, E. H. (2016). Engaging methodological pluralism. In D. Gitomer & C. Bell (Eds.), *Handbook of research on teaching* (5th ed., pp. 127–247). American Educational Research Association.

National Reading Panel (U.S.), & National Institute of Child Health and Human Development (U.S.). (2000). *Report of the National Reading Panel: Teaching children to read: An evidence-based assessment of the scientific research literature on reading and its implications for reading instruction: Reports of the subgroups*. National Institute of Child Health and Human Development, National Institutes of Health.

National Research Council. (1999). *Improving student learning: A strategic plan for education research and its utilization*. National Academies Press.

National Research Council. (2002). *Scientific research in education*. In R. J. Shavelson & L. Towne (Eds.), *Committee on scientific principles for education research*. National Academies Press.

National Research Council. (2003). *Strategic education research partnership*. National Academies Press.

National Research Council. (2004). *Learning and instruction: A SERP research agenda*. National Academies Press.

Neal, Z. P., Neal, J. W., Lawlor, J. A., & Mills, K. J. (2015). Small worlds or worlds apart? Using network theory to understand the research–practice gap. *Psychosocial Intervention 24*(3), 177–84.

Nelson, L. D., Simmons, J., & Simonsohn, U. (2018). Psychology's renaissance. *Annual Review of Psychology*, *69*(1), 511–534.

Nosek, B. A., & Bar-Anan, Y. (2012). Scientific utopia: I. Opening scientific communication. *Psychological Inquiry*, *23*(3), 217–243.

Nosek, B. A., Spies, J. R., & Motyl, M. (2012). Scientific utopia: II. Restructuring incentives and practices to promote truth over publishability. *Perspectives on Psychological Science*, 7(6), 615–631.

Open Science Collaboration. (2015). Estimating the reproducibility of psychological science. *Science*, *349*(6251), aac4716.

Otte, E., & Rousseau, R. (2002). Social network analysis: A powerful strategy, also for the information sciences. *Journal of Information Science*, *28*(6), 441–453.

Penuel, W. R., Briggs, D. C., Davidson, K. L, Herlihy, C., Sherer, D., Hill, H. C., Farrell, C. C., & Allen, A. R. (2016). *Findings from a national survey of research use among school and district leaders* (Technical Report No. 1). National Center for Research in Policy and Practice.

Penuel, W. R., Briggs, D. C., Davidson, K. L., Herlihy, C., Sherer, D., Hill, H. C., Farrell, C. C., & Allen, A. R. (2017). How school and district leaders' access, perceive, and use research. *AERA Open, 3*(2).

Penuel, W. R., Gallagher, L. P., & Moorthy, S. (2011). Preparing teachers to design sequences of instruction in earth systems science: A comparison of three professional development programs. *American Educational Research Journal, 48*(4), 996–1025.

Peurach, D. J. (2016). Innovating at the nexus of impact and improvement: Leading educational improvement networks. *Educational Researcher, 45*(7), 421–429.

Peurach, D. J., Penuel, W. R., & Russell, J. L. (2018). Beyond ritualized rationality: Organizational dynamics of instructionally-focused continuous improvement. In C. James, D. E. Spicer, M. Connolly, & S. D. Kruse (Eds.), *The SAGE handbook of school organization* (pp. 465–488). SAGE.

Pianta, R., Hamre, B., Downer, J., Burchinal, M., Williford, A., LoCasale-Crouch, J., Howes, C., La Paro, K., & Scott-Little, C. (2017). Early childhood professional development: Coaching and coursework effects on indicators of children's school readiness. *Early Education and Development, 28*, 956–975.

Portes, A. (2000). The hidden abode: Sociology as analysis of the unexpected. *American Sociological Review, 65*(1), 1–18.

Powell, D. R., & Diamond, K. E. (2011). Improving the outcomes of coaching-based professional development interventions. In S. B. Neuman & D. K. Dickinson (Eds.), *Handbook of early literacy research* (Vol. 3, pp. 295–307). Guilford.

Pyrczak, F. (2017). *Evaluating research in academic journals: A practical guide to realistic evaluation* (6th ed.). Routledge.

Redding, C., Cannata, M., & Taylor Haynes, K. (2017). With scale in mind: A continuous improvement model for implementation. *Peabody Journal of Education 92*(5), 589–608.

Rockoff, J. E. (2004). The impact of individual teachers on student achievement: Evidence from panel data. *American Economic Review, 94*(2), 247–252.

Russell, J. L., Bryk, A. S., Dolle, J., Gomez, L. M., LeMahieu, P., & Grunow, A. (2017). A framework for the initiation of networked improvement communities. *Teachers College Record, 119*(7), 1–36.

Santagata, R., Kersting, N., Givvin, K. B., & Stigler, J. W. (2011). Problem implementation as a lever for change: An experimental study of the effects of a professional development program on students' mathematics learning. *Journal of Research on Educational Effectiveness, 4*, 1–24.

Schmidt, R., Young, V., Cassidy, L., Wang, H., & Laguarda, K. (2017). Impact of the New Teacher Center's new teacher induction model on teachers and students. SRI international.

Schwartz, H. L., McCombs, J. S., Augustine, C. H., & Leschitz, J. T. (2018). *Getting to work on summer learning: Recommended practices for success* (2nd ed.). RAND Corporation.

Society for Research on Educational Effectiveness. (2019). *Mission statement.*

Spillane, J. P. (1998). State policy and the non-monolithic nature of the local school district: Organizational and professional considerations. *American Educational Research Journal, 35*(1), 33–63.

Tournaki, N. (2003). The differential effects of teaching addition through strategy instruction versus drill and practice to students with and without learning disabilities. *Journal of Learning Disabilities, 36*(5), 449–458.

Tschannen-Moran, M., & Hoy, W. K. (2000). A multidisciplinary analysis of the nature. meaning, and measurement of trust. *Review of Educational Research, 70*(4), 547–593.

van Velzen, J. H. (2018). Students' general knowledge of the learning process: A mixed methods study illustrating integrated data collection and data consolidation. *Journal of Mixed Methods Research, 12*(2), 182–203.

Wentworth, L., Mazzeo, C., & Connolly, F. (2017). Research practice partnerships: A strategy for promoting evidence-based decision-making in education. *Educational Research, 59*(2), 241–255.

Xie, S., & Li, H. (2018). Perspectives on readiness for preschool: A mixed-methods study of Chinese parents, teachers, and principals. *Children and Youth Services Review, 95*, 19–31.

Yin, R. K. (2017). *Case study research and applications: Design and methods* (6th ed.). SAGE.

CHAPTER 5

QUANTITATIVE RESEARCH DESIGN AND EDUCATION POLICY EVALUATION

Pedro Reyes and Michael R. Scott
University of Texas at Austin

The purpose of this chapter is to present and discuss some of the most prevalent quantitative research strategies used by education policy evaluation researchers. Although the purpose of any study may vary, there are some common strategies researchers use to ascertain the effectiveness of any policy goal. Usually, such a policy objective has a program with a theory embedded, providing a roadmap that outlines the activities that allege to produce certain outcomes. As a consequence of program implementation, the outcomes should produce what the specific policy goal intended (Stone, 1997). In doing policy evaluation, researchers often evaluate these programs that have been created to support the specific policy objective. For example, a specific policy may be one that the government desires to improve the mortality rates of children from families with a low economic status. Thus, the legislature may dictate a particular policy direction and allocate resources to improve child mortality. Then, a state agency operationalizes this policy by building a specific health program to target that specific population. Later the program is implemented, and after some

Maximizing the Policy Relevance of Research for School Improvement, pp. 109–135
Copyright © 2021 by Information Age Publishing
All rights of reproduction in any form reserved.

time, a policy evaluator is hired to make sense of its effectiveness. The policy evaluator uses a standardized set of techniques to assesses the policy/program goals, documents, and outcomes according to the strategy used in the implementation of it.

Our approach to this chapter is to present the most prevalent methods of policy evaluation research and then show an example of each method's use. Our hope is that by the end of the chapter, the reader can understand the proper application of each research strategy and raise critical questions about their utility. This chapter is geared for the casual user (consumer) of research strategies, mostly practitioners. It should help them understand the process, limitations, as well as the outcomes of specific research strategies. We first present the framework behind this quantitative thinking. Second, we discuss experimental and quasi-experimental research approaches as policy evaluation research strategies. Then, we continue with the use of survey research in policy evaluation. Finally, we present some advice regarding statistical considerations, limitations, and ethics of this type of research.

THE FRAMEWORK

In order to use the quantitative tradition of social science research properly (under which education policy evaluation falls), researchers must first appropriately frame one or more research questions. To do this, they employ the social research process (Crotty, 1998). This process was developed over the years by philosophers, social scientists, and researchers to provide legitimacy to this type of research. It is a philosophical perspective of research, as it has a set of major assumptions about what makes up the "world" of research. In fact, most researchers using this tradition follow these assumptions in order to claim legitimacy in producing any new knowledge. There are multiple perspectives as to how a researcher may address these assumptions, including post-positivism, interpretivism, constructivism, and critical perspectives (Crotty, 1998). Although all these perspectives may be used to do policy evaluation, the one discussed in this chapter is the "post-positivist" perspective (Creswell, 2003; Popper, 1972).

The post-positivist perspective makes three major assumptions about the world of research in the areas of ontology, epistemology, and methodology. The first area, *ontology*, concerns how researchers define reality; this perspective assumes that "the state of being" or reality is concrete and that it can be measured given certain precautions. In other words, "reality is independent of human perception" (Sale et al., 2002, p. 44). This means that the concept of interest can be defined specifically and then measured regardless of any other perception. We do so by developing and testing an instrument which was created and carefully designed from a particular theory. If using the concept of *leadership* as an example, in the post-positivist perspective, we are defining a reality of "leadership" via an instrument that has embedded the theoretical properties defined by a particular theory. We prove that the instrument is legitimate (i.e., is real) by subjecting the instrument to several statistical tests that provide evidence through reliability and validity processes used by the creator of the test or instrument. In this way, the researcher claims that the instrument measures the concept of leadership and thus, a leadership reality has been constructed.

The second area, *epistemology*, concerns a theory of knowledge. It is the way knowledge is acquired. This theory outlines the reasons as to what, how, and why we learn when doing social science research. This assumes that the researcher and the researched are independent entities. This assumption embeds the theoretical perspective of meaning we use and attribute to develop new knowledge (Crotty, 1998). The most prominent characteristic in the post-positivistic tradition is objectivism (Popper, 1972). This theory of knowledge posits that "all things exist as meaningful entities independently of consciousness and experience, that they have truth and meaning residing in them as objects; and that careful research can attain that objective and meaning" (Crotty, 1998, pp. 5–6). Therefore, researchers studying leadership have decided that the concept of leadership exists as a meaningful entity, and that by using careful research they can develop the psychometric properties that provide validity to the instrument. Once validity has been established, they may use a particular methodology to present new claims of knowledge concerning leadership.

The third and final area making up the post-positivist tradition of the social process of research is about the *methodology*, or the procedures used to conduct research. The methodology is the strategy or design along with the methods needed within the post-positivistic perspective. It is a theoretical perspective that embeds the assumptions about ontology and epistemology presented above. Except that in this case, it outlines the specific methodology and related methods to follow in order to develop any new knowledge. There are different methodologies appropriate to different research problems. For example, if one wanted to evaluate a school intervention, such as a new literacy program, the researcher may want to consider an experimental design that rules out all kinds of potential effects that are not actually associated with the program. The experimental design (discussed below in greater detail) includes a series of assumptions, such as random assignment of subjects to the experimental group, carefully validated measures of the outcome variables, strict internal validity, and so on. Similarly, a correlational design may require many controls to really understand how a particular variable affects the variable of interest. Gersten et al. (2005) offer a checklist as a resource that allows researchers plan their research in a way that is valid and reliable. Above all, the researcher's methodology is designed upfront and carefully, in order to take all precautions to make sure any inference is valid and appropriate to a large population. This methodology is carefully crafted to make sure that all the potential biases are eliminated before one executes the data collection and analyses. It is important to know that methodology is line with the epistemology and ontology as described above. Thus, all the assumptions together guide and provide the parameters to follow to create knowledge. They are consistent and systematic, and if not followed, one cannot use those assumptions to claim the "legitimacy" that they provide.

One final other piece important to discuss upfront is a theoretical perspective. Typically, this is the theory that informs the context, the logic, and the processes being measured and used to explain and predict phenomena. The theory or theoretical model includes so-called variables or key concepts that are articulated in the theory. Once these are identified, tested, and measured with precision, then the researcher is ready to conduct the research. The theory provides for hypotheses development and testing. In most instances, the theory guides how the concepts are to be developed, tested, and analyzed. For example, when doing policy evaluation research, researchers first start with the theory. They then define the inputs, such as the activities or interventions designed to improve a situation like child mortality. Next, they identify the key concepts or variables to be assessed and the concrete ways to measure of these variables. Researchers then validate the variables, first conceptually, and then they empirically test them on a small group (i.e., sample) representative of the larger group (i.e., population). If the measurements are well executed—meaning consistent and valid—then they are ready to conduct research and develop new knowledge. Otherwise, they may experience failure in predicting and explaining the phenomena they are trying to understand.

Now, we focus on three of the most common strategies when doing research focused on policy evaluation research: experimental, quasi-experimental, and survey research designs.

EXPERIMENTAL RESEARCH

Policy evaluation research often seeks to understand causal relationships. For example, does moving from a high-poverty neighborhood improve opportunities for job attainment? Does implementing trauma-informed practices in the classroom improve a student's probability of graduating from high school? Does increasing funding for HIV education reduce infections to the virus? In each of these questions, researchers ask if a change in policy *causes* a difference in outcomes that matter to school practitioners and policymakers. These questions are important to answer but answering them properly requires making several assumptions. In order to ensure that we are conducting research in an environment in which these assumptions can be met, we follow the tenets of *experimental design*. In this section, we describe how experimental design can be used to inform policy. First, we explain the reasons why experimental design is important to make causal claims, including the assumptions that must be met to make such a claim. Second, we describe how a social experiment should be conducted. Finally, we provide two examples of policy-related experiments. For additional discussion of these topics, we suggest that the reader refer to Borman (2012).

Experiments as the "Gold Standard"

We often want to know if a certain intervention will make an impact. In order to be able to make such a determination, researchers should follow an experimental design. Without following these principles that we describe, arguments could be made by different people that a particular intervention is positive, negative, or has no effect. What is important to know though, is precisely this—is there an effect, and if so, is it positive or negative? The reason experiments are so important is because they reduce the number of potential confounders. Confounders are factors unrelated to the intervention of interest that may be unobserved but still partially explain the phenomenon being studied.

As a hypothetical example, let us say we want to know if a student learning accountability policy improves student mastery of the content. A district decides to use the new accountability structure in one school and the old structure with another school. In comparing the results, the district finds that the students master the material at a higher rate under new structure. However, in this case, prior student understanding was not taken into account, which confounds the results. Another district decides to compare the same new structure for accountability against the same old structure. But by following an experimental design, the second district finds that there is actually a lower rate of mastery using the new structure than the old one. The effects that the two districts find are exactly the opposite. This could lead to erroneous decision making.

Assumptions in Experimental Inference

In any experimental inference, the three most important assumptions that researchers make include random assignment and that their measures are *reliable* and *valid*. Reliability assumes that random error is reduced—

meaning that if the same experiment were replicated, the researchers would get the same result. Mitchell and Jolley (2012) describe reliability as a prerequisite for the second assumption: validity. In its most basic definition, ensuring validity asks if the researcher is measuring what they intend to measure. We now discuss briefly random assignment and why reliability and validity are fundamental to experimental design.

Random Assignment. Random assignment of subjects to any intervention is critical to generate credible results. Random assignment eliminates error by selecting subjects from a larger population as a sample, thus making sure that each subject in the population, regardless of frequency, has an equal chance of being selected and assigned to either the intervention or to the control group. Simple random selection is a good strategy. In this scenario, each participant has an equal chance of being placed in an experimental group without regard to other factors. When a simple random sample is employed of a large number of participants, confounding variables that may skew results are limited. The reason is that we can assume there is an equal mix of the different factors between the two groups; the only difference between the two groups is that one received the different intervention (Shadish et al., 2002). But, when one needs to ensure a specific group is represented, stratified random sample is a better approach. In this case, participants are separated into different groups (such as by gender and socioeconomic status), and then a random sample is taken from each of the groups (Good & Hardin, 2012). This may be more appropriate in cases where these factors are important. For example, in an adolescent socialization study, if the theory states that boys and girls are socialized differently, then researchers will want to ensure that they account for the gender differences in the intervention.

Reliability. At its essence, reliability means that any random error that may influence a result is removed. Although removing all random error is nearly impossible due to the innate differences in human and organizational behavior, researchers should still take care to assess the reliability of their measures. More error in an experimental model increasingly reduces the precision of our estimates of the effect. Random error can be introduced due to the observer or researcher, the measure or instrument used to assess the outcome, or the participants. Researchers cannot entirely remove all random error, but there are ways in which they can ensure error minimally impacts the estimates. However, measures cannot be valid if they are not reliable.

Validity. As described previously, attuning to validity means ensuring that the researcher is testing what is intended. It also means that the measures are absent of bias. Those aspects of validity can be broken down in several different components that are often placed in distinct categories. We describe some of the most important categories of validity below. For a more detailed discussion, we recommend Shadish et al. (2002) and Mitchell and Jolley (2012) as resources.

- *Construct validity* focuses on if the measure that researchers use tests the intended outcome. This is related to the theoretical concept itself; it is a definition that includes all the theoretical dimensions of a concept as indicated in the theory. Researchers must first ensure they are using a sound theory to meet the assumption of face validity. Mitchell and Jolley (2012) further categorize construct validity into four domains: face validity, content validity, convergent validity, and discriminant validity.

    - o *Face validity* refers the construct reasonably appearing to measure what is intended. This generally is accomplished if the research team appropriately utilizes a sound theory in developing their measure. That is, it serves as a check on how the relevant questions measuring the concept "appear" to be related to the theoretical concept.
    - o *Content validity* assesses if the entire construct is included in the measure. For example, if the theory driving a research team's measure includes three parts, they must ensure that all parts are included in their measure.
    - o *Convergent validity* addresses if the multiple parts of a measure "agree" with each other. Even if these various constructs might differ slightly because they all are a part of one construct, they should somewhat be in agreement with each other.

Discriminant validity refers to the "disagreement" of measures with unrelated constructs.

- *Internal validity* assesses if the research was performed in a way that reduces confounding variables. Gerber and Green (2012) describe a measure as valid when the treatment effect is based *solely* on intervention and that the effect is based on participant *himself* who receives the treatment. This means that the outcomes do not depend on the treatments that other participants receive or the research design.
- *External validity* is also described as "generalizability." If a research team's construct is generalizable, it will apply across time, across all members of the population, and across contexts (Mitchell & Jolley, 2012).

Although there is much to consider in experimental design, much of this can be addressed by ensuring randomization, which we discuss in the next section.

Ensuring Reliability in Experimental Design

Now that we have described the two main assumptions and their various components, we discuss how researchers ensure that their measures are reliable. Remember that assessing for reliability means reducing random error as much as possible. Many times, research teams check for reliability by assessing test-retest reliability. In practice, this means that the research is conducted on a sample, and the same study is performed on the same sample at a later time. The scores of the test are compared to the score of the retest for each participant. If these scores are highly correlated (around 90% is the best-case scenario in social science research), researchers can assume that random error is small, and the measure is reliable. If the correlation coefficient is low, researchers must assess why random error is present (Shadish et al., 2002).

There are three ways in which random error may result in low test-retest reliability. First, if there are multiple experimental observers measuring the outcome, inter-rater reliability must be assessed. This correlation assesses to what extent different researchers correspond in their scoring. If there is low inter-rater reliability, the research teams should train each other to ensure that no matter whom the rater is, a participant would receive the same score. Second, inter-item correlation should be assessed. Also called internal consistency, scores on each item measuring the same thing should be related in similar ways. Statistically speaking, they should be correlated with each other using a statistical technique such as Cronbach's alpha. In this measure, a correlation is calculated for each pair of items in the same measure, and the average of each correlation is taken. If $\alpha < 0.7$, the researcher should either add more items or eliminate those items that may not be internally consistent with the rest of the measure. However, if inter-rater reliability and internal consistency are both high and the test-retest correlation is low, it is likely that the error is due to bias, rather than randomness, and the design of the experiment itself must be reassessed (Mitchell & Jolley, 2012). These design issues are also ones that ensure validity, which we discuss next. As we have described, there are many components to meeting the validity assumption of an experimental design. Although construct validity is assessed using the measure of internal consistency as described above, researchers who are not careful with their design and do not ensure internal validity, such as by not using a random design, might introduce bias into their results.

Predominant Models of Experimental Design

Although we do not discuss each experimental design in detail, we now turn to the two predominant models of designing an experiment in policy evaluation and research: independent measures and repeated measures. Regardless of the model employed, the tenets of reliability and validity previously described apply.

Independent measures. In the independent measures design, each participant is randomly assigned to a level of the intervention. In a study with two levels (i.e., a treatment and a control), each participant is assigned to receive only the treatment or the control. Although this model has the benefit of reducing participant fatigue and limits potential biases related to having participated in multiple iterations of the study, it does require a larger sample size than using the repeated measures design. If the sample size in an independent measures study is low, results may be more prone to bias due to underlying student or school characteristics that a large random sample may be able to avoid.

Repeated measures. In the repeated measures design, each participant receives both (or all) conditions of the experiment. In a study with two levels, half of the participants receive the treatment and the other half receive the control first. After some time, the participants receive the opposite level. Although there may be some effects due to the order in which participants receive the treatment, researchers can statistically control for this effect. The benefit of a repeated measures design is therefore that fewer participants are needed, which can save time in obtaining consenting participants.

Two Examples of Experimental Design in Policy Evaluation

We now turn to two examples of experiments designed to improve different outcomes. The first experiment was designed to examine the social opportunity of families living in public housing communities (Shroder & Orr, 2012). The second experiment we discuss involves the incorporation of green exercise as a means to improve student self-esteem (Reed et al., 2013).

Moving to opportunity example. In the 1990s, the U.S. Congress authorized the Department of Housing and Urban Development (HUD) to conduct a social experiment to see if providing housing vouchers to low-income families to move from public housing projects to middle-class neighborhoods would improve their social opportunity to find and maintain stable housing, employment, and education. This independent measures design, which was named Moving to Opportunity (MTO), randomly assigned each of the families to one of three groups: receiving a housing voucher with counseling to support appropriate placement, receiving a voucher with no counseling, and a control group that only offered the families the standard governmental programs for housing. Over 15,000 individuals, clustered by family unit, agreed to participate in the study.

Although it was at first questioned if an experiment was the most appropriate method given its costs, as well as the number of potential confounders, it was determined that it was indeed the most appropriate model. Previous research employed a quasi-experimental design, which we discuss next, but the number of confounders exacerbate the problems associated with non-random sampling. Although the MTO study produced a variety of results, some in conflict with each other, it does appear that housing vouchers improve the long-term economic opportunity for families (Chetty et al., 2016). Despite conflicting findings, Shroder and Orr (2012) report that HUD has learned a lot about the neighborhood effects of poverty and how mobility impacts one's social opportunity. This in turn has provided them with suggestions on how to improve policy related to poverty and public housing.

Green exercise example. The second study evaluates a program that incorporates exercise in green environments (i.e., parks or rural settings) to see if it improves self-esteem compared to exercising in strictly urban settings (Reed et al., 2013). Although similar research had been done on an adult population, the researchers wanted to see if this also transferred to children. Children were randomly assigned to run in a green setting or an urban setting, and one week later they each completed a run in the opposite condition. Researchers then assessed their self-esteem after the run, controlling for levels of physical activity. In this experiment, although self-esteem improved after all exercises, there was no difference between the setting of the run. However, more children did enjoy green exercise more, which the authors suggested might be a beneficial finding to improve overall child physical activity.

QUASI-EXPERIMENTAL RESEARCH

Oftentimes, in studying policy, conducting an experiment is not possible. Ensuring an adequate sample size that can be appropriately randomized to infer causality is costly. Even in the MTO study (Shroder & Orr, 2012), a cost-benefit analysis was conducted to see if an experiment was needed to understand the impact of the program. Although they decided in that case that it was, at other times it may not be necessary. Furthermore, in policy analysis this is not always even possible. Social variables are much more complicated to control, as one could in a laboratory. Therefore, while they may implement an experiment that compares groups, they do not often randomize. In yet other instances, researchers may want to study the impact of a policy using data that have already been collected. Many lessons can be learned from conducting these studies. In fact, especially given the robust statistical tools, quasi-experimental designs can offer us a plethora of knowledge to better inform policy and practices. Although we must be careful about making causal claims in these types of studies, by employing the appropriate statistical analysis we still are able to explore causality despite the non-random nature of the data. In this section, we discuss the procedures of conducting quasi-experimental research and provide an example of each of the techniques.

Quasi-Experiments in Policy Evaluation Research

As we previously discussed, experimental design is often costly. Randomization requires a large number of participants who must be assigned to one of several groups in order to make an inference. In other cases, the phenomenon of interest simply does not allow for randomization. For example, in one study, the effects of military veteran status on postsecondary outcomes were explored (Steele et al., 2018). The researchers could not randomize for being in the military. However, in quasi-experiments, we cannot conduct simple statistical comparisons due the various potential confounders. Specifically, were there characteristics of the population who moved versus those who stayed? In order to account appropriately for potential confounders in quasi-experiments or other observational studies (those that use existing data), we must employ an appropriate statistical technique.

There are many different approaches that allow the researcher to account for confounding variables. We briefly describe five of the most common: propensity score matching and weighting, instrumental variables, fixed effects, differences-in-differences, and regression discontinuity. Although there are various assumptions related to each method that we do not cover below, we give a broad overview to provide a general understanding of the different types of methods that are available to assess causality if we are not able to conduct a randomized experiment. For a more technical description of these methods, see Morgan and Winship (2014) and Wooldridge (2002). For another discussion of quasi-experimental designs in education policy research, see Kaplan (2012).

Propensity Score Matching and Weighting. One of the more commonly used approaches in observational or quasi-experimental designs, matching allows the researcher to approximate equality of the potential confounding variables. In this process, each observation (i.e., person) received as a score for their propensity (or, probability) for being part of the treatment group, given a set of covariates that may be considered confounding. Researchers can then either match someone in the treatment group to the control group who has similar propensity scores, or the inverse of that probability can be used to weight the effects of being in the program. This allows the researchers to remove out potential selection bias that could impact the treatment effect.

As an example, Steele et al. (2018) examined the higher education outcomes of U.S. military veterans, compared to similar non-veteran higher education graduates. Using a nationally representative sample, their research explored the extent of student debt, employment status, and employment earnings 1, 4, and 10 years after graduation. By creating a propensity score weight for veteran status, they were able to account for selection bias: people do not randomly join the military. The weights account for age, race/ethnicity, socioeconomic status, sector of college attended, and major, as veterans may differ in these characteristics from non-veterans. After accounting for these differences in these two groups, Steele et al. (2018) find that although veterans have higher earnings and rates of employments 1 and 4 years after graduation, they are at greater odds for being unemployed 10 years after graduation. However, for those who are employed, veterans still have an earnings benefit 10 years later. Additionally, despite the Montgomery GI Bill, veterans are as likely as non-veterans to graduate with student debt.

Instrumental Variables. In other quasi-experimental designs, we may find that the effect we are interested in studying might be also affected by other external factors. Econometricians refer to these factors as *exogenous variables*. Although we may not be interested in the effects of these exogenous variables, they may obstruct our ability to understand the relationship between our treatment and outcome of interest. For example, let us say we are interested in understanding the relationship between attending an after-school tutoring program (READ 180) and reading achievement (example from Kim et al., 2011). However, because the program is voluntary, not all students who were offered the reading program attended. This could be for a variety of background characteristics, such as student socioeconomic background. Therefore, if we were to assess the effect of the program on those who attended, we might find skewed results. Instrumental variables analysis functions to control for these background factors. This design is thus conducted in two stages. In the first stage, we calculate the predicted number of days one attends the program (Z) regressed on if they were offered to attend the program (D) and a set of the covariates, such as socioeconomic status (X). In the second stage, our outcome of interest, reading score (Y) is then regressed on the predicted number of days from the first stage (Z') and the covariates (X). In this way, rather than assessing the effect on being assigned to attend the program, which may give dubious results, we seek to understand the effect of being assigned to participate in the program and of following through with it.

The two-step approach to an instrumental variables approach allows the researcher to control for exogenous variables, in this case, attending the after-school tutoring program. Kim et al. (2011) found that attending READ 180 improved reading in some areas (e.g., reading comprehension and spelling) but not in other areas (e.g., oral reading fluency and spelling). The positive effects for some areas of literacy showed that READ 180 was a promising after-school program that should be considered. However, the authors also suggest that the study needed to be conducted longitudinally and at a larger scale to understand broad-range and long-term impacts. If additional research finds similar effects, it would be worthwhile to promote the program to improve literacy in the population that READ 180 serves.

Fixed Effects. If we want to look at the impact of a policy over time, we can use data that is collected on a sample of individuals over time, also known as panel data. However, there are also stable characteristics of the individuals that we observe which do not change over time. For example, a student of a lower socioeconomic background may have a lower reading score, but may also respond differently to the policy intervention, due to that background. Therefore, it is important to control for these stable characteristics of individuals so that we can approximate the effect of the policy (*X*) on the outcome of interest (*Y*). In calculating fixed effects, we are controlling for each individual to ensure that the effect which is found is only related to the policy.

In examining the segmented labor market of teacher attrition in charter schools and traditional public schools, Gulosino et al. (2019) examined the role of timing on a new teacher's decision to exit the profession or transfer to a different school. Because they are trying to explore the reasons for leaving the teaching profession, and there are various school-level factors in each school year that may impact a teacher's decision to exit. By fixing the effects of the schools, Gulosino et al. find that new charter schoolteachers are more likely to leave the profession, while new traditional public-school teachers who leave more often transfer to a different school.

Differences-in-Differences. In another scenario where we are interested in the effect of policy over time, we might want to compare how two different groups react a policy. For example, we may want to see how different school lunch programs affect student achievement. If we are to calculate the achievement of students in all schools before the different programs begin and again after a year of the program, controlling only for the treatment may not capture the effect of the program. We may find that students who do not receive school lunch also perform better in class as the year progresses. The difference-in-differences technique allows us to explore how both time and the program affect student achievement. In this model, we calculate the difference in attention between the two timepoints for both groups. We then take the difference of change from the group that receives breakfast from the change of the group that does not. What remains is the effect of the program.

Anderson et al. (2018) examined to see if schools with a large proportion of students receiving free or reduced-price lunch (FRL) perform better on standardized tests if they are provided with healthy school lunches over those who are provided a standard school lunch. By estimating the differences of scores for schools with a high FRL rate within the differences of those receiving a healthy school lunch, Anderson et al. find that students attending schools providing a healthy lunch perform better on standardized tests. What is more, students in high FRL schools benefit from the healthy lunch program more than students not in high FRL schools. The authors also performed a similar analysis on obesity rates, but they did not find an effect.

Regression Discontinuity. One final method to assess causality in quasi-experimental research is known as regression discontinuity. In many policy decisions, groups research a treatment due to a threshold (or cut-off score). For example, students receive free or reduced-price lunch (FRL) based on their level of income. Students below a certain income receive benefits, but those who make more than the specified threshold do not. To assess the effect of FRL on one's health, it would not be useful to compare all people who receive FRL to those who do not. Many people who do not receive benefits have sufficient income to purchase their food and are also more likely to have improved health (for a variety of reasons). Therefore, this research design assesses the effect of a treatment such as FRL on the sample around the threshold. The treatment effect estimates the difference between the outcome just below threshold and the outcome just above it. Although the outcome is only generalizable to around the threshold, it does give us a better understanding of the impact of a particular policy or program. In the research study that examines the effects of the National School Lunch Program on child health, Gundersen et al. (2012) use a type of regression discontinuity design to explore if students who receive free lunch have improved health outcomes. Indeed, their extension of the regression discontinuity finds evidence for better health outcomes.

These different designs allow us to infer causality even when it is not feasible to conduct a randomized experiment. Although the results of these studies still only infer causality, they allow us to understand how certain mechanisms operate, which provides evidence for improving educational policies and systems.

SURVEY RESEARCH

Now, we discuss survey research as a strategy to evaluate policy initiatives. Surveys are used to collect data that we cannot obtain from existing data, such as experiments or other administrative data sources (Robinson & Leonard, 2019). Surveys are used extensively to understand social and behavioral characteristics of people; one of the most famous examples is the U.S. Decennial Census (Fowler, 2013). We can then use the survey data we collected to describe the sample or make inferences on the population. Two common techniques are cross-sectional designs and longitudinal designs.

One of the most common survey designs is the cross-sectional design (Babbie et al., 2019). This design assumes that the data are collected on each participant at a single point in time. However, the data collection is administered to multiple groups. This strategy may help understand how a policy program affects different groups at the same time, assuming of course they received the same intervention. For example, one may compare the effects of a vaccine among three or four groups of different social statuses. As another example, one may evaluate a local school district policy on the effectiveness of a curriculum program. Using a cross-sectional design, one compares attitudes towards a certain math curriculum among third, fourth, and fifth graders.

Another variation of survey design is the longitudinal design (Babbie et al., 2019). This type of design collects data from the same group or cohort at several points over a period of time. For example, a policy evaluator may want to assess the effectiveness of a program to reduce illiteracy, along with learning and labor outcomes, on a specific segment of the population. The cohort or groups receiving the intervention is followed for 10 years. Every year or so for that period, a survey is conducted on the same group. The data may be analyzed every year or every other year, assuming that the cohort or group is approximately the same over that extended period of time. Of course, subjects may drop out or simply are not found for subsequent data collection. If there is a significant subject dropout, then that eventuality may affect the outcome of the study.

Cross-sectional designs are popular because they take less time than longitudinal designs. But we must be careful to attend to issues of maturation, history, and subject selection challenges which we cannot control in these types of designs. Maturation can be a problem, for example, if the survey is done on teenagers, 1 year or 2 years out of a specific program. The period of growth that takes place may affect the way they respond to the specific survey and may not reflect the program itself. The challenge with history is problematic as well. Some of us still recall when President Kennedy was assassinated. That year was particularly traumatic among school children, particularly in their observation of how the adults were affected by such a dramatic event. Conducting a cross-sectional survey on depressive symptoms of children before and after Kennedy's assassination may provide different results between these two groups. Finally, subject selection may also present challenges when comparing groups. The time when the teenager was in eighth grade may be totally different than when he/she was in 12th grade. So, history, maturation, and the selection of respondents may affect our inferences, either in how subjects respond to surveys or how we compare the groups. It is important to consider these factors when doing policy evaluation research. The fact that the survey was well constructed and has excellent properties does not mean that it always provides solid information. At least, one must recognize the challenges in interpreting such data.

In addition to a research design, survey research can also be viewed as a tool for data collection within another research design (Babbie et al., 2019). As a design tool, most of the work using survey data occur at a single point in time ("one-shot" survey designs), but surveys can also be used in a time series, collecting data over several timepoints. At its essence, surveys provide a description of a group on specific social and/or behavioral characteristics. For example, policy evaluators may take a program that prevents suicide among men who served on active duty (war) in the military and design a survey instrument to collect data on the suicidal feelings among the target sample. One would assess the effectiveness of the program by collecting survey data on the target sample, including those who participated in the program and those who did not. The research team could then describe the distribution of responses and understand to what extent the program is associated with reduced suicidal feelings among the population of active duty personnel. We could then use quasi-experimental methods, as described above, to approximate the causal effects of the program.

Strategies in Survey Research Design

One of the most important issues in survey design is the defining the objective of the survey. For example, some of us are interested in describing specific events taking place in social settings. Others are interested in explaining abstract ideas or concepts. In a policy context, we may want to describe the distribution of a particular financial aid program on first-generation students. One may devise an instrument that records such a data across individuals and groups to understand the distribution of financial aid among those individuals. On the other hand, if one wants to understand the concept of status differential and how those statuses are related to financial aid distribution, then the nature of the survey design is a bit more complex than for the previous example. One must develop a survey that is based on the concept of social statuses. This concept is defined theoretically or based on some social theory. Then, the concept is defined or operationalized; and then in turn such concept is broken down by dimensions which are also defined in terms of specific questions. Once we have a "bank of items" available to assess the concept, then all the items are tested to understand the psychometric properties of the survey. Thus, the objective of the survey determines the type and design of the instrument to be used. Therefore, it is critical that one defines the parameters to design the questions necessary to answer the objective of the survey research.

Once the objective of the survey has been well-defined, the next step is the construction of survey questions. Questions must be asked in a way that will yield accurate responses. However, they must also be engaging so that that as many participants as possible complete the survey. This involves asking questions that clearly address your objective and that are sensitive to your participant's background. For more information and guidance, see Robinson and Leonard (2019).

Critical to any survey is the concept of measurement. Measurement provides the rationale for claiming significance of findings. The principles of measurement that we discussed in the experimental design section also apply here. Specifically, reliability is absolutely essential in survey research. Reliability is the test's "ability" to measure the concept or the event consistently. If the test or survey elicits different responses from the same individuals at any given point, then it is said that the test is unreliable (Mitchell & Jolley, 2012). One must provide evidence that the reliability coefficient is adequate before one can use the survey instrument with some confidence.

Similarly, one must establish validity in order to test a concept. In technical terms this is called "construct validity," which simply means that its concrete definition is based on a theoretical definition. There is a process to test for content validity and it must be done upfront if one wants to claim that the survey instrument is measuring such a theoretical construct. Most of this process is done by experts in the subject matter area. Once the items have been developed, the instrument is subjected to some statistical or item analyses to understand if the questions developed "hang together" to measure the different dimensions of the concept. Finally, one develops the index that will provide a numerical score that represents the concept empirically. That number is used to covary or correlate it with another concept. For example, the concept of individual happiness may be correlated with receiving (or not receiving) access to social welfare benefits. The concept of happiness must be theoretically defined and then empirically developed in order to conclude that such a relationship exists.

Example of Survey Research in Policy Analysis

We now turn to an example of survey research conducted to analyze a policy change. In this example, we show how survey research can be used as a tool to supplement the data collected, rather than a survey design itself. Henry et al. (2006) explore the potential concerns related to the 2003 decision to allow states to control much of early childhood education, a change from the Head Start program largely overseen by the federal government. In this study, the researchers document the kindergarten readiness of children who attended Head Start compared to Georgia's prekindergarten program. Henry et al. collected various sources of data to understand each student's kindergarten readiness, including parental and teacher surveys. These surveys provided important characteristics about the families and the classrooms, which could also affect a child's readiness. These were linked to observations and assessment data about the children, and propensity score techniques were used to compare the two groups. The researchers found that attending either program was helpful in preparing a child for kindergarten. Although the researchers employed various data collection techniques to generate their findings, the surveys provided the researchers with additional measures related to the social and behavioral characteristics that might otherwise be missed if they had only used observational data.

ADDITIONAL CONSIDERATIONS IN QUANTITATIVE POLICY ANALYSIS

Now that we have explored the primary methods that are used in quantitative research related to education policy evaluation, we discuss important topics that the researcher or consumer of that research must consider. First, we explain the fundamental statistical principles of power, significance, and effect sizes. These three principles are important to understand the extent to which it is possible to trust our inferences. We then turn to a discussion of the limitations of quantitative research. Finally, we discuss the role of ethics in designing and carrying out quantitative policy evaluation.

Power, Significance, and Effect Sizes

All statistical inferences rely on the scientific principle of the hypothesis. When we perform statistical analyses, we rely on two types of hypotheses: the null hypothesis and the alternative hypothesis. The null hypothesis is the basis of our statistical inference and states that there is no difference between the groups being compared. The alternative hypothesis is the opposite of the null—that there is a difference between the groups. Although our policy evaluations are more interested in the alternative hypothesis, our statistical inferences are based on the null hypothesis. We can then infer the results of the alternative hypothesis based on the null hypothesis. In order to make inferences, hypotheses require evidence for the purposes of proof. It is important to discuss the extent to which researchers have sufficient evidence to make their inferences. Herein lies the concepts of power, significance, and effect sizes.

Part of the process of statistical inference is controlling for potential errors. Remember that statistics rely on using a sample of data to make an inference about the population. Because the techniques we have discussed above are robust to making these inferences, there is still a chance that the researcher's inference has an error. There are two types of errors: Type I errors are where we infer there is an effect in the population where there is not (i.e., a false positive), and Type II errors are where we infer there is not an effect in the population where there is (i.e., a false negative) (Hedberg, 2018). Therefore, it is important to minimize the probability of committing either type of error.

Researchers can minimize the risk through increasing the power and effectively using significance testing. Power refers to the probability that we reject the null hypothesis when the alternative hypothesis is true, or, the probability that we do not commit a Type II error. There are several factors related to power, including the amount of uncertainty of the phenomenon, the effect size, and the sample size (Hedberg, 2018). One way researchers can assuredly increase the power of their study is by increasing the size of their sample, although it is important to recognize that this is not always possible given limited resources.

The significance test is how researchers can minimize the probability of committing a Type I error. When we conduct a statistical analysis, the resulting probability test is the level at which we risk committing a Type I error. The level the researchers set is signified by the Greek letter alpha (α), and social scientists conventionally use the threshold of $\alpha = 0.05$. That is, if the probability test of our analysis (also denoted as the p value) is less than α, then we are willing to reject the null hypothesis because our risk of committing a Type I error is sufficiently low.

Once we have determined that we have statistical significance, it is also important to understand if our study has practical significance. The amount of practical significance in our inference is referred to as the effect size (Hedberg, 2018). Although each inference requires a different estimator of effect size, the general notion of effect size is that it is the significance test divided by the sample size (Rodriguez, 2007). That is, the larger the sample size, the larger our significance test should be in order to have a practically significant inference. In means comparison tests, Cohen's *d* is the measure of effect size often reported (Rodriguez, 2007), which is the standardized difference between the two means. By focusing only on power and statistical significance, researchers may find that there is a significant nonzero result. However, given that this result may be very close to zero, it is important to understand the practical significance (McCartney & Rosenthal, 2000; Sullivan & Feinn, 2012). This is particularly important in policy evaluation. Given that policies and programs are often costly, in evaluation of these policies it is important to understand the practical significance. In essence, this would be a mechanism to examine the exchange between the costs and the benefits (McCartney & Rosenthal, 2000). Regardless of any of these methods, researchers must be clear in their decision-making process. Effect sizes and significance tests may be misinterpreted, allowing for incorrect findings to be reported (Robinson & Levin, 1997). We discuss other ethical issues in a following section.

Limitations

As with any methodologies, there are limitations to experimental, quasi-experimental, and survey methodologies. Let us address the most salient limitations affecting each of the strategies. As indicated, experimental designs are delicate designs in that if one does not meet the assumptions of random selection, reliability, and validity, then the experiment is flawed. Any problems with sampling may derail the outcomes of any experiment. Let us say that the sample is biased because the researcher was not careful in the sampling process, then the outcome of the study may be attributed to other factors than those associated with the intervention. Similarly, if the instruments used to measure the outcome variables are not reliable and valid, then the researcher may be introducing significant variation because of measurement error. Of course, error in measurement will have significant negative effects on the outcome of any experiment.

Quasi-experiments suffer from similar limitations as experimental designs, with the exception that quasi-experiments do not require random assignment to the intervention. In this case the researcher must use as many controls as possible to avoid concluding that there are differences due to the intervention when in fact there are not differences at all. Accordingly, researchers must compensate on a comparison group to make sure the comparison groups seem as "equal" as possible. Thus, the researcher is forced to look into characteristics such as socioeconomic status and ethnicity, among others. One must offer different tests of significance (test of variance) to assure the reader that the groups are somewhat similar. Sometimes we use repeated measures designs on a single subject to make judgments about an intervention. But even that strategy has some challenges. How does one control or measure "maturity," for example? Subjects have many stimuli that affect how they respond to any intervention. The researcher must be careful to make sure he/she takes those issues into account.

Finally, survey research methods also have some significant limitations. Survey research can give you only a snapshot view of the reality. It helps us understand how subjects are thinking at that particular moment in time. One may consider a longitudinal survey to understand how attitudes vary over time. But a longitudinal design also has limitations. Subjects may drop out, affecting the overall validity of any study. The researcher then has to compensate for all these problems associated with survey work. Another major limitation, particularly for cross-sectional survey designs is how carefully the sample is selected. It is quite clear that a minor error in sampling would lead to untenable conclusions. A recent example that illustrates this case is when, in the 2016 presidential election, the researchers predicted that one of the candidates would win a particular state. The researchers forgot to include a significant section of the population in the model, and the outcome was the opposite of what was predicted by the researchers. Thus, one cannot underestimate how important sampling is when using survey as a method to explain policy outcomes. Despite these limitations, they are still powerful tools to evaluate policy. Researchers must be cognizant of these limitations to realize that their inferences are not steadfast. However, through careful, honest design, they may reduce any potential problems that may arise.

Ethical Considerations

When doing social science research, one must consider conflicts of interest that arise. There are ethical issues that one must be concerned about and which may affect the outcome of any policy evaluation. Most of us abide by such considerations, but not all social scientists do. Thus, we are proposing a simple set of recommendations that constitute good practices in doing this type of research. It does not mean that we have a comprehensive set of recommendations. For additional information, one such source is Israel and Hay (2006).

One of the most important recommendations is to have voluntary participation in research. Whether one uses survey, experimental, or quasi-experimental research, we must make sure that no individual should be forced to participate in any research. Why is this important? The answer is quite simple; the research may generate negative effects on individuals or groups. That potential outcome may affect the participants in significant ways. Even if the survey is anonymous, groups and individuals may be identified and thus may potentially be in some precarious situation. Recall that a researcher may require information that is totally private to be provided to a total stranger (Babbie et al., 2019). This particular recommendation may go against the rules espoused in statistical theory, which recommends that all participants of a random sample must participate to ensure full representation of the sample. How does one comply with two expectations that are pulling the researcher in opposite directions?

The researcher has options. In the case of a survey research project, the research can always oversample to accomplish the goal of "representativeness." This means that a sample may include many more cases than necessary for the research, and as participants decline to participate, the researcher may include more participants from the initial sampling process. This way will ensure that the researcher has enough sample units to still accomplish the goal of the research and not force individuals to participate. Similarly, if we use interviewers to conduct an evaluation of a particular program which generated from a policy, then the interviewers should be trained to persuade individuals to participate in the research project. Yet, one must be careful to not use techniques that may force an individual to participate in the study. Babbie et al. (2019) indicated that there is a very "fine line between ethical persuasion and coercion" (p. 340). Therefore, our advice is that we should always keep the participants in mind as we engage in any type of research.

Another equally important ethical recommendation is to "do no harm to respondents." This is a fundamental rule for types of research, including survey, experimental, quasi-experimental, and other types. But how does one create harm in an interview or survey? Harm comes in many shapes. As the participant reveals information, they may "endanger their home life, friendships, jobs, and so forth" (Babbie et al., 2019, p. 65). Revealing sensitive information to a complete stranger may put participants in some risk, even if the research assures the participant of confidentiality. This is particularly the case when one is dealing with small samples of individuals. Let us take for example a study of the effectiveness of bilingual education in a school district. Most of the teachers know the individuals who teach bilingual education. Thus, the findings may reveal that the program may or may not be as effective. Then, the bilingual teachers may experience embarrassment or harm because of the outcome of the research. Similarly, if one is studying the effectiveness of a food stamps program in eradicating malnutrition, a potential finding may be that the program has not fully accomplished its goal and thus may recommend the program be suspended. That recommendation may have impact for a significant number of individuals participating in that program; if cut, we are creating substantial harm to those individuals affected by the program.

The next ethical issue we discuss is "anonymity and confidentiality." This principle is perhaps the key to protect individuals and their identities, particularly when potential risks are associated with the outcome of the research. Typically, we associate the two with one another. But there is a difference in their conceptions. Confidentiality is "at work" when you the researcher can identify the participants' response but essentially promise that the researcher will never divulge the identity of the individual (Babbie et al., 2019). On the other hand, anonymity is "at work" when even the researchers cannot identify a respondent from any particular response (Babbie et al., 2019). When doing policy analysis work, we must be cautious about both of these important issues. For example, should the study call for survey research as the preferred technique to obtain data, how does one conduct a survey and protect anonymity of participants? It is almost impossible to do so. The reason is that the researcher must have a follow up plan and thus will have a list of individuals who responded to the initial data collection step. If the researcher is not familiar with who responded in the first place, it will be difficult to achieve a good response rate from the initial sample. To avoid anonymity problems, the researcher can re-survey the sample again, stating that those who responded do not have to respond again. But that technique is inefficient and expensive. Thus, this is where confidentiality comes into play. The researcher must use both principles to assure the respondents that their identity will be protected at all costs. This is complicated when the researcher has to do face-to-face or telephone interviews as part of the evaluation. But, again, the researcher must use confidentiality as a way to ensure anonymity and prevent any harm to the participants.

One of the typical practices to improve anonymity and confidentiality is to create a code of numbers that can be used to track who has responded and who has not responded to a survey. Researchers must remove any personal identifying information from the survey. In that way, one assures the participant that his/her responses will be kept anonymous and confidential.

Finally, it is important to clearly state the purpose and the sponsor of the investigation/evaluation of a program. There are two connected issues with doing so. On the one hand, should the researcher clearly explain the purpose, the respondent may be influenced to answer in some "socially approved" way, thus biasing the outcome of the study. On the other hand, if one explains the purpose clearly, one may compel certain individuals to participating and other individuals from not participating (Babbie et al., 2019). Thus, where do we go from here? We fall on the side of honesty. It is more important to be honest about the purpose and sponsor of the research than not. We must avoid deception at all costs. The truth will always come out sooner or later; therefore, we would err on the side of honesty. This position may affect the completeness of the study; but it better to recognize those issues as limitations to the study than to deceive the participants regarding the purpose and sponsorship of the research study.

CONCLUSION

In summary, doing policy research is important and a valuable process that produces information to improve or to develop new policy. In this chapter we discussed three major strategies to conduct policy evaluation research: Experiments, quasi-experiments, and survey research. We did it within a single perspective—post-positivism. This theoretical perspective followed here has rules and norms that must be followed faithfully. Our presenting of this perspective does not mean that that is the only viable perspective. On the contrary, we appreciate different perspectives that inform the social sciences. We urge all policy researchers to consider the various and sundry worldviews as it allows for a more complete picture of a complicated and challenging policy world.

We discussed the utility of experimental design. In doing so, we also outlined the challenges associated with this design. It is dubbed as the "gold standard" when it comes to designs in the social sciences. But it is also difficult to meet all the assumptions required by this design. Thus, the researcher as well as the practitioner must be careful in interpreting the findings of any experimental research. One must clearly understand the sampling strategy and the reliability and validity of the measurements at use. Any error introduced in those areas may deeply affect the outcome of any study, particularly those studies being used to make cause-and-effect relationships. It is quite easy to hide behind an experimental study and make statements that may not be warranted.

Similarly, we discussed quasi-experiments as a strategy to do policy evaluation research. We indicated that these designs are a solid replacement for experiments when it is not possible to use random assignment to the intervention. But the fact that quasi-experiments do not require random assignment makes it even more challenging to draw sound conclusions about any policy analysis. We can make statements of trends and opportunities, and we can make tentative cause-and-effect statements. There are too many environmental effects that cannot be controlled for; thus, we cannot be as conclusive as we would like to be. Despite those limitations, we can still make meaning of studies. But one has to be intellectually honest and describe the limitations of any study.

Finally, we described the use of survey as a potential data gathering tool along with its significant advantages and limitations. As a policy analyst/researcher, one must be aware of those advantages and limitations and account for those limitations in reporting results to policymakers in particular. There is no perfect tool in social sciences to generate perfect information about any policy, individuals, or groups. Therefore, we recommend researchers follow a code of ethics in doing any research (e.g., American Educational Research Association, 2011). We hope this summary can help practitioners not only understand the tools that are available to do policy evaluation, but we hope the reader understands the limitations and advantages related to the strategies discussed in this chapter. One must interpret the outcomes of these studies with great care, particularly when we are making decisions to keep a program or disband it. Many times, we have seen practitioners believe a "salesman" promoting a particular program without asking those fundamental questions that affirm the validity of different studies. We believe this chapter can be helpful in that regard.

REFERENCES

American Educational Research Association (2011). *Code of ethics.* http://www.aera.net/Portals/38/docs/About_AERA/CodeOfEthics(1).pdf

Anderson, M. L., Gallagher, J., & Ritchie, E. R. (2018). School meal quality and academic performance. *Journal of Public Economics, 168,* 81–93.

Babbie, E. R., Wagner, W. E., & Zaino, J. (2019). *Adventures in social research* (10th ed.). SAGE.

Borman, G. D. (2012). The use of randomized trials to inform education policy. In G. Sykes, B. Schneider, & D. N. Plank (Eds.), *Handbook of education policy research* (pp. 145–154). Taylor & Francis.

Chetty, R., Hendren, N., & Katz, L. F. (2016). The effects of exposure to better neighborhoods on children: New evidence from the Moving to Opportunity experiment. *American Economic Review, 106*(4), 855–902.

Creswell, J. W. (2003). *Research design: Qualitative, quantitative, and mixed methods approaches.* SAGE.

Cronbach, L. J., & Shavelson, R. J. (2004). My current thoughts on coefficient alpha and successor procedures. *Educational and Psychological Measurement, 64*(3), 391–418.

Crotty, M. (1998). *The foundations of social research: Meaning and perspective in the research process.* SAGE.

Fowler, F. J. (2013). *Survey research methods* (5th ed.). SAGE.

Gerber, A. S., & Green, D. P. (2012). *Field experiments: Design, analysis, and interpretation.* London: WW Norton.

Gersten, R., Fuchs, L. S., Compton, D., Coyne, M., Greenwood, C., & Innocenti, M. S. (2005). Quality indicators for group experimental and quasi-experimental research in special education. *Exceptional Children, 71*(2), 149–164.

Good, P. I., & Hardin, J. W. (2012). *Common errors in statistics* (4th ed.). John Wiley & Sons.

Gulosino, C., Ni, Y., & Rorrer, A. K. (2019). Newly hired teacher mobility in charter schools and traditional public schools: An application of segmented labor market theory. *American Journal of Education, 125*(4), 547–592.

Gundersen, C., Kreider, B., & Pepper, J. (2012). The impact of the National School Lunch Program on child health: A nonparametric bounds analysis. *Journal of Econometrics, 166*(1), 79–91.

Hedberg, E. C. (2018). *Introduction to power analysis: Two-group studies*. SAGE.

Henry, G. T., Gordon, C. S., & Rickman, D. K. (2006). Early education policy alternatives: Comparing quality and outcomes of Head Start and state pre-kindergarten. *Educational Evaluation and Policy Analysis, 28*(1), 77–99.

Israel, M., & Hay, I. (2006). *Research ethics for social scientists*. SAGE.

Kaplan, D. (2012). Causal inference in non-experimental educational policy research. In G. Sykes, B. Schneider, & D. N. Plank (with T. G. Ford) (Eds.), *Handbook of education policy research* (pp. 155–169). Taylor & Francis.

Kim, J. S., Capotosto, L., Hartry, A., & Fitzgerald, R. (2011). Can a mixed-method literacy intervention improve the reading achievement of low-performing elementary school students in an after-school program? Results from a randomized controlled trial of READ 180 enterprise. *Educational Evaluation and Policy Analysis, 33*(2), 183–201.

McCartney, K., & Rosenthal, R. (2000). Effect size, practical importance, and social policy for children. *Child Development, 71*(1), 173–180.

Mitchell, M. L., & Jolley, J. M. (2012). *Research design explained* (5th ed.). Cengage Learning.

Morgan, S. L., & Winship, C. (2014). *Counterfactuals and causal inference.* Cambridge University Press.

Popper, K. R. (1972). *Objective knowledge: An evolutionary approach*. Clarendon Press.

Reed, K., Wood, C., Barton, J., Pretty, J. N., Cohen, D., & Sandercock, G. R. (2013). A repeated measures experiment of green exercise to improve self-esteem in UK school children. *PLoS One, 8*(7).

Robinson, D. H., & Levin, J. R. (1997). Research news and comment: Reflections on statistical and substantive significance, with a slice of replication. *Educational Researcher, 26*(5), 21–26.

Robinson, S. B., & Leonard, K. F. (2019). *Designing quality survey questions.* SAGE.

Rodriguez, W. (2007). Effect size. In N. J. Salkind (Ed.), *Encyclopedia of measurement and statistics* (pp. 301–304). SAGE.

Sale, J. E., Lohfeld, L. H., & Brazil, K. (2002). Revisiting the quantitative-qualitative debate: Implications for mixed-methods research. *Quality and Quantity, 36*(1), 43–53.

Shadish, W. R., Cook, T. D., & Campbell, D. T. (2002). *Experimental and quasi-experimental designs for generalized causal inference*. Houghton Mifflin.

Shroder, M. D., & Orr, L. L. (2012). Moving to Opportunity: Why, how, and what next? *Cityscape, 14*(2), 31–56.

Steele, J. L., Buryk, P., & McGovern, G. (2018). Student veterans' outcomes by higher education sector: Evidence from three cohorts of the baccalaureate and beyond. *Research in Higher Education, 59*(7), 866–896.

Stone, D. A. (1997). *Policy paradox: The art of political decision making*. W. W. Norton.

Sullivan, G. M., & Feinn, R. (2012). Using effect size—or why the P value is not enough. *Journal of Graduate Medical Education*, *4*(3), 279–282.

Wooldridge, J. M. (2002). *Econometric analysis of cross section and panel data*. MIT Press.

CHAPTER 6

QUALITATIVE RESEARCH DESIGNS FOR POLICY-RELEVANT RESEARCH

Amanda U. Potterton
University of Kentucky

Joel R. Malin
Miami University of Ohio

INTRODUCTION

Qualitative research can—and, to some extent, currently does—play a key role in guiding and informing education policy. This chapter provides an exploration of the ways in which qualitative research designs can be useful in education and, more specifically, how they might better inform school improvement efforts at both the national and international levels. First, we consider the marginalization of qualitative research, discuss quality and rigor, and provide an overview of prominent qualitative research designs. Next, we pay particular attention to "what works" research, describing limitations associated with these approaches and suggesting ways that new roles can be carved out.

Maximizing the Policy Relevance of Research for School Improvement, pp. 137–162
Copyright © 2021 by Information Age Publishing
All rights of reproduction in any form reserved.

We then explore qualitative, case-specific research for examples of public scholarship and policy knowledge and recognize evaluation, with the incorporation of qualitative research designs, as an especially policy-relevant mechanism. As we detail later, our understanding of "relevance" (i.e., *to have a bearing upon*) in this context is quite broad, for instance moving beyond narrow conceptions of "what works" and inclusive of more diffuse, conceptual influences on policy/policymakers. Next, we acknowledge some existing qualitative studies that have extended relevant theoretical and conceptual knowledge in the field of education. We suggest that researchers and practitioners can continue to learn from qualitative studies like those described through critical engagement with the designs, findings, and conceptual contributions.

In the second portion of the chapter, we posit that qualitative research and knowledge mobilization are key components for addressing and enhancing policy relevance, and we point to some under-investigated education issues that could benefit from further exploration using qualitative research designs. In doing so, we provide suggestions about how researchers might move forward with their studies, especially if they are interested in ways that their findings can be policy relevant for a variety of education audiences. Finally, we conclude with a discussion and an appendix of resources that might be helpful for researchers and practitioners who are interested in developing and carrying out qualitative research. Throughout, some examples we provide (to illustrate or elaborate on points we make) are in the area of school choice research, given that we both operate in this research space.

UNDERSTANDING THE MARGINALIZATION OF QUALITATIVE RESEARCH, AND CARVING OUT NEW ROLES

Various arguments surrounding the relative utility of qualitative and quantitative research approaches exist, and we begin this section by explaining our standpoint. We align with those who encourage us to move beyond debates that promote the use of one approach over the other, and we push forward in thinking about how both qualitative and quantitative methods are valuable (e.g., Dumas & Anderson, 2014; Tierney & Clemens, 2011; Westmarland, 2001). Even more, we believe quantitative and qualitative approaches to a research problem can be interrelated and more strategically coordinated to understand specific cases (and, ultimately, to build theory). We believe that there is good potential, when thinking about these strategic approaches, to build *complementary* knowledge and a deeper understanding of the complexity and richness of education policy and social science problems. Nonetheless, it is important to understand the past in order to move forward.

Whereas quantitative research generates numerical data for the purpose of understanding education problems and often describes the "what" of a problem, qualitative research tends to explore the "how" and "why" of a research problem through the collection and analysis of textual data. There are clear differences, then, between quantitative and qualitative research, including inferential statistics that are possible because of quantitatively-generated data. Qualitative research, on the other hand, examines underlying questions surrounding context and can provide helpful insight into problems. As stated above, quantitative and qualitative research can be complementary, and it is through the creative and careful consideration of social science research problems that researchers can work together to build a strong picture, or a more holistic view, of a particular problem.

This potential is different from the benefits of singular mixed methods studies, which are also valuable in many contexts. What we are envisioning here, instead, is illustrated by what is now occurring at Tulane University in the research organization Education Research Alliance for New Orleans (ERA-New Orleans). Researchers at ERA-New Orleans are working to provide a multi-faceted view of the education reforms in New Orleans post-Katrina. Their research agenda includes but is not limited to trying to "understand [Charter Management Organization] CMO policies and practices and how these shape the options available to families in New Orleans" (Education Research Alliance for New Orleans, 2020). The organization's publications include reports from experts that are both quantitative and qualitative in design, and they are archiving their work to build a summary of findings for policy knowledge and relevance.

Another example of the way in which qualitative inquiry can work alongside quantitative research studies is by providing supplemental explanations. For example, Scott and Villavicencio (2009) created a contextual framework with the aim of better explaining charter school achievement. At the time of their writing, Scott and Villavicencio explained how issues related to quantitative studies about charter school achievement included in some cases, as examples, single point-in-time limitations, selection biases, and value-added measures concerns (Scott & Villavicencio, 2009). Of course, qualitative studies also carry limitations related to generalizability since sample sizes are smaller and bound in specific context. Scott and Villavicencio suggest, however, that:

> Qualitative studies of school context can enrich the research and policy debates on charter school achievement, though those who want to simply ascertain if charter schools are "working" tend to neglect such scholarship. Although research on school contexts cannot establish causal relationships

> between school characteristics and school outcomes, it can inform and broaden our understanding of quantitative measures of student performance. (p. 228)

Qualitative studies are needed, for one, to support the important work being done quantitatively (e.g., by assessing contexts, variances, and in-depth perceptions that are likely to be missed in larger-scale quantitative designs). Overall, we believe that, broadly speaking, we can do a better job as researchers to more strategically examine a phenomenon in one area, through studies that explore different aspects of education problems and with different projected outcomes, to more holistically understand complex issues in education, policy, and practice.

Quality, Rigor, and Prominent Qualitative Designs

There are numerous options to choose from when approaching qualitative work, as well as specific methods. In terms of analytic approaches and research design, Creswell and Poth (2018) describe five main choices: (1) narrative research, (2) phenomenology, (3) grounded theory, (4) ethnography, and (5) case study. Within each of these approaches, there are subjective but largely-supported criteria for "good" study, which are based around issues like transparency, acknowledgement of positionality, and staying within the bounds of generalizability. These quality criteria are relevant for both quantitative and qualitative studies, and we encourage researchers to maintain strict levels of rigor and transparency when developing, carrying out, and reporting on qualitative designs. Given the above, below we also provide a very brief overview of the five main qualitative analytical approaches (please see our Appendix for a list of useful resources for further exploration).

Narrative research focuses on individual experiences and their lived and told stories, and can include life history, biographical studies, autoethnography, or oral histories (Creswell & Poth, 2018). Phenomenology is an approach wherein researchers examine what individuals or groups have in common (a phenomenon) and is useful for better understanding shared experiences (Creswell & Poth, 2018). In grounded theory, researchers move beyond description and actually generate new theory after a process of fully developing (or saturating) the data to best understand a problem (Cresswell & Poth, 2018). Ethnographers focus on culture-sharing groups, observing patterns, and providing thick descriptions of the group (Cresswell & Poth, 2018). Finally, case study research differs from ethnography because, even though ethnographers may study a group, which might in some instances be considered a case, they focus on the culture rather than using a case as a specific illustration to explore an issue (Cresswell & Poth, 2018). Within all these approaches, researchers choose methods that help them understand the problem in question. They might conduct interviews and focus groups, analyze documents and other artifacts, conduct participant observation, and/or create journals and memos.

Most importantly, it is important for researchers to ensure that interpretation of data is clear and transparent, as this will improve overall rigor and is key to establishing trustworthiness in relation to study findings. As Brooks and Normore (2015, 2018) explain:

> While each research design has a specific approach to establishing rigor, there are a few issues specific to qualitative studies of educational leadership that scholars should consider. It is critical that scholars are aware of the ways that various research designs establish rigor and then even more important that they do not violate these norms and rather meet various thresholds for quality and rigor.... If triangulation is the technique scholars use, then they should actually follow through and explain how they approached this aspect of the study ... if a study claims that data were gleaned from an analysis of documents, interviews and observation, all three forms of data should be evident in the findings. (2015, p. 802; see also 2018, p. 26)

"WHAT WORKS" RESEARCH, LIMITATIONS, AND POSSIBILITIES

To the extent that qualitative research has been marginalized in terms of its "policy relevance," it is important to briefly consider *why* this has happened as well as *how* it might appropriately assume a more prominent place. We do assert that an overly narrow "what works" agenda has privileged quantitative over qualitative research in some arenas and at considerable cost. We also point to recent developments suggesting there is strong opportunity to move forward differently. We draw from fundamental research utilization scholarship (e.g., Weiss, 1979) and from others such as Dumas and Anderson (2014), Tierney and Clemens (2011), and Westmarland (2001) to point out several key roles of qualitative research (for example, various ways of understanding and *utilizing* qualitative research that clearly underscore its actual or potential policy relevance).

Emphasizing "what works" relative to education policy and educational improvement decisions is appealing and not entirely misplaced. Ultimately, though, in United States education we have, since the early 2000s, seen a hyper-focus on "what works" that is, overall, counterproductive and that fails to illuminate the assorted ways in which research can beneficially link with practices and/or policies. Tseng and Coburn (2019) detail how and why the "what works" agenda has been dominant in education policy since the early 2000s (p. 351). In brief, several key federal policies and developments—such as the No Child Left Behind Act of 2001 (NCLB), the Education Sciences Reform Act of 2002, and the development and initial charge of the Institute for Education Sciences (IES)—coalesced to ensure that particular research designs and forms of evidence (read: evidence-based programs as shown via quantitative, experimental designs) would be privileged by educational decision makers. For instance, educators seeking to select/adopt particular programs were now required (if they desired federal funds) to select only those that were sufficiently supported by "scientifically based research" (a term introduced in NCLB). Gathered studies from IES accordingly show a clear focus on replicability and randomized trials (Wallechinsky, 2016).

Of course, we do not see all of this as universally bad and these efforts are indeed important. We do not deny the potential usefulness, for instance, of the U.S. Department of Education's "What Works Clearinghouse." However, we argue that its existence carries with it the possibility of misrepresenting a vast and rigorous list of peer-reviewed research studies surrounding topics that are also relevant for education policy and social science problems. To highlight Tseng and Coburn's (2019) explanation, Figure 6.1 is sourced from the IES (2020) website when we searched for "What Works Clearinghouse" studies on charter schools (since this topic is an example that is familiar to our personal areas of research scholarship):

In Figure 6.1, aside from these nine topics and their associated small number of studies that meet the site's "What Works" standards, there are many more examples of evidence-based research (both quantitative and qualitative) that address programs that are about or like the ones noted, which include the Knowledge is Power Program (KIPP), Green Dot Public Schools, Reading Mastery, SuccessMaker®, Academy of Reading®, Bridges in Mathematics, CompassLearning, Harlem Children's Zone (HCZ) Promise Academy Charter School, and Youthbuild. Of course, we acknowledge that the research studies provided in the site are also valuable for better understanding how charter schools may or may not be impacting students, parents, and surrounding district public schools that already exist. However, our key point here is that there is also *a vast body of* evidence-based research that is *not* included in this list. Aside from many robust and peer-reviewed quantitative studies that are not included (which we will not expand on here given our chapter's focus), other qualitative studies also robustly address charter schools and various effects for stakeholders. They, too, are undeniably rigorous and policy relevant, and have only been published after adhering to strict peer-review standards and revisions.

Figure 6.1

What Works Clearinghouse

Source: U.S. Department of Education, Institute of Education Sciences (2020).

An Example: Qualitative Case-Specific Research for Public Scholarship and Policy Knowledge

To provide an example, among some qualitative charter school research studies missing in the "What Works" list are those that capture the perceptions and experiences of individuals who make sense of education policy and implementation in many different settings. The list of missing studies is long. To demonstrate this, Table 6.1 details a small number of evidence-based studies related to charter schools that used qualitative research designs to explore and analyze local, "on the ground" experiences of parents, teachers, school leaders, and community members, as well as other stakeholders who are invariably affected by (and who also affect) policies. We chose these studies because they address various aspects related to charter schools, as do the studies in the "What Works" list. The studies below indeed provide information about "what works" (and what may not be working well) for charter schools and the stakeholders impacted by them[1] (see Table 6.1).[1]

Aside from providing peer-reviewed evidence about charter schools, several of the articles highlighted in Table 6.1 also introduce new concepts and typologies that can inform future, evidence-based charter school, school choice, education reform, and education policy studies.

Encouragingly, Tseng and Coburn (2019) also claim that the landscape is undergoing a shift, as shown for example by the somewhat loosened criteria for evaluating whether particular programs are "evidence-based" within the Every Student Succeeds Act of 2015 (even if they are not yet recognized by the IES at the U.S. Department of Education). Tseng and Coburn suggest that "the pendulum" may be "swinging towards more pluralistic approaches in US education" (p. 363). By this, they explain that they identified a partial shift from primarily top-down strategies (e.g., research into practice) and more toward bottom-up strategies (e.g., connecting research and practice). Dumas and Anderson (2014) also poignantly recommend thinking critically about policymaking as a process that is built from the bottom up. In our view, and as we will further articulate, such shifts would enable qualitative research to assume meaningful, and more practice- and policy-relevant, roles.

Turning to research-use scholarship for public scholarship and policy knowledge, we can further see that the "what works" emphasis is limiting and inconsistent with the real world. The process of influencing policy through research is complex and nonlinear, with decision-making occurring as a process rather than an event (e.g., Datnow et al., 2002; Oliver & Cairney, 2019). Policymakers—construed broadly here and inclusive of district officials, for instance—ultimately must consider a variety of information about particular issues and collectively integrate it with their values

Table 6.1

A List (Not Exhaustive; Alphabetized by Author) Providing 12 Examples of Evidence-Based Charter School Qualitative Studies Published in Peer-Reviewed Journals Between the Years 2016–2019

Author and Title	Peer-Reviewed Journal and Year	Relevant Context	Approach	Sample of Findings
Gawlik, M. A. (*Principalship Socialization in Charter Schools*)	*Journal of School Leadership*, 2019	three charter elementary schools in Florida (FL) during the 2012–2013 school year	exploratory qualitative case study (including semistructured interviews, observations, and document analysis)	principal transitions into schools and subsequent socialization were varied among the charter school principals, and they differed between network-based and stand-alone charters
Golann, J. W. (*Conformers, Adaptors, Imitators, and Rejecters: How No-Excuses Teachers' Cultural Toolkits Shape Their Responses to Control*)	*Sociology of Education*, 2017	"no excuses" charter schools in a northeastern U.S. city	ethnographic	revealed teachers' adaptation strategies in response to school control, wherein they either imitated, conformed, adapted or rejected expected approaches in the schools
Henry, K. L., & Dixson, A. D. (*"Locking the Door Before We Got the Keys": Racial Realities of the Charter School Authorization Process in Post-Katrina New Orleans*)	*Educational Policy*, 2016	charter schools and stakeholders in New Orleans, Louisiana (LA)	drawn from two qualitative case studies (2014-2015 in New Orleans, LA and a long-term ethnographic study of community responses to school reform); semi-structured interviews with African American educational stakeholders who applied to open and operate a charter school or who were familiar with the charter context and reforms post-Katrina; critical race theory	the charter the authorization and application process was racialized and reproduced White dominance

(Table continued on next page)

Table 6.1 (Continued)

A List (Not Exhaustive; Alphabetized by Author) Providing 12 Examples of Evidence-Based Charter School Qualitative Studies Published in Peer-Reviewed Journals Between the Years 2016–2019

Author and Title	Peer-Reviewed Journal and Year	Relevant Context	Approach	Sample of Findings
Hornbeck, D., & Malin, J. (*State Auditors in Education Policy*)	*Educational Policy*, 2019	Ohio and Pennsylvania as state case contexts	multiple-case study design; policy and document analyses	executive-level state auditors' powers have expanded substantially since the proliferation of brick-and-mortar and online charter schools and due to other factors related to political motivations, auditors' power, and auditing oversight
Jabbar, H. (*Recruiting "Talent": School Choice and Teacher Hiring in New Orleans*)	*Educational Administration Quarterly*, 2018	New Orleans, LA	94 interviews with principals, district leaders, and charter network leaders	school choice posed challenges for leaders related to teacher recruitment and hiring practices
Marsh, L. T., & Noguera, P. A. (*Beyond Stigma and Stereotypes: An Ethnographic Study on the Effects of School-Imposed Labeling on Black Males in an Urban Charter School*)	*The Urban Review*, 2018	"no excuses" charter school	ethnographic	a language of deficit and pathology impacted Black male students' schooling experiences as they negotiated racial stigma as racialized bodies
Potterton, A. U. (*Leaders' Experiences in Arizona's Mature Education Market*)	*Journal of Educational Administration*, 2019	one Arizona district public school and its surrounding community, including nearby charter schools	ethnographic	schools leaders' decision-making processes were influenced by competitive pressures, and district public school leaders responded differently to competition than did the charter school leaders

(Table continued on next page)

Table 6.1 (Continued)

A List (Not Exhaustive; Alphabetized by Author) Providing 12 Examples of Evidence-Based Charter School Qualitative Studies Published in Peer-Reviewed Journals Between the Years 2016–2019

Author and Title	Peer-Reviewed Journal and Year	Relevant Context	Approach	Sample of Findings
Thomas, K. A., & Lacey, C. H. (*A Phenomenological Study of the Leadership Experiences of the Charter School Founder-Administrator in Florida*)	*The Qualitative Report*, 2016	four founder-administrators of charter schools in FL	open-ended interviews	areas of accountability and compliance were common critical factors dictated by districts' and charters' rules for defining quality
Torres, A. C. (*Teacher Efficacy and Disciplinary Expectations in Charter Schools: Understanding the Link to Teachers' Career Decisions*)	*Journal of School Choice*, 2016	New York City, New York	interviews with 20 Charter Management Organization (CMO) and non-CMO teachers	strict disciplinary methods may benefit teachers in creating orderly environments but may undermine efficacy and increase teacher turnover
Torres, A. C., & Weiner, J. (*The New Professionalism? Charter Teachers' Experiences and Qualities of the Teaching Profession*)	*Education Policy Analysis Archives*, 2018	Northeastern region of the United States.	interviews with 20 new and novice teachers teaching in high profile charter organizations in the northeast (such as Uncommon Schools, KIPP, MATCH, and Boston Collegiate); 17 different schools represented	teachers embraced managed professionalism ("new professionalism") and spoke positively of climate and colleagues, they felt pressures from competition, and they questioned efficacy

(Table continued on next page)

Table 6.1 (Continued)

A List (Not Exhaustive; Alphabetized by Author) Providing 12 Examples of Evidence-Based Charter School Qualitative Studies Published in Peer-Reviewed Journals Between the Years 2016–2019

Author and Title	Peer-Reviewed Journal and Year	Relevant Context	Approach	Sample of Findings
Waitoller, F. R., Nguyen, N., & Super, G. (*The Irony of Rigor: 'No-Excuses' Charter Schools at the Intersections of Race and Disability*)	*International Journal of Qualitative Studies in Education*, 2019	Chicago, Illinois Public Schools (CPS)	partnership with a law advocacy group; in-depth, semi-structured interviews with 24 parents (83% Black, 17% Latinx, and all women); document reviews of students' Individual Education Plans (IEPs) and other charter school documents	"no-excuses" charter schools in the study utilized mechanisms that excluded students with disabilities, and in particular Black and Latinx students
Weixler, L. B., Lincove, J. A., & Gerry, A. (*The Provision of Public Pre-K in the Absence of Centralized School Management*)	*American Educational Research Journal*, 2019	charter school leaders in New Orleans, LA	mixed methods (longitudinal student enrollment and performance records) and interviews with school leaders from 10 case studies	Pre-K seats substantially fell as budgeting and decision-making mechanisms were decentralized, there were few benefits for charter schools to offer Pre-K programs since Pre-K graduates are very mobile, and there was an observable disinvestment in Pre-K programs which are intended to advance social goals for education systems

and professional judgment to make decisions (Brighouse et al., 2018). Further, as Nutley et al. (2007) summarized, research is much more often used *conceptually* (i.e., shaping how one views their professional worlds and thinks about problems) than *instrumentally* (i.e., directly influencing policy or prompting a change in practice).

Operating from this understanding, we can see more clearly the potential roles of qualitative research. Dumas and Anderson (2014), for example, pointed to overlapping issues and suggested the need to move our focus from "policy prescription" to "policy knowledge" (p. 8). They argued that qualitative research was particularly well-suited to supply the latter, defined as "information and ideas useful in framing, deepening our understanding of, and/or enriching our conceptualization of policy problems" (p. 8). Qualitative research, for example, can help us to understand what McLaughlin (2006) termed "the problem of the problem" (p. 210). For example, why are a subset of a school's students experiencing disappointing math outcomes? What are the problem(s) related to this problem? Of course, answers to these questions have profound policy implications—we should decide differently depending upon the specific problem that is operating. Dumas and Anderson argue—and we concur—that qualitative research can be particularly valuable in such regards.

We take the position that qualitative research designs are a necessary consideration when researchers are aiming to gain a deeper understanding of the social, cultural, political, and economic contexts that all work together to assist in shaping schools and the students within them. Ultimately, we are rooting and aiming for research that moves forward to consider how all our work can interrelate if we are thoughtful and diligent. Indeed, as public researchers, we believe that we have, as does the wider field of researchers, a service responsibility to commit ourselves to thinking about how our work across the whole field can do this better.

Program Evaluation as a Policy-Relevant Mechanism

As an important point relating to this chapter, there is a very helpful body of research focused on program evaluation, and learning about these policy-relevant evaluations can be of great value for scholars who want to gain a better understanding about how research can be practically useful for and centered upon specific programs and policies (Fitzpatrick et al., 2012). For example, deliberative democratic evaluation (House & Howe, 1999) is an evaluation approach that centers democracy and social justice as primary goals. Program and policy evaluations center stakeholders, whether they use quantitative, qualitative, or mixed methods designs. Fitzpatrick et al. (2012) explain that:

> Research and evaluation seek different ends. The primary purpose of research is to add to knowledge in a field, to contribute to the growth of theory. A good research study is intended to advance knowledge ... that is a secondary concern in evaluation. Evaluations' primary purpose is to provide useful information to those who hold a stake in whatever is being evaluated (stakeholders), often helping them to make a judgment or decision.... Research seeks conclusions; evaluation leads to judgments. (pp. 9–10)

There are multiple approaches to program evaluation, including branches of Methods, Use, Values, and Social Justice (Mertens & Wilson, 2012). Such branches, especially in the areas of Values and Social Justice, are particularly well-positioned for qualitative research since a social justice framework includes evaluators who might, "develop theoretical frameworks based on cultural responsiveness, race/ethnicity, human rights, feminist, disability rights, deafness, postcolonial/indigenous, and queer theories" (Mertens & Wilson, 2012, p. 40). We want to acknowledge the potentially troubling notion that there may be a necessary and true, yet sometimes unhelpful, divide that can separate the work of evaluators who are researchers and more traditional university-based academic researchers. We hope that program evaluators and more traditionally-based researchers can continue to better align themselves with each other, in the same ways that we hope quantitative and qualitative researchers can better align themselves, for strategic purposes in social science research and for the greater overarching purposes of learning, building better policy knowledge, and understanding complex issues.

In other words, we value the mixing of quantitative and qualitative methods to better inform topics and similarly encourage the development of more cohesive communication between the fields of evaluation and research occurring in more traditional settings. This will benefit everyone, perhaps especially those policymakers and stakeholders who have a level of distrust of academic institutions. We think it is our responsibility to help break down these walls. As we grow in the ability to share knowledge and move research from the "ivory tower" into the communities where our work matters, such distinctions between evaluators and researchers might soften.

LEARNING FROM WHAT ALREADY EXISTS[2]

Here, we emphasize the importance of researchers and practitioners accessing, reading, and critiquing existing studies and then moving forward with potentially new ideas and designs. Research may or may not be policy relevant, and we argue that it is in the accessing, reading, understanding, and acting upon what we have learned where good potential lies for improving its relevance. In this section, we give attention to some powerful qualitative research studies that can help to inform and build knowledge. The conceptual frameworks, methodological approaches, and deep analyses used in the studies we discuss below have critically pushed boundaries to build upon educational theories and concepts. Existing and in-depth qualitative research studies, many that are ethnographic, can provide rich conceptual contributions that are both informative and ongoing. Not all these examples described below are recent, nor are they exhaustive, of course. Yet, their contributions are lasting and still relevant, with good potential to have policy-relevant implications for school improvement today (depending, of course, on how they are accessed, read, understood, critiqued, and then built and acted upon).

In the 1970s, Paul Willis (1977) conducted an ethnography in England, illustrating in rich detail how a group of lads from working class backgrounds experienced and acted within a contradictory culture both inside and outside of school. Willis's book, *Learning to Labour: How Working Class Kids Get Working Class Jobs*, unveils students' agency and students' intentional opposition to authority and, although they sometimes penetrated the conformity expected of them in the system, they were also limited by an oppressive class structure within which existed sexism, racism, and, centrally, strong labor reproductive power. These experiences all worked in complicated ways to ultimately reproduce working class jobs. Such depth of understanding was made possible through rich engagement and data collection in the lads' setting and then also through in-depth immersion and time spent analyzing and building upon previous conceptual frameworks surrounding social class reproduction (see, for example, Bowles & Gintis, 1976). Readers of Willis's work will gain a stronger understanding of agency and power, and conscious consideration of this study can sharpen educators, our research, and our practice in nearly every way.

Peter McLaren's (1986/1999) book, *Schooling as a Ritual Performance: Toward a Political Economy of Educational Symbols and Gestures*, offers social theory contributions developed from a project about student and teacher life in an inner-city Catholic school in Toronto, Canada. McLaren's poststructuralist, anthropological, critical ethnographic study provides excellent material for both researchers and practitioners to think deeply (and with policy relevance as a goal) as they read about systems and cultures in educational institutions, either individually or in group studies (Lankshear, 1999). Indeed, Apple (1988) wrote a review of the work that highlighted its strength and potential:

> McLaren's work goes inside the institution. He illuminates the interaction between the students and the rituals that organize day-to-day life in a largely working-class school in Toronto and links these to family and "street

> corner" life as well. Furthermore, where Willis draws his interpretations from culturalist Marxist work, McLaren incorporates some of these interpretations within a framework of analysis taken from the anthropological work of Victor Turner and others who stress the importance of symbol and ritual in the organization of institutions and culture. The books' roots are in "ritology." ... McLaren is the first to apply these insights in such a thorough and detailed manner to the ordinary working of the school. (p. 122)

Apple's description is important because it highlights how McLaren's book was a first of its kind and can continue to provide important, educational theory insights. Similarly to Willis's (1977) piece, McLaren's study captures a culture, within and surrounding a school site, and a conscious consideration of this in-depth ethnography can help both researchers and practitioners as they consider power dynamics within daily rituals that take place in schools.

Annette Lareau's (2000) conceptual contributions provide researchers and practitioners with a better understanding of the role of social class as it relates to both positive and negative impacts of parent involvement in schools. Lareau includes a helpful appendix in *Home Advantage: Social Class and Parental Intervention in Elementary Education* that details her process of gaining research site access and struggling through decisions about data analysis. Such transparency provides an excellent model for existing and aspiring qualitative research designers and can help both researchers and practitioners understand some of the nuts and bolts of a study. Lareau's (2011) later in-depth qualitative fieldwork with a research team in her book *Unequal Childhoods: Class, Race, and Family Life* further develops notions of class differences, and, in this study's case, in terms of how these differences relate to raising children. Again, this is a body of work that provides illustrations for researchers' and practitioners' critically conscious consideration.

Eve Ewing's (2018) *Ghosts in the Schoolyard* provides an in-depth critical analysis of Chicago Public Schools closings and slated closings. In an important sense, it was built to uncover and understand why many Chicago residents were resisting the closure of schools that, according to dominant discourse, were clearly "failing" and "underutilized" and so on. Ewing provides an historical analysis, contextualizing the situation not in terms of the stale and often objective-sounding rationales for closing the schools, but more deeply in terms of longstanding racism and racist policies (e.g., education, housing, and criminal justice policy). She also provides a discourse analysis, aiming to understand the evidence that various parties marshalled to support their claims and to understand how certain citizens and groups resisted these policy plans and responded to challenges that arose along the way. For example, they faced inadequate and shifting opportunities to voice their experiences in formal settings. Out of Ewing's analysis emerged several key theoretical constructs, including that of institutional mourning, which is the idea that "individuals might mourn institutions or intangible entities, much as we mourn people" (p. 181). For us this work was rich, broadening our sense of public education in relation to culture, race, and power, while also (on a microlevel) helping us to better understand the disparate, meaningful evidence that different stakeholders bring to bear about the value (or nonvalue) of particular schools. This is important for policy-relevance because it is through a conscious consideration of racist policies that practitioners and researchers might gain a more critical lens through which to work.

Such works are models that we suggest can be collectively and intentionally read, analyzed, and critiqued by researchers and practitioners in order to build a deeper repertoire of theoretical knowledge for their own policy and practice understanding and relevance. We included the specific examples above because we think that they, similarly to how Apple (1988) described McLaren's (1986/1999) work, build upon and challenge findings in some ways, include qualitative research designs that have created new theories and ways of thinking about systems, institutions, culture, agency, social class, and race, and have pushed boundaries in terms of critically examining the political, social, cultural, and economic spaces in schools.

QUALITATIVE RESEARCH AND KNOWLEDGE MOBILIZATION: A KEY TO POLICY RELEVANCE

If research is to be integral to school improvement and to have policy relevance, it is key that we understand (or contribute to the understanding of) the construction, use, and mobilization of knowledge in policy and practice (see Malin & Brown, 2020). On the practice side, for instance, we must consider: What school improvement ideas are being communicated, adjusted, and adopted in multiple settings? How and why are these ideas being mobilized? What knowledge is key to educational decision-makers in these settings? To what extent and how are these new approaches being evaluated, and how are the results being communicated and utilized? Similar questions can and should be asked on the policy side and, in fact, there are considerable similarities between evidence use in policy and in practice (Rickinson et al., 2018).

We want to make a couple of points here, in relation to this chapter. First, it is clear that qualitative research is essential for understanding knowledge construction, use, and mobilization in education. As Gitomer and Crouse (2019) detail, researchers studying the use of research (a related area) tend to be pragmatic in nature and often rely on multiple methods to address their questions. Invariably essential are "up close" qualitative methods like observation (e.g., while deliberations are occurring or as decisions are being made) and interviewing (e.g., to understand why a person has made a particular decision and what evidence they weighed during the decision process). Recently, Malin et al. (2019) qualitatively analyzed educators' written requests for grant funding to purchase desired educational resources or services. Their goals were to understand "to what extent, and how, educators utilized research and other forms of evidence to support their decision-making" (p. 1). Such research, which examines research and other evidence use *in situ*, has potential to generate insights into educators' key concerns, needs, and reasoning around core aspects of their work.

Second, it becomes clear that there are few direct lines between research and practice or research and policy. Rather, these connections tend to be mediated or brokered (e.g., see Malin & Brown, 2020). It is thus critically important to understand this mediation process, from a research perspective, and/or to learn how to leverage it (e.g., for researchers who wish to make particular impacts). And, as with the above, it is important to consider not only presence and communication of research evidence, but other forms of evidence as well, and how evidence use might shift over time. For example, on the policy side, Malin et al. (2020) qualitatively examined media-based coverage, deliberation, and knowledge use/framing as school choice reforms were advanced and accelerated in Indiana. They noted that shifting justifications and arguments were more ideological than empirical in nature. Further, they reported that advocates were routinely and successfully dominating the media space to frame problems and associated solutions as they desired. On the practice side, Malin et al. (2018) conducted a (primarily qualitative) multiple case study of brokerage in education. Their study revealed two distinctive types of knowledge brokerage (one that is primarily one-way in nature, and one that is more interactive), and this analysis led them to suggest ways in which research engagement could be increased in education. Drawing upon extant research, they suggested that interactive approaches are favorable, and they encouraged researchers and other stakeholders to join the ongoing conversations that were already underway on certain platforms, even though they are predominantly populated by educators.

Overall, qualitative research designs, alongside the examination of how research is (or is not) being mobilized for the purposes of education improvement, appear to be crucial for those concerned with policy relevance. For researchers who are interested in conducting studies related to knowledge mobilization, qualitative research designs as demonstrated above do provide an opportunity to take close looks into the ways actors in various school-related settings are impacting practice. Fischman and Tefera (2014a) recommend that an important way to move away from "ivory tower" limitations of research is to "stop complaining and engage with knowledge mobilization strategies (KM)" (p. 1; see also, for a related argument, Vasquez Heilig & Brewer, 2019). We agree, and elsewhere Fischman and Tefera (2014b) state:

> we believe it is important to consider how the knowledge produced by qualitative researchers could contribute in more effective ways to the educational policy debate ... we do not think that there are universal or magic formulas, but we believe that one of the first steps is to intentionally and deliberately reclaim and become part of the education policy debate. To do this, we believe that explicit strategies aimed at increasing knowledge mobilization (KM) are an important avenue for education researchers to improve the use and impact of research in education policy and practice. (p. 9)

EDUCATIONAL POLICY TOPICS FOR QUALITATIVE INVESTIGATION

We acknowledge that not all educational policy research is necessarily high in policy relevance. That said, we think that, with a concerted effort to better connect research projects using various methodological approaches, we might be able to, as researchers, gain an overall better understanding of a case study, an area, or a topic of concern. Within this concerted effort, there will be studies that are quantitatively focused and those that are qualitatively designed. To be truly relevant, and as argued above, we think that it is imperative to move past debates that suggest any hierarchical positionality of certain methods over others and suggest, instead, that we learn as much as we can from as many angles as we can, and by including as many stakeholders as we can (Fitzpatrick et al., 2012; House & Howe, 1999). The following is a list that is not exhaustive (since possibilities are endless) of areas that we think are particularly in need of further qualitative investigation:

- stakeholders' perceptions of education reforms, especially those that are focused on marginalized contexts and groups
- school choice reforms in local settings
- school leaders' experiences with education reforms and changes
- stakeholders' perceptions of the access to or restriction from research knowledge (accessibility/usefulness)
- district-level studies of policy changes, perhaps especially including those reforms that require extensive cross-sector (including PK–16) collaboration

- studies related to higher education educational leadership, educational policy, and teacher/leader practitioner graduate degree and certificate programs' use of existing qualitative literature to encourage critically conscious exploration of education issues
- more on the sociocultural contexts of education reforms (See, for example, a set of articles that examine sociological contributions to school choice policy and politics around the globe in the 2020 Politics of Education Yearbook in *Educational Policy* [Potterton et al., 2020])
- international-level studies related to all of the above

DISCUSSION

Dimensions of education policy, and the sensemaking associated with policymaking and implementation, are complex and reliant on many local variables, including those that are historical, political, social, cultural, and economic (Spillane et al., 2011). As we illustrated in this chapter, there are rich possibilities for qualitative research designs when it comes to understanding education policies and practices at the federal, state, and local levels, and much can be gained from exploring local contexts and from communicating with stakeholders. Both evaluation and research have good potential to be policy relevant, and even more so when researchers and evaluators learn from each other's fields. Dumas and Anderson (2014) challenge researchers to think about policymaking from the "ground up" (p. 6), and conducting qualitative research studies is an excellent first step to better understanding what is happening for people who are experiencing a wide variety of education reforms. Dumas and Anderson assert that, rather than considering the building of policy as only the work of policymakers,

> policy can sometimes come from the ground up. That is, we may do just as well, if not better, thinking about using qualitative and participatory action research to impact policy by communicating directly with communities, families, teachers and young people. (p. 6)

The real policy experiences that stakeholders make sense of in local settings matter tremendously, and we could do well to qualitatively learn from these communities, families, teachers, and young people (Dumas & Anderson, 2014). Indeed, for policy implementation to occur in some form or another, it is dependent upon the actions of those who are affected by many variables and interpretations of policies. As researchers think about the ways in which qualitative research designs might be beneficial for policy-relevant studies, it is necessary to understand the contexts for which the studies have been made in the first place. Of course, the writing of a policy and actual implementation are two different, yet interrelated situations, and, as we discussed in this chapter, it can be argued that the creation of educational policies *actually* occurs in the process of implementation (Datnow et al., 2002). These are also developed in the many, complex ways that knowledge is or is not mobilized. Spillane et al. (2002) explain policy implementation in this way:

> What a policy means for implementing agents is constituted in the interaction of their existing cognitive structures (including knowledge, beliefs, and attitudes), their situation, and the policy signals. How the implementing agents understand the policy's message(s) about local behavior is defined in the interaction of these three dimensions. (p. 388)

Further, Joyce and Cartwright (2019) address the important gap that exists between what works in practice as compared to "what works" in research. Specifically, local "what works" efforts are often disrupted when scaling-up attempts are not fitted to contextual settings (Joyce & Cartwright, 2019). When applying this explanation to qualitative research studies, and while acknowledging that qualitative studies cannot generalize in the traditional sense of the word as pertaining to quantitative methods, there is power and great potential for readers to gain insight from case studies and specific contexts and to consider how findings may have potential for naturalistic generalizations (Stake & Trumbull, 1982).

Perhaps this is a better way of thinking about the ways in which we can read, critique, and eventually take action based on what we learn from qualitative research studies and the contexts in which they occur. Stake and Trumbull (1982) state that, "The naturalistic researcher observes and records what readers are not placed to observe for themselves, but who, when reading the descriptive account, can experience vicariously the various perplexities" (p. 3). Likewise, we think that qualitative research can provide a useful springboard for better understanding people's lived contexts. We hope that more researchers and practitioners can engage with the plethora of qualitative research designs that currently exist (or have yet to be designed) for the purposes of increasing policy relevance and for considering the ways in which knowledge can be examined and mobilized for improvement in education.

REFERENCES

Apple, M. W. (1988). Schooling as ritual performance: Towards a political economy of educational symbols and gestures. Peter McLaren. *Comparative Education Review*, *32*(1), 122–124. https://doi.org/10.1086/446745

Bowles, S., & Gintis, H. (1976). *Schooling in capitalist America: Educational reform and the contradictions of economic life*. Basic Books.

Brighouse, H., Ladd, H. F., Loeb, S., & Swift, A. (2018). *Educational goods: Values, evidence, and decision-making*. University of Chicago Press. https://doi.org/10.7208/chicago/9780226514208.001.0001

Brooks, J. S., & Normore, A. H. (2015). Qualitative research and educational leadership: Essential dynamics to consider when designing and conducting studies. *International Journal of Educational Management, 29*(7), 798–806. http://dx.doi.org/10.1108/IJEM-06-2015-0083

Brooks, J. S., & Normore, A. H. (2018). Qualitative research in educational leadership studies: Issues in the design and conduct of studies. In C. R. Lochmiller (Ed.), *Complementary research methods for educational leadership and policy studies* (pp. 19–32). Palgrave Macmillan. https://doi.org/10.1007/978-3-319-93539-3

Creswell, J. W., & Poth, C. N. (2018). *Qualitative inquiry & research design: Choosing among five approaches*. SAGE.

Datnow, A., Hubbard, L., & Mehan, H. (2002). *Extending educational reform: From one school to many.* RoutledgeFalmer.

Dumas, M., & Anderson, G. L. (2014). Qualitative research as policy knowledge: Framing policy problems and transforming education from the ground up. *Education Policy Analysis Archives, 22*(11). http://dx.doi.org/10.14507/epaa.v22n11.2014

Education Research Alliance for New Orleans. (2020). Charter schools. https://educationresearchalliancenola.org/research-areas/charter-schools

Ewing, E. L. (2018). *Ghosts in the schoolyard*. The University of Chicago Press. https://doi.org/10.7208/chicago/9780226526331.001.0001

Fischman, G. E., & Tefera, A. (2014a). If the research is not used, does it exist? *Teachers College Record, 17570*, 1–10.

Fischman, G. E., & Tefera, A. (2014b). Qualitative inquiry in an age of educationalese. *Education Policy Analysis Archives, 22*(7). https://doi.org/10.14507/epaa.v22n7.2014

Fitzpatrick, J. L., Sanders, J. R., & Worthen, B. R. (2012). *Program evaluation: Alternative approaches and practical guidelines* (4th ed.). Pearson.

Gawlik, M. A. (2019.) Principalship socialization in charter schools. *Journal of School Leadership, 29*(1), 3–24. https://doi.org/10.1177%2F1052684618825089

Gitomer, D. H., & Crouse, K. (2019). *Studying the use of research evidence: A review of methods*. William T. Grant Foundation. wtgrantfoundation.org/studying-the-use-of-research-evidence-a-review-of-methods

Golann, J. W. (2017). Conformers, adaptors, imitators, and rejecters: How no-excuses Teachers' cultural toolkits shape their responses to control. *Sociology of Education, 91*(1), 28–45. https://doi.org/10.1177%2F0038040717743721

Henry, K. L., & Dixson, A. D. (2016). "Locking the door before we got the keys": Racial realities of the charter school authorization process in post-Katrina New Orleans. *Educational Policy, 30*(1), 218–240. http://dx.doi.org/10.1177/0895904815616485

Hornbeck, D., & Malin, J. (2019). State auditors in education policy. *Educational Policy. 33*(7), 1047–1075. http://dx/doi.org/10.1177/0895904818755469

House, E. R., & Howe, K. R. (1999). *Values in evaluation and social research*. SAGE.

Jabbar, H. (2018). Recruiting "talent": School choice and teacher hiring in New Orleans. *Educational Administration Quarterly, 54*(1), 115–151. http://dx.doi.org/10.1177/0013161X17721607

Joyce, K. E., & Cartwright, N. (2019). Bridging the gap between research and practice: Predicting what will work locally. Advance online publication, *American Educational Research Journal.* https://doi.org/10.3102%2F0002831219866687

Lankshear, C. (1999). Foreword. In P. McLaren, *Schooling as a ritual performance* (2nd ed.) (pp. viii–xxii). Routledge.

Lareau, A. (2000). *Home advantage: Social class and parental intervention in elementary education.* Rowman & Littlefield.

Lareau, A. (2011). *Unequal childhoods: Class, race, and family life (*2nd ed.) University of California Press.

Malin, J. R., & Brown, C. (Eds.). (2020). *Connecting the dots between research and practice: The role of knowledge brokers, mobilizers and boundary spanners in education.* Routledge. https://doi.org/10.4324/9780429462436

Malin, J. R., Brown, C., & Saultz, A. (2019). What we want, why we want it: K–12 educators' evidence use to support their grant proposals. *International Journal of Education Policy and Leadership, 15*(3), 1–19. https://doi.org/10.22230/ijepl.2019v15n3a837

Malin, J. R., Brown, C., & Trubceac, A. (2018). Going for broke: A multiple case study of brokerage in education. *AERA Open, 4*(2), 1–14. http://journals.sagepub.com/doi/10.1177/2332858418769297

Malin, J. R., Lubienski, C., & Mensa-Bonsu, Q. (2020). Media strategies in policy advocacy: Tracing the justifications for Indiana's school choice reforms. *Educational Policy, 34*(1), 118–143. https://doi.org/10.1177%2F0895904819881187

Marsh, L. T., & Noguera, P. A. (2018). Beyond stigma and stereotypes: An ethnographic study on the effects of school-imposed labeling on Black males in an urban charter school. *The Urban Review, 50*(3), 447–477. http://dx.doi.org/10.1007/s11256-017-0441-x

McLaren, P. (1999). *Schooling as a ritual performance: Toward a political economy of educational symbols and gestures* (3rd ed.). Rowman & Littlefield. (Original work published 1986)

McLaughlin, M. W. (2006). Implementation research in education: Lessons learned, lingering questions and new opportunities. In M. I. Honig (Ed.), *New directions in education policy implementation: Confronting complexity* (pp. 209–228). State University of New York Press.

Mertens, D. M., & Wilson, A. T. (2012). *Program evaluation theory and practice: A comprehensive guide.* The Guilford Press.

Nutley, S. M., Walter, I., & Davies, H. T. (2007). *Using evidence: How research can inform public services*. The Policy Press. https://doi.org/10.2307/j.ctt9qgwt1

Oliver, K., & Cairney, P. (2019). The dos and don'ts of influencing policy: a systematic review of advice to academics. *Palgrave Communications, 5*(1), 21. https://doi.org/10.1057/s41599-019-0232-y

Potterton, A. U. (2019). Leaders' experiences in Arizona's mature education market. *Journal of Educational Administration, 57*(1), 21–35. https://doi.org/10.1108/JEA-02-2018-0043

Potterton, A. U., Edwards Jr., D. B., Yoon, E., & Powers, J. M. (2020). Sociological contributions to school choice policy and politics around the globe: Introduction to the 2020 PEA Yearbook. *Educational Policy*, *34*(1), 3–20. https://doi.org/10.1177/0895904819881150

Rickinson, M., de Bruin, K., Walsh, L., & Hall, M. (2017). What can evidence-use in practice learn from evidence-use in policy? *Educational Research*, *59*(2), 173-189. https://doi.org/10.1080/00131881.2017.1304306

Scott, J., & Villavicencio, A. (2009). School context and charter school achievement: A framework for understanding the performance "Black Box." *Peabody Journal of Education*, *84*, 227–243. http://dx.doi.org/10.1080/01619560902810161

Spillane, J., Reiser, B., & Reimer, T. (2002). Policy implementation and cognition: Reframing and refocusing implementation research. *Review of Educational Research*, *72*(3), 387–431. http://dx.doi.org/10.3102/00346543072003387

Stake, R. E., & Trumbull, D. J. (1982). Naturalistic generalizations. *Review Journal of Philosophy and Social Science*, *7*(1), 1–12.

Thomas, K. A., & Lacey, C. H. (2016). A phenomenological study of the leadership Experiences of the charter school founder-administrator in Florida. *The Qualitative Report*, *21*(9), 1594–1614. https://nsuworks.nova.edu/tqr/vol21/iss9/3

Tierney, W. G., & Clemens, R. F. (2011). Qualitative research and public policy: The challenges of relevance and trustworthiness. In J. C. Smart & M. B. Paulsen (Eds.), *Higher education: Handbook of theory and research* (pp. 57–83). Springer. https://doi.org/10.1007/978-94-007-0702-3_2

Torres, A. C. (2016). Teacher efficacy and disciplinary expectations in charter schools: Understanding the link to teachers' career decisions. *Journal of School Choice*, *10*(2), 171–199. https://doi.org/10.1080/15582159.2016.1152528

Torres, A. C., & Weiner, J. (2018). The new professionalism? Charter teachers' experiences and qualities of the teaching profession. *Education Policy Analysis Archives*, *26*(19). https://doi.org/10.14507/epaa.26.3049

Tseng, V., & Coburn, C. (2019). Using evidence in the US. In A. Boaz, H. Davies, A. Fraser, and S. Nutley (Eds.), *What works now? Evidence-informed policy and practice* (pp. 351–368). Policy Press.

U.S. Department of Education. Institute of Education Sciences, National Center for Education Evaluation and Regional Assistance. (2020). Find what works based on the evidence. https://ies.ed.gov/ncee/wwc/FWW/Results?filters=,Charter-Schools

Vasquez Heilig, J., & Brewer, T. J. (2019). Making the case for academia's engagement in knowledge: Mobilization and purposeful public scholarship in social media. *Critical Questions in Education*, *10*(2), 81–91.

Waitoller, F. R., Nguyen, N., & Super, G. (2019). The irony of rigor: 'No-Excuses' charter schools at the intersections of race and disability. *International Journal of Qualitative Studies in Education*, *32*(3), 282–298. https://doi.org/10.1080/09518398.2019.1576939

Wallechinsky, D. (2016). Institute of Education Sciences. *AllGov: Everything our government really does*. http://www.allgov.com/departments/department-of-education/institute-of-education-sciences?agencyid=7358

Weiss, C. H. (1979). The many meanings of research utilization. *Public Administration Review*, *39*(5), 426–431. https://doi.org/10.2307/3109916

Weixler, L. B., Lincove, J. A., & Gerry, A. (2019). The provision of public pre-K in the absence of centralized school management. *American Educational Research Journal*, *55*(6), 2439–2473. https://doi.org/10.3102%2F0002831219845623

Westmarland, N. (2001). The quantitative/qualitative debate and feminist research: A subjective view of objectivity. *Forum qualitative Sozialforschung = Forum: qualitative social research*, *2*(1). https://doi.org/10.25595/455

Willis, P. (1977). *Learning to labour: How working class lads get working class jobs*. Routledge. https://doi.org/10.4324/9781351218788

APPENDIX

Some Helpful (Not Exhaustive) Qualitative Research Design Resources and Other Chapter-Relevant Resources That Are Not Already Noted in the References

Creswell, J. (1998). *Qualitative inquiry and research design: Choosing among five traditions*. SAGE.

Doucet, F. (2019). *Centering the margins: (Re)defining useful research evidence through critical perspectives*. William T. Grant Foundation.

Emerson, R. M., Fretz, R. I., & Shaw, L. L. (2011). *Writing ethnographic fieldnotes*. (2nd ed.). The University of Chicago Press. http://dx.doi.org/10.7208/chicago/9780226206868.001.0001

Fetterman, D. M. (2010). *Ethnography: Step-by-step* (3rd ed.). SAGE.

Fischman, G., & McLaren, P. (2005). Rethinking critical pedagogy and the Gramscian and Freirean legacies: From organic to committed intellectuals or critical pedagogy, commitment, and praxis. *Cultural Studies Critical Methodologies*, *5*(4), 425–447. http://dx.doi.org/10.1177/1532708605279701

Geertz, C. (1973). *The interpretation of cultures*. Basic Books.

Gibton, D. (2016). *Researching education policy, public policy, and policymakers: Qualitative methods and ethical issues*. Routledge. https://doi.org/10.4324/9781315775722

Ginsberg, M. & Gorostiaga, J. (2001). Relationships between theorists/researchers and policy makers/practitioners: Rethinking the two cultures thesis and the possibility of dialogue. *Comparative Education Review*, *45*(2), 173–196. http://dx.doi.org/10.1086/447660

Glaser, B., & Strauss, A. (1967). *The discovery of grounded theory: Strategies for qualitative research*. Aldine. https://doi.org/10.1097/00006199-196807000-00014

Greene, M. (1995). *Releasing the imagination: Essays on education, the arts, and social change*. Jossey-Bass.

Hardy, I. (2009). The politics of educational policy studies: A preliminary analysis of leading educational policy journal publications. *Critical Studies in Education*, *50*(2), 173–185. http://dx.doi.org/10.1080/17508480902859441

Honig, M. I. (2006). Complexity and policy implementation: Challenges and opportunities for the field. In M. I. Honig (Ed.), *New directions in educational policy implementation: Confronting complexity* (pp. 1–23). SUNY.

Lather, P. (2004). This IS your father's paradigm: Government intrusion and the case of qualitative research in education. *Qualitative Inquiry, 10*(1), 15–34. http://dx.doi.org/10.1177/1077800403256154

Lincoln, Y., & Guba, E. (1985). *Naturalistic inquiry*. sage. https://doi.org/10.1016/0147-1767(85)90062-8

Maxwell, J. A. (2013). *Qualitative research design: An interactive approach*. SAGE.

Miles, M. B., Huberman, M. A., & Saldaña, J. (2014). *Qualitative data analysis: A methods sourcebook*. SAGE.

Nowell, L. S., Norris, J. M., White, D. E., & Moules, N. J. (2017). Thematic analysis: Striving to meet the trustworthiness criteria. *International Journal of Qualitative Methods, 16*, 1–13. http://dx.doi.org/10.1177/1609406917733847

Olson, M. R., & Craig, C. J. (2009). "Small" stories and meganarratives: Accountability in balance. *Teachers College Record, 111*(2), 547–572.

Somekh, B., & Schwandt, T. (Eds.). (2007). *Knowledge production: The work of educational research in interesting times*. Routledge.

Smagorinsky, P. (2008). The method section as conceptual epicentre in constructing social science research reports. *Written Communication, 25*(3), 389–411. http://dx.doi.org/10.1177/0741088308317815

Stake, R. E. (2005). Qualitative case studies. In N. K. Denzin & Y. S. Lincoln (Eds.), *The SAGE handbook of qualitative research* (pp. 443–466). SAGE.

Weaver-Hightower, M. (2008). An ecology metaphor for educational policy analysis: A call to complexity. *Educational Researcher, 37*(3), 153–167. http://dx.doi.org/10.3102/0013189X08318050

Welner, K. (2010). Scholars as policy actors: Research, public discourse, and the Zone of judicial constraints. *American Educational Research Journal, 49*(1), 7–29. http://dx.doi.org/10.3102/0002831211415253

Wiseman, A. (2010). The uses of evidence for educational policymaking: Global contexts and international trends. *Review of Research in Education, 34*, 1–24. http://dx.doi.org/10.3102/0091732X09350472

NOTES

1. Please also see our note in the Discussion about the importance of acknowledging the power and potential for naturalistic generalizations (Stake & Trumbull, 1982) in qualitative research.
2. Thank you to Dr. Gustavo Fischman for his committed leadership and teaching practice at Arizona State University. The majority of the readings that are included as examples in this section come directly from coursework in his class about power, policy, and politics, and they continue to be influential still.

CHAPTER 7

THE ROLE OF MIXED METHODS IN INCREASING THE RELEVANCY OF EDUCATION POLICY RESEARCH AND EVALUATION

Kim Kappler Hewitt and Katherine Cumings Mansfield
University of North Carolina at Greensboro

INTRODUCTION

Since the 1960s, there has been increased federal involvement in educational policy and practice that has translated into both increased federal spending and a growing demand for evidence of policy and program effectiveness (Burch & Heinrich, 2016). In this evidence-based milieu, there has been a parallel call for advances in state data systems as well as the need for more complex research methodologies to ascertain not only whether policies and programs are working, but how and why they are effective or how they could be improved (Burch & Heinrich, 2016; Mertens & Wilson, 2012; Spillane et al., 2018; Timans et al., 2019). This, in turn, has led to a growing consensus about the need for more diverse methodologies, such

Maximizing the Policy Relevance of Research for School Improvement, pp. 163–187
Copyright © 2021 by Information Age Publishing
All rights of reproduction in any form reserved.

as mixed methods research (MMR; Timans et al., 2019) and evaluation in federal grantmaking (Burch & Heinrich, 2016; Curry & Nunez-Smith, 2015). Meanwhile, there has been increased attention in educational research journals on articles that challenge the quantitative-qualitative binary and advocate for more integrated approaches (Firestone, 1987; Johnson & Onwuegbuzie, 2004; Madey, 1982; Onwuegbuzie & Leech, 2005; Morgan, 2007; Sale et al., 2002; Teddlie & Tashakkori, 2003).

Additionally, policy involves and impacts humans, who are complex, and that complexity is best examined through the complementarity that mixed methods can provide. Policy-relevant research involves understanding human thinking, perceptions, reactions, behaviors, and reasoning. Additionally, policy research is more context-dependent than some other research types, especially historically and politically. Further, there are often sizable and complicated governance issues that need to be explained, even in quantitative heavy studies. For these reasons, we argue that research for and about educational policy can sometimes best be understood through the pairing of quantitative and qualitative approaches. We agree with others that mixed methods research is especially well-suited for policy research that aims to provide stakeholders with aggregate findings at the national or state level while also attending to local contextual complexities that add precision and depth to findings. (Burch & Heinrich, 2016; Weaver-Hightower, 2014).

The purpose of this chapter is to explore the role MMR might play in increasing the relevancy of policy research, analysis, and evaluation for school improvement. First, we define *what* mixed methods research is and how it differs from monomethod approaches that singularly emphasize either quantitative or qualitative methods. Then, we discuss reasons *why* mixed methods approaches can potentially strengthen our policy research efforts. In the next section, we share how MMR can be used in policy-relevant research by first describing distinct MMR designs for consideration. We then share illustrative examples to further strengthen our understandings of how MMR is used in policy-relevant research. In the last section, we discuss the implications of MMR for those who work in organizations centered around school improvement, such as university preparation programs, school districts, and policy think tanks. Then, we share suggestions for expanding our conceptions of research methods courses before concluding.

WHAT IS MMR AND WHY SHOULD WE USE IT?

The most basic way to define mixed methods research (MMR) is to describe it as an empirical endeavor that includes at least one quantitative and one qualitative data collection method in its design (Burch & Heinrich, 2016; Creswell & Clark, 2011; Curry & Nunez-Smith, 2015; Greene et al., 1989; Johnson & Onwuegbuzie, 2004; Sale et al., 2002; Timans et al., 2019; Welton et al., 2015), prompting some to refer to MMR as *integrative research* (Johnson & Onwuegbuzie, 2004). Others have described MMR as a process that creates a sum greater than its parts: "In terms of methods, one plus one equals three. And what's the three? The interplay between the two types of methods; the interaction, the synergistic coming together, which creates something that never existed before" (Madey, 1982, p. 235). Indeed, Tashakkori and Teddle (2003) refer to this fusion of quantitative and qualitative approaches as the *third methodological movement.* While this combination is generally focused on the integrated use of numerical (quantitative) and non-numerical (qualitative) data, MMR can also incorporate other elements drawn from both traditions (Creswell & Clark, 2011), such as establishing criteria for credibility of a particular study or drawing from multiple epistemologies.

While some scholars promote the *incompatibility thesis* (Howe, 1988), the claim that qualitative and quantitative paradigms are incommensurate, Teddlie and Tashakkori (2003) outline five foundational theses regarding the relationship between quantitative and qualitative paradigms within MMR:

1. A-paradigmatic thesis: The assertion that paradigms and methods can be independent of one another;
2. Complementary strengths thesis: The assertion that MMR is possible if the approaches are kept separate such that the strengths of each can be realized;
3. Single paradigm thesis: The assertion that one paradigm can serve as the foundation for MMR—typically pragmatism or a transformative-emancipatory paradigm;
4. Dialectic thesis: The assertion that MMR should intentionally engage multiple paradigms as partial, yet valuable, worldviews held dialectically in tension with one another such that the juxtaposition is synergistic; and
5. Multiple paradigms thesis: The assertion that one paradigm might be best for one study or element of a study while a different paradigm might be best for another element of a study such that, while different from one another, the multiple paradigms are used in conjunction with one another.

Johnson and Onwuegbuzie (2004) contend that not only are qualitative and quantitative paradigms *commensurate* but that MMR is superior to monomethod studies:

> In some situations the qualitative approach will be more appropriate; in other situations the quantitative approach will be more appropriate. In many situations, researchers can put together insights and procedures from both approaches to produce a superior product.... We are advocating a needs-based or contingency approach to research method and concept selection. (p. 17)

Indeed, our review of the literature showed that MMR can be leveraged to strengthen monomethod research in numerous ways that are particularly valuable for policy-relevant research. For example, MMR has the capability to answer a wide variety of research questions. That is, while quantitative studies typically aim to answer whether change has occurred and if so, to what degree, qualitative studies focus on understanding why and how these changes occurred (Bryman, 2006; Burch & Heinrich, 2016; Creswell & Clark, 2011; Firestone, 1987; Mertens & Wilson, 2012). Moreover, MMR studies can be designed such that one approach is used to support the other (Burch & Heinrich, 2016; Creswell & Clark, 2011; Greene et al., 1989; Onwuegbuzie & Leech, 2005; Welton et al., 2015). For example, interview (qualitative) data might be used to inform survey development (quantitative). Conversely, responses on a survey (quantitative) can be used to inform sampling for interviews (qualitative). In the interest of limited space, Table 7.1 summarizes some of the main findings from our examination of the literature on MMR.

As an example of how these benefits of MMR can be applied in policy-relevant research, consider Hewitt's (2015) mixed methods survey study of teacher perceptions of the use of value-added data (student growth data) as a component of their evaluations. (The benefits of MMR as applied in the study are italicized for emphasis in the following paragraphs.) The use of closed-ended (quantitative) data allowed Hewitt to get a broad sense of teachers' perceptions, and open-ended (qualitative) data allowed her to get a sense of why teachers held the views they did, especially as a function of their values and experiences. Both quantitative and qualitative data allowed her to address the first purpose of the study in a *complementary* or *additive* way,

> 1) To examine educators' perceptions of the use of the Education Value Added Assessment System (EVAAS)—a type of value-added model—for educator evaluation, in particular what effects educators predict these systems will have on teaching and learning and what, if any, consequences of implementing these systems they have observed in their own schools.

Quantitative methods (specifically inferential statistics) were required to address the second purpose: "2) To determine how perceptions vary by educator familiarity and experience with the use of value-added for

Table 7.1

Examples From the Literature Highlighting the Benefits of Using MMR

Themes	References
Answers variety of questions (what, scale, why, how)	Bryman (2006); Burch & Heinrich (2016); Creswell & Clark (2011); Firestone (1987); Johnson & Onwuegbuzie (2004); Mertens & Wilson (2012); Timans, Wouters, & Helbron (2019)
Expands comprehensiveness (breadth and depth)	Burch & Heinrich (2016); Creswell & Clark (2011); Mertens & Wilson (2012); Timans, Wouters, & Helbron (2019); Welton, Mansfield, Lee, & Young (2015)
Attends to contextual complexity; encourages holistic view	Burch & Heinrich (2016); Creswell & Clark (2011); Mertens & Wilson (2012); Onwuegbuzie & Leech (2005); Welton, Mansfield, Lee, & Young (2015)
Supports study development; one approach supports the other	Burch & Heinrich (2016); Creswell & Clark (2011); Greene, Caracelli, & Graham (1989); Mertens & Wilson (2012); Onwuegbuzie & Leech (2005); Welton, Mansfield, Lee, & Young (2015)
Compensates for limitations; draws on strengths of each	Bryman (2006); Burch & Heinrich (2016); Creswell & Clark (2011); Firestone (1987); Johnson & Onwuegbuzie (2004); Mertens & Wilson (2012); Onwuegbuzie & Leech (2005); Welton, Mansfield, Lee, & Young (2015)
Complementary and/or additive outcomes	Burch & Heinrich (2016); Firestone (1987); Johnson & Onwuegbuzie (2004); Onwuegbuzie & Leech (2005); Sale, Lohfeld, & Brazil (2002)
Strengthens triangulation and corroboration	Bryman Greene, Caracelli, & Graham (1989); Burch & Heinrich (2016); Creswell & Clark (2011); Firestone (1987); Johnson & Onwuegbuzie (2004); Mertens & Wilson (2012); Onwuegbuzie & Leech (2005); Timans, Wouters, & Helbron (2019); Welton, Mansfield, Lee, & Young (2015)
Increases credibility/confidence	Bryman (2006); Burch & Heinrich (2016); Firestone (1987)
Increases reliability/validity/relevance	Burch & Heinrich (2016)
Reveals contradictions; leads to question reframing	Mansfield (2014); Onwuegbuzie & Leech (2005)
Encourages representation and voice	Mansfield (2014); Mertens & Wilson (2012)
Promotes collaboration	Burch & Heinrich (2016); Mansfield (2014); Mertens & Wilson (2012); Onwuegbuzie & Leech (2005)
Strengthens relationships	Burch & Heinrich (2016); Mansfield (2014); Mertens & Wilson (2012)
Enables researcher flexibility	Burch & Heinrich (2016); Onwuegbuzie & Leech (2005); Timans, Wouters, & Helbron (2019)
Increases utility of findings	Bryman (2006); Burch & Heinrich (2016); Creswell & Clark (2011); Johnson & Onwuegbuzie (2004); Mansfield (2014); Mertens & Wilson (2012); Morgan, 2007
Provides logical, practical alternative; uses what works	Johnson & Onwuegbuzie (2004); Mertens & Wilson (2012); Morgan, 2007;

educator evaluation" (p. 3). As such, MMR allowed her to *answer different types of questions* within the study. Indeed, she found that teachers who had received value-added scores the previous year, compared to those who did not, perceived themselves to be more knowledgeable about value-added and were significantly more opposed to the use of value-added for educator evaluation.

Arguably the most concerning finding, which was *corroborated* in the quantitative and qualitative data and more powerfully illustrated through the qualitative data, was the finding that the use of value-added data in teacher evaluations, according to respondents, led teachers to avoid teaching certain students and to the segregation of students with disabilities:

> I have experienced Regular Education Teachers not wanting to have EC students [exceptional children/students with disabilities] in their classrooms since their jobs are on the line if their students are not making growth. They are less inclined to want to do inclusion. (p. 28)

Additionally, the use of value-added appeared to result in teachers avoiding certain schools and in the segregation of students who struggled academically:

> I personally am requesting to NOT teach an intensive class [for students whose achievement is multiple years below grade level] next year and will likely try to move to another school because I am scared of what taking on the lowest students in my grade, and really the lowest students in my district, will do to my evaluation. I have the heart to teach these kids, but they are not the kids that show the scores on [value-added], and I am scared if I stay too long then I will get trapped and will not be able to find another job.... We have created "intensive" classes basically to separate the low kids from the high kids, all with the goal of improving test scores. What it does is create segregation. (pp. 28–29)

Hewitt concluded that policy to incorporate value-added data into teachers' evaluations resulted in "several unintended and unanticipated consequences" (p. 33), and MMR *increased the utility* of Hewitt's findings such that she was able to recommend five "urgent and substantive midcourse policy corrections" (p. 34).

As argued by Onwuegbuzie and Leech (2005) and exemplified in the Hewitt study, "neither tradition is independent of the other, nor can either school encompass the whole research process. Thus, both quantitative and qualitative research techniques are needed to gain a more complete understanding of phenomena" (p. 380) in policy-relevant studies. Another consideration is the growing demand for more rigorous evidence of program and policy effectiveness that has been spurred on by an evidenced-based political climate (Burch & Heinrich, 2016). In the past, quantitative methods were emphasized in policy-relevant research endeavors. While experimental and quasi-experimental designs are still considered the gold standard in educational research (e.g., as defined by the federal What Works Clearinghouse), lessons learned from policy implementation research include going beyond statistics to better understand *why* participants behaved as they did and what could be done to improve implementation results (Datnow & Park, 2009; Honig, 2009). Thus, MMR is a compelling approach to identify and explain policy and program impacts (Mertens & Wilson, 2012). Additionally, MMR is ideal for studies "where processes and outcome measures will be used by diverse stakeholders and where enhancing learning and communication is an important part of the research process" (Burch & Heinrich, 2016, p. 20).

In addition to studying the implementation and effects of policy or what one might refer to as research *on* policy, MMR can also be used to research *for* policy, which is done at the front end of policy research. Research *for* policy is important because it informs policy stakeholders and researchers of the nature of a problem and raises awareness around undesirable conditions that demand policy action (Weimer, 2009). Examples of this type of research might take the form of a context analysis or input analysis (Mertens & Wilson, 2012). On the other hand, research *on* policy could examine policy implementation fidelity or evaluate the intended or unintended consequences of policy (Mertens & Wilson, 2012).

HOW CAN MMR BE USED IN POLICY-RELEVANT RESEARCH?

Prior to designing a policy-relevant study that leverages the power of MMR, it behooves researchers to construct a theory of action (ToA) that reflects the assumptions and values that underpin educational policy for school improvement. The next section describes the purpose and benefits of constructing a ToA to inform MMR design.

Alleviating Design Challenges by Leading With a Theory of Action

While often implicit and invisible, policy formation is informed by and dependent upon values and assumptions held by policymakers. Thus, it is important to start with a ToA or visual theory of change to clarify the underlying assumptions and beliefs behind a policy, along with stakeholder assumptions about causal linkages (Burch & Heinrich, 2016; Mertens & Wilson, 2012). As an example, Figure 7.1 illustrates the theory of action

(ToA) behind policy involving the use of measures of student growth such as value-added scores in teacher evaluations. In their book on new generation teacher evaluation policy that incorporates student growth measures (SGMs), Hewitt and Amrein-Beardley (2016) explain:

> According to the ToA, teacher evaluation systems that involve SGMs will primarily affect teacher quality by promoting the voluntary and involuntary exit (dismissal) of ineffective teachers and motivating remaining teachers to work harder and smarter. The result would be increased teacher quality which will lead to increased student learning, as reflected in increased student achievement, which will elevate U.S. education and increase the nation's global competitiveness. This ToA has a *prima facie* logic to it, yet it assumes that a) SGMs can reliably and accurately distinguish effective from ineffective teachers; b) that these data, together, will be appropriately used to inform personnel (dismissing, hiring) decisions; c) that remaining teachers will be motivated to work harder and smarter in response to the data (as opposed to moving to other grade levels, schools, or leaving teaching altogether); and d) that changes in test scores as a function of these policies will reflect increases in student learning and—more importantly—increase the type of student learning that will make the U.S. more globally competitive. The legitimacy of the ToA will ultimately be determined in the years and decades to come as the effects of teacher accountability policies become clearer. (pp. 13–14)

Hewitt and Amrein-Beardley built the ToA based on previous policy studies involving SGMs, including Amrein-Beardsley (2014), Harris and Herrington (2015), and Holloway-Libell and Amrein-Beardsley (2015).

Developing a ToA informed by previous policy studies also helps policy stakeholders and the research team better understand contextual features that create challenges, such as policy and institutional history, formal and informal governance, and intra-/inter-organizational influences (Burch & Heinrich, 2016). Theories of action help us understand political, social, and historical forces that are embedded in policy and help shape problem definition, policy implementation, and assessment of outcomes. The process of developing the ToA also reveals the complex tangle of governance affiliations and helps the researcher understand the interplay between multiple policy levels, including the federal government, state education agencies, state law, and local school board policy.

MMR Designs

Informed by a ToA, quantitative and qualitative approaches can be integrated in a number of ways, resulting in a variety of MMR research designs. Scholars from a number of disciplinary traditions have developed various

Figure 7.1

Theory of Action Underpinning Teacher Accountability From Hewitt and Amrein-Beardsley (2016) That Maps the Underlying Values and Assumptions Behind Policy Involving Student Growth Measures (SGMs) Such as Value-Added Scores in Teach Evaluations

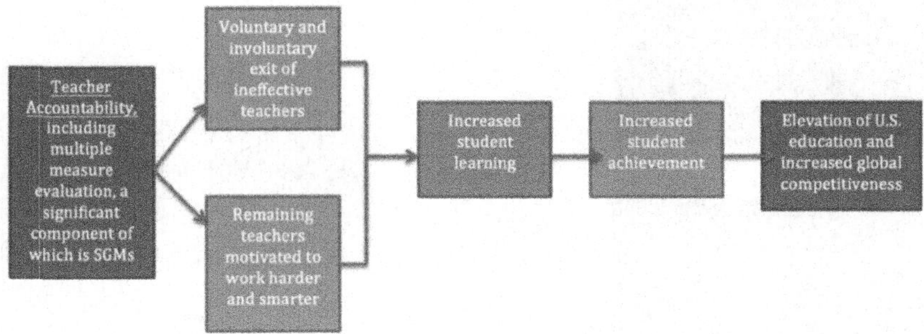

typologies to classify MMR designs (Creswell & Clark, 2011; Teddlie and Tashakkori, 2003). In the paragraphs that follow, we use the typology presented by Creswell and Clark (2011) and provide an illustrative example of a recent educational policy study for five of the MMR design types.

Convergent Parallel Design

In convergent parallel design, the quantitative and qualitative strands of the study occur concurrently (at the same time), are typically prioritized about equally, and are independent of one another (one strand does not rely on the other). The integrative mixing of the two approaches occurs at the interpretation stage (see Figure 7.2).

Illustrative example (research *of* policy; state level). In 2010, the legislature of the State of Illinois required a complete redesign of principal preparation programs. The state policy required five main shifts in principal preparation:

- A targeted principal endorsement, instead of a general administrative certificate
- Partnerships with school districts in preparation program design and delivery
- Selective admissions criteria
- P–12 licensure (adding prekindergarten to the leadership training)
- A competency-based internship (White et al., 2016)

Figure 7.2

Convergent Parallel Design (Independent; Concurrent; Equal Prioritization; Mixing During Interpretation)

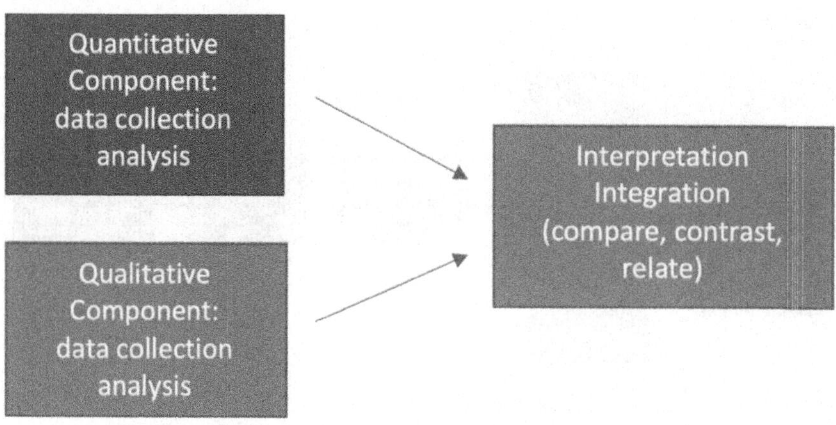

In their research *of* policy, White et al. (2016) studied navigation and policy enactment of the 2010 statute by Illinois principal preparation programs, specifically focusing on changes that occurred in preparation programs as a function of the policy. Their "mixed methods study was designed to investigate the degree to which the implementation of Illinois' redesigned principal preparation programs live up to the aspirations presented in the new policy" (p. 14) and involved site visits to 12 preparation programs. Site visits (qualitative) included observations, document analysis, and interviews of various stakeholders (e.g., faculty, external/district partners, students, and program directors). A second component of the study included a syllabus review (qualitative) of the syllabi from 14 principal preparation programs. Concurrently with the qualitative components of the study, the research team administered a quantitative survey to the coordinators of all principal preparation programs that had been approved at that point in time, and 21 of 28 program coordinators completed the survey for a 75% response rate. The three datasets were analyzed separately, and then the findings were integrated during the interpretation stage to yield the following key findings:

- Most programs reported strong partnerships with districts after the redesign (p. 6).
- Most programs experienced a dramatic drop in enrollment, as anticipated by moving from general administrative training [for

any administrative role in a district] to a principal-specific endorsement (p. 6).

- Instructional leadership [became] a clear program focus in terms of coursework and internship competencies (p. 7).
- Special student populations (students with disabilities, [English Language Learners], and early childhood students) have received increased coverage in both coursework and internships, per redesign requirements (p. 7).
- Competency-based internships have brought a welcomed depth, clarity, and authenticity to candidates' internship experiences that many [stakeholders] believe will better prepare candidates for the principalship (p. 7).
- Many programs collect data on current candidates, but outcome data on graduates are lacking (p. 7).

While the White et al. study reflects the way in which quantitative and qualitative components of a convergent parallel design run concurrently to yield policy recommendations, other MMR designs involve sequencing the quantitative and qualitative components one after the other, as described it the following sections.

Sequential Explanatory Design

In sequential explanatory design, the researcher begins with a quantitative phase that holds the priority (emphasis) in addressing the research question(s). The subsequent qualitative phase is informed by the quantitative phase and is used to explain and make meaning of the quantitative results. Sequential explanatory design is interactive in the sense that the second phase (qualitative) is dependent upon the first phase (quantitative) in that results from the quantitative phase are used to develop research questions and data collection protocols for the qualitative phase. For example, quantitative results might be used to generate items in interview protocols, for the purpose of exploring the "why" and "how" behind the quantitative data.

In this respect, the first phase (quantitative) is also dependent upon the second phase (qualitative) to make meaning of or explain the findings. This design is sequential in that one phase (qualitative) must follow the other (quantitative), and it involves mixing or integration at the data collection phase because the collection of quantitative data is imperative to inform the collection of the qualitative data of the study. Additionally, there is mixing at the interpretation phase because qualitative results are used to explain and make meaning of quantitative results (see Figure 7.3).

Figure 7.3

Explanatory Sequential Design (Interactive/Dependent; Sequential; Quantitative Prioritization)

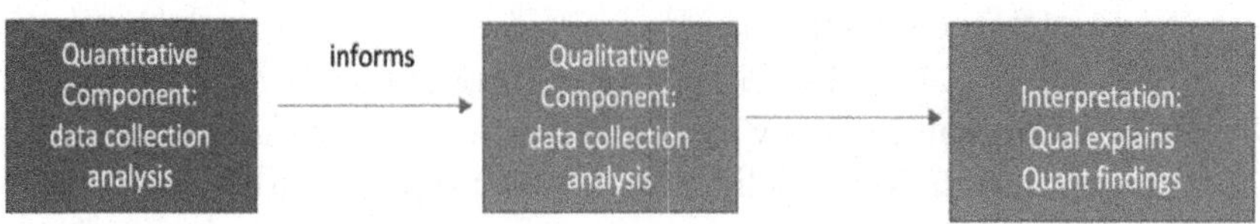

Illustrative example (research *of* policy; local level). In their longitudinal MMR study, Spillane et al. (2018) drew on five years of data from a midsized, suburban school district to examine the relationship between indicators of teacher quality and who teachers saw as experts and sought out for advice. The team posed three research questions:

1. "What information do teachers and school leaders draw on when constructing their understandings of the most expert or 'best' teachers of mathematics among their colleagues?" (p. 589). This question was addressed through qualitative interview data in the second stage of the study.
2. "How, if at all, do the test scores of their colleagues' students figure into these constructions of the 'best' teachers of mathematics?" (p. 589). This question was addressed through qualitative interview data in the second stage of the study.
3. "Does teacher performance, as measured by their students' test scores, predict being sought out or seeking work-related advice about mathematics?" (p. 589). This question was addressed through quantitative data from two sources—student test scores and teacher social network data—in the first stage of the study.

The district in which the study was situated had engaged in a multi-year effort to implement an inquiry-based math curriculum and had instituted infrastructure to support the implementation, including revised district-level assessments that were scored by teachers and discussed in professional learning communities (PLCs), professional development through a master's program for strategically selected teachers from each school, math coaches in some schools, organizational routines including PLCs and weekly team meetings, and an online data dashboard where teachers could see their own data as well as that of their colleagues.

In each year between 2011–2015, Spillane et al. (2018) administered a quantitative survey to teachers and administrators that included items about their roles, backgrounds, and experiences. Additionally, respondents were asked to list the names of up to 12 colleagues from whom they sought advice about mathematics instruction. For each, they indicated whether they received information and advice about math. The researchers utilized latent space network models to map networks of expertise. Additionally, the researchers utilized three quantitative measures of teacher performance: (1) proportion of proficient students; (2) class average test score; and (3) teacher value-added (growth model developed by the research team and not utilized by the district).

The quantitative analysis of the social network data and student test data yielded the following results:

> School staff were not more likely to seek out colleagues for instructional advice when those colleagues' students performed better on tests; instead, we find that higher performing teachers were more likely to *seek* advice and information than were lower performing teachers. (Spillane et al., 2018, p. 588)

The quantitative results, while powerful, yielded no understanding of why teachers do not seek guidance from colleagues whose students perform well on state and district tests, nor did it provide insight into what does matter in terms of teachers' reasons for seeking out the colleagues whom they do. The research team integrated the interview (qualitative) data collection in the last year of the study, which was informed by the quantitative findings, with the quantitative findings to explain that:

> While school staff report knowing the best mathematics teachers among their peers, they generally do not rely on student test scores to identify those experts. Instead, in identifying experts they rely on their own direct or indirect knowledge of their colleagues' teaching approaches; their colleagues' excitement about, knowledge of, and understanding of mathematics, as demonstrated in meetings; and their colleagues' subject-specific formal positions and/or training. (p. 587)

The team further found that "various components of the district's educational infrastructure to support elementary math education created opportunities for teachers to build this direct and indirect knowledge about colleagues' math expertise" (pp. 587–588). As such, the infrastructure that the district put into place intentionally to support the implementation of the inquiry-based mathematics curriculum had an important impact on how teachers came to make determinations about peers' expertise. These determinations typically were not based on the test data accessible through the online data dashboard, as teachers reported in interviews, because they were skeptical that test scores could accurately determine good teachers, although some respondents made determinations about teacher expertise based on how teachers used data. The integration of the qualitative analysis to explain the quantitative findings yielded important policy-relevant conclusions:

> District policymakers can influence teachers' access to their expert peers, but relying solely on making student test data widely available to teachers is likely to be insufficient.... Instead, policymakers should attend carefully to the various ways that school staff use different sorts of information . . . to figure out instructional expertise ... and design educational infrastructures that maximize opportunities for teachers to *see* and *engage* with these experts. (p. 608; italics in the original)

The integration of quantitative and qualitative methods and analyses yielded policy-amenable insights; in other words, the findings from the explanatory sequential design can be used to inform policy that will affect the very types of teacher connections and interactions that served as the focus of the study. The MMR design provided productive policy input.

Further, these findings are externally generalizable. Although Spillane et al. (2018) situated their study within one district, they argued that the study provides *external generalizability* in two forms: *transferability*, which is the applicability of findings to other settings that are similar in relevant ways; and *theoretical* or *analytical generalizability*, in the sense that findings from the study can contribute to refinement of theory regarding teacher peer interactions. While the concept of generalizability has long been associated with—and some would argue limited to—quantitative methodology, these concepts of transferability and theoretical (analytical) generalizability come from the discourse of qualitative methodology. This is another way in which this study integrates quantitative and qualitative research traditions.

Exploratory Sequential Design

Essentially, exploratory sequential design flips the sequence of stages from explanatory sequential design. The qualitative stage both precedes the quantitative stage and is prioritized over it in exploratory sequential design. The results of the qualitative stage are used to inform the development of the quantitative stage, which serves to test and/or attempt to generalize findings from the qualitative stage (see Figure 7.4). In other words, descriptive findings from the qualitative stage (e.g., themes, patterns, negative case findings) are used to generate research questions and items for a quantitative instrument or protocol. For example, if a researcher were interested in studying the role of an instructional coach in cultivating mature professional learning communities (PLCs), she might interview PLC team members from two teams at each of three schools within a district. She might use what she learned from the interviews to inform the construction of a closed-item (such as Likert scale) survey instrument (quantitative) that she then administers to a stratified (based on student demographics) random sample of other districts across the state that also use instructional coaches to facilitate PLCs. She could then draw conclusions about the generalizability and utility of her qualitative findings to inform policy (research *for* policy) regarding funding for instructional coach positions and district practices regarding PLC facilitation.

Figure 7.4

Exploratory Aequential Design (Interactive/Dependent; Sequential; Qualitative Prioritization; Mixing During Data Collection)

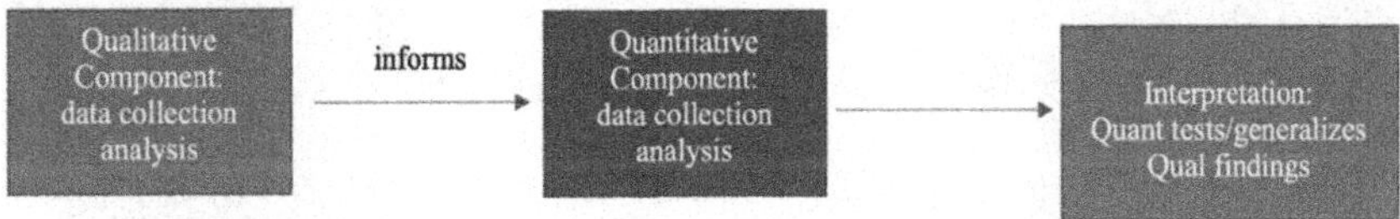

Embedded Design

Embedded design involves a modest, supplemental element of quantitative data within a qualitative study or vice versa. The embedded (supplemental) component is in support of or enhances the main (priority or emphasized) approach. While embedded design is interactive/dependent, it can be concurrent or sequential, and the main component can be qualitative or quantitative. The mixing occurs at the design stage, as the embedded, supplemental component is necessary for the design of the main component. Figure 7.5 reflects the embedding of a modest quantitative component within a predominantly qualitative study (left-hand side of figure) and, alternatively, the embedding of a modest qualitative component within a predominantly quantitative study (right-hand side of figure); in each example, the supplemental method can be concurrent with or sequential to the predominant method. An illustrative example from Koyama and Chang (2019) appears below, as their study is also an example of transformative MMR.

Transformative Design

The distinguishing feature of transformative design is its situation within a critical, transformative, or emancipatory theoretical framework

Figure 7.5

Embedded Design (Interactive/Dependent; Concurrent or Sequential; Quantitative or Qualitative Prioritization; Mixing During Design)

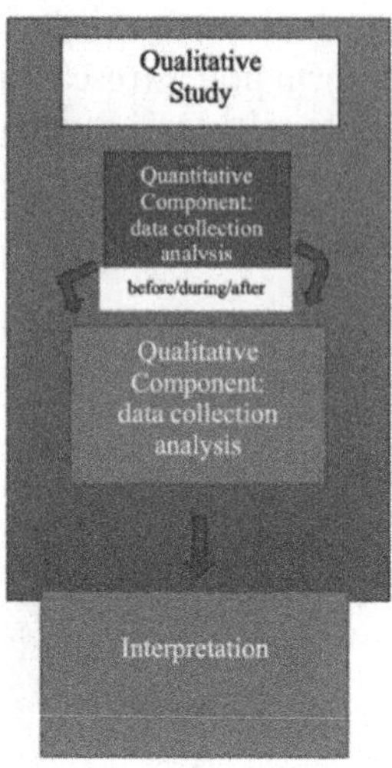

OR

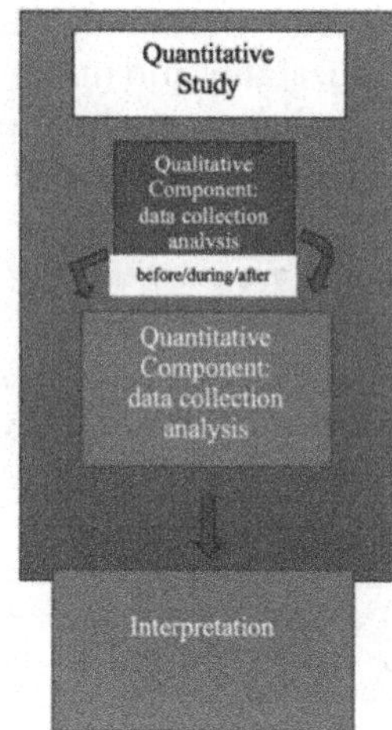

that surfaces and examines issues of power, oppression, and inequity. The framework is the key element of transformative design, and the mixing of qualitative and quantitative elements occurs at the design level. While the quantitative and qualitative components are interactive, transformative design can be concurrent or sequential and can prioritize qualitative or quantitative. That said, most transformative MMR will prioritize qualitative elements, as examining and interrogating counter-narratives and the role of language and discourse in establishing, reinforcing, and reproducing unequal power arrangements are common practices in transformative epistemologies (see Figure 7.6) (Weaver-Hightower, 2014).

Illustrative example of Embedded Design and Transformative Design (research of policy; state-level and district-level). Koyama and Chang (2019) utilize Critical Policy Analysis (CPA) in their study of the way in which stakeholders make meaning of and enact two Arizona state policies regarding refugee education: (1) the state Strategic Plan for educating refugees invokes a discourse of *belonging* as reflected in its goals to increase the safety and belonging of refugee students, "increase refugee student directed activities" (p. 144), and increase awareness among the general population about refugee resettlement in Arizona. In tension with the Strategic Plan is Proposition 203, which invokes an *othering* discourse and isolates refugees and Spanish-speaking immigrant students in Structured

Figure 7.6

Transformative design (interactive/dependent; concurrent or sequential; quantitative or qualitative prioritization; mixing during design).

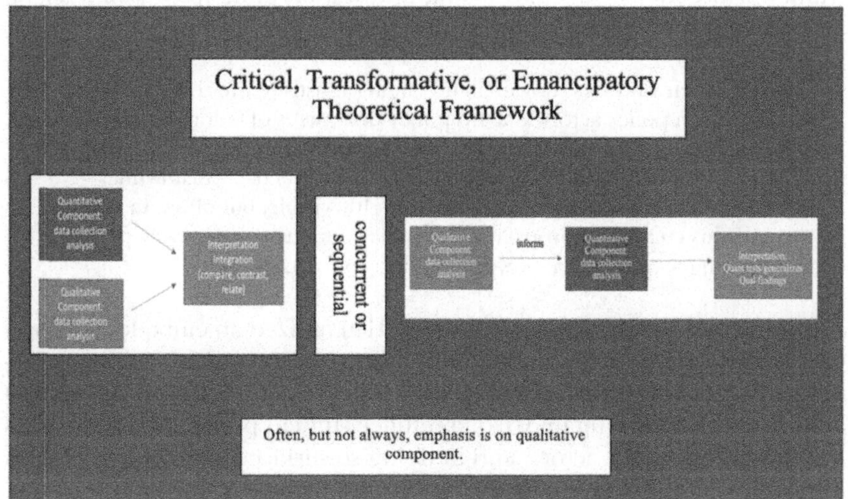

English Immersion (SEI) courses for 4 hours per day, despite research indicating that the approach excludes, isolates, stigmatizes, and misserves students (Koyama & Chang, 2019).

Additionally, Koyama and Chang (2019) utilize Critical Discourse Analysis (CDA), which positions language as "social practice, a mode of action that mutually shapes and is formed through the social ... language works within, and because of, power relations" (p. 140). They also draw upon tenets of actor network theory, which "guides examinations of how things, people, and ideas come to be connected into larger units, called networks, to perform actions" (p. 140). Their use of CPA and CDA defines the Koyama and Chang study as transformative MMR because they utilized critical theoretical frameworks.

Koyama and Chang (2019) engaged in a 3-year ethnography of refugee networks within the Desert United School District (DUSD) area of Arizona. As an ethnography, their study was qualitative; however, embedded in it was a survey (quantitative[1]) component that was part of the overarching ethnography, which primarily focused on observations, interviews, and document analysis of three key stakeholder groups: Members of the Refugee Services Department of DUSD; principals, teachers, and refugee parents of sample schools within the district; and community-based refugee organizations, agencies, and programs. In this respect, Koyama and Chang used an embedded design in that the survey (quantitative) was embedded into the larger ethnography (qualitative). In their analysis, Koyama and Chang developed etic (*from outside* perspective of researchers/theoretical framework) codes from survey data and added emic (*from within* social group being studied) codes from interviews:

> Based on their findings, Koyama and Chang illustrate the contradictory ways in which policy actors take up policy discourses of belonging and othering. Formal school actors, namely teachers and administrators, engaged in acts ... that rendered refugees invisible and isolated.... Meanwhile, refugee mentors positioned refugees as highly visible, but often, in need of saving. This creative appropriation of policy discourses effectively perpetuates existing asymmetrical power relations. (pp. 152–153)

In their study, Koyama and Chang (2019) utilized an embedded design (quantitative survey within qualitative ethnography) within their transformative MMR study that leveraged CPA and CDA to examine discourses of belonging and othering in Arizona refugee student policy and enactments by educational policy actors, and in doing so surfaced and analyzed issues of asymmetrical power, marginalization, and inequity.

Multiphase Design

Multiphase designs are used for a "program of study addressing an overall program objective" (Creswell & Clark, 2011, p. 72). The program, which takes place over a period of time, involves multiple phases that include quantitative and qualitative approaches, each of which can be concurrent or sequential. The distinguishing feature is that the various phases each serve as building blocks for the program of inquiry (see Figure 7.7).

Illustrative Example (research for policy; international/global level). In 2004, Michael Cowie and colleagues from 15 countries across five continents created a research network named the International Study of Principal Preparation (ISPP). The network conducted a program of inquiry comprised of three phases of research centered on the challenges that new principals face, guided by the "chief question of the study [which] was: How can principal preparation programs be useful to novice principals?" (Slater et al., 2018, p. 127). The program of inquiry took place over the course of a number of years, resulting in numerous publications and the development of two principal preparation frameworks (Slater et al., 2018).

Phase one of the project (qualitative) involved case studies and interviews and was focused on mapping the terrain of formal and informal principal

Figure 7.7

Sample MMR Multiphase Design Illustrating a Program of Study Over Time That Is Comprised of Substudies of Various Designs

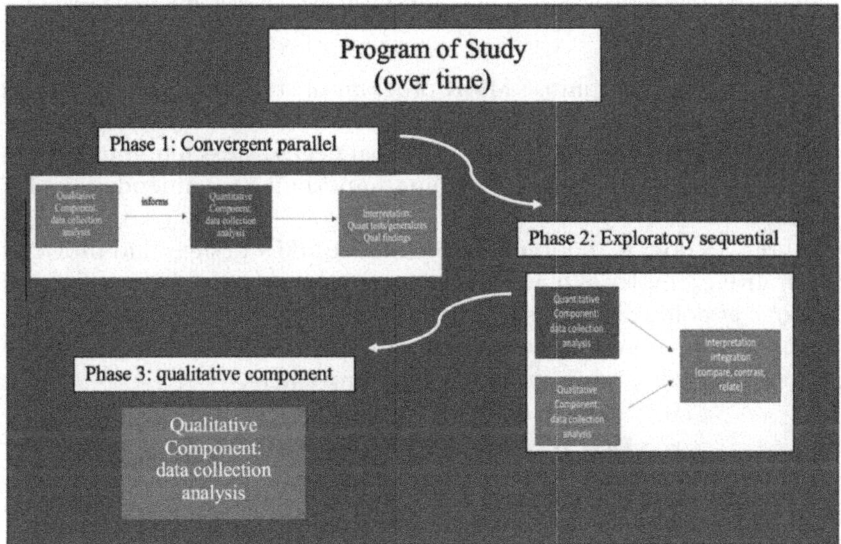

preparation programs and opportunities across network nations (Slater et al., 2018). Comparative case studies on principal preparation programs illustrated that programs in only four of the network countries—Canada, England, Scotland, and the United States—had formal principal preparation programs. In the second phase (qualitative), researchers conducted individual and group interviews, and cross-cultural analyses to examine the realities, experiences, and challenges of new principals within their first three years of service.

The third and final phase involved development of a survey instrument (quantitative and qualitative) that was informed by the results of phases one and two and that focused on new principals' perceptions regarding their experiences, challenges, and the adequacy of their preservice preparation. Findings from across the three phases were used to develop policy recommendations, including:

> 1) Formal principal preparation programs should be expanded to both developed and developing countries; 2) Principal preparation programs should not [emphasis original] be standardized across countries, as they need to be responsive to context and varying needs; 3) Preparation programs should include an emphasis on instructional leadership; 4) At the

> same time, based on new principals' stated needs across a variety of settings and nations, preparation programs should also provide instruction on budgeting, accountability paperwork, and implementation of policy mandates; and 5) Additionally, in developing nations, findings reveal a need to prepare preservice principals to address issues of absenteeism (students and teachers), union challenges, and procurement of materials and facilities. (Slateret al., 2018, p. 131)

As such, the multiphrase MMR program of study over multiple years conducted in three phases allowed the network of researchers to study principal preparation and novice principal needs across multiple settings throughout network nations, yielding important recommendations for policy.

In this section, we outlined six prominent MMR designs and provided illustrative examples of how they can be applied in research *for* policy and research *of* policy at local, state, national, and global/international levels. In the next section, we discuss implications of MMR for increasing the relevance of policy research for school improvement.

DISCUSSION AND CONCLUSIONS

In this chapter, we explained the unique qualities of mixed methods research (MMR) and the potential contributions MMR can make toward increasing the robustness and usefulness of policy-relevant research in education. We first answered questions around what MMR is and explained the many reasons MMR is considered an often superior way to study policies and practices embedded in complex systems such as schools. We then shared specific MMR designs, offering graphic representations to enhance understanding. Additionally, we provided illustrative examples to demonstrate how MMR can be used in policy-relevant school improvement inquiries. We now turn our attention to the implications of our reasoning for those who do research of and for policy and those who teach research coursework in the university setting. (For an excellent discussion of these issues, we direct the reader to the book, *Mixed Methods for Policy Research and Program Evaluation* by Burch and Heinrich [2016] which informs the discussion that follows.)

Recommendations for Policy Researchers

Regardless of the sophistication, rigor, and compelling findings of policy-relevant research, it is unlikely to be taken up by policymakers and to influence policy unless researchers find effective ways to engage with policymakers (Burch & Heinrich, 2016). Weimer (2009) goes further by advocating for a more analytical way of studying policy to increase its usefulness earlier in the inquiry process. That is, Weimer distinguishes between *policy research* as that which informs policy and *policy analysis* as that which systematically assesses policy alternatives that might be used to address an identified need.

In addition to taking a more analytical approach to education policy research, it is also important to do more than just hand a policy community, such as a school district, a final report. Rather, including formative feedback as well as summative feedback can do much to strengthen school improvement (Burch & Heinrich, 2016; Mertens & Wilson, 2012). Along with formative feedback, policy researchers might also work with stakeholders to build capacity toward sustainable change (Burch & Heinrich, 2016; Mertens & Wilson, 2012).

In terms of effectively communicating policy research/analysis findings, it is important for researchers to select a variety of dissemination platforms and tools that will speak to a variety of audiences. For example, policy researchers can create executive summaries[2] that can be more easily digested by a busy superintendent or school board member. Moreover, research findings can be translated to short, colorful booklets or pamphlets to be used with parents and other community members. Similarly, researchers might design one-page policy briefs that can be used when conversing with federal, state, and local policy makers, including elected officials. We urge readers to consult Section III of this volume, "Traditional and Alternative Outlets for Research Dissemination"—and in particular Price's Chapter 12, "Communicating to Policymakers"—for additional ideas and a thorough discussion about communicating with policy stakeholders.

Recommendations for Research Coursework

Given that MMR began to gain prominence only within the first decade of the 21st century, and with the advocacy and use of MMR on the rise, its institutionalization as a distinct approach is relatively new (Timans et al., 2019). Thus, it is important to consider what the implications might be for the ways universities organize and provide their required research courses, as well as how they teach graduate students to conduct research. While it was beyond the scope of this chapter to adequately discuss, there are still strong feelings among some intellectual learning communities about the value of MMR and whether it is possible really to do MMR if one adheres to a strict post-positivist or constructivist paradigm. (See Burch & Heinrich, 2016; Firestone, 1987; Howe, 1988; Johnson & Onwuegbuzie, 2004; Morgan, 2007; Onwuegbuzie & Leech, 2005; and Pallas, 2001 for a substantive discussion around the incompatibility thesis.) We agree with Onwuegbuzie and Leech (2005) that "a false dichotomy exists between quantitative and qualitative research" (p. 384), but as Burch and Heinrich (2016) point out:

> The polarization of methods is still powerfully embedded in the culture of academic institutions, as reflected in graduate training programs across the disciplines that specialize in either quantitative or qualitative methods ... we need training programs that will build capacity among the next generation of policy researchers in both qualitative and quantitative methods. (p. 202)

We agree with Burch and Heinrich (2016) that graduate programs need to incorporate coursework on both quantitative and qualitative methodologies. Given the value-added that mixed methods research contributes to policy research (Hendren et al., 2018), doctoral education training programs should include instruction on MMR and policy research. It is unclear how common mixed methods coursework is in doctoral education programs and public policy programs, given a dearth of extant research on the topic. That said, in their study of 20 top-ranked doctoral education programs in the United States, Capraro and Thompson (2008) found that none of them required mixed methods coursework. A 2015 study by Leech and Haug of graduate research coursework across 28 U.S. institutions did not even collect data on mixed methods coursework.

Given that the rise of mixed methods research began in earnest around 2006 and that scientific institutionalization (e.g., journals, associations, textbooks, handbooks, and readers) tends to precede academic institutionalization (e.g., degrees, faculty, and curricula; Timons et al., 2019), we speculate that the academic institutionalization of mixed methods, in the form of coursework requirements, is still a work in progress. As such, education doctoral programs that do not as of yet include mixed methods research and policy research coursework could make MMR a component of a course on policy research or—conversely—policy research could be taught as a component of a course on MMR. As we consider ways to make policy research more accessible to a variety of policy actors, we also realize the importance of changing some of the andragogical strategies used in university classrooms and in-service professional development. Future training must include explicit attention to how policy research can be designed to support policy impact (Burch & Heinrich, 2016).

Finally, but not exhaustively, future research should identify exemplary university programs that have managed to move beyond the politicization of research collection tools, communicate the value of different research methods for different purposes, and offer mixed methods as a legitimate approach to policy-related theses, capstone, and dissertation work. We recommend that exemplars serve not just to legitimate but to *prioritize* mixed methods as a key tool for conducting policy relevant research for school improvement where communication with policymakers and school stakeholders is key to interpreting and using research findings.

REFERENCES

Amrein-Beardsley, A. (2014). *Rethinking value-added models in education: Critical perspectives on tests and assessment-based accountability*. Routledge.

Bryman, A. (2006). Integrating quantitative and qualitative research: How is it done? *Qualitative Research, 6*(1), 97–113. https://doi.org/10.1177/1468794106058877

Burch, P., & Heinrich, C. J. (2016). *Mixed methods for policy research and program evaluation.* SAGE.

Capraro, R. M., & Thompson, B. (2008). The educational researcher defined: What will future researchers be trained to do? *The Journal of Educational Research, 101*(4), 247–253.

Cowie, M., & Crawford, M. (2007). Principal preparation—still an act of faith? *School Leadership & Management, 27*(2), 129–146. https://doi.org/10.1080/13632430701237198

Creswell, J. W., & Clark, V. L. P. (2011). *Designing and conducting mixed methods research* (2nd ed.). SAGE.

Curry, L. & Nunez-Smith, M. (2015). *Mixed methods in health sciences research: A practical primer.* SAGE http://dx.doi.org/10.4135/9781483390659

Datnow, A. & Park, V. (2009). Conceptualizing policy implementation: Large-scale reform in an era of complexity. In G. Sykes, B. Schneider, & D. N. Plank (with Ford, T. G.) (Eds.) *Handbook of education policy research* (pp. 348–361). Routledge.

Firestone, W. A. (1987). Meaning in methods: The rhetoric of quantitative and qualitative research. *Educational Researcher, 16*(7), 16–21.

Greene, J. C., Caracelli, V. J., & Graham, W. F. (1989). Toward a conceptual framework for mixed-methods evaluation designs. *Education Evaluation and Policy Analysis, 11*(3), 255–274.

Harris, D. N., & Herrington, C. D. (2015). The use of teacher value-added measures in schools: New evidence, unanswered questions, and future prospects. *Educational Researcher, 44*(2), 71–76. https://doi.org/10.3102/0013189X15576142

Hendren, K., Luo, Q. E., & Pandey, S. K. (2018). The state of mixed methods research in public administration and public policy. *Public Administration Review, 78*(6), 904–916.

Hewitt, K. K. (2015). Educator evaluation policy that incorporates EVAAS value-added measures: Undermined intentions and exacerbated inequities. *Education Policy Analysis Archives, 23*(76), 1–49.

Hewitt, K. K., & Amrein-Beardsley, A. (Eds.). (2016). *Student growth measures in policy and practice—Intended and unintended consequences of high-stakes teacher evaluations.* Palgrave Macmillan.

Holloway-Libell, J., & Amrein-Beardsley, A. (2015). "Truths" devoid of empirical proof: Underlying assumptions surrounding value-added models in teacher evaluation. *Teachers College Record*, (ID#: 18008), 1–10. http://www.tcrecord.org/Content.asp?ContentId=18008

Honig, M. (2009). What works in defining "what works" in educational improvement: Lessons from education policy implementation research, directions for future research. In G. Sykes, B. Schneider, & D. N. Plank (with T. G. Ford) (Eds.), *Handbook of education policy research* (pp. 333–347). Routledge.

Howe, K. R. (1988). Against the quantitative-qualitative incompatibility thesis, or, Dogmas die hard. *Educational Research, 17*(8), 10–16.

Koyama, J., & Chang, E. (2019). Schools as refuge? The politics and policy of educating refugees in Arizona. *Educational Policy, 33*(1), 136–157.

Johnson, R. B., & Onwuegbuzie, A. J. (2004). Mixed methods research: A research paradigm whose time has come. *Educational Researcher, 33*(7), 14–26.

Leech, N. L., & Haug, C. A. (2015). Investigating graduate level research and statistics courses in schools of education. *International Journal of Doctoral Studies, 10*, 93–110. http://ijds.org/Volume10/IJDSv10p093-110Leech0658.pdf

Madey, D. L. (1982). Some benefits of integrating qualitative and quantitative methods in program evaluation, with illustrations. *Educational Evaluation and Policy Analysis, 4*(2), 223–236.

Mertens, D., & Wilson, A. (2012). *Program evaluation theory and practice: A comprehensive guide*. Guilford Press.

Morgan, D. L. (2007). Paradigms lost and pragmatism regained: Methodological implications of combining qualitative and quantitative methods. *Journal of Mixed Methods Research, 1*(1), 48–76. https://doi.org/10.1177/2345678906292462

Onwuegbuzie, A. J., & Leech, N. L. (2005). On becoming a pragmatic researcher: The importance of combining quantitative and qualitative research methodologies. *International Journal of Social Research Methodology, 8*(5), 375–387.

Pallas, A. M. (2001). Preparing education doctoral students for epistemological diversity. *Educational Researcher, 30*(5), 6–11.

Sale, J. E. M., Johfeld, L. H., & Brazil, K. (2002). Revisiting the quantitative-qualitative debate: Implications for mixed-methods research. *Quality & Quantity, 36*, 43–53.

Spillane, J. P., Shirrell, M., & Adhikari, S. (2018). Constructing "experts" among peers: Educational infrastructure, test data, and teachers' interactions about teaching. *Educational Evaluation and Policy Analysis, 40*(4), 586–612. https://doi.org/10.3102/0162373718785764

Slater, C. L., Garduno, J. M. G., & Mentz, K. (2018). Frameworks for principal preparation and leadership development: Contributions of the International Study of Principal Preparation (ISPP). *Management in Education, 32*(3), 126–134.

Tashakkori, A., & Teddlie, C. (2003). *Handbook of mixed methods in social and behavior research*. SAGE.

Teddlie, C., & Tashakkori, A. (2003). Major issues and controversies in the use of mixed methods in the social and behavioral sciences. In A. Tashakkori & C. Teddlie (Eds.) *Handbook of mixed methods in social and behavior research* (pp. 3–50). SAGE.

Timans, R., Wouters, P., & Heilbron, J. (2019). Mixed methods research: What it is and what it could be. *Theory and Society, 48*(2), 193–216.

Weaver-Hightower, M. B. (2014). A mixed methods approach for identifying influence on public policy. *Journal of Mixed Methods Research, 8*(2), 115–138.

Weimer, D. L. (2009). Making education research more policy-analytic. In G. Sykes, B. Schneider, & D. N. Plank (with T. G. Ford) (Eds.), *Handbook of education policy research* (pp. 93–100). Routledge.

Welton, A. D., Mansfield, K. C., Lee, P. L., & Young, M. D. (2015). Mentoring educational leadership doctoral students: Using methodological diversification to examine gender and identity intersections. *International Journal of Educational Leadership Preparation, 10*(2), 53-81.

White, B. R., Pareja, A. S., Hart, H., Klostermann, B. K., Huynh, M. H., Frazier-Meyers, M., & Holt, J. K. (2016). *Navigating the shift to intensive principal preparation in Illinois: An in-depth look at stakeholder perspectives* (IERC 2016-2). Illinois Education Research Council at Southern Illinois University.

NOTES

1. Surveys can contain quantitative (closed items), qualitative (open-ended items), or mixed items. Koyama and Chang (2019) categorized their survey as quantitative.
2. An executive summary is an abridged version of a longer report designed to allow readers quickly to become familiar with a large body of material without having to read the final report in its entirety.

CHAPTER 8

THE POTENTIAL FOR IMPROVEMENT SCIENCE AND RESEARCH PARTNERSHIPS TO MAXIMIZE THE POLICY RELEVANCE OF SCHOOL IMPROVEMENT RESEARCH

Sarah Winchell Lenhoff, Jeremy Singer, and Ben Pogodzinski
Wayne State University

Increased demands by policymakers for evidence-based practices and rigorous impact evaluations in education offer researchers an unprecedented opportunity to influence policy (Tseng, 2012). Yet, academic research has an infamous reputation for not addressing the real problems of policy and practice (Bevan, 2017; López Turley & Stevens, 2015; Polikoff & Conway, 2018; Thompson et al., 2017), being difficult to understand (Penuel et al., 2018), and being slow to adapt to changing circumstances in implementation (Penuel et al., 2015; Polikoff & Conway, 2018). The increasing complexity of the educational policy landscape (Lubienski, 2018) threatens to exacerbate the disconnect between researchers and policymakers. Researchers interested in school improvement cannot

Maximizing the Policy Relevance of Research for School Improvement, pp. 189–216
Copyright © 2021 by Information Age Publishing
All rights of reproduction in any form reserved.

be content to "illuminate and critique these processes of knowledge production and use;" rather, we must seek ways to "become more effective operators within the knowledge-exchange environments that surround contemporary policymaking" (Lupton & Hayes, 2018, p. 203).

This chapter addresses Lupton and Hayes's (2018) call for educational researchers "to develop our own pedagogical dispositions and strategies towards policymaking" (p. 203) by considering the opportunities offered by improvement science and research partnerships. Both improvement science and research-practice partnerships (RPPs) are increasingly popular approaches to improving practices within schools, and a growing body of research demonstrates their potential to improve educational outcomes (see Bryk et al., 2015; Coburn & Penuel, 2016). Little research has investigated how these approaches might be beneficial in improving the quality and influence of research itself. By turning these approaches inward, can researchers use the principles of improvement science and RPPs to maximize the policy-relevance of school improvement research?

We seek to address this question in three parts. We begin this chapter with a review of the literature on improvement science and RPPs, and we consider how their core principles align with the interests of researchers seeking to produce policy-relevant work. Then, we analyze the key opportunities and challenges of enacting these principles by reflecting on our own research partnership grounded in improvement science. We conclude with important lessons for researchers who seek to influence policy through partnerships and suggest directions for future research and applications of improvement science in policy-focused research teams.

POLICYMAKERS, RESEARCHERS, AND RESEARCH USE IN EDUCATION

Education is a complicated field for the use of research in policymaking. Because education is inherently ideological, policymakers may be particularly skeptical of empirical claims (Lubienski, 2018). Further, ideology, politics, and power play significant roles in shaping both the production of educational research and how different types of knowledge are valued in the field of education (Lupton & Hayes, 2018; Gerrard, 2015). Practitioners often react with skepticism to research and evidence that is not specific to their context, and sparse social networks among and between educators can weaken the uptake of research (Daly et al., 2014; Finnigan et al., 2013).

The terrain for research-use in educational policymaking has only become more complex with the shift from "government" to "governance" and the increasing influence of a variety of non-governmental actors (Scott et al., 2017). Intermediary organizations, which "seek to assemble, interpret, and advance information for policymakers to use in the policymaking process," often "operate in a space largely removed from more traditional forms of expertise, with increasingly obsolete forms of quality control to evaluate information claims" (Lubienski, 2018, pp. 160–161). The growing influence of intermediary organizations (e.g., research consortia, advocacy groups, and education-focused philanthropies) (Scott et al., 2017; Tseng, 2012) signals a disruption to the "iron-triangle" of interest groups, the Department of Education, and Congressional committees in education policymaking (Scott & Jabbar, 2014) as well as a decrease in the influence of school boards and other traditional policymakers (Henig, 2013). As a result, "an infrastructure of rapid production and dissemination of data," has given policymakers more opportunities than ever to learn about research evidence and apply that learning in their policymaking (Lubienski, 2018, p. 157).

Empirical research casts doubt, however, on whether knowledge that passes through this information landscape is actually used by policymakers. For instance, studying the policy landscape in New Orleans, Jabbar et. al (2015) "found that policymakers primarily used personal anecdotes to justify their position and explain the success of reforms, and they relied on blogs or non-peer-reviewed sources for background information" (p. 1). These dynamics are further complicated by their local contexts. From place to place, levels of cohesiveness, consensus, mobilization, resource allocation, and trust between key policy actors can vary widely (Lubienski, 2018; Scott et al., 2017), making studies of research use difficult to generalize to other contexts, with different policy players and histories. Thus, although there is an unprecedented stated demand and opportunity for research-based policies, the complexities of the current educational policymaking landscape threaten to expand the divide between researchers and policymakers.

In addition, while researchers might use the terms "research" and "evidence" interchangeably, policymakers often define evidence beyond "empirical findings derived from scientific methods"—including student achievement data, expert testimony, practitioner knowledge, community input, personal experiences, experiences of others, and constituent feedback (Tseng, 2012, p. 6). This tendency toward a broad definition of evidence carries risks, as policymakers and educational leaders consider investing in programs and policies that claim to be research-based (Penuel et al., 2018). Intermediary organizations with a high degree of influence and access to policymakers and educational leaders exacerbate these risks as they offer their own data, which may be inappropriately conflated with professional judgment and ultimately yield to ideological commitments (Trujillo, 2014).

Importantly, barriers to high-quality research use do not solely arise from the policymaking side. Indeed, Farley-Ripple et al. (2018) conceptualize a bidirectional gap between communities of research and practice, pointing to competing assumptions and perspectives on the products, inquiry, problems, structures, and processes of knowledge use (see Dunn, 1980) that can grow or shrink the gap along six different dimensions of "depth," from the conceptualization of research design through the use of evidence at the decision-making stage. Tseng (2012) argues that "connecting research and practice should be more of a two-way street" (p. 6) and points toward defining, acquiring, interpreting, and using research as four areas where research producers and research users diverge. However, academics have tended to operate under a producer-push model (Nutley et al., 2007) that shifts responsibility for policy learning from research producers onto research users. As Lupton and Hayes (2018) note, researchers use these "traditional modes of academic dissemination" to "'throw it over the wall' and see what gets picked up, and complain that our lack of influence is someone else's fault" (p. 203). This mode of operating has left researchers with a poor understanding of how policymakers "pull" research (Dearing & Kreuter, 2010) and ultimately undermines efforts to create policy-relevant research.

IMPROVEMENT SCIENCE AND THE POLICY RELEVANCE OF RESEARCH

The emergence of improvement science in education research has introduced new frameworks within which academic researchers can expand the policy relevance of their work and develop common practices for making research more relevant across contexts (Lewis, 2015). Improvement science is a theory of improvement that gained popularity in the medical field as a way to develop quality improvements in common practices, such as how to respond to potential cardiac arrests (Berwick, 2008). The auto industry has also embraced improvement science as a way to systematically improve efficiency and productivity (Womack & Jones, 2003).

As an approach to continuous improvement, improvement science is organized around identifying problems in work processes that are associated with key outcomes. By systematically designing improvements to those work processes, testing innovations, making adjustments based on evidence, and implementing the innovations in more and varied contexts, workers may be able to improve desired outcomes at scale (Bryk et al., 2015; Grunow et al., 2018). This approach to improvement is a complement to large-scale impact evaluations that rely on fidelity in implementing a common reform model across many sites. While these evaluations are useful for understanding the average impact of a reform, they have been critiqued for their lack of usefulness in early stages of improvement and their inattention to uneven implementation or necessary adaptations (Peurach et al., 2016).

Researchers have promoted several methods to enact improvement science, such as networked improvement communities (Bryk et al., 2015), design-based implementation research (Fishman et al., 2013), and Six Sigma (Aboelmaged & Lichtman, 2010). A set of core principles links these and other continuous improvement methods together: (a) systems, rather than individuals, create outcomes; (b) processes within systems can be changed to improve outcomes; (c) improvement requires "collective learning and discovery;" (d) the people who are directly responsible for the practices that need improving are in the best position to identify problems and potential solutions; and (e) effective practices are eventually codified into "standard work processes" throughout the system (Grunow et al., 2018, p. 12).

The principles of improvement science lend themselves to collaborative work between researchers and practitioners. As researchers seek to inform educational improvement, they can support teams of educators by bringing research evidence to bear in designing changes to practice, introducing tools of measurement to track progress, and evaluating implementation of scale-up across sites (Cohen-Vogel et al., 2014). There are several examples of successful practice improvements that have emerged out of these types of research partnerships, including improving developmental mathematics instruction in community colleges (Edwards et al., 2015; Gomez et al., 2015), strengthening the early career experiences of teachers (Hannan et al., 2015), and designing professional supports for the enactment of the Next Generation Science Standards (Anderson et al., 2018).

In most examples of continuous improvement in education, the principles of improvement are used to support the design, measurement, and scale up of instructional innovations in classrooms. This makes sense: improving the "core of educational practice" is both essential and historically very difficult (Elmore, 1996, p. 2). Yet, many of the most persistent problems in education stem from structural and social issues that require large-scale policy changes. To strengthen the ability of researchers to influence system-level policy changes, the research process itself may benefit from a disciplined inquiry approach, grounded in the principles of improvement science. For education researchers, producing policy-relevant research could be conceived as an *outcome* that is produced through *processes* within their *practice* as researchers. Framing the work of researchers in this way allows us to consider how to organize research teams with a continuous improvement management philosophy, drawing on the tools and methods of improvement science to get better at producing policy-relevant research.

A commitment to the core principles of improvement science in education policy poses a challenge to policymakers. Policymakers must actively resist the tendency of "going fast and learning slow," in favor of modest and gradual policy increments informed by "learning quickly and cheaply ... while also generating empirical guidance as to what to try next" (Bryk et al., 2015, pp. 6, 16). Further, education policymakers must resist the silver-bullet thinking pervasive in contemporary policymaking (see Peck & Theodore, 2015) and must consider not only what works on average but also what works for whom and under what conditions. Indeed, as Bryk et al. (2015) argue, "quality improvement challenges policy actors toward more prudent aspirations" and to "recognize the limits of what they actually know and are able to directly affect in a complex system" (p. 191).

Likewise, improvement science may prompt researchers to address the dispositional barriers that can diminish the policy relevance of their work. Academic researchers are likely to hesitate to move beyond uncertainties (Heimans & Singh, 2018; Polikoff & Conaway, 2018) and may point to instances where certain types of evidence do not necessarily form a good basis for decision making (e.g., Sanderson, 2003; Simons, 2003). They are reluctant to offer a decisive recommendation (Polikoff & Conway, 2018), and often proceed slowly through cycles of inquiry and analysis before recommending action (Penuel et al., 2015). While improvement science prompts policymakers to slow down, it prompts researchers to speed up. As policymakers embrace a more prudent policy approach, researchers must embrace "unforesee-ability" in education research (Heimans & Singh, 2018) and the reality that "failures are unavoidable when one is trying to change complex social systems" (Bryk et al., 2015, p. 179). Thus, researchers must be willing to make specific and concrete recommendations to policymakers as an ongoing part of the policymaking process (Polikoff & Conway, 2018).

In addition, improvement science may help address the structural barriers that researchers face in seeking to make their work more useful and relevant for policymakers. Researchers are not always interested in questions that would yield the most actionable information for practitioners and policymakers (Thompson et al., 2017), and research that is valued in academia is often not the most useful research for practitioners and policymakers (Bevan, 2017; Lubienski, 2018; Penuel et al., 2018). Indeed, the primacy many universities put on "intellectually interesting questions" and academic publications can disincentivize researchers from pursuing applied work (López Turley & Stevens, 2015). Improvement science may help researchers take a problem-specific and user-centric approach that prioritizes the needs of practitioners and policymakers. In doing so, it may encourage universities to "embrace a mission that directs intellectual resources both to advancing basic understanding about education problems and actively contributing to their solutions" (Bryk et al., 2015, p. 190).

Adopting principles of improvement science that school improvement researchers have increasingly promoted for practitioners and policy-makers may help them advance the policy relevance of their research. These principles call upon researchers interested in informing policy to ask "three core improvement questions" about their own work: "What is the specific problem I am now trying to solve? What change might I introduce and why? And, how will I know whether the change is actually an improvement?" (Bryk et al., 2015, p. 9). On one hand, these questions—and a deliberate commitment to the principles of improvement science that they necessitate—may offer a starting point for researchers as they develop dispositions and strategies to influence policy. However, the professional incentives, training, and interests of researchers pose threats to the use of improvement science to inform policy-relevant work in traditional research institutions. One long-term goal of this project is to explore the possibilities of orienting university-based research activities around the principles of improvement science and documenting the challenges and opportunities in that approach within both the policy sphere and our professional outlets.

RESEARCH PARTNERSHIPS AND THE POLICY-RELEVANCE OF RESEARCH

Research-practice partnerships (RPPs) in education also offer a useful set of principles and practices for advancing the policy-relevance of research (Farrell et al., 2018). Coburn and Penuel (2016) note that many forms of partnerships exist between researchers and practitioners and define RPPs as one "very specific form of partnership" (p. 49) with a set of distinguishing features (see Coburn et al., 2013). In contrast to "smash-and-grab" or one-off arrangements between researchers and practitioners (Bevan, 2017), RPPs are long-term: "researchers and system leaders share an open ended commitment to build and sustain a working collaboration over multiple projects" (Coburn & Penuel, 2016, p. 49). Aligned with the principles of improvement science, RPPs set their research priorities based on challenges that practitioners face, rather than gaps in existing theory or research (Coburn & Penuel, 2016; Coburn et al., 2013).

The emphasis on practitioner needs does not mean that RPPs simply reverse the one-directional relationship between researchers and practitioners. Rather, as Penuel et al. (2015) theorize, RPPs represent "joint work at boundaries"—"both district goals for improvement and aspects of the research are defined and evolve through interaction, rather than being planned fully ahead of time or defined by either researchers or practitioners independently of one another" (p. 183). In this way, RPPs challenge the translation metaphor that the research community has predominantly used to characterize the gap between research and practice (Penuel et al., 2015). Penuel et al. note that framing the gap between research and practice as a problem of translation inappropriately depicts the work of bridging that gap as a directional movement from research to practice. Further, they demonstrate that the translation metaphor inaccurately describes when interventions and programs are replicated in new settings, betrays the possibility of mutualism and reciprocity, and offers too narrow a conception of research use by practitioners. Indeed, RPPs produce original analyses of data, going "beyond the focus of many current organizations on making data accessible to district leaders" (Coburn et al., 2013, p. 4).

The long-term, responsive, and jointly negotiated nature of RPPs serve as an important complement to the principles of improvement science. Improvement science maintains that "it is essential that all involved in the work be active agents in its improvement" (Bryk et al., 2015, p. 34). Because researchers' social networks of influence tend to be removed from the levers of power in policymaking, RPPs are important for creating the circumstances that make such collaboration possible (Boyask & Vigurs, 2018). Researchers in RPPs can use improvement science to more actively and effectively engage with those decision-makers when preparing, conducting, and disseminating research.

Against the backdrop of a highly complex and contentious educational policymaking landscape, the structure of RPPs can help researchers and policymakers productively engage each other in the research and policymaking process (Lubienski, 2018). As joint work at boundaries, RPPs push researchers and practitioners to define, acknowledge, and cross boundaries that are cultural, professional, and organizational as well as navigate the political context in which those boundaries are situated (Coburn & Penuel, 2016; Penuel et al., 2015). Penuel et al. (2015) call for RPPs to employ "boundary practices"—"new routines that bridge the practices of researchers and those of practitioners as they engage in joint work" (p. 190)—that reframe the surfacing of cultural differences and conflict inherent in "boundary crossing" as a routine part of practice that can productively contribute to the partnership's success. The pervasive challenges of turnover, political tension, and shifting priorities in education threaten the ability of researchers and policymakers to engage in disciplined cycles of inquiry (Thompson et al., 2017). However, as researchers and practitioners jointly negotiate their work, they develop a stronger commitment to partnership and the production of research for informing improvements (Farrell et al., 2018; Bevan et al., 2015).

Further, these intentional strategies for boundary-crossing play an important role in establishing and maintaining the mutual benefit for researchers and policymakers. Partnerships between researchers and policymakers in education offer tremendous benefits for both parties, because each party's needs and assets complement each other (López Turley & Stevens, 2015). The possibility for mutual benefit in these partnerships can be disrupted, however, by diverging interests and issues of power and voice (Bevan, 2017; Conaway et al., 2015; Thompson et al., 2017). The RPP principles of jointly negotiated work and shared authority can help establish a relationship between researchers and policymakers in which "the problem being addressed and the opportunity to work together is seen as benefiting both parties equally if not identically" (Bevan, 2017, p. 139).

While a growing body of research demonstrates that RPPs lead to effective educational interventions (see Coburn & Penuel, 2016), important questions remain unanswered. As Coburn and Penuel (2016) note, "Most research on the outcomes of RPPs in education and other fields has focused on the impact of interventions developed in the context of a partnership. Thus, they do not investigate the impact of the partnership itself or other outcomes of RPPs" (p. 49). More research is needed on the effect of participating in RPPs on practitioners' and policymakers' understanding of the research process or the value of research in decision-making, and whether they further disseminate and scale-up the innovations they codesign (Coburn & Penuel, 2016). Notably, the literature on RPPs inadequately addresses their ability to promote greater knowledge use by practitioners and policymakers. Coburn and Penuel (2016) note that "there is mixed evidence about whether participation in partnerships is associated with increased use of this research for making decisions" (p. 50) and argue that "we need to better understand when and under what conditions RPPs foster research use and when they do not" (p. 51).

These gaps in the literature are even more pronounced when considering partnerships that focus on influencing educational policy rather than educational practice. These partnerships can exist at the district level (e.g., the Houston Education Research Consortium), city level (e.g., Education Research Alliance for New Orleans), or the state level (e.g., Policy Analysis for California Education). Some of these partnerships assess and offer recommendations for a broad range of educational policies (e.g., Michigan Consortium for Educational Research), while others focus more narrowly on a particular policy issue (e.g., Massachusetts Consortium for Innovative Education Assessment). Studying these partnerships is complicated by the blurred distinction between researchers and policymakers. While researchers and practitioners are more easily sorted into two distinct communities (see Farley-Ripple et al., 2018), foundations and intermediary organizations can be both the "hubs" of an educational research and policymaking landscape, as well as "spokes" that produce their own educational research and lobby for particular policies that they favor (Scott & Jabbar, 2014). Indeed, our own research partnership (the Detroit Education Research Partnership) is supported by a Detroit-based foundation that also produces and disseminates its own research and is one of the primary stakeholders represented in a new quasi-governmental policymaking group organized by the Detroit mayor. The lack of research on the impact of such partnerships—as well as the extent to which their research is relevant to policymakers and the mechanisms through which it successfully influences research-use in policymaking—point to an opportunity for research that considers whether the principles of improvement science and RPPs can help advance the policy relevance and use of research produced by those partnerships.

THE CASE OF THE DETROIT EDUCATION RESEARCH PARTNERSHIP

We explore the potential for improvement science and RPPs to maximize the policy relevance of education research by reflectively examining the case of our own research partnership, the Detroit Education Research Partnership. The hub of our partnership is the Wayne State University College of Education (WSU) in Detroit, Michigan. The Detroit Public Schools Community District (DPSCD) became a formal research partner with WSU in 2017 and a citywide steering committee focused on reducing chronic absenteeism, called Every School Day Counts Detroit, joined the partnership in 2018. Although these institutions constitute the formal partners, the policymaking and advocacy audiences for our research also included grassroots community organizing group 482Forward, Detroit's branch of the Campaign for Grade Level Reading, and the public-private Community Education Commission (CEC) formed by Mayor Duggan. The latter brings together educational, non-profit, and business leaders from across the city, including the superintendent of DPSCD and a leader in Detroit's charter school community. The Michigan branch of the American Federation of Teachers, Michigan Department of Education, and the Skillman Foundation also have representatives on the board. The Skillman Foundation is one of the funders of our partnership and has played a significant role in education policymaking in Detroit for the last two decades. Most recently, the foundation was the organizing hub for the Coalition for the Future of Detroit Schoolchildren, which issued recommendations for citywide school reform when Detroit Public Schools was near bankruptcy in 2015. One specific recommendation was for the creation of a commission similar to the CEC that would manage accountability, openings, and closures for all Detroit public schools (Lenhoff et al., 2019).

Unlike RPPs that are focused on specific problems of classroom- or school-level practice, our RPP might better be called a "research policy partnership." Although policy partnerships share many principles with

RPPs, they differ in important ways. Rather than focus on one school or school system, the goal of research policy partnerships is to produce research that informs broad improvements across educational systems. Our partnership, for instance, is designed to inform citywide policy in order to improve educational conditions and, in turn, outcomes for Detroit students, with a specific focus on reducing chronic absenteeism and improving the quality and stability of city schools. That means that our research must be useful not only for the traditional public-school district, but also for the more than 50,000 Detroit students who attend either public schools in other districts or charter schools in and outside the city limits.

We have organized our research policy partnership around a continuous improvement framework, borrowing key concepts and organizational routines from improvement science in education. In order to "learn fast" about what to study and how best to communicate our findings to partners, we have focused our attention on high-leverage practices for improving our key outcome—the relevance of our research for policy decision-making in Detroit. This means, for instance, that although we recognize that politics shapes policymaking, the focus of our improvement work is not changing political loyalties in the Detroit education landscape. By developing organizational routines, like reflective memo-writing after meetings with external partners and plan-do-study-act (PDSA) cycles to determine and measure changes in our practice, we have begun implementing elements of improvement science to serve as a method for improving the policy relevance of research in complicated political landscapes.

Because there are no existing models for how to incorporate improvement science into the enhancement of research partnership activities, we approached our work with some organizing principles and structures that allowed us to get feedback, learn, adapt, and hopefully improve over time: (a) we consider the needs, priorities, and levers for change available to all of our policymaking partners when deciding what to study; (b) how we communicate our research is shaped by the diversity of our partners and their potential use cases; (c) we collect data from our partners to measure our success in providing research that can inform policy improvements; and (d) we adapt our research, communication, and outreach practices based on the data we collect. Coming out of the first year of our RPP, we learned many lessons from the improvement science and partnership process we applied. In the following sections, we share what we learned from our partners, how we approached adaptation, and our reflections on what this means for this approach both in our context and in the broader field.

REFLECTIONS ON USING IMPROVEMENT SCIENCE AND RPPS IN DETROIT

During the 2018–19 school year, we collected feedback from our partners to inform improvement in our research practices and to generate new knowledge on the efficacy of improvement science and research partnerships for informing policy. These data were generated through 11 semistructured interviews with representatives from partner organizations, meeting minutes from 13 internal research meetings, online feedback surveys from 31 respondents, and reflective memos from nine meetings with key policymakers or influencers in Detroit, including the CEC, the Skillman Foundation, the mayor's office, and several nonprofit education groups. These data were used to help us reflect on how we were fulfilling the goal of our partnership and whether the research we were producing was relevant to the policymakers who were closest to the problems we investigated. This process allowed us to consider new ways of organizing our work and communicating with our partners. The following sections report on what we heard and how we responded to this feedback by adapting our research design and communication activities in subsequent studies.

Who Are Our Partners and What Do They Need?

What We Heard

In Detroit, the Skillman-backed Coalition for the Future of Detroit Schoolchildren recently issued a report with sweeping recommendations for how Detroit educators, policymakers, and community members should be working together to improve education in the city. Focused on improving early literacy, school attendance, and systems coordination, the report created incentives for the creation and philanthropic support of several new or emerging education-focused organizations, including some of our partners. One partner told us that the early stage of these organizations was one reason why our work was important:

> Especially when you look at the newness of so many of the institutions that were being built: 313Reads, Every School Day Counts—not new, but still reforming in a new context—DPSCD, CEC. How can you be providing them and equipping them in a capacity that they need to be able to really understand and do an analysis of their work in the context of what's actually happening with Detroit kids? That's why I think it's so important and what our working theory was around it.

The same partner went on to describe the needs of one of these groups, the CEC:

> I think ... it's being grounded in the reality, and so really making sure that they're using data and research to understand the context and the problems that they're trying to solve. I think us, that have been staring at these things, or working on these things for years, have an inherent understanding of some of the patterns that happen in the kids' lives and how they interact with the school district.

For this stakeholder, one essential need was for key policy partners to be brought into the community of stakeholders who had been working on educational problems in Detroit for years. These new actors, many of whom were in formal positions of power, did not always understand the history of Detroit educational reform or the context in which many Detroit students have attended school. Another partner echoed this concern, saying how important research was in filling knowledge gaps among key stakeholders who might be making policy decisions, such as members of the mayor's staff or people involved in the CEC.

At the same time, our research policy partnership needed to fill the role of more traditional research entities, such as answering questions that school districts do not have the capacity to answer. A school district leader told us that their team "can't address everything that we want to," so they see a benefit to "research partners who are aligned around helping us address other areas of our strategic planning or our goals." Many of the partners we spoke to expressed the need for our work to answer many questions, across audiences and for different purposes. One community partner told us how they hoped our exploration could help shift the narrative around research and data in education, from punitive accountability measures to useful information:

> When I think of, especially your research, it's like, it's informative to, like where it can be an indicator for so many things, and ... people who are in schools currently, teachers, the union, like the principals, and like allowing people to see data not just as a punitive. Because I think that's like, that has been something harped into, not just to ... our public education systems in general, in Michigan and across the country, of like, there's no real incentive to look at research with a lens of like, "I'm not going to be fired. This doesn't define me."

One of our partners told us they heard someone in the mayor's office say that our research "was changing the way that we're thinking." The partner went on to say, "To me, that's what success is looking like, is through this process, people are feeling of value, are changing the way that they're thinking, and are feeling more informed about what they're working on." A key lever aiding our ability to inform multiple audiences was our orientation toward improvement science. One partner mentioned this in their response to a question about how we will know we are successful:

> Because you have to remember, in what you're doing, everyone's now thinking about ... you know? That's the whole continuous improvement part. I think you're being really successful. And I also think part of it is for you to reflect on, "What value am I bringing? And what value could I bring after doing this?"

These sentiments were also reflected in our feedback survey data, where 83% of respondents agreed with the statement "I learned a lot from this research." In addition, participants responded to the question "What new questions do you have about education in Detroit after learning about this research?" with questions about whether a common curriculum might help mitigate the impact of mobility and what interventions could help to end chronic absenteeism. One respondent said:

> I would like to see more information about school culture, teacher tenure, academic climate, etc. I am interested in how behavior impacts absence and school mobility, particularly considering how that school responds/manages behavior issues. Similarly, in the world of positive youth development, we think in terms of risk factors and protective factors—is there a way to study the protective factors that might reduce rates of chronic absence and/or school exit? How does the existence of special needs/learning disabilities impact absences and student mobility?

This type of feedback encouraged us to continue giving explicit attention to improving our practice as a research collaborator via the lens of our partners. Further, statements like these suggested an increasing alignment with our partners, in terms of valuing our research and the process we collectively used to produce, disseminate, and improve research.

How Feedback Shaped Adaptation

The feedback that our research should be useful for a broad array of stakeholders led us to consider how to shape our topics and communication to reach audiences that are multidimensional—spanning school systems, municipal government, advocacy groups, and the community at large. While formal partnership with one or two key educational institutions was important to gain legitimacy in the policy landscape and identify the most pressing questions, these institutions could not be the only audiences for our research. Policy change occurs over time and through the sometimes uncoordinated work of multiple actors at different levels of the system (Baumgartner & Jones, 2010; Marsh & Wohlstetter, 2013). For instance, we began this stage of the RPP thinking of the CEC as the primary policy-influencing body. However, the CEC itself represents multiple institutions (e.g., traditional public-school system, charter schools, parents, philanthropy) and, therefore, its members have varying needs. At the same time, the CEC is but one policy-influencing organization. In the Detroit context, grassroots community groups are also very important in shaping the conditions for and promoting specific policy changes. Given the highly volatile political context—with Detroit Public Schools recently released from emergency management and the city just a few years out of municipal bankruptcy—local organizing groups are some of the most stable and consistent education-focused entities in the city.

Thus, rather than bidirectional (Farley-Ripple et al., 2018), we increasingly began to think about the ways in which our research policy partnership needed to be multidirectional. Multiple audiences, or partners, in our research required us to be disciplined in learning about the perspectives, areas of concerns, and levers for change that existed within our policy environment. Proactively engaging partners in determining a research agenda is a key principle of RPPs (Coburn et al., 2013), yet this process became both more essential and more challenging in a complex policy environment with changing centers of policy activity.

Feedback from our partners spurred us to reconsider how to communicate with the multiple audiences for our work and to consider their different potential use cases. For instance, one of our initial research projects was a study of chronic absenteeism in Detroit schools. Our DPSCD partners wanted detailed information on barriers to attendance in particular neighborhoods and schools, as well as student subgroup data to help them refine their approach to reducing absenteeism. While we created research products that helped DPSCD leaders with their needs, we also created different ways of presenting our research findings for our CEC partners, who were interested in which neighborhoods had the most potential for a new public-charter bus loop. These partners did not initially see how chronic absenteeism research would be helpful to their goals. However, when we presented data that showed neighborhood characteristics with chronic absence rates and student exit rates side-by-side, they could see the connection between these issues. Months later, our CEC partners requested additional data on chronic absenteeism across the city, suggesting that we were successful in communicating our findings effectively to this audience. Based on this feedback, we have also adjusted our approach to research reporting, focusing on more frequent short policy briefs that will allow us to tailor reports for specific audiences without having to make every report useful for every stakeholder.

The Complexities of "Neutrality"

What We Heard

Although many partners acknowledged that no one can ever be truly objective or neutral, several told us that it was important that we represented a perspective that was perceived as unbiased with regard to what research and data indicates are key policy problems and potential solutions in Detroit. For instance, one partner mentioned how some of the policymakers had already invested in pilots of potential policy reforms, so "these interventions that are actually tied more personally to them, ... I mean can anyone look at data from a not, like, objective lens? But, especially when you want something. Especially when something was formed around an individual project." This stakeholder argued that having a research partner that was not invested in any particular policy outcome was beneficial in bringing more objective evidence to bear on policy problems. Contrasting our approach to that of other research teams, this partner's comments reflected that the ways we "jointly negotiated" the research process contributed to a greater degree of trust in us and our work.

Similarly, another partner framed our work within the context of mistrust among many community members after years of state control of DPSCD and the proliferation of charter schools, noting:

> You're also providing a neutral perspective for them to be able to interpret and share their individual perspectives. That creates almost like a mechanism in which I'm not having to prove my point to you, you know? ... It's very much like, "Hey, how can we all be looking at these patterns and then learning from that?"

Another partner cited "neutrality" as one of the reasons research was important in helping him, a school district leader, make policy decisions:

> I think research in general provides new knowledge and insights around issues and opportunities. It looks at the impossible maybe to find out that it's impossible, and maybe to validate that it's impossible at this point. So, it takes an objective look at the world and tries to understand it honestly.

For this leader, who had struggled to get others within his organization to care about the problems he saw in the system, research was essential for objectively describing the reality of educational conditions and outcomes in order to gain support for necessary changes in policy and practice.

Yet, one partner raised the concern that the typical methods of communication researchers use to present research "neutrally" can often alienate the very audiences we were trying to reach. Alluding to the racialized nature of cultural norms like "objectivity" (Jones & Okun, 2016), our partner said:

> The way that I would actually reframe it, but it means a lot of work for you, is I think in the academic world, we have this sense that's kind of rooted in white supremacy, in all honesty, of like, "This is how you present neutral information." So, it's just, it's a different way of looking at it, but when you really think about it in a way of what culture sets and values am I just inherently bringing in to how I think this needs to be presented, and how I'm defining neutral, it really shifts a way that you free yourself up from being like, "Oh, I don't have to have it presented this, this, and this way. I could be doing things this way and it doesn't mean that I'm swaying the data." It doesn't have to be these black and white squares for it to be neutral. It's actually, if I'm working with community, that doesn't have a Ph.D., it's doing them a disservice by keeping it in this very coded language, in all honesty.

Another partner observed that our external presentations were focused on what we could learn: "I feel like it was, the presentation allowed for people to have multiple voices and multiple interpretations of that data, and creating a space just like rooted in learning, and really thinking different, and how can we think." She went on to tell us that we did a "good job" being "pretty neutral" in presenting the information and gathering feedback from community members. However, she considered ways in which that neutral positioning may have interfered with participants' engagement. She said:

> Then I was thinking about it in a more instructional way.... You could have done even something, like giving people more choice of which topic is more interesting for you, and then start there. Maybe people in the room, let's start in chronic absence, let's do that."

This feedback on guarding against bias and the perception of bias and about how we might shape our presentations to better serve the needs of our various partners, led us to adapt our practice in several ways, described below.

How Feedback Shaped Adaptation

While we recognized that we had a particular perspective on our research and on the direction that we believed policymakers should be going, we also benefited from our partners' trust that the data and research we presented were accurate and reflective of the experiences of Detroit students. This trust emerged both out of our position as "neutral" researchers in the policy landscape and out of our openness and explicit attention to the interests and goals of our partners.

The feedback that our understanding of neutrality may have narrowed our reach to certain audiences led to important reflections within our team. We discussed different ways of presenting data, different forums we might design to engage community members, and perhaps other "products" beyond traditional policy reports. At the same time, we recognized the tension that our partner mentioned—that doing this will mean "a lot of work." One way we might apply the principles of improvement science would be to use this feedback to develop common practices of engagement with different stakeholder groups, which would include codifying templates for outreach meetings, visual and oral presentations, and mechanisms to solicit feedback. Like the "standard work processes" that Bryk et al. (2015) promote, these could include guidance and presentation templates that we test out in different forums, refine over time, and eventually promote to standard practices that any member of our team would use when engaging certain audiences. The observations and recommendations from our partners helped us understand how our research would have more relevance if we did not think about it as "our" research alone. While it needed to include some boundaries that sustained its research validity and objectivity in the minds of our partners, it also needed to be interpreted and therefore coconstructed with our partners.

Cocreation of the Policy Narrative

What We Heard

All of the partners we spoke with emphasized the importance of cocreating the narrative about the policy implications of our research. While they agreed that we do have a role in framing how the main takeaways from our research are presented, they also wanted to ensure that community partners were deeply involved across the research cycle. For instance, one partner said, "I think it starts with real conversations between community partners and researchers before any research happens. Like, asking like, 'What do we want researched?' " The partners argued that the findings of our research were most powerful and potentially influential when combined with the narratives of community members, including students, parents, educators, and other community stakeholders in Detroit schools. One partner said,

"When research and community experience can be really powerful is when they amplify, when research amplifies community experience." Not only was this cocreation important for community-based policy change, but it was also necessary in ethically supporting the social justice objectives of our partners. A school district leader framed the importance of improving the city's schools as connected to the community's long struggles for educational equality:

> My goal is ultimately to get to the performance phase, where we're making an impact on students. I've been looking at this for a long time, I've been leveraging the knowledge of other folks. I know we have pervasive 40% poverty across the city, with a third of the resources and all the infrastructure requirements. I'm personally a person who came from that space, in the city of Detroit in Black Bottom, so when I think about where I am, my belief in what's achievable or not, I see a city full of students, families like me, that have this unrealized potential. So, the goal is to unleash that potential across the city.

Connecting our work to the history of Detroit's struggles for educational equality was important in helping us think about how to coconstruct our findings with our partners. As we have engaged community members, there have been times when our data seemed to contradict what they have experienced in their own lives. These moments represented "joint work at boundaries" (Penuel et al., 2015, p. 184) that are important in analyzing the practices within research partnerships. They helped us reconsider how to interpret our findings, generate potential policy recommendations, and connect those findings to the varied experiences of our community, which we also considered as "data" in our research. As one partner said, "In my mind, your report, the end report was definitely going to come out with some recommendations," which would be informed by the feedback we have gathered from community partners, since "the interpretation that you're getting is also data."

Another important takeaway with implications for our improvement science orientation is the tradeoff between quickly reporting out research to get feedback and the time that it takes to prepare engaging presentations that solicit the most useful feedback or that generate the best ideas for improving policy from multiple partners. Other suggestions included a "mini guide" for how to interpret quantitative research results and other "data visualization" techniques to make our research more user-friendly.

How Feedback Shaped Adaptation

In reflecting on feedback that encouraged us to think about how we were co-constructing research interpretations with our partners, we began to implement small changes in our research process. For instance, after completing our main analyses, but before releasing our latest public report, we presented our findings to two stakeholder groups—one representing parents and one representing nonprofit partners. We used these presentations to share what we were learning and to solicit feedback on our hypotheses about the mechanisms driving the associations we found. We were also able to hear their interpretations of our research and its implications for their work. This helped us frame our final written report in a way that would be accessible to our partners and reflect their use cases, and it also helped us identify and explain alternative explanations for our findings that are worth further exploration, either in our future research projects or in projects initiated by our partners.

We are also in the process of implementing new methods of displaying geographic patterns that have emerged out of our research. We plan to measure policymakers' responses to the graphics and maps in our reports and public documents by generating different visual representations of the same concept and asking stakeholders to respond with their interpretations, takeaways, and questions through an online feedback survey and interviews. We will measure how changing geographic unit boundaries that are displayed or the units of analysis in our map keys influence how policymakers interpret, respond to, and act upon our research. In turn, we will use this information to make additional adaptations that we will continue to test, with the goal of developing a template for how best to present mapping data to policymakers for maximum policy relevance.

Assumptions About the Nature of Research

What We Heard

Farley-Ripple et al. (2018) note that the gap between practitioners and researchers can be a product of differing assumptions and perspectives about the nature and quality of research. Our first year of research was built around a large-scale administrative data set from the state. Whereas these data enabled us to look at broad patterns and associations longitudinally and for entire student populations, its specificity was limited at the student-level to individual demographics and a geocode for their residential block. Our partners, however, did not have a good understanding of the data environment in the state, often assuming at first that our data had to have come from direct data collection from students and parents.

In the early stages of our research, our partners tended to ask questions or seek conclusions from the data that did not fit with the analyses we were able to conduct. An illustrative example comes from a CEC staff member's introductory e-mail to us:

> I agree that the board is very interested in the topics proposed (mobility, absenteeism, and school choice exit). I think it would also be powerful to also incorporate student performance into the mix to strengthen the argument of why it's important that we address these issues. Some of that is obvious *but if we can call out the causal relationship*, I think that could be powerful [emphasis added].

A particular focus was the motivations of students and parents. One high-level administrator in the public-school district, for example, said her main interest in our research was "the motivations for students' families to move [to suburban schools] or to stay." Likewise, another district leader was "looking at students leaving the city" and wanted to know "why are they making that choice?" These sentiments—wanting concrete evidence of "why" absenteeism, mobility, and exit were happening—were shared by many of our partners. From a continuous improvement perspective, we recognized the need to think carefully not only about how we should present our findings but also how we would frame them with an overview of our data and methods, including their limitations and possibilities.

How Feedback Shaped Adaptation

Recognizing that our partners were inclined to take a casual leap when reading our research, we dedicated extra time in public presentations and private meetings to explain where our data came from and what we could and could not learn from them. We sought to position research in this first year of our partnership as a strong starting point for future work that could incorporate surveys or interviews with parents, or even use experimental or quasi-experimental research design. This approach drew upon the RPP approach to research partnerships as long-term and open-ended commitments (Coburn & Penuel, 2016). In all our periodic updates with partners, we set aside time to ask what else they would want to know. We would also discuss which parts we thought we could answer with our current data and the kinds of data and methods we would need in order to answer the rest.

As we published our first major report and solicited feedback from our partners, we saw evidence that this open communication about data and methods was effective. As one CEC board member commented after the release of our first report, "I think the value of this report is it says, 'Student mobility and chronic absenteeism are real,' right? Like this is what's happening. So, I think this can become a launchpad for other studies that start to get at the root cause and why." Indeed, not only had we built a shared understanding of the limits and possibilities of our first round of research, but we also began to develop a shared vision for future work together. A CEC staff member expressed excitement about "really digging in" next year "with focus groups and more qualitative research":

> because people who are on the ground in these various spaces are living these realities day in and day out. And so, it doesn't even have to just be talking to parents, but talking to the people who work with parents, they're going to know some of the why as well. It can start to paint a broader picture around the data. That might also make it more actionable.

Likewise, as we discussed variation in school chronic absenteeism rates with one member of the CEC board, he asked, "How did that happen? Why and what's going on inside those [schools]?" He suggested that we needed "other studies that sort of dig deeper into that because that's where we can start to make cleaner policy decisions." In fact, this feedback led us to include new data collection through parent surveys and interviews in a subsequent grant application to continue the research partnership. Incorporating our partners' expressed interest in new data collection and research methods both strengthened our application for continued funding and demonstrated to our partners that we would genuinely respond to their needs and interests.

This gap between us and our partners—around the nature and quality of our research—could have jeopardized our ability to maximize the policy relevance of our work. Using PDSA cycles to reflect on our work allowed us to directly address that gap, instead of continuing to conduct and publish research without information on how our partners were receiving it. As a result, we created more trust and stronger relationships with our partners, demonstrated a knowledge of the local context, and aligned our goals for future work—all of which are foundational for effective research partnerships (Connolly, 2019).

DISCUSSION

Research presented in traditional academic outlets (e.g., academic journals, conference presentations) often does not reach an audience in the position to shape and implement policy. When researchers do want to increase the relevance of their work to policymakers, there are few evidence-based approaches to doing so. Engaging in a disciplined approach to policy-relevant research requires researchers to communicate differently depending on the audience, and it also demands that they continue to use their research expertise to better understand how and why research informs policy. Our research partnership, grounded in the principles of improvement science, is an emerging model for developing pedagogical dispositions and strategies to improve the policy relevance of academic research in education and, in turn, shaping policy itself. We contribute to the research on continuous improvement and research partnerships, and we offer new insights into how frameworks from each of these areas can be helpful in improving the research process—from origination of research questions to dissemination of findings. We advance the field of policy-relevant research in education in three ways: (a) we demonstrate how researchers can turn the tools of improvement science inward to improve their own research practices; (b) we show how RPPs can facilitate the collection of feedback data useful in refining research practices; and (c) we establish systems to test and evaluate the impact of our approach on policymaking in the future.

Partnerships meant to influence policy improvement are different than those focused on instructional improvement. They require a multi-directional arrangement that goes beyond one research partner and one practice partner and includes stakeholders who create and enact policy (e.g., superintendent, mayor, lawmakers), as well as those who advocate for policy change (e.g., community organizers, students, parents). This means that improvement work must be attentive to the outcome of creating research which is relevant across multiple audiences with different needs. With this in mind, process improvements might include practices for engaging diverse audiences in conversation around what research they need in order to make policy decisions, the practices for identifying key policy stakeholders and communicating with them, for quickly producing accurate research, and for presenting findings in a way that policymakers can understand and act on.

As with most work in schools, research partnerships depend on building trust between partners and establishing the valued contribution of each partner, which then contributes to the "created value" within the partnership (Connolly, 2019). We set out to build alignment, trust, and local knowledge as a strong foundation with our partners. We were able to do that more effectively because of our use of improvement partnership principles (i.e., an iterative approach to research focus and design, intentionally requesting feedback from partners).

One final consideration is how to measure our key outcome—policy relevance. There is a clear tension between wanting policymakers to use research in making decisions and not wanting them to make decisions based on inaccurate or underinformed interpretations of research (Lubienski, 2018). Therefore, researchers must be thoughtful about how to define and measure their influence. We believe that research teams should aim to improve in the following ways: (a) increase the number of people in positions of influence over policy who read our work; (b) increase the interest of policymakers and community members in the key findings we identify in our research; and (c) increase the number of new research questions generated by policymakers.

Our research partnership is but one example, and our ability to reflect on its strengths and weaknesses is limited by our own positions within it. Coburn and Penuel (2016) note that, although there are some exceptions (e.g., Cooper, 2007), the majority of work on the dynamics of research partnerships has been first-person accounts written by researchers in partnerships, not practitioners (e.g., Roderick et al., 2007). We fall into the same category. These insider accounts often describe strategies that partnerships use to organize their work and learn from each other. As such, they provide insight into the workings of RPPs that others can use to inform their own partnerships. However, they do not derive from systematic research design, data collection, and analysis. They also typically involve retrospective analyses, making them subject to hindsight bias. Our research attempts to mitigate some of these concerns by intentionally collecting data in real-time and implementing changes in response to those data, but we acknowledge that this process is imperfect because of our positions as both partners and researchers.

This work is difficult, and it presses researchers to reconsider traditional ways of knowing and producing research evidence. We are still in the early phases of our work, so it is as yet unclear how our attempts to establish trust, respond to feedback, and adapt our research processes will bear out in terms of policy adoption and enactment. There may be mitigating factors that ultimately make these efforts ineffectual or complicate their potential impact. Building trust with partners must be balanced with research integrity and accuracy. In highly politicized contexts, where ideologues often arm themselves with carefully selected data to support their prior positions, education researchers must develop processes to navigate these complex dynamics while not betraying their professional commitments. In addition, the structural barriers within institutions of higher education may continue to pose threats to this way of working. Although some leading researchers are pushing the field to recognize the value of partnerships in research (Gordon, 2019; Scott, 2019), the time and resources required to be a good partner are too often not valued in traditional metrics of academic success. More must be done to align researchers' professional incentives with the requirements of doing partnered research that has relevance for policy.

Academic researchers have unprecedented potential to influence policy and make their work matter for improving educational experiences and outcomes. Research partnerships, grounded in the principles of improvement science, are one way academic researchers can get better at navigating the policy world and improve how they use their expertise to improve policy in education. As more partnerships launch, researchers can take a disciplined approach to understanding their impact and adapting their practice to meet their goals. As evidence grows on how to do this work well, other research partnerships—and policy contexts—may benefit from the improved approaches to communication, dissemination, explanation of findings and limitations, and coconstruction of implications that we have begun to develop.

REFERENCES

Aboelmaged, M. G., & Lichtman, R. (2010). Six Sigma quality: A structured review and implications for future research. *The International Journal of Quality & Reliability Management, 27*(3), 269–318. http://dx.doi.org/10.1108/02656711011023294

Anderson, C. W., Santos, E. X. de los, Bodbyl, S., Covitt, B. A., Edwards, K. D., Hancock, J. B., Lin, Q., Thomas, C. M., Penuel, W. R., & Welch, M. M. (2018). Designing educational systems to support enactment of the Next Generation Science Standards. *Journal of Research in Science Teaching, 55*(7), 1026–1052. https://doi.org/10.1002/tea.21484

Baumgartner, F. R., & Jones, B. D. (2010). *Agendas and instability in American politics*. University of Chicago Press.

Berwick, D. M. (2008). The science of improvement. *JAMA, 299*(10), 1182–1184. https://doi.org/10.1001/jama.299.10.1182

Bevan, B. (2017). Research and practice: One way, two way, no way, or new way? *Theory/Practice Forum, 60*(2), 133–141.

Bevan, B., Gutwill, J., Petrich, M., & Wilkinson, K. (2015). Learning through STEM-rich tinkering: Findings from a jointly negotiated research project taken up in practice. *Science Education, 99*, 98–120.

Boyask, R.. & Vigurs, K. (2018). Developing a methodology for public engagement with critical research. *Policy Futures in Education, 16*(2), 21–231.

Bryk, A. S., Gomez, L. M., Grunow, A., & LeMahieu, P. (2015). *Learning to improve: How America's schools can get better at getting better.* Harvard University Press

Coburn, C. & Penuel, W. (2016). Research-practice partnerships in education: Outcomes, dynamics, and open questions. *Educational Researcher, 45*(1), 48–54.

Coburn, C., Penuel, W., & Geil, K. (2013). *Research-practice partnerships: A Strategy for leveraging research for educational improvement in school districts.* William T. Grant Foundation.

Cohen-Vogel, L., Tichnor-Wagner, A., Allen, D., Harrison, C., Kainz, K., Socol, A. R., & Wang, Q. (2014). Implementing educational innovations at scale: Transforming researchers into continuous improvement scientists. *Educational Policy, 29*(1), 257–277. https://doi.org/10.1177/0895904814560886

Conaway, C., Keesler, V., & Schwartz, N. (2015). What research do state education agencies really need? The promise and limitations of state longitudinal data systems. *Educational Evaluation and Policy Analysis, 37*(1S), 16S–28S.

Connolly, F. (2019). *Measuring the value of a research-practice partnership.* Retrieved March 19, 2019, from http://nnerppextra.rice.edu/measuring-the-value-of-an-rpp/

Cooper, L. A. (2007). Why closing the research-practice gap is critical to closing student achievement gaps. *Theory Into Practice, 46*(4), 317–324.

Daly, A. J., Finnigan, K. S., Jordan, S., Moolenaar, N., & Che, J. (2014). Misalignment and perverse incentives: Examining the politics of district leaders as brokers in the use of research evidence. *Educational Policy, 28*(2), 15–174. https://doi.org/10.1177/0895904813513149

Dearing, J. & Kreuter, M. (2010). Designing for diffusion: How can we increase uptake of cancer communication innovations? *Patient Education and Counseling, 81,* S100–S110.

Dunn, W. N. (1980). The two-communities metaphor and models of knowledge use. *Knowledge, 1*, 515–536.

Edwards, A. R., Sandoval, C., & McNamara, H. (2015). Designing for improvement in professional development for community college developmental mathematics faculty. *Journal of Teacher Education*, *66*(5), 466–481. https://doi.org/10.1177/0022487115602313

Elmore, R. (1996). Getting to scale with good educational practice. *Harvard Educational Review*, *66*(1), 1–27. https://doi.org/10.17763/haer.66.1.g73266758j348t33

Farley-Ripple, E., May, H., Karpyn, A., Tilley, K., & McDonough, K. (2018). Rethinking connections between research and practice in education: A conceptual framework. *Educational Researcher, 47*(4), 235–245.

Farrell, C. C., Davidson, K. L., Repko-Erwin, M. E., Penuel, W. R., Quantz, M., Wong, H., Riedy, R., & Brink, Z. (2018). *A descriptive study of the IES Researcher-Practitioner Partnerships in Education Research Program: Final report* (Technical Report No. 3). National Center for Research in Policy and Practice.

Finnigan, K. S., Daly, A. J., & Che, J. (2013). Systemwide reform in districts under pressure: The role of social networks in defining, acquiring, using, and diffusing research evidence. *Journal of Educational Administration, 51*(4), 476–497. https://doi.org/10.1108/09578231311325668

Fishman, B. J., Penuel, W. R., Allen, A.-R., Cheng, B. H., & Sabelli, N. (2013). Design-based implementation research: An emerging model for transforming the relationship of research and practice. *Yearbook of the National Society for the Study of Education, 112*(2), 136–156.

Gerrard, J. (2015) Public education in neoliberal times: Memory and desire. *Journal of Education Policy, 30*(6), 855–868.

Gomez, K., Gomez, L. M., Rodela, K. C., Horton, E. S., Cunningham, J., & Ambrocio, R. (2015). Embedding language support in developmental mathematics lessons: Exploring the value of design as professional development for community college mathematics instructors. *Journal of Teacher Education*, *66*(5), 450–465. https://doi.org/10.1177/0022487115602127

Gordon, N. (2019, January 16). *To become a public scholar, I had to face a reality.* Education Week. https://www.edweek.org/ew/articles/2019/01/16/to-become-a-public-scholar-i-had.html

Grunow, A., Hough, H., Park, S., Willis, J., & Krausen, K. (2018). *Towards a common vision of continuous improvement for California* (Getting Down to Facts II). Stanford University. https://www.gettingdowntofacts.com/publications/towards-common-vision-continuous-improvement-california

Hannan, M., Russell, J. L., Takahashi, S., & Park, S. (2015). Using improvement science to better support beginning teachers: The case of the Building a Teaching Effectiveness Network. *Journal of Teacher Education, 66*(5), 494–508. https://doi.org/10.1177/0022487115602126

Heimans, S., & Singh, P. (2018). Putting the steam back into critique? 'Gathering' for critical-dissensual collaborations in education policy research. *Policy Futures in Education, 16*(2), 185–201.

Henig, J. (2013). *The end of exceptionalism: The changing politics of school reform*. Harvard Education Press.

Jabbar, H., LaLonde, P.G., DeBray-Pelot, E. Scott, J., & Lubienski, C. (2015). How policymakers define "evidence": The politics of research use in New Orleans. In L. Miron, B. Beabout, & J. Boselovic (Eds.), *Only in New Orleans: School choice and equity post-hurricane Katrina* (pp. 285–304). Sense.

Jones, K., & Okun, T. (2016). *Dismantling racism workbook*. https://resourcegeneration.org/wp-content/uploads/2018/01/2016-dRworks-workbook.pdf

Lenhoff, S. W., Lewis, J. M., Pogodzinski, B., & Jones, R. D. (2019). 'Triage, transition, and transformation': Advocacy discourse in urban school reform. *Education Policy Analysis Archives, 27*(32). http://dx.doi.org/10.14507/epaa.27.4230

Lewis, C. (2015). What is improvement science? Do we need it in education? *Educational Researcher, 44*(1), 54–61. https://doi.org/10.3102/0013189X15570388

López Turley, R. N., & Stevens, C. (2015). Lessons from a school district-university research partnership: The Houston Education Research Consortium. *Educational Evaluation and Policy Analysis, 37*(1S), 6S–15S.

Lubienski, C. (2018). The critical challenge: Policy networks and market models for education. *Policy Futures in Education, 16*(2), 156–168.

Lupton, R., & Hayes, D. (2018). Think tanks and the pedagogical dispositions and strategies of socially critical researchers: A case study of inequalities in schooling. *Policy Futures in Education, 16*(2), 202–216.

Marsh, J. A., & Wohlstetter, P. (2013). Recent trends in intergovernmental relations: The resurgence of local actors in education policy. *Educational Researcher, 42*, 276–283.

Nutley, S., Walter, I., & Davies, H. T. O. (2007). *Using evidence: How research can inform public services*. Policy Press.

Peck, J., & Theodore, N. (2015). *Fast policy: Experimental statecraft at the thresholds of neoliberalism*. University of Minnesota Press.

Penuel, W., Allen, A., Coburn, C., & Farrell, C. (2015). Conceptualizing research–practice partnerships as joint work at boundaries. *Journal of Education for Students Placed at Risk (JESPAR), 20*(1–2), 182–197.

Penuel, W., Farrell, C., Allen, A., Toyama, Y., & Coburn, C. (2018). What research district leaders find useful. *Educational Policy, 32*(4), 540–568.

Peurach, D. J., Glazer, J. L., & Lenhoff, S. W. (2016). The developmental evaluation of school improvement networks. *Educational Policy, 30*(4), 606–648._https://doi.org/10.1177/0895904814557592

Polikoff, M., & Conaway, C. (2018, September 25). *Getting beyond "did it work?": Proposing a new approach to integrate research and policy*. Brookings, Brown Center Chalkboard. www.brookings.edu/blog/brown-center-chalkboard/2018/09/25/

getting-beyond-did-it-work-proposing-a-new-approach-to-integrate-research-and-policy/

Roderick, M., Easton, J. Q., & Sebring, P. B. (2007). *Developing new roles for research in new policy environments: The Consortium on Chicago School Research.* University of Chicago

Sanderson, I. (2003). Is it 'what works' that matters? Evaluation and evidence-based policy-making. *Research Papers in Education, 18*(4), 331–345.

Scott, J. (2019, January 16). *Public scholarship is about more than edu-celebrity.* Education Week. https://www.edweek.org/ew/articles/2019/01/16/public-scholarship-is-about-more-than-edu-celebrity.html

Scott, J., DeBray, E., Lubienski, C., Goel LaLonde, P., Castillo, E., & Owens, S. (2017). Urban regimes, intermediary organization networks, and research use: Patterns across three school districts. *Peabody Journal of Education, 92*(1), 16–28

Scott, J., & Jabbar, H. (2014). The hub and the spoke: Foundations, intermediary organizations, incentivist reforms, and the politics of research evidence. *Educational Policy, 28*(2), 233–257.

Simons, H. (2003). Evidenc-based practice: Panacea or over promise? *Research Papers in Education, 18*(4), 303–311.

Thompson, K., Martinez, M., Clinton, C., & Diaz, G. (2017). Considering interest and action: Analyzing types of questions explored by research-practitioner partnerships. *Educational Researcher, 46*(8), 464–473.

Trujillo, T. (2014). The modern cult of efficiency: Intermediary organizations and the new scientific management. *Educational Policy, 28*(2), 207–232.

Tseng, V. (2012). *The uses of research in policy and practice* (Social Policy Report, Vol. 26, No. 2). Society for Research on Child Development.

Womack, J. P., & Jones, D. T. (2003). *Lean thinking: Banish waste and create wealth in your corporation, revised and updated* (2nd ed.). Free Press.

CHAPTER 9

SOCIAL NETWORK ANALYSIS FOR POLICY-RELEVANT EDUCATION RESEARCH

Yinying Wang
Georgia State University

INTRODUCTION

This chapter describes how social network analysis (SNA) has been applied in education policy research. While SNA is not a traditionally taught methodological course in colleges of education, it has been increasingly used in education policy research. The *2017 Politics of Education Yearbook* presents a series of case studies that highlighted the competing networks with different visions for public education goals and governance (Marshall et al., 2017). SNA conceptualizes a policymaking or implementation process as a network of actors mobilized through coalition ties. We can conduct SNA to examine whether a policy actor (e.g., an individual or a group) occupies a central position within a policymaking network, whether the policy actor belongs to various coalitions, or whether the policy actor plays a brokering role between different stakeholders to influence the policymaking process. SNA can also be applied to study policy implementation by examining the social networks forged over the policy implementation processes and assess

Maximizing the Policy Relevance of Research for School Improvement, pp. 217–240
Copyright © 2021 by Information Age Publishing
All rights of reproduction in any form reserved.

how the social networks facilitate or impede the policy implementation. In addition to analytical results, SNA generates graphs as part of network illustration. Such graphs can grab readers' attention, offering a reader-friendly way to present analytical results to readers.

To facilitate the application of SNA in education policy research, in this chapter I first introduce different types of policy networks, then elucidate the theoretical groundings of network analysis by presenting salient network theories (e.g., network theory of social capital, the strength of weak tie theory, and advocacy coalition framework) as well as network constructs (e.g., structural holes, brokerage, and closure). I then introduce the mathematical foundation of social network analysis—a branch of mathematics called graph theory. Next, I assemble a collection of network analysis articles as examples to demonstrate how network data were collected and how the networks were constructed and analyzed in the research on state reading policymaking, teacher education, charter school reform, Common Core State Standards, the opt-out movement, and the implementation of Every Student Succeeds Act. Like all research methods, SNA has its limitations, I therefore conclude with some recommendations for advancing the theoretical groundings, optimizing SNA methodological approaches, and guiding education policymaking and leadership practices.

TYPES OF POLICY NETWORKS

If we want to understand a policy network, we need to know first how the network is constructed and then how different parts of the network interact with one another. To do so, we conceptualize a policy process as a set of policy actors (i.e., nodes) and the interactions (i.e., ties) among them (Coleman & Perl, 1999; Rhodes, 2006). In political science, a policy network refers to "sets of formal and informal institutional linkages between governmental and other actors structured around shared interests in public policymaking and implementation" (Rhodes, 2007, p. 1244). Applying this definition to education policy research, policy actors can be the U.S. Department of Education, state education agencies, local school districts, interest groups, philanthropic foundations, and individuals who are affiliated with those organizations and groups. Their interactions and the resultant influence over a policymaking and implementation process can be assessed by applying SNA. In policy networks, what ties represent can differ greatly. In this sense, the nature of ties determines the nature of policy networks. Depending on what the ties represent, there are five types policy networks: (1) information/advice network, (2) resource network, (3) ally network, (4) coordination network, and (5) policy networks in the digital world. Table 9.1 summarizes network types in education policy.

To demonstrate how different types of policy networks have been studied in policy research, the studies in Table 9.1 are not exhaustive, but rather illustrative. In Table 9.2, I introduce each of these network types in turn.

Table 9.1

Summary of Education Policy Networks

Authors	Network	Network Types	Nodes	Ties
Song & Miskel (2006)	reading policymaking in eight states	information/ advice network	policy actors active in shaping state reading policy	collaboration or interaction between actors regarding the state reading policy
Au & Ferrare (2014)	the campaign to pass the charter school Initiative 1240 in the state of Washington	resource network	wealthy individuals and their affiliated philanthropic organizations	financial donations, endorsement, and a technical report written in support of the campaign
Kretchmar et al. (2014)	TFA's role in charter school reform	resource network	organizations and individuals	partnerships, funding, leading, or employment, serving on advisory/ governance board, fellowship
Reckhow & Snyder (2014)	grant making in K–12 education	resource network	grantees received at least $2 million in grants from three or more major education funders	sharing the same funders
Wallis & Dockett (2015)	online hyperlinks of a key landmark document on early childhood policy in Australia	digital network	webpage	hyperlinks
Ferrare & Reynolds (2016)	grant making in K-12 education	resource network	non-major philanthropic foundations and their grantees	grant funds
Young et al. (2016)	reading policymaking in California, Connecticut, Michigan, and Utah	information/ advice network	policy actors active in shaping state reading policy	policy actors active in shaping state reading policy

(Table continued on next page)

Table 9.1

Summary of Education Policy Networks (Continued)

Authors	Network	Network Types	Nodes	Ties
Wang & Fikis (2017	communication on Common Core on Twitter	digital network	Twitter users who mentioned and/or replied to others on the topic of Common Core	mentioning or replying to on Twitter
Wang (2017)	the opt-out movement in the state of New York	coordination network	policy actors active in the opt-out movement	collaboration, co-participation in an event, and sharing the same sentiment regarding the opt-out movementcitation
Baek et al. (2018)	TFA's social networks of the deregulation of teacher education	resource network, coordination network	TFA and its connections	TFA and organizations that are connected by personnel ties (i.e., founded by, in partnershipwith, or staffed by TFA members and alumni)
Parsons (2018)	collaboration in autism policy	information/ advice network	government and nongovernmental organizations	collaboration
Wang (2018)	implementation of ESSA	ally network	witnesses at congressional hearings on ESSA	sharing the same policy preferences

Information/Advice Networks

The most common policy network is information/advice network (Weible & Sabatier, 2005). As the name suggests, in information/advice networks, the ties represent the exchange of information and advice related to policy issues among policy actors. Information/advice networks are particularly important when the policy issues are complex and each policy actor is knowledgeable about only a small amount of the information/advice. In a reading policymaking network in eight states (Alabama, California, Connecticut, Indiana, Maine, Michigan, Texas, and Utah), the ties indicate collaboration or interaction among policy actors who were active in shaping state reading policy (Song & Miskel, 2006). In a network engaged in implementing the Common Core State Standards, the ties indicate seeking advice concerning the implementation of Common Core in a district in California (Liou, 2016). In a network of autism policymaking in Virginia, the ties indicate seeking information with relevant education or health expertise about autism (Parsons, 2018). In the network of Teach for America (TFA) alumni and their organizations supporting charter school agendas, the ties indicate serving on the advisory or governance board (Kretchmar et al., 2014).

Resource Networks

In resource networks, the ties represent resources that flow within the networks. The resources could be financial donations, grant funding, and personnel. In the resource network of the campaign to pass charter school Initiative 1240 in the state of Washington, the ties indicate cash and in-kind contributions to the campaign (Au & Ferrare, 2014). In a study on the influence of philanthropy in K–12 education policy, the resource network was composed of philanthropic foundations and their grantees that were connected by grant funds (Ferrare & Reynolds, 2014). Notably, personnel sharing involves much stronger commitment than simply providing financial resources; therefore, it is rare to see personnel-sharing networks, let alone research being done on them (Robinson & Gaddis, 2012).

Ally Networks

In ally networks, the ties represent alliances and coalitions. In policy research, a coalition is formed by policy actors sharing the same policy reference (Salisbury et al., 1987). Policy actors' policy preference can be revealed in many forms, such as through press releases, legislative testimonies, and co-sponsoring legislation. For instance, 12 national civil and human rights group formed a coalition with the New York State Education Department in the opt-out movement, after they announced their opposition to the movement in a press release, because they argued that standardized testing was the only objective measure of student progress and teacher and student accountability (Wang, 2017a). In congressional hearings on the Every Student Succeeds Act (ESSA), the Civil and Human Rights and Education Group, Congressional Hispanic Caucus, Congressional Black Caucus, and Congressional Asian Pacific American Caucus formed a coalition based on their shared policy preference that the decision about how to identify consistently underperforming subgroups should be left to states (Wang, 2018). Policy preference can also be revealed when legislators publicly express their support for a piece of legislation by cosponsoring it (Fowler, 2006). With such a legislative cosponsorship network, influential legislators can be detected by how central they are in the network.

Coordination Networks

In coordination networks, the ties represent coordinated behavior that a pair of policy actors demonstrate to influence policymaking processes. Coordination can assume many forms, ranging from synchronizing action to developing a joint strategy on a policy issue. Take the opt-out movement—the grassroots, organized efforts to refuse to take high-stakes standardized tests—as an example. The coordination ties were established between the two policy actors (e.g., the Long Island Opt Out group and the teachers unions), when the teachers unions helped distribute the Long Island Opt Out group's event fliers about boycotting state standardized tests (Wang, 2017a). Further, in the social networks accounting for the rise of civil society in Mexico, the coordination ties were operationalized as coparticipation in protest campaigns together in the rising civil society (Wada, 2014). The actors (e.g., workers, peasants, students, civic associations, and nongovernmental organizations) were thus connected by the coordination ties if they coattended a protest campaign. The aforementioned policy preferences do a fairly good job to predict the formation of both the coordination networks and the ally networks (Weible & Sabatier, 2005).

Policy Networks in the Digital World

With the proliferation of digital data, interaction ties can be formed online. The interaction ties can represent who talks or responds to whom on social media. In a study of the tweets with #CommonCore, Supovitz and his colleagues identified three types of elite actors on Twitter (i.e., those who posted large number of tweets, those whose tweets were frequently retweeted, and those who were mentioned frequently and extensively by others), and then manually coded a random sample of tweets posted by the elite actors as either informational or opinion-based (Supovitz et al., 2017). In another study of Common Core on Twitter, instead of examining the retweeting networks in Supovitz et al.'s study, researchers focused on the communication network on the Common Core on Twitter—a pair of Twitter users were connected by a communication tie if one Twitter user mentioned and/or replied to another Twitter user in the tweets containing #CommonCore and #CCSS (Wang & Fikis, 2019). Wang and Fikis

(2019) argued that if a Twitter user sent out retweets, such retweets were not considered as communication, since mentions and/or replies indicate two-way *communication*, whereas retweets are considered as one-way information *broadcasting*. Notably, Wang and Fikis used the Twitter application program interface (API) to collect social media data. The Twitter API is a program that provides the public with efficient access to a random sample of approximately 1% of all real-time tweets (Murthy, 2013; Twitter, 2019). This data collection approach can be automated and scaled-up, presenting itself as a new method of collecting digital data in a timely manner, a point I will return to shortly.

The interaction ties can also represent hyperlinks that connect the websites of policy actors and policy issues. Many policy actors (e.g., government agencies, advocacy groups, and philanthropic foundations) have their own websites. In a study on the Tampa Bay water policy, 72% of policy actors had websites (Berardo & Scholz, 2010). In a study on a key landmark document on early childhood policy in Australia (*Transition to School: Position Statement*), a Google search was run on the online document *Transition to School: Position Statement* to identify the websites that were linked to the online document (Wallis & Dockett, 2015). Once a list of policy actor websites or policy issue websites (i.e., "seed sites") is compiled, automated web crawler software programs can methodically scan the seed sites to identify the hyperlinks from one website to another. In a hyperlink policy network, a tie suggests which websites are connected by hyperlink. Therefore, the ties are "directed," showing how information flows from one website to another. The ties can also be "weighted," if Website A has multiple hyperlinks to Website B, but only one hyperlink to Website C (Yi & Scholz, 2016). In fact, building hyperlink ties is one strategy to build alliances among policy actors (Park et al., 2004). By doing so, the interlinked websites around a given policy issue thus bear a resemblance to offline interactions among policy actors who interact with one another on a policy issue (Howlett, 2002; McNutt, 2010; Rogers & Ben-David, 2010). Hyperlink ties also express recognition of expertise when hyperlinks provide research reports or journal articles as the authoritative sources of information of a policy issue.

It is important to note that even though each of the aforementioned five types of policy networks has a different focus, the distinction between them is not clear-cut. Ally networks and coordination networks are sometimes not mutually exclusive. Resource networks and ally networks can even be considered two sides of the same coin. Nevertheless, these policy networks enrich our understanding of policymaking and implementation processes. I now turn to the theoretical tenets of social network analysis in policy research.

THEORETICAL GROUNDINGS

Social network theories and the related constructs lay theoretical groundings to study education policy through a social network lens. Social network theory is a school of thought that shares the conceptual roots of social networks but focuses on different aspects of the networks. Here I introduce some dominant theories (e.g., network theory of social capital, the strength of weak tie theory, and advocacy coalition framework) as well as network constructs (e.g., structural holes, brokerage, and closure).

Network Theory of Social Capital (Lin, 1999)

According to the network theory of social capital, social capital is conceptualized as the relational assets: the "resources embedded in a social structure which are accessed and/or mobilized in purposive actions" (Lin, 1999, p. 35). To that end, to generate social capital is to gain access to socially embedded resources through social ties. The social ties function as the conduits through which the policy actors can access their social contacts' resources. A policy actor's access to the embedded resources is subject to the social ties in a network: the more ties a policy actor has, the easier the access to the resources. As such, a policy actor needs to be an active agent to access and mobilize the resources embedded in the social networks and to instrumentally forge and sustain social ties. On that note, whether a policy actor's beliefs and preferences are represented in policies is a function of the quality and quantity of resources controlled by whom the policy actor has ties with.

Strength of Weak Ties Theory (Granovetter, 1973)

In comparison with network theory of social capital, Granovetter's (1973) strength of weak tie theory places more focus on the network structure. The term "weak tie" is misleading, however, as a weak tie is not weak at all. To differentiate the strong ties from the weak ties, let us consider our friendship network. Our ties to the close friends are the strong ties, because we might meet face-to-face at least three times a week, or we have a quite strong emotional attachment to one another. By contrast, our ties to the acquaintances are the weak ties, because we might only meet once or twice over the last six months, or we do not have a strong emotional attachment to them. Granovetter's empirical study on the relationship between personal contacts and job search produced a strikingly counterintuitive finding: our *weak* ties (acquaintances) are more likely to provide information that leads to landing a job successfully than our strong ties (close friends), despite the fact that our close friends are arguably more motivated in helping us find a job. Weak ties are so valuable because novel information is more likely to come from the weak ties because of their bridging function in information flow between different groups; whereas the strong ties are unlikely to be the sources of novel information, as our close friends tend to know one another and thus share the same information source. If we apply the strength of weak tie theory to the lobbying networks of healthcare policymaking, the policy information passed more through the weak ties (i.e., acquaintances) than through the strong ties (i.e., close, trusted contacts; Carpenter et al., 1998).

Network Closure and Structural Holes (Burt, 2005)

How does network structure influence social capital? To explain the relationship between them, two theoretical constructs— network closure and structural holes—have been developed. First, network closure refers to the idea that a well-connected network is instrumental to the performance at both the individual level and the collective level. Consider that network ties function as the conduit of social contagion (Borgatti & Foster, 2003; Wasserman & Faust, 1994). What is contagious via the ties is subject to how the ties are defined and operationalized. Ties are the channels to spread not only tacit knowledge (e.g., ideas, practices, information, advice, and expertise), but also psychological influences (e.g., beliefs, attitude, trust, and distrust; Burt, 2005). Individually, whether one adopts tacit knowledge or whether one is influenced by a psychological effect is subject to the social ties surrounding the individual (i.e., the proportion of the people who have adopted it and how strong the social ties are). Further, the timing of adoption is a function of the lengths of paths in the social networks—how many intermediary people it takes to connect an individual to other adoptees. Seen from the vantage point of a group as a whole, people mutually influence and inform each other in a socially contagious process that creates the increasing homogeneity within the group. Thus, collective norms, rules, and values emerge, promoting collective behavior in the policymaking process. To that end, network closure facilitates collaboration and information sharing among policy actors (Schneider et al., 2003). The network measures that capture the structure of network closure are network density and network centralization. Density is calculated by dividing the actual number of ties within a network with the maximum number of possible ties (Borgatti et al., 2013). A higher network density means a higher level of network closure, if the number of nodes remains constant. The second indicator of network closure is network centralization (see Borgatti et al.,

2013, for a thorough explication of how network centralization is calculated).

Second, the construct of a structural hole has its theoretical root in the strength of weak ties theory (Granovetter, 1973). The difference, albeit subtle, is that Granovetter (1973) emphasized the value of tie strengths, but Burt highlighted the importance of nonredundant ties (Sandström & Carlsson, 2008). Structural holes are the break in the network structure that can be identified by the absence of ties or the presence of weak ties. The policy actors in a position to bridge such holes are expected to have a strategic advantage as they have access to new and diversified information or resources that can be used in the policymaking processes. That is, the policy actors who position themselves as a bridge across distinct groups tend to have more social capital than those who interact with those in the same group. In comparison to those who are in the same group, the policy actors who function as a bridge are more likely to generate new ideas, because "opinion and behavior are more homogeneous within than between groups" (Burt, 2004, p. 349). As such, new ideas are likely to emerge from the policy actors who have access to alternative ways of thinking and behaving in different groups, thus formulating new ideas through the selection and synthesis of diverse information embedded in different groups. Accordingly, a network that spans many structural holes is a network rich in social capital. Administrative agencies appear to have more structural holes than interest groups, thereby often acting as policy brokers or intermediaries between coalitions (Sabatier, 1998). The structural holes can be identified by calculating network heterogeneity in network analysis (Reagans & Zuckerman, 2001).

The two network constructs—network closure and structural holes—seem contradictory. Yet they are unique and important in their own ways. Burt (2005) summarized that the brokerage across structural holes is the source of new, innovative ideas, and that network closure offers a convergence on attitudes and practices within the network. Network closure and structural holes enforce one another in the process of policymaking and implementation. The structure of policy networks—with their network closure and structural holes—reflect how information/advice, resource, alliances, and coordination are shaped, shifted, and evolved over the policymaking processes. If we follow this logic, examining the structures of policy networks can reveal how distinct patterns of ties—the existence or absence of brokerage and structural holes—influence the network performance, i.e., policy outcomes. This view is supported by empirical evidence: structural holes are positively correlated with mobilizing resources, whereas network closure is positively correlated with prioritizing resources in policymaking (Sandström & Carlsson, 2008).

Advocacy Coalition Framework

The advocacy coalition framework is another salient theoretical framework that explains policymaking processes (Sabatier & Weible, 2007). The advocacy coalition framework views a policymaking process as a competition between coalitions of policy actors (e.g., interest groups, administrative agencies, journalists, and scientific representatives) who advocate their beliefs about a policy preference. Policy preferences are revealed and articulated in public by policy actors in many ways, including press releases, newspapers, congressional testimonies, and social media (Leifeld, 2017). In doing so, other policy actors feel encouraged to support them or reveal their oppositions. Similar policy preferences therefore lay the ground to form coalitions. The shared policy preferences function as the glue holding a coalition together (Pierce, 2011). This is because policy actors tend to reach out to and create ties with those who have similar policy preferences with the goal of forming winning coalitions (Sabatier et al., 1987; Weible, 2005). In that sense, convergent and divergent belief systems among actors can be expressed in a relational fashion in policy networks. More important, policy actors' belief systems and resources drive the network structure of policy networks (Henry et al., 2010). The centrality and tie strength of a policy preference imply how strong a coalition is formed around a particular policy preference.

An advocacy coalition in a policymaking process is subject to the resources garnered by the coalition (Sabatier, 1998). In situations where the policy beliefs of two or more coalitions are in conflict, seeking and accumulating resources becomes important, and the power balance among coalitions might alter considerably. The coalition with the greatest resources and policy power might thus have a crucial impact on policymaking, and the policy output might change. One example of how power seized by policy actors can influence the future of policy coalitions is the opt-out movement (Wang, 2017a). Generally speaking, nongovernment policy actors usually have less power than government agencies in the policymaking processes. However, in the case of the opt-out movement in the state of New York, some opt-out parents were elected and won their seats in the districts' school board. In doing so, they gained the power to advocate for "a more holistic" education approach aimed at going beyond test scores and placing focus on the whole child. In one district, three Long Island Opt Out-endorsed board members were elected in 2015 to serve on the nine-member board (Franchi, 2016). In addition to amassing power at the local level, the Long Island Opt Out group was active at the state level by strongly supporting the election of Todd Kaminsky (D-Long Beach) to the state senate, who sponsored the bill that untethered teacher evaluation from standardized testing scores and wrote a letter to the then-Secretary of

Education John King to urge the U.S. Department of Education to reconsider its decision to punish school districts with the high opt-out rate (The New York State Senate, 2016).

METHODOLOGICAL APPROACHES

After an overview of five types of policy networks, dominant theories, and theoretical constructs of SNA, in this section we zero in on the analytical aspects of SNA. First, I briefly introduce the mathematical foundations of SNA: a branch of mathematics called graph theory. Next, I use a set of articles to demonstrate how policy networks have been analyzed in empirical studies. Frequently used SNA software include UCINET, *R*, Stata, Pajek, StOCNET, SIENA, and KlinqueFinder.

Graph Theory

Graph theory conceptualizes that a graph can be used to illustrate a network—a mathematical object that can be represented in a matrix (Harary, 1969). By applying graph theory to education policy research, a policymaking and implementation process can be considered as a policy network which can be graphically represented as a set of policy actors who interact over the policymaking process (Coleman & Perl, 1999). In doing so, a policy network can be represented as a graph *G* (A, T), which is composed of policy actors *A* (also called nodes or vertices) and ties *T* (also called edges or links). When two policy actors are connected by a tie, the actors are considered adjacent in the policy network. As a result, a policy network can be represented as an adjacency matrix, as seen in Figure 9.1. Consider a policy network *G* of six policy actors (A1, A2, A3, A4, A5, and A6), and nine interaction ties. In the network *G1*, *A* = {A1, A2, A3, A4, A5, and A6}, *T* = {(A1, A2), (A1, A3), (A1, A6), (A2, A3), (A2, A6), (A3, A4), (A3, A6), (A4, A5), (A4, A6)}. Thus, the network *G1* (upper left in Figure 9.1) can be represented as the adjacency matrix 1 (upper right in Figure 9.1).

It is sometimes not enough to know the existence of an interaction tie. We might also be interested in who initiates an interaction with whom. To differentiate the sender and the recipient of the communicated messages, the interaction tie (A1, A6), as seen in *G2* (lower left in Figure 9.1), can be interpreted as A1 sends a message to A6; thus the network becomes directed, suggesting the interaction is asymmetric—the interaction starts from A1 and ends with A6. Further, we might be interested in how often the policy actors interact with one another and the extent of influence derived from their ties. To search for answers to these questions, we can differentiate the strength of an interaction tie. Specifically, the value in each cell, as seen in the adjacency matrix 2 (lower right in Figure 9.1), represents the frequency and/or quality of the tie; therefore, the network becomes weighted, suggesting the tie strength. In the directed, weighted network *G2* in Figure 9.1, the A6-A3 tie is stronger (tie strength = 3) than the one in the undirected, unweighted network *G1* (tie strength = 1). As such, the directed, weighted network *G2* provides more fine-grained details than the undirected, unweighted network *G1* on how the communicated message flows within the network.

Figure 9.1.

Illustration of Graph Theory

An unweighted, undirected network *G1*

The adjacency matrix 1

	A1	A2	A3	A4	A5	A6
A1	0	1	1	0	0	1
A2	1	0	1	0	0	1
A3	1	1	0	1	0	1
A4	0	0	1	0	1	1
A5	0	0	0	1	0	0
A6	1	1	1	1	0	0

A weighted, directed network *G2*

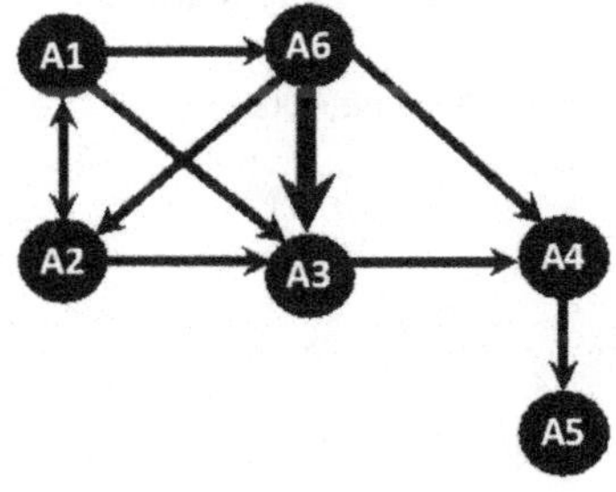

The adjacency matrix 2

	A1	A2	A3	A4	A5	A6
A1	0	1	1	0	0	1
A2	1	0	1	0	0	0
A3	1	1	0	1	0	0
A4	0	0	1	0	1	0
A5	0	0	0	0	0	0
A6	0	1	3	1	0	0

The graphs discussed so far are all one-mode networks. That is, all nodes in the network are in the same category (policy actors in this case). When the nodes in a network are in two different categories—such as policy actors as one category and their opinions as another category, such a network is called a two-mode network. For example, in Figure 9.2, the graph on the left is a two-mode network: squares represent tweets; dots represent the hashtags used in the tweets. For further network analysis, the two-mode network on the left can be converted into a one-mode network on the right, in which dots represent the hashtags and the ties represent which hashtags co-occur in tweets. The similar techniques of converting a two-mode network to a one-mode network can be used to study which policy actors advocate for or are opposed to which policy preferences. In the two-mode network, the two categories of nodes are policy actors and their policy preferences. After converting the two-mode network to the one-mode network, policy actors become the only categories of nodes that are connected by the co-occurrence ties indicating which policy actors have the same policy preferences in the network (Wang, 2018).

Figure 9.2.

An Example of Converting a Two-Mode Network to a One-Mode Network

Network construction

- Tweet1: @GOP the ppl spoke LOUDLY against **#Amnesty** and **#Obamacare** and **#Commoncore** this = NO to JEB BUSH for 2016!!!!!
- Tweet2: Jeremy Spencer talking about the coming storm Nathan Deal will face with **#CommonCore #gagov #StopCommonCore #gagop** http://t.co/oyM0WIBBsw
- Tweet3: @tedcruz understands the threat of **#CommonCore** @JebBush SUPPORTS the big government nanny state **#Cruz2016 #CruzCrew** http://t.co/IMWkRM0DWN
- Tweet4: Common Core in Action: Manipulating Shapes in the Elementary Math Classroom **#CCSS #ipaded #edtech** http://t.co/TD1X4wnasR
- Tweet5: Turn Your Public Library Into a Kid Coding Community https://t.co/N3SP1Bxipk **#edtech #corporateworkers #commoncore #stopcommoncore**

Converting two-mode network to one-mode co-occurrence network

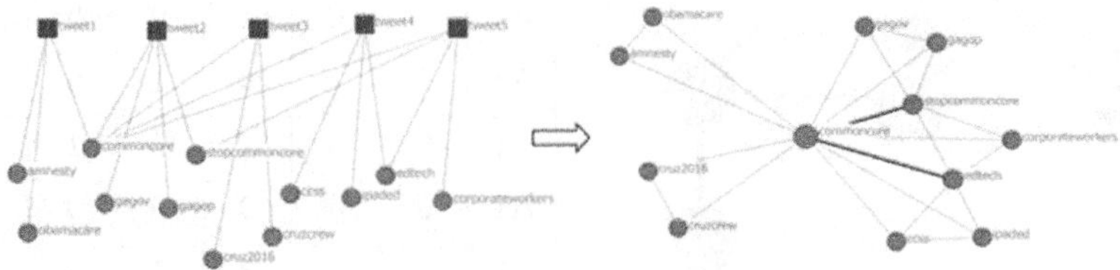

Two-mode network
Nodes: tweets + hashtags
Ties: occurrence

One-mode network
Nodes: hashtags
Ties: co-occurrence

Though the terms of "network" and "graph" have been sometimes used interchangeably in the literature, it is important to add a nuanced methodological note here. A network is represented by an adjacency matrix and can be visualized by a graph. Yet a network has much more fine-grained information than a visualized graph. Moreover, unlike the visualized graph, the network, which is grounded in graph theory, can be further analyzed through sophisticated matrix manipulations (see Newman, 2013, for a thorough explication of matrix manipulations in network analysis).

Levels of SNA

After illustrating graph theory, here I introduce how SNA has been applied to education policy research. There are three levels of network analysis: the network– (n^0),the node– (n^1), and the dyadic– n^2), levels, where n is the number of nodes in the network, and the notations indicate the level of network analysis (Borgatti et al., 2013).

At the network level (n^0), the network analysis primarily focuses on the network size, density, centralization, fragmentation, reciprocity, and core-periphery analysis. The SNA at the subgroup level—such as calculating the subgroup density—is also considered as the analysis at the network level. At the network level, the analysis outcomes are how many nodes and ties are in the network (i.e., network size), how dense the network is (i.e., network density), how fragmented the network is (i.e., network fragmentation), the proportion of reciprocal ties in the total number of ties (i.e., reciprocity), and which nodes are at the center and periphery of the network (i.e., core-periphery analysis; Borgatti et al., 2013). These network analysis outcomes are calculated to identify which network (or subgroup) is well-connected. For example, in a study on the local autism policy networks, Parson (2018) differentiated two types of networks: information-sharing network and financial resource network. It was found that the information-sharing network (density = 0.039) was less dense than the financial resource network (density = 0.086). This is because most of the financial resources were provided by one policy actor (the state government), whereas the information-sharing network was comprised of governmental organizations (e.g., Virginia Department of Education and Virginia Department of Aging and Rehabilitation Services) and an array of non-government organizations (e.g., the Blue Ridge Autism and Achievement Center, Commonwealth Autism, and Carilion Clinic).

At the node level (n^1), the analysis focus is placed on how central a given node is in the network. This is the most prevalent level of network analysis in education policy research, as most of the SNA articles on education policy analyzed the networks at the node level. Node centrality is the analysis outcome. An array of centrality measures have been developed to quantify how central a node is from different perspectives (for technical details on different centrality measures, see Newman, 2013). The commonly used centrality measures are degree centrality, betweenness centrality, and closeness centrality. The centrality measures are calculated to identify how central a policy actor is in a policy network, which implies the policy actor's influence. In state reading policymaking networks across eight states, government actors occupied significantly more central positions than nongovernment actors (Song & Miskel, 2005). Overall, the nongovernment actors had much less influence than the government actors in education policy networks. Generally speaking, "more diffused and weaker interest are less likely to organize effective groups to represent their 'latent' opinions" (Glynn et al., 2015, p. 98). However, in the opt-out movement network, the central actors were pro-opt-out teachers, opt-out parents, opt-out advocacy groups, the parent teacher associations, and opt-out students (Wang, 2017a).

At the dyadic level of network analysis (n^1), the analysis focuses on the dyadic, pairwise relationships between the nodes. At this level of network analysis, the researchers use statistical models to investigate the distribution of ties and examine the probabilities of tie formations in a network. The SNA studies on education policy rarely analyzed networks at this level. One example was found in a study on the resource network of an adult basic education policy from 1998 to 2005: the decreased resource dependence not only led to network fragmentation but also changed the nature of ties among the policy actors (Park & Rethemeyer, 2012). Another example was a study on charter schools. Jabbar (2015) conceptualized schools as nodes and conducted the dyadic level of analysis to report that public schools in New Orleans were more likely to compete with charter networks, even after controlling for school performance levels.

In addition to analyzing policy networks at the above three levels, SNA can be accompanied by quantitative and/or qualitative analysis to study education policy networks. In the studies that used both SNA and quantitative methods, the network analysis outcomes at three levels—the network– (n^0), the node– (n^1), and the dyadic– (n^2), levels—can be used as either dependent variables or independent variables for further statistical analysis. Take a study on the state reading policy networks as an example. The researchers used degree centrality as the outcome variable in multiple regression analysis and found that a policy actor's influence and policy preferences were the significant predictors of the policy actor's centrality in the policy networks (Young et al., 2016). Moreover, to investigate the trust and school leaders' social networks in a midsize underperforming urban school district, Daly and Finnigan (2012) calculated each school leader's centrality (how central a leader is in districtwide social networks), the E-I index (the extent of ties within groups and between groups), and the reciprocity (the extent of mutual relationships), and then used the outcomes of reciprocity as the dependent variable in multiple regression. The researchers found that a leader's years in administration and trust in central office were the significant predictors of how many reciprocal ties a leader had.

One of the inherent limitations of SNA is that it does not provide fine-grained information on *why* and *how* the ties are forged. Qualitative approaches thus provide a complementary methodological approach (Frank & Yasumoto, 1998). Many researchers first conduct SNA to examine the networks and provide a social context, and then analyze the qualitative data—such as interview data or archival data—to understand and interpret why and how the ties are forged. For example, policy actors can be interviewed to provide supplementary information. In one study, the interview data suggested that the minuscule influence of the teachers union in the state reading policy networks was because reading was not an important issue for teachers unions, whose priorities were money, supplies, and salaries (Song & Miskel, 2006). Moreover, after identifying competing coalitions in the opt-out movement to further understand how the coalition ties were forged, Wang (2017a) drew on Stone's (2001) framework of policy paradox to analyze how the movement goals were articulated, how the movement was framed, and what policy solutions were mobilized by the movement actors.

RECOMMENDATIONS FOR FUTURE RESEARCH

After introducing the methods of SNA and what they can accomplish in education policy research, I offer some recommendations for advancing the theoretical groundings, optimizing SNA methodological approaches, and guiding education policymaking and leadership practices. In doing so, this chapter aims to lay the ground for future applications of SNA in education policy research.

Theoretical Recommendations

Future researchers are recommended to use the findings from SNA studies to refine current theoretical constructs and develop new theories. To date, most of the SNA studies in education policy have remained at the theory application level. That is, most studies applied the theories and constructs introduced earlier, but did not use the empirical findings to advance the theory development in the field of education policy. An example that future researchers can follow is a study that proposed a theory explaining information sharing among lobbyists, members of Congress, and government agencies (Carpenter et al., 2004). After analyzing over 40,000 information-sharing relationships among lobbyists, congressional staff, and government agencies in both health and energy policy domains, Carpenter et al. (2004) developed a theory positing that information-sharing relationships prevail between organized interests themselves and are heavily dependent on their mutual relationships to third parties. The theory development—along with research methods and evaluation—are three essential components in the advancement of a field (Kuhn, 2012). With the accumulation of empirical findings in education policy, some theories and constructs need to be either refined with subtle adjustments or refuted with radical changes to better explain the phenomenon in education policy. Applying social network analysis to advance theory development in education policy would be fertile territory for future researchers.

Methodological Recommendations

In education policy research, many studies used SNA as a visualization tool to illustrate policy processes, identify salient policy actors by centrality measures, and assess policy actors' interactions. These methodological approaches, albeit valuable, have not fully capitalized on the predictive power of SNA in education policy research. Specifically, in addition to using network analysis outcomes as the variables in conventional statistical models (e.g., regression analysis and *t*-test), there are network statistical models developed specifically to analyze the networks. A fundamental difference between conventional statistical models and network statistical models lies in the fact that the nodes, which mostly represent policy actors in policy networks, are interdependent on one another (Robins et al., 2012). The *interdependence* of policy actors does not meet the assumption of independence in conventional statistical models; therefore, new statistical techniques have been developed to analyze the networks. Such network statistical models have already been applied to policy networks (Lubell et al., 2012).

For instance, to compare the changes in centrality of teacher leaders and non-teacher leaders in 12 elementary schools' teacher advice/information-seeking networks over three years, Hopkins et al. (2013) conducted the node-level *t*-test based on permutations because the centrality measures in social networks did not meet the normal distribution assumption in the conventional statistical analysis. To test the differences between the teacher interaction networks on lesson planning, reform knowledge, and recognition reform efforts, Daly and his team (Daly et al., 2010) used quadratic assignment procedure correlations because the network data, which were inherently interdependent, did not meet the assumption of independence of observations in the conventional statistical models. The quadratic assignment procedure correlation tests were also applied to test the differences between policy networks, such as the networks of policy actors' website hyperlinks, policy actors coparticipating events and activities, and policy actors' partnerships (e.g., offering technical, financial, political, or regulatory assistance) in the Tampa Bay water policy process (Yi & Scholz, 2016). Further, Spillane et al. (2015) used the *p2* model—a network statistical model that tests the effect of node variables and dyadic variables on the presence of ties (for technical details, see van Duijn et al., 2004)—to investigate what factors significantly predicted the dyadic tie formations between schools. Jabbar (2015) used the exponential random graph model (ERGM), another network statistical model testing the homophily effect—whether two individuals sharing a given characteristic are more likely to forge a dyadic tie (for technical details, see Lusher et al., 2012)—to predict the principals' perceived competitive ties between schools.

In addition to applying network statistical models, emerging methods of collecting digital data offer new methodological tools in education policy research. A common data acquisition approach is to use application programming interfaces (APIs) to retrieve data generated on the Internet. Many technology companies (e.g., Google, Facebook, and Twitter) use the APIs to grant others limited access to their data so that more applications can be created using the data. The Twitter API is one of the most popular APIs among researchers. In education policy, Wang and Fikis (2017) used the Twitter API to collect the tweets containing the hashtags #CommonCore and #CCSS. Moreover, with ready access to digital data, web crawlers, as noted earlier, are a valuable tool for collecting the network data of hyperlinks of policy actors' websites and documents (Wallis & Dockett, 2015).

Practical Recommendations

SNA serves as a valuable tool for policymakers. In education, many scholars share the concern over the limited use of research in policymaking (Neal, Mills et al., 2019). Malouf and Taymans (2016) lamented, "the transformation of education into an evidence-based field has been proclaimed for over a decade ... the degree to which it is actually taking place remains an open question" (p. 454). To address this concern, the first recommendation for education policy researchers is to assess their social networks with policymakers (Neal, Neal et al., 2019). Are there strong ties and/or weak ties between policy researchers and policymakers? What does it take to forge such ties? Is there network closure or structural holes in the social networks of policy researchers and policymakers? Network ties and network structure are the conduits through which policy actors access their social contacts' resources and thus build influence on policymaking and implementation. In this case, education policy researchers can apply SNA to assess the social ties and network structure, or lack thereof, that impede the flow of research evidence from policy researchers to policymakers.

The second recommendation for education policy researchers is to use SNA for real-time or near real-time analysis. Digital data are generated in a constant stream, providing troves of data for education research. How do people discuss an education policy on social media and blogs? How do the press (i.e., traditional media) cover an education policy? Are the arguments supporting and opposing a policy on social media different from the ones in the traditional media? Who are the opinion leaders of a policy preference? Who are in the policy actors' coalitions? SNA can answer all these questions. When digital data are collected in real-time (e.g., via a web crawler and API) and analyzed (e.g., via *R* or Python programming language), SNA has great potential to process the constant incoming data and produce timely results and visualization for education policymakers (Wang, 2017b). All the methodological approaches introduced in this chapter can be automated or semi-automated. Real-time analytics is definitely an area those interested in using digital data in education policy research should be aware of.

To conclude, this chapter discusses how SNA has been applied in education policy research. Needless to say, as an alternative method, SNA lends much support toward answering the research questions related to identifying policy actors and the interactions within and across them which help explain a policy outcome. The theoretical groundings and methodological approaches introduced in this chapter aim to set the stage for future research. It is the hope that this chapter could invite future researchers to apply SNA to advance education policy research, propel theory development, and optimize research methods.

REFERENCES

Au, W., & Ferrare, J. J. (2014). Sponsors of policy: A network analysis of wealthy elites, their affiliated philanthropies, and charter school reform in Washington State. *Teachers College Record, 116*(8), 1–24.

Berardo, R., & Scholz, J. T. (2010). Self-organizing policy networks: Risk, partner selection, and cooperation in estuaries. *American Journal of Political Science, 54*(3), 632–649.

Borgatti, S. P., Everett, M. G., & Johnson, J. C. (2013). *Analyzing social networks*. SAGE.

Borgatti, S. P., & Foster, P. C. (2003). The network paradigm in organizational research: A review and typology. *Journal of Management, 29*(6), 991–1013.

Burt, R. S. (2004). Structural holes and good ideas. *American Journal of Sociology, 110*(2), 349–399.

Burt, R. S. (2005). *Brokerage and closure: An introduction to social capital.* Oxford University Press.

Carpenter, D. P., Esterling, K. M., & Lazer, D. M. (2004). Friends, brokers, and transitivity: Who informs whom in Washington politics? *The Journal of Politics, 66*(1), 224–246.

Carpenter, D. P., Esterling, K. M., & Lazer, D. M. (1998). The strength of weak ties in lobbying networks: Evidence from health-care politics in the United States. *Journal of Theoretical Politics, 10*(4), 417–444.

Coleman, W. D., & Perl, A. (1999). Internationalized policy environments and policy network analysis. *Political Studies, 47*(4), 691–709.

Daly, A. J., Moolenaar, N. M., Bolivar, J. M. & Burke, P. (2010). Relationships in reform: The role of teachers' social networks. *Journal of Educational Administration, 48*(3), 1–38.

Daly, A. J., & Finnigan, K. S. (2012). Exploring the space between: Social networks, trust, and urban school district leaders. *Journal of School Leadership, 22*(3), 493–530.

Ferrare, J. J., & Reynolds, K. (2016). Has the elite foundation agenda spread beyond the Gates? An organizational network analysis of nonmajor philanthropic giving in K–12 education. *American Journal of Education, 123*(1), 137–169.

Fowler, J. H. (2006). Legislative cosponsorship networks in the US House and Senate. *Social Networks, 28*(4), 454–465.

Franchi, J. (2016, May 25). *Long Island's opt out movement has made the grade—now what?* Long Island Press. https://www.longislandpress.com/2016/05/25/long-islands-opt-out-movement-has-made-the-grade-now-what/

Frank, K. A., & Yasumoto, J. Y. (1998). Linking action to social structure within a system: Social capital within and between subgroups. *American Journal of Sociology, 104*, 642–686.

Glynn, C. J. Herbst, S., Lindeman, M., & O'Keefe, G. J., & Shapiro, R. Y. (2015). *Public opinion* (3rd ed.). Westview Press

Granovetter, M. S. (1973). The strength of weak ties. *American Journal of Sociology, 78*(6), 1360–1380.

Harary, F. (1969). *Graph theory*. Addission-Wesley.

Henry, A. D., Lubell, M., & McCoy, M. (2010). Belief systems and social capital as drivers of policy network structure: The case of California regional planning. *Journal of Public Administration Research and Theory, 21*(3), 419–444.

Hopkins, M., Spillane, J. P., & Jakopovic, P., & Heaton, R. M. (2013). Infrastructure redesign and instructional reform in mathematics: Formal structure and teacher leadership. *Elementary School Journal, 114*(2), 200–224.

Howlett, M. (2002). Do networks matter? Linking policy network structure to policy outcomes: Evidence from four Canadian policy sectors 1990-2000. *Canadian Journal of Political Science/Revue Canadienne de Science Politique, 35*(2), 235–267.

Jabbar, H. (2015). Competitive networks and school leaders' perceptions: The formation of an education marketplace in post-Katrina New Orleans. *American Educational Research Journal, 52*(6), 1093–1131.

Kretchmar, K., Sondel, B., & Ferrare, J. J. (2014). Mapping the terrain: Teach for America, charter school reform, and corporate sponsorship. *Journal of Education Policy, 29*(6), 742–759.

Kuhn, T. (2012). *The structure of scientific revolutions: 50th anniversary edition*. University of Chicago Press.

Leifeld, P. (2017). Discourse network analysis: Policy debates as dynamic networks. In J. N. Victor, M. N. Lubell, & A. H. Montgomery (Eds.), *The Oxford handbook of political networks* (pp. 301–326). Oxford University Press.

Lin, N. (1999). Building a network theory of social capital. *Connections, 22*(1), 2851.

Liou, Y. (2016). Tied to the Common Core: Exploring the characteristics of reform advice relationships of educational leaders. *Educational Administration Quarterly, 52*(5), 793–840.

Lubell, M., Scholz, J., Berardo, R., & Robins, G. (2012). Testing policy theory with statistical models of networks. *Policy Studies Journal, 40*(3), 351–374.

Lusher, D., Koskinen, J., & Robins, G. (2012). *Exponential random graph models for social networks: Theory, methods, and applications*. Cambridge University.

Malouf, D. B., & Taymans, J. M. (2016). Anatomy of an evidence base. *Educational Researcher, 45*(8), 454–459.

Marshall, C., Johnson, M., & Tichnor-Wagner, A. (2017). Neoliberal policy network governance and counter-networks of resistance: Actions and reactions from across policy arenas. *Peabody Journal of Education, 92*, 1–3.

McNutt, K. (2010). Virtual policy networks: Where all roads lead to Rome. *Canadian Journal of Political Science/Revue canadienne de science politique, 43*(4), 915–935.

Murthy, D. (2013). *Twitter: Social communication in the Twitter age*. Polity Press.

Neal, J. W., Neal, Z. P., Mills, K. J., Lawlor, J. A., & McAlindon, K. (2019). What types of brokerage bridge the research-practice gap? The case of public school educators. *Social Networks, 59*, 41–49.

Neal, J. W., Mills, K. J., McAlindon, K., Neal, Z. P., & Lawlor, J. A. (2019). Multiple audiences for encouraging research use: Uncovering a typology of educators. *Educational Administration Quarterly, 55*(1), 154–181.

Newman, M. E. J. (2013). *Networks: An introduction*. Oxford University Press.

New York State Senate. (2016, July 8). *Senator Kaminsky pens letter to U.S. Department of Education re: Opt out movement.* https://www.nysenate.gov/newsroom/articles/todd-kaminsky/senator-kaminsky-pens-letter-us-dept-education-re-opt-out-movement

Park, H. W., Kim, C. S., & Barnett, G. A. (2004). Socio-communicational structure among political actors on the web in South Korea: The dynamics of digital presence in cyberspace. *New Media & Society, 6*(3), 403–423.

Park, H. H., & Rethemeyer, R. K. (2012). The politics of connections: Assessing the determinants of social structure in policy networks. *Journal of Public Administration Research and Theory, 24*(2), 349–379.

Parsons, B. M. (2018). Local autism policy networks: Expertise and intermediary organizations. *Educational Policy, 32*(6), 823–854.

Pierce, J. J. (2011). Coalition stability and belief change: Advocacy coalitions in US Foreign policy and the creation of Israel, 1922–44. *Policy Studies Journal, 39*(3), 411–434.

Reagans, R., & Zuckerman, E. W. (2001). Networks, diversity, and productivity: The social capital of corporate R&D teams. *Organization Science, 12*(4), 502–517.

Reckhow, S., & Snyder, J. W. (2014). The expanding role of philanthropy in education politics. *Educational Researcher, 43*(4), 186–195.

Rhodes, R. A. W. (2006). Policy network analysis. In M. Moran, M. Rein, & R. E. Goodin (Eds.), *The Oxford handbook of public policy* (pp. 425–447). Oxford University Press.

Rhodes, R. A. (2007). Understanding governance: Ten years on. *Organization Studies, 28*(8), 1243–1264.

Robins, G., Lewis, J. M., & Wang, P. (2012). Statistical network analysis for analyzing policy networks. *Policy Studies Journal, 40*(3), 375–401.

Robinson, S. E., & Gaddis, B. S. (2012). Seeing past parallel play: Survey measures of collaboration in disaster situations. *Policy Studies Journal, 40*, 256–273.

Rogers, R., & Ben-David, A. (2010). Coming to terms: A conflict analysis of the usage, in official and unofficial sources, of 'security fence', 'apartheid wall', and other terms for the structure between Israel and the Palestinian territories. *Media, War & Conflict, 3*(2), 202–229.

Sabatier, P., Hunter, S., & McLaughlin, S. (1987). The devil shift: Perceptions and misperceptions of opponents. *Western Political Quarterly, 40*(3), 449–476.

Sabatier, P. A. (1998). The advocacy coalition framework: Revisions and relevance for Europe. *Journal of European Public Policy, 5*(1), 98–130.

Sabatier, P. A., & Weible, C. M. (2007). The advocacy coalition framework. *Theories of the Policy Process, 2*, 189–220.

Salisbury, R. H., Heinz, J. P., Laumann, E. O., & Nelson, R. L. (1987). Who works with whom? Interest group alliances and opposition. *American Political Science Review, 81*(4), 1217–1234.

Sandström, A., & Carlsson, L. (2008). The performance of policy networks: The relation between network structure and network performance. *Policy Studies Journal, 36*(4), 497–524.

Schneider, M., Scholz, J., Lubell, M., Mindruta, D., & Edwardsen, M. (2003). Building consensual institutions: Networks and the National Estuary Program. *American Journal of Political Science, 47*(1), 143–158.

Song, M., & Miskel, C. G. (2005). Who are the influentials? A cross-state social network analysis of the reading policy domain. *Educational Administration Quarterly, 41*(1), 7–48.

Spillane, J., Hopkins, M., & Sweet, T. M. (2015). Intra- and interschool interactions about instruction: Exploring the conditions for social capital development. *American Journal of Education, 122*(1), 71–110.

Stone, D. (2001). *Policy paradox: The art of political decision making*. W. W. Norton.

Supovitz, J. A., Daly, A. J., Del Fresno, M. (2017). *#CommonCore: How social media is changing the politics of education* (Consortium for Policy Research in Education). http://repository.upenn.edu/hashtagcommoncore/1

Twitter. (2019). *REST APIs*. https://dev.twitter.com/rest/public

van Duijn, M. A. J., Snijders, T. A. B., & Zijlstra, B. J. H. (2004). P2: A random effects model with covariates for directed graphs. *Statistica Neerlandica, 58*(2), 234–254.

Wada, T. (2014). Who are the active and central actors in the 'rising civil society' in Mexico? *Social Movement Studies, 13*(1), 127–157.

Wallis, J., & Dockett, S. (2015). Stakeholders, networks and links in early childhood policy: Network analysis and the Transition to School: Position Statement. *Contemporary Issues in Early Childhood, 16*(4), 339–354.

Wang, Y. (2017a). The social networks and paradoxes of the opt-out movement amid the Common Core State Standards implementation: The case of New York. *Education Policy Analysis Archives, 25*(34), 1–27.

Wang, Y. (2017b). Education policy research in the big data era: Methodological frontiers, misconceptions, and challenges. *Education Policy Analysis Archives, 25*(94), 1–24.

Wang, Y. (2018). *Mapping the coalitions of ESSA implementation: A discourse network analysis of congressional hearings*. Paper presented at the 2018 Annual Meeting of American Educational Research Association

Wang, Y., & Fikis, D. J. (2019). Common Core State Standards on Twitter: Public sentiment and opinion leaders. *Educational Policy, 33*(4), 650–683.

Wasserman, S., & Faust, K. (1994). *Social network analysis: Methods and applications*. Cambridge University Press.

Weible, C. M. (2005). Beliefs and perceived influence in a natural resource conflict: An advocacy coalition approach to policy networks. *Political Research Quarterly, 58*(3), 461–475.

Weible, C. M., & Sabatier, P. A. (2005). Comparing policy networks: Marine protected areas in California. *The Policy Studies Journal, 33*(2), 181–201.

Yi, H., & Scholz, J. T. (2016). Policy networks in complex governance subsystems: observing and comparing hyperlink, media, and partnership networks. *Policy Studies Journal, 44*(3), 248–279.

Young, T. V., Wang, Y., & Lewis, W. D. (2016). Explaining how political actors gain strategic positions: Predictors of centrality in state reading policy issue networks. *Educational Policy, 30*(6), 799–819.

CHAPTER 10

CRITICAL APPROACHES FOR POLICY-RELEVANT RESEARCH

Derek A. Houston
University of Oklahoma

T. Jameson Brewer
University of North Georgia

Meredith L. Wronowski
University of Dayton

We write together on the land placed by its Creator in the care and protection of the Cherokee and Creek Nations in Georgia, the Myaamia and Shawnee Nations in Ohio, and the Caddo Nation and the Wichita & Affiliated Tribes (Waco, Keechi, and Tawakoni Peoples) in Oklahoma and originally shared by many Indigenous Nations—including the Kiowa, Comanche and Apache Tribes—as places of gathering and exchange.

[Educational] Policy is political: it is about the power to determine what is done. It shapes who benefits, for what purpose and who pays. It goes to the very heart of educational philosophy—what is education for? For whom? Who decides? (Bell & Stevenson, 2006, p. 9)

Maximizing the Policy Relevance of Research for School Improvement, pp. 241–263
Copyright © 2021 by Information Age Publishing
All rights of reproduction in any form reserved.

INTRODUCTION

We open this chapter with the understanding that educational policy is political and that the issues and realities within American public education have historical roots that remain largely unchanged and power dynamics that continue to reproduce inequity and inequalities. Given the oversized role that power dynamics and inequality play in educational policy, the scope of this chapter is to briefly define and address critical approaches to relevant educational policy research. Because educational policy is political, the study of educational policy is inherently political. Thus, it is important to study educational policy and educational policy research through critical lenses that center the systematic critique of systems of power and amplify the need for justice. We argue that a critical approach to educational policy is vital given that ignoring—willfully or ignorantly—power dynamics will always work to provide support and cover for the status quo that has fostered decades of systematic racial, economic, and gendered inequality in schools and, subsequently, in the broader society.

In order to address the systemic ills that have plagued and continue to plague U.S. education, it is imperative that researchers who want to inform educational policy address the systems of power and injustice critically, with a keen eye on the effects of policy on the most marginalized and disenfranchised. Regardless of the macro or micro policy topic or reform being examined, educational policy research must, at its core, position itself within the arena of critical theory. Failure to explore and challenge inequitable power structures that reproduce social and racial injustices within educational policy research serves to likewise reinforce those same injustices through willful ignorance.

In this chapter, we briefly outline foundational conversations of critical theory that have been applied to education, with specific attention to the historical canons of DuBois, Marx, Friere and the more contemporary works of hooks, Crenshaw, Bell, and Ladson-Billings. Next, the chapter provides examples of critical approaches used in policy-relevant research. The chapter specifically avoids the methodological qualitative/quantitative binary and focuses, instead, on the epistemological foundations of critical research. However, it must be said that, historically, critical theory has been noticeably absent from the broad landscape of educational policy—particularly as policy work has centered around false narratives of positivism and claims of unbiased scientific inquiry by way of employing quantitative methods. As Diem et al. (2014) note,

> As part of the policy studies field, educational policy research has tended to operate within a traditionalistic (i.e., positivist) paradigm and, over time, has developed a group of taken-for-granted assumptions, norms, and tradi-

> tions that institutionalize conventional ontological, epistemological, and methodological traditions. (p. 1068)

Moreover, while not all quantitative research has fallen prey to such tenants, the broad body of quantitative educational policy research has operated within the ideology of positivism and an acontextual disposition that, by definition, actively ignores relevant power dynamics and reduces economic stratification and racial inequities to statistical background noise. The fields of policy analysis and evaluation are experiencing an emergence of critical work that accesses frameworks designed to interrogate dominant cultural and value assumptions that undergird policy, as well as the likelihood that a policy will exacerbate or mitigate long-standing and systemic inequities (Diem et al., 2014; Marshall, 1999; Taylor, 2006). To highlight the use of critical frameworks in policy research, this section includes examples from multiple research paradigms, each with a critical focus on educational research.

Finally, the chapter provides a call to action on the need for, and use of, critical approaches in policy-relevant research. A critical approach to policy-relevant research does not have a focus on outcomes but rather a focus on disproportionate opportunity which effects the outcomes (Howe, 1997). Outcomes-based policy research largely relies on myths of meritocracy and centers, for example, on student academic and economic outcomes as the result of individual effort and that are not explainable through critical analysis of power imbalances, classism, and racism. We argue that what is most important in the conversation of educational policy research and schooling is the accumulated educational debt of historic systemic inequalities faced by the most marginalized (Ladson-Billings, 2006) and the educational opportunity gaps (Carter & Welner, 2013; Milner, 2010), not achievement gaps, that are still present. As such, in the growing age of racial and socioeconomic inequality, it is imperative that policy-relevant research incorporate a critical approach to examining where inequitable access to opportunity results in inequitable educational outcomes, and thus, inform policy that impacts the most marginalized.

WHAT IS CRITICAL THEORY? AND WHY IT'S USEFUL

As noted above, we operationalize this chapter from the understanding and perspective that educational policy (laws, debates, pedagogy, methods, curriculum, etc.) are innately political in nature and, as a result, are impacted and influenced by power dynamics and power imbalances. Purportedly, public schools are the cornerstone of American democracy, providing a level and equal playing field for all students to achieve academically despite their socioeconomic, racial, and parental educational attainment backgrounds.

Though, while such arguments have been thoroughly problematized (Bowles & Gintis, 1976; Brewer & Myers, 2015; Carter & Welner, 2013; Coleman, 1990; Coleman et al., 1966; Ennis, 1976; Jencks & Phillips, 1998; Jencks et al., 1972; Ladson-Billings, 2006; Piketty, 2014; Rothstein, 2004; Wilkinson & Pickett, 2010), the power and political dynamics of the American legislative and policy environment reinforce and reproduce the entrenched power dynamics by the very nature of our political process (e.g., voter suppression). The imbalance within the American political structures reflects centuries of racist, classist, and sexist systems that privilege some (namely the affluent and White) while disenfranchising, disparaging, and oppressing others (namely Black, Latinx,[1] and Indigenous persons, as well as the low and middle class) (Feagin, 2013). These historical roots of class and racial dynamics continue to be made manifest through myriad artifacts within educational policymaking that, both overtly and covertly, do not provide an equal educational opportunity (Carter & Welner, 2013; Ladson-Billings, 2006; Marx, 1867/1987; Piketty, 2014). Because schools and schooling are understood in terms of providing the mechanism by which and through which students, regardless of background, can realize the "American Dream" of economic and social mobility and the extent to which an unequal system may hide systemic inequalities, analysis of educational policy decisions mandates that we interpret policymaking through a critical theory and social justice framework. A failure to critique educational policies without making use of a critical theory and social justice perspective accomplishes two things: (1) it reinforces the myth of meritocracy and shifts the blame for generational poverty, for example, onto the shoulders of "bad" or "lazy" students (Thernstrom & Thernstrom, 2003) or cultural/racial deficits (Payne, 2003) rather than an unjust system; and, (2) bolsters a policymaking landscape that can, and often does, operate outside of the systemic realities and contexts faced by students—specifically Black, Latinx, Indigenous, and students in poverty (see Table 10.1).

Given this imperative, researchers should strive to incorporate a critical lens whenever possible in their works and in their consultations with policymakers. While critical approaches can be, and often are, dismissed as biased or opinionated, we must ask ourselves who dismisses such critiques and what power, if any, they seek to retain through the dismissive nature of ignoring valid critical theory critiques. A failure to challenge unfair and inequitable power structures—with data—will silently reinforce those very power imbalances and, in the process, contribute to the reproduction of systemic class and racial injustices made possible through schools.

Critical theory is, in short, a "specific scholarly approach that explores the historical, cultural, and ideological lines of authority that underlie

Table 10.1

Methods and Motivations for Research Paradigms

Research Methods	Critical	Critical Quantitative	Positivist–Postpositivist
Scope	In-depth	Broad	Broad
Findings	Interpretive	Generalizable	Generalizable
Data	Idiographic	Aggregate	Aggregate
Results	Context dependent	Context dependent	Context dependent
Research Motivation			
Questions	Model questioning	Model questioning modification	Model verification confirmation
Goals	Description	Investigation	Explanation
Outcomes	Equity	Equity	Fairness

Note. Adapted from Stage (2007).

social conditions" (Sensoy & DiAngelo, 2017, p. 23) that fosters a disposition in which "awareness and analysis involve identifying places where the normalization of systems of privilege and disadvantage should be questioned, resisted, and changed at all levels—social, cultural, institutional, and personal" (Adams & Zúñiga, 2016, p. 113). Educational research often fails to account for the systems of privilege that inform educational opportunities, and thus inform educational outcomes. For example, funding structures for public education in the United States rely primarily on local property tax revenue (Baker & Corcoran, 2012). As is the case, the wild variations among property values across geographic locales—not only statewide and nationwide but varied even across counties and school districts—naturally and necessarily create an unjust system (Baker et al., 2014). Viewing this type of funding structure through a Marxist critical theoretical lens allows researchers, policymakers, teachers, and parents alike to problematize the system as a mechanism by which, and through which, socioeconomic stratification is maintained (Bowles & Gintis, 1976). If schools are to be understood as a level playing field, as suggested above, then the very nature of school funding challenges the myth of the American Dream at the outset of policy examination, well before additional and useful examinations of other policies through varied lenses within critical theory (e.g., feminist criticism, LGBTQ criticism, post-colonial criticism, etc.) begin to highlight layers of stratified power and the resulting oppression.

Conversations surrounding equal opportunities versus equal outcomes have long been contentious. In their seminal work, Bowles and Gintis (1976) explicated the massive impact that socioeconomic status had on student opportunities and, therefore, student outcomes. Drawing on a growing body of research of the time (Coleman et al., 1966; Jencks et al., 1972), Bowles and Gintis' research declared definitively that economic power imbalances in American society that were the natural result of capitalism informed inequitable educational experiences for students across the United States. Their examination through a Marxist lens remains the bedrock of critical policy analysis centering around the implications of economic inequality on school opportunities. And this is important considering that "as a site for the reproduction of capitalist values and White supremacist capitalist patriarchy classroom spaces themselves are rife with constraints and restraints that impose the values and actions which work toward the reproduction of the status quo" (Freire, 2013, p. 263).

WHY IS CRITICAL THEORY RELEVANT TO POLICY RESEARCH?

It is crucial for an understanding of American educational history ... to recognize that within American democracy there have been classes of oppressed people and that there have been essential relationships between popular education and the politics of oppression. Both schooling for democratic citizenship and schooling for second-class citizenship have been basic traditions in American education. (Anderson, 1988, p. 1)

A critical theory approach to policy research is necessary given that the context of education does not exist in a vacuum. People are impacted by the policies and practices that are currently implemented in education and the sociocultural and historical inequities of the status quo, writ large. In his discussion of Harold Lasswell's mid-20th century views on the subject of policy orientation that valued context, Torgerson notes that "the increasing importance of intellectuals comes, in [Lasswell's] view, with both promise and threat. Intellectuals could simply form part of the oligarchic and bureaucratic structures operating for the benefit of the few at the cost of the oppression and indignity of the many.

"A policy profession devoted to democracy would depend on a critical stance toward context, and crucial to this posture would be a questioning of the obvious" (Torgerson, 2007, p. 17). Gillborn (2005) further argues that education policy is an act of White supremacy or institutionalized White power and in the context of the American power and policy landscape (including, but not limited to, education policy), the legacy and status quo deriving from historical power inequities favoring White people must be acknowledged and understood. Uncritical analysis of policy and practice reinforces the status quo. Without a doubt, a significant portion of American history and contemporary society relies on and reinforces a power structure wrought with institutionalized White supremacy (DiAngelo, 2018; Sensoy & DiAngelo, 2017). In order to understand where opportunity gaps may exist and to begin to address these policies, we must examine the educational context in which we currently exist.

Since the 1990s, the policy context of education has been dominated by an accountability-based reform agenda with No Child Left Behind promised as a panacea for addressing both perceived poor global performance and inequities of outcomes in the U.S. educational system (Vasquez Heilig et al., 2014). While school accountability reform has been successful in *highlighting* achievement gaps between White, economically-advantaged students and students living in marginalized communities, the accountability policy paradigm has done little to systematically address the entrenched and historical opportunity gaps that are at the root of those achievement gaps. In some cases, the implementation of accountability policy in school settings that are at risk of being labeled as "failing" due to long-standing and systemic inequities within and outside the school setting, may have exacerbated these opportunity gaps by ignoring systemic inequities, narrowing curriculum and instruction, and creating an environment in which marginalized students are viewed as liabilities (Jacob, 2005; Vasquez Helig, 2011; Vasquez Heilig & Darling-Hammond, 2008; Vasquez Heilig et al., 2012).

The National Center for Education Statistics publishes annually their Condition of Education Report (McFarland et al., 2018), providing a longitudinal snapshot of the United States' educational system, broadly defined. Over a nearly 20 year period, educational achievement (NAEP reading and mathematics scores) and attainment (postsecondary enrollment rates) measures have seen increases, with the increases being representative across racial and class groups. However, these achievement gaps (gaps in outcomes) have remained relatively constant. An ample body of literature has generally focused on outcomes-based models and studied policies that were designed to help close those gaps. Yet, the gaps remain. Gap gazing (Gutiérrez, 2008; Gutiérrez & Dixon-Roman, 2010; Rodriguez, 2001)[2] has not helped reduce the achievement gaps (Carter & Welner, 2013). Instead of focusing on achievement gaps, a critical though not novel approach would be to address the opportunity gaps (gaps in inputs), as Milner (2012) would call them. Gap-gazing is one example of how a lack of criticality, or a critical-theory informed approach, has allowed a policy agenda centered on individualism and meritocracy to thrive, increasing the educational debts (Ladson-Billings, 2006) owed to Black, Latin, Indigenous, and students in poverty. However, the two dominant reform agendas—accountability and choice—have fallen short in their ability to address these opportunity gaps.

The inequitable conditions are not lost on many educational researchers. These school conditions disproportionately impact the most marginalized in the U.S. context, namely Black, Latinx, Indigenous, and people living in poverty. Additionally, the inequitable conditions are disproportionately seen across the K–20 spectrum (McFarland et al., 2018). For many conditions—such as Black preschool children being suspended at rates higher than their peers, public school Students of Color receiving less money per pupil, the rising costs of higher education access, and women being paid 23% less for the same work—Black, Latinx, Indigenous, women, and students in poverty are disproportionately affected. Critical approaches to policy-relevant research centers on the study of systems, systemic and systematic issues, how inequalities of opportunity come into existence, perpetuate, impact policy outcomes, and how their outcomes disproportionately impact some more than others.

What is also not lost within critical approaches to policy-relevant research is the systemic and systematic links between race, poverty, gender, and education. Thus, an intersectional (Crenshaw, 1989) critique of policy addresses how power dynamics impact individuals from different intersecting identities differently. Furthermore, an intersectional critique recognizes that those occupying multiple marginalized identities are they, themselves, more marginalized. Because of this, a critical intersectional approach to policy-relevant research is warranted. This approach helps account for the interrelatedness of power dynamics at the intersection of multiple marginalized identities. For example, in reference to school funding inequalities, a critical intersectional approach to policy-relevant research could look not only at the decline in public education funding but also address at who is impacted at the margins, highlighting inequalities at the intersection of race, gender, and poverty.

Evidenced above is the relevance of critical theory in policy-relevant research. Moving forward, we provide examples of the application of critical approaches in policy-relevant research.

WHAT ARE SOME CRITICAL APPROACHES THAT HAVE BEEN USED IN POLICY-RELEVANT RESEARCH?

Next, the chapter provides examples of critical approaches used in policy-relevant research. Additionally, we provide examples of policy-relevant research that lacked a critical approach and discuss how a critical approach could have changed facets of the analyses used and conclusions drawn. This section includes examples from multiple research paradigms, each with a critical focus on educational research. Instead of specifically focusing on the methodological qualitative/quantitative binary, we highlight how the research takes steps to critically examine policy, the types of questions that were asked, the discussion of data limitations, any critiques made, and suggestions offered. We spend time examining research that spans three educational levels of policy-relevant research: K–12, higher ed, and P–20.

Critical Policy Approaches

Critical policy analysis and evaluation can occur using a variety of data sources and qualitative and quantitative methodologies/methods. The defining feature of critical policy analysis is a stance that interrogates dominant cultural assumptions and examines the likelihood that policy will empower, democratize, and/or redistribute good and opportunities to oppressed groups and communities (Diem, et al., 2014; Marshall, 1999). Taylor (2006) has suggested that critical policy evaluation must be oriented in a values approach that considers both the external political values of a wide-range of stakeholders, including maintaining the status quo or emancipation from oppressive power structures, as well as the intrinsic values indicated by the policy itself. In this respect, critical policy evaluation can serve as a counter-strategy to "evidence" based technical-rational evaluation. Technical-rational policy evaluation is grounded in a post-positivist paradigm in which the policy observer is external to the evaluation and, therefore, their selection, analysis, and presentation data can be considered value-free. However, critical policy evaluation has the ability to center both policy observers and stakeholders within the evaluation, and, by doing so, allows for explicit identification and uncovering of their values that serve as foundations of the policy evaluation process. Below we describe examples of critical policy analysis and evaluation that span methodological approaches.

Qualitative methods have a lengthy history in policy research, particularly with regard to interpretive policy analysis (IPA). However, IPA scholars approach their work from an inductive, often policy-neutral stance. In contrast, critical policy analysis (CPA) uses a deductive approach from a critical theory foundation (Mansfield & Thachik, 2016). An analysis of the Texas *Closing the Gaps 2015* policy using both IPA and CPA reveal that the policy message was one emphasizing the human capital and economic paradigm of education and evoking affective terms such as achievement of the American Dream as policy salesmanship. Analyzing the same policy from a CPA perspective highlights the failure to acknowledge the systemic inequities that created achievement gaps, the emphasis on meritocracy, and the positioning of diversity as valuable in the context of economic competition but not valuable in terms of community cultural wealth (Mansfield & Thachik, 2016). Overall, findings from this study indicate reforms can aim to increase educational access and achievement for people of color, while still failing to acknowledge cultural values or address systemic inequities.

Similar themes are present in the analysis of the foundational policy writings of Wendy Kopp, founder of Teach for America. The explicit policy goal of TFA is to reduce achievement gaps and reduce inequitable access to quality education for students of color and economically disadvantaged students. However, applying a CPA approach reveals three counterstories to the policy narrative. The first counterstory is the presence of latent institutional racism in TFA that prioritizes dominant culture corps members, degrades existing teachers, and excludes the voices of students, families, and communities of color (Barnes et al., 2016). The second counterstory is the advancement of neoliberal reforms and privatization that runs counter to culturally relevant pedagogy in favor of standardized definitions of achievement. The third counterstory is the identification of cultural repossession and a poverty of culture in exchange for a culture of achievement (Barnes et al., 2016). Even when policy texts advocate for social justice work, the failure to support appropriate enactment of policies can lead to failure in this work.

In an analysis of transgender student and staff policies in Ontario school district boards, Omercajic (2015) uses critical gender theories to uncover hegemonic gender norms in policy texts and enactment. The written policies examined emphasized the presence of students struggling with gender identity and the need for schools to reduce dangers and alienation that transgender or gender fluid students experience. However, the policies also emphasized "accommodation when requested," forcing students to out themselves, and offered little to no guidance for administrators and teachers in enactment. Thus, the policies, as enacted, did little to create inclusive spaces or address problematic heteronormative curriculum and instruction (Omercajic, 2015). As illustrated in these three examples, applying critical frameworks to the uses of traditional qualitative methods in educational policy analysis can uncover latent oppressive stances in the policies and empower voices silenced in the policy process. Qualitative methods will continue to be valuable to policy analysis. But enhancing these methods by incorporating critical theoretical underpinnings allows them to deduce dominant culture values present in educational policies, tell counterstories to dominant narratives present in the salesmanship and promotion of educational policies, and uncover hegemonic norms embedded in educational policy texts and their enactment by policy actors. The reframing of qualitative methods is an important step forward because considerable policy analysis work depends on qualitative data. However, quantitative and mixed methods have a long-standing history in the field of policy and program evaluation.

Quantitative methods are an important tool for both quasi-experimental and causal policy evaluation. However, these methods have been viewed as incongruent with critical theory given their historical roots in the eugenics movement. More recently two bodies of scholarship, critical quantitative inquiry (Stage, 2007) and QuantCrit (see Gillborn et al., 2018), have emerged as sets of principles for applying a critical lens to quantitative methods and for reclaiming quantitative methods for social justice work. This is accomplished through a "principled ambivalence" to numbers, recognizing that statistical research is not value-free or politically neutral (Crawford et al., 2019; Zuberi & Bonilla-Silva, 2008). QuantCrit is not a theory on its own, rather it is a methodological framework that is grounded in the tenets of critical race theory (CRT), including the centrality of racism and white supremacy, challenging dominant white narratives by including the knowledge and perspectives of marginalized groups, and a commitment to social and racial justice (Garcia et al., 2018). A deep examination of the principles of QuantCrit are beyond the scope of this chapter (see Gillborn et al., 2018); rather, we describe the ways in which these principles have been applied.

The ways that students' and families' race, ethnicity, and languages are coded by K–12 schools are not politically or perception neutral and can be connected to White, dominant norms (Crawford et. al., 2019; Gillborn et al., 2018). Racism is deeply entrenched within official processes, reports, and statistical reporting (Garcia et al., 2018). Specifically, an interrogation of race and language categories widely used in Florida revealed that student race was "re-formed" due to a policy that allowed families who identified as "Latino" to identify *only* in that category, disregarding families who identified as members of indigenous Latino or Black Latino race groups. Compared to multiple group assignment data strategies, this reduced the number of "American Indian" students to 0% – 1% from 3% – 10% and reduced the number of Black students from 1% – 7% from 2% – 11%. In addition, indigenous Mexican languages were "re-formed" as Spanish by registrars who were instructed that any language from Mexico should be recorded as Spanish. In addition, registrars did not routinely record the language of families who identified as Black or White, assuming that these families were "English Proficient" or not multilingual (Campbell-Montalvo, 2019).

In addition to problematic data collection and handling that is grounded in White-normative perceptions of diverse families, quantitative data can also be used to construct narratives that: (1) fail to accurately represent the counterstories and everyday realities of minoritized communities, and (2) inappropriately and selectively use data to frame white students and families as oppressed in political narratives (Crawford, 2019). A particularly public example of this use of data occurred in Britain where the *Race Disparity Audit* of 2017 was used to publicize the claim that "White working-class" students in Britain were being disadvantaged in the educational system. The report, frequently cited in a variety of conservative media outlets in Britain, used descriptive statistics to show that White students claiming free school meals (FSM) had lower achievement compared to Indian, Pakistani, Bangladeshi, Black Caribbean, Black African, and Chinese students. However, these claims failed to acknowledge that only 11.5% of White students claim FSM, compared to 23% to 45% of Pakistani, Bangladeshi, Black Caribbean, Black African students and that, when comparing success rates of non-FSM students, Black Caribbean students were the student subgroup with the lowest academic success rate. Additionally, by framing White students claiming FSM as "working class," the Conservative party intentionally used language that would make the issue speak to the majority of the White voting base, 60% of whom considered themselves "working class" even though they do not claim FSM (Crawford, 2019).

The two examples highlighted above provide clear cases of using QuantCrit as a post hoc critique of educational policy and politics; however, Sablan (2019) demonstrates how QuantCrit can also be applied as a methodology and research design. Cultural capital (Bourdieu, 1986) is a theory of social reproduction of the dominant class through schools rewarding their normative behaviors and tastes. While cultural capital can be considered a critical theory, the way that the theory has been operationalized and used in quasi-experimental models has been deficit-minded and used to blame students' academic "failures" on their nondominant cultures (Dixon-Román, 2014; Ladson-Billings, 1998; Yosso, 2005). However, nondominant cultural capital and community cultural wealth (CCW) provide counterstories to the dominant culture narrative of cultural capital. Sablan (2019) demonstrates the application of a QuantCrit framework to operationalize CCW in a way that indicates four distinct forms of capital—aspirational, familial, navigational, and resistant (Yosso, 2005)—that people from nondominant cultures possess in higher education settings. Sablan created items for each of Yosso's (2005) forms of cultural capital through a review of critical literature, and a collaboration with both academics with expertise in cultural capital theory and community leaders from Pacific Islander cultures. The items such as, "I am connected to my extended family members," and "I know about my family's history," were used to operationalize the concept of familial capital. Items like, "I believe there are injustices in my ethnic/racial/cultural community," and "I want to make a difference in my racial/ethnic/cultural community," represent the concept of resistant capital, while items like "I have succeeded despite by barriers to success," and "Even when I have limited resources, ... I find ways to secure the essentials for my education," are used to operationalize navigational and aspirational capital. In addition, the four CCW scales created to better understand the non-dominant cultural capital of Native Pacific Islander and Asian American undergraduate students centered them in the questions, asking them to identify if qualities were "Not at all like me" to "Exactly like me." This process of operationalization shows congruence between the counter-story approach of qualitative CRT research and measurement theory by embedding the collection of counter-stories of marginalized Asian American and Pacific Islander students including Filipino, Chamorro, Micronesian, and multiethnic students (groups that are frequently included in a blanket "Asian" label) within the validation and reliability process. The study resulted in creation and validation of critical CCW constructs that can be used in future quasi-experimental and causal models that seek to counter deficit-minded results historically reported from similar models.

Critical latent variable modeling has been extended to structural models examining the relationship of student race, income, parental education, and high school student achievement to SAT scores. These explanatory models were able to uncover an intersectional effect of Black students living in poverty on their SAT scores mediated by their high school achievement. While both Black and White students living in poverty had lower SAT scores, the effect was nearly twice as large for Black students living in poverty. The difference between Black and White students was so large that even increasing high school achievement by a full point on a four-point scale could not reduce this gap, a clear argument against the idea of meritocracy and pulling oneself up by their "bootstraps" (Dixon-Roman, McArdle, & Everson, 2013).

Lastly, Malcom-Piqueux (2015) proposes that person-centered, rather than variable-centered, quantitative approaches can make an important contribution to critical quantitative work. Methods such as latent class analysis (LCA) or latent profile analysis (LPA) can be used to highlight inequities between groups of students by using their responses to items related to complex, underlying constructs. These constructs can emerge from critical frameworks and can be related to intersectional demographic variables after the latent profiles are developed, which offers a more critical approach compared to using demographic variables to explain outcomes. The latter approach frequently reinforces deficit mindsets about marginalized students and communities. Applying this method to higher education financing survey data, Malcom-Piqueux found that Latinx and Black students were more likely to self-finance or rely on financial aid to fund their college education, compared with the Asian and White students who were more likely to receive parental financial support. LCA and LPA are also methods that are congruent with quasi-experimental and causal modeling, both of which are currently viewed as powerful policy evaluation tools. However, QuantCrit has yet to be effectively applied in these causal models, an important next step for the growth of this framework (Sablan, 2019).

(Un)critical Causal Policy Approaches

The use of causal inference in policy-relevant research has grown in sophistication with the growth in the tools to carry out the research. The causal theory discussed in the 1980s has gained broader acceptance across a wide variety of disciplines and is viewed as a foundational work in policy-relevant research. Increasingly, policymakers want to know if a policy has a direct and causal effect on outcomes. In their seminal work on the theory and methods behind causal inference, Murnane and Willett (2011) highlight four quasi-experimental techniques that could be used to make causal inferences: difference-in-differences, regression discontinuity, instrumental variables estimation, and the use of the propensity score. These quasi-experimental approaches provide researchers with the methods, while upgraded technology provides them with the tools, to make causal inferences. However, there are few, if any, published examples of causal research that take critical approaches. Because of this, we offer examples of policy-relevant research that uses causal approaches and discuss how a critical approach could have shaped both the methods/analyses used and the conclusions drawn. We also discuss the possible underlying assumptions of each article and how a critical approach would shape those assumptions.

In a causal regression discontinuity design, Carlson and Lavertu (2018) find that an infusion of School Improvement Grant (SIG) monies and application of federal Turnaround and Transformation models of school improvement yielded significant improvement in academic achievement in the first 3 years after the SIG award with diminishing increases in the 4th year. The authors also conclude that the Turnaround model, where 50% of a school's faculty and administration is replaced, is less costly than the Transformation model which focuses on changes in school governance and teacher evaluation. What is absent from this work are the counterstories that have emerged from critical school accountability and improvement scholars. For example, the work is based on the assumption that "achievement" should be narrowly defined using a standardized test criterion. A narrow definition of achievement has been linked to a narrowing of curriculum and instruction educational triage concentrated in "failing" schools that are frequently located in economically disadvantaged communities and communities of color (Booher-Jennings, 2005; Jacob, 2005). In addition, a singular focus on "school improvement" which views students and communities in human capital terms delegitimizes community-based knowledge and represents another form of postcolonial surveillance and punishment on oppressed communities and the educators that serve them (Green, 2018; Vasquez Heilig et al. 2014). In essence, we do not contend that evaluations of federal and state policy programs should not be conducted, rather we propose that researchers should create space for subaltern ways of knowing.

Lacoe and Steinberg (2019) demonstrate the use of an instrumental variable approach to causal modeling to examine the relationship of out-of-school suspensions (OSS) on achievement and attendance following a discipline policy change in a large, urban school district. The authors find OSS has a significant effect on decreased math and ELA achievement and on increased absences. While the authors interrogate the validity of OSS in light of its negative effects on achievement, they fail to question whether punitive practices such as suspension policies, regardless of disproportionate impacts, are just and address justice. Although the authors demonstrate higher proportions of OSS for Black, male, economically disadvantaged, and special education students compared to their percentages of overall enrollment, they fail to discuss the implications of this disproportionality even when a significant amount of critical scholarship has previously addressed these issues and their implications. From a methodological and analytical perspective, the authors include these student identity characteristics in their models only as a fixed effects control vector. The data set utilized offered an opportunity for critical quantitative analysis to uncover the effects of student identity characteristics and intersectional identities even when examining the causal effect of a discipline policy change. An example of a QuantCrit reframing of the analysis could include using multilevel models to examine fixed effects of intersectional student identity (Lopez et al., 2018) while simultaneously examining a policy effect through cross-level identity characteristics-policy interaction terms (Heck et al., 2013). Finally, a critical approach to evaluation of discipline may identify different sets of research questions. For example, what questions would be asked if the authors viewed the causes of the suspensions as a district, school, or personnel problem and not that of a student problem? What conclusions would be made if the cause of outcome was centered in examining inequities and problematic features of the discipline system and not on the "misbehavior" of the students?

Critical approaches are equally about the methods or modes of inquiry, the questions that are asked, and the critiques offered. The methodological approaches and examples offered here are not distinctly critical. As we have discussed, the use of critical theory as a framework to understand policy research presupposes an analysis that is "unabashedly political" in its quests for socially just practices, policies, and outcomes (Baez, 2007). Furthermore, under a critical theory framework, the research not only addresses the question but offers a critique of systems that operate unjustly and limit emancipatory opportunity, particularly for marginalized and disenfranchised populations. Thus, although we offer some critical approaches to policy-relevant research, they are but examples of how the application of the tools of research, grounded in critical theory, can inform policy. As such, how these tools are used can help determine if oppressive and unjust systems are dismantled or reinforced, torn down or propped up, reversed or revered and, thus, lead to a more socially just world or not—emancipation or objectification, freedom or continued restraint, resistance or complacency.

THE CURRENT STATE OF EDUCATIONAL POLICY RESEARCH

There is truly only one certainty when considering social phenomena: there is little to be certain about. Just as humans differ from one another, so too are there differences in lived realities and understandings that derive from context. And while a statistician may purport methods that "control" for messy factors like poverty, there can never be a full—or perhaps close enough—understanding of how poverty impacts lives without a consideration of context. That is, two students living in poverty, both receiving governmental aid, with both parents living at home, with two siblings, equidistant from the schoolhouse will necessarily have different experiences, perspectives, interactions, outputs, and outcomes when considering their educational realities.

In short, educational policy research—or any other form of social inquiry—that does not center contextual factors such as culture within the process of casting value decisions is myopically interested in engaging in reductionistic science that does not begin to understand the lived experiences of individuals and groups. Yet, this type of work is difficult and often requires more resources and time than are readily available in this hyper realm of inquiry that seeks to label best practices, brand them, and then seek out venues for profit. With this understanding, policy research that is culturally responsive requires the researcher to have and operate within an in-depth understanding of the context of the research. This, as suggested above, requires the researcher to forgo the illusions proffered by other forms of inquiry and evaluation, which insist that social phenomena are a-contextual and that the results of educational research are widely generalizable outside of their specific context. Said another way, Hood, Hopson and Frierson note that "for too long the broad, established evaluation community has either ignored or been reluctant to engage in a meaningful scholarly dialogue about the roles of culture and context in evaluation"

(Hood et al., 2005). In short, some education policy researchers and evaluators seemingly have intentionally ignored context and culture (often the culture of communities of color and/or impoverishment) and, thus, upheld cultural imperialism as the worldview. As such, the assumptions of the researcher that follow are thus substituted for the palpable realities that are taken as sterile.

In other words, engagement with the stakeholders (students, parents, community members, teachers, and staff) involved in educational programs prior to the development of the research or evaluation project accomplishes much. For example: (a) it indicates a general disposition of honoring more than one vantage perception; (b) it situates the content of the evaluation within the particular context of an educational program; and (c) it likely will lead to a better and more accurate understanding of the outcomes of a particular program within the unique situation in which the program is enacted.. Of great concern is the desire to generalize "best practices" across all contexts by either ignoring contextual realities or attempting to statistically control for them—a mathematical ignoring of context. By systemically ignoring context, such policy research or evaluation seeks to standardize both the service as well as the recipient; call it the McDonaldization of social inquiry and social reform.

The quest for certainty operates from a perspective that individual, school, and community culture is meaningless, and it should be controlled or ignored at all costs. The quest for the reproduction of a-contextual certainty may very well be the currency of our age, yet, what we need is contextually and culturally responsive evaluations that acknowledge and honor the differences and diversity among us. Social scientists forfeit a truly rich opportunity to understand the human condition as dictated by context when they attempt to generalize. Contextually and culturally relevant policy research and evaluation stands as the only holistic manner by which to gain insightful and meaningful understandings of social and school phenomena.

Research that does not employ a critical theory lens posits a position of meritocracy—that is, there is no power imbalance, there is no classism, no racism, and so forth. It assumes that students are receiving education in a vacuum where reform treatments can be tested (often as solutions in search of a problem). For too long, quantitative methods that purport to sterilize contextual factors and bias have ignored power structures inherent in schooling and society at large. And while we are not arguing for the abandonment of quantitative methods, we are suggesting, as David Berliner (2002) has, that educational policy analysis and research be broadened to not only allow for more nuanced methods that account for contextual factors but for those that specifically speak directly towards exposing inequality and power dynamics that have for too long reinforced racial and class inequality. This is vital as "the interpretive policy analyst ... cannot stand outside the policy issue being analyzed. Indeed, analysts have to immerse themselves in the beliefs (ideas, values, feelings, and meanings) of both the participants and the researchers" (Fischer, 2003).

A VISION FOR CHANGE IN EDUCATIONAL POLICY RESEARCH

> There is no magic, either in mixed schools or in segregated schools. A mixed school with poor and unsympathetic teachers with hostile public opinion, and no teaching of truth concerning black folk, is bad. A segregated school with ignorant placeholders, inadequate equipment, poor salaries, and wretched housing, is equally bad. (DuBois, 1935, p. 335)

Academics and educational-policy researchers engaging in educational policy research must have, at their core, a shared sense of obligation to students and student opportunities. This commitment can no longer be met with claims of bias. Yet, to the extent that we are accused of being biased in favor of equality and equity, we are guilty as charged. And to that point, we recognize, as many have before us, that taking a critical theoretical approach to policy research is the only method through which we can expose and challenge power imbalances that largely favor the white affluent power hierarchy in American society and schools. Failure to challenge these realities and contexts in our work will, by definition, work to reinforce the status quo of inequality. We must challenge policy and political assertions that do not acknowledge power, race, and/or class.

Where do we go from here? In conversation with his student Luke Skywalker, noted orator Master Yoda stated, "You must unlearn what you have learned." In response, Luke mumbled, "Oh, alright, I'll give it a try." In retort, Master Yoda exclaimed, "Try not, do or do not. There is no try" (Kershner, 1980). We draw upon these words to issue a challenge. For those who center the examination of power and systems of power, the choice of doing so critically or uncritically is nonexistent. When it comes to critical policy work, work that challenges and seeks to disrupt systems of power and oppression, it is either done or not done. There is no trying. Failure is a part of the doing. Doing critical research is a way of existing, constantly thinking about how power and systems of power impact their ways of being, their worldview, and the ways of being for those that are systematically marginalized, disenfranchised, and oppressed. Thus, we challenge those who engage this work and who start to think about how this chapter informs their work, research, and life. If you choose to explore this work, do so mindfully. Do so with the understanding and expectation that critical work is an existence and not just an approach. Do so knowing that this work is hard and that your socialization, your ways of knowing (ontological and epistemological assumptions) will likely be challenged. Do so knowing that even the choice to do critical policy research is political and is rooted in power structures that may delegitimize the contributions of some scholars more than others. Do so with the understanding that you are doing this work while standing on the shoulders of giants and recognize those shoulders appropriately. Finally, regardless of the methodological approach you choose to use, be mindful that critical work is communal and approach this work with the understanding that you are working with and for communities.

We leave you the following: In the growing age of racial and socioeconomic inequality, it is imperative that policy-relevant research incorporates a critical approach to examining where inequitable access to opportunity results in inequitable educational outcomes, and, thus, informing policy that impacts the most marginalized. Policy research or the doing of research is, in and of itself, a technology or a tool—a tool that has been used to reinforce acritical policies and practices. As we have noted, the application of critical theory to this research asks the actor to not change the method but change how the method or tool is applied conceptually, theoretically, and in practice. In their discussion of using colonial technologies as tools of decolonization, La Paperson (2017) suggests that we must "Figure out how technologies operate" and that "Technologies can be disrupted and reorganized" in order to "operate on ourselves and other technologies and turn these gears into decolonizing operations." We suggest the same.

REFERENCES

Adams, M., & Zúñiga, X. (2016). Getting started: Core concepts for social justice education. In M. Adams & L. A. Bell (Eds.), *Teaching for diversity and social justice* (pp. 95–130). Routledge.

Anderson, J. D. (1988). *The education of Blacks in the South, 1860–1935.* University of North Carolina Press.

Baez, B. (2007). Thinking Critically about the. *New Directions for Institutional Research, 133,* 17–23.

Baker, B. D., & Corcoran, S. P. (2012). *The stealth inequities of school funding: How state and local school finance systems perpetuate inequitable student spending.* Center for American Progress.

Baker, B. D., Farrie, D., & Sciarra, D. G. (2014). *Is school funding fair? A national report card.* Education Law Center.

Barnes, M., Germain, E., & Valenzuela, A. (2016). Teach for America's long arc: A critical race theory textual analysis of Wendy Kopp's works. *Education Policy Analysis Archives, 24,* 1–14.

Bell, L., & Stevenson, H. (2006). What is education policy? In *Education policy* (pp. 23–40). Routledge

Berliner, D. C. (2002). Educational research: The hardest science of all. *Educational Researcher, 31*(8), 18–20.

Booher-Jennings, J. (2005). Below the bubble:"Educational triage" and the Texas accountability system. *American Educational Research Journal, 42*(2), 231–268.

Bourdieu, P. (1986). The forms of capital. In J. G. Richardson (Ed.), *Handbook of theory and research for the sociology of education*. Greenwood Press.

Bowles, S., & Gintis, H. (1976). *Schooling in capitalist America*. HarperCollins.

Brewer, T. J., & Myers, P. S. (2015). How neoliberalism subverts equality and perpetuates poverty in our nation's schools. In S. N. Haymes, M. V. D. Haymes, & R. Miller (Eds.), *The Routledge handbook of poverty in the United States* (pp. 190–198). Routledge.

Campbell-Montalvo, R. (2019). Linguistic and racial re-formation of indigenous Mexicans' languages and races in Florida Heartland K–12 schools. *Proceedings of the Linguistic Society of America, (4)*1, 1–9. http://dx.doi.org/10.3765/plsa.v4i1.4556

Carter, P. L., & Welner, K. G. (Eds.). (2013). *Closing the opportunity gap: What America must do to give every child and even chance*. Oxford University Press.

Coleman, J. (1990). *Equality and achievement in education*. Westview Press.

Coleman, J., Campbell, E. Q., Hobson, C. J., McPartland, J., Mood, A. M., Weinfeld, F. D., & York, R. L. (1966). *Equality of educational opportunity*. U.S. Department of Health, Education, and Welfare.

Crawford, C. E. (2019) The one-in-ten: Quantitative critical race theory and the education of the 'new (White) oppressed'. *Journal of Education Policy, 34*(3), 423–444, http://dx.doi.org/10.1080/02680939.2018.1531314

Crawford, C. E., Demack, S., Gillborn, D., & Warmington, P. (2019). Quants & crits: Using numbers for social justice (Or, how <u>not</u> to be lied to with statistics). In J. DeCuir-Gunby, T. K. Chapman, & P. A. Schutz (Eds.), *Understanding critical race research methods and methodologies: Lessons from the field* (pp. 125–137). Routledge.

DiAngelo, R. (2018). *White fragility: Why it's so hard for White people to talk about racism*. Beacon Press.

Diem, S., Young, M. D., Welton, A. D., Mansfield, K. C., & Lee, P. L. (2014). The intellectual landscape of critical policy analysis. *International Journal of Qualitative Studies in Education, 27*(9), 1068–1090. http://dx.doi.org/10.1080/09518398.2014.916007

Dixon-Román, E. (2014). Deviance as pedagogy: From non-dominant cultural capital to deviantly marked cultural repertoires. *Teachers College Record, 11*, 1–30.

Dixon-Román, E. J., Everson, H. T., & McArdle, J. J. (2013). Race, poverty and SAT scores: Modeling the influences of family income on black and white high school students' SAT performance. *Teachers College Record, 115*(4), 1–33.

Du Bois, W. E. B. (1935). Does the Negro need separate schools? *Journal of Negro Education*, 328–335.

Ennis, R. H. (1976). Equality of educational opportunity. *Educational Theory, 26*(1), 3–18.

Feagin, J. (2013). *Systemic racism: A theory of oppression*. Routledge.

Fischer, F. (2003). *Reframing public policy: Discursive politics and deliberative practices*. Oxford University Press.

Freire, C. (2013). "Class" discussion: Social class, communication and the classroom environment. In C. S. Malottt, M. Cole, & J. Elmore (Eds.), *Teaching Marx: The socialist challenge* (pp. 259–272). Information Age Publishing.

Garcia, N. M., López, N., & Vélez, V. N. (2018). QuantCrit: Rectifying quantitative methods through critical race theory. *Race Ethnicity and Education, 21*(2), 149–157. http://dx.doi.org/10.1080/13613324.2017.1377675

Gillborn, D. (2005). Education policy as an act of White supremacy: Whiteness, critical race theory and education reform. *Journal of Education Policy, 20*(4), 485–505.

Gillborn, D, Warmington, P., & Demack, S. (2018). QuantCrit: Education, policy, 'big data' and principles for a critical race theory of statistics. *Race Ethnicity and Education, 21*(2), 158–179. http://dx.doi.org/10.1080/13613324.2017.1377417

Green, T. L. (2018). School as community, community as school: Examining principal leadership for urban school reform and community development. *Education and Urban Society, 50*(2), 111–135.

Gutiérrez, R. (2008). A "gap-gazing" fetish in mathematics education? Problematizing research on the achievement gap. *Journal for Research in Mathematics Education, 39*(4), 357–364.

Gutiérrez, R., & Dixon-Román, E. (2010). Beyond gap gazing: how can thinking about education comprehensively help us (re) envision mathematics education? In B. Atweh, M. Graven, W. Secada, & P. Valero (Eds.), *Mapping equity and quality in mathematics education* (pp. 21–34). Springer.

Heck, R. H., Thomas, S. L., & Tabata, L. N. (2013). *Multilevel and longitudinal modeling with IBM SPSS*. Routledge.

Heilig, J. V., & Darling-Hammond, L. (2008). Accountability Texas-style: The progress and learning of urban minority students in a high-stakes testing context. *Educational Evaluation and Policy Analysis, 30*(2), 75–110.

Heilig, J. V., Young, M., & Williams, A. (2012). At-risk student averse: Risk management and accountability. *Journal of Educational Administration, 50*(5), 562–585.

Hood, S., Hopson, R., & Frierson, H. (2005). Introduction: This is where we stand. In S. Hood, R. Hopson, & H. Frierson (Eds.), *The role of culture and cultural context: A mandate for inclusion, the discovery of truth, and understanding in evaluative theory and practice* (pp. 1–5). Information Age.

Jacob, B. A. (2005). Accountability, incentives and behavior: The impact of high-stakes testing in the Chicago Public Schools. *Journal of Public Economics, 89*(5-6), 761–796.

Jencks, C., & Phillips, M. (Eds.). (1998). *The Black-White test score gap*. Brookings Institution Press.

Jencks, C., Smith, M., Acland, H., Bane, M. J., Cohen, D., Gintis, H., Heyns, B., & Michelson, S. (1972). *Inequality: A reassessment of the effect of family and schooling in America*. Basic Books.

Kershner, I. (Director). (1980). *Star wars: Episode V—The empire strikes back* [Film]. Lucasfilm.

la paperson. (2017). *A third university is possible*. University of Minnesota Press.

Lacoe, J., & Steinberg, M. P. (2019). Do suspensions affect student outcomes? *Educational Evaluation and Policy Analysis, 41*(1), 34–62.

Ladson-Billings, G. (1998). Just what is critical race theory and what's it doing in a nice field like education? *International Journal of Qualitative Studies in Education, 11*, 7–24.

Ladson-Billings, G. (2006). From the achievement gap to the education debt: Understanding achievement in U.S. Schools. *Educational Researcher, 35*(7), 3–12.

López, N., Erwin, C., Binder, M., & Chavez, M. C. (2018). Making the invisible visible: advancing quantitative methods in higher education using critical race theory and intersectionality. *Race Ethnicity and Education, 21*(2), 180–207. http://dx.doi.org/10.1080/13613324.2017.1375185

Malcom-Piqueux, L. (2015). Application of person-centered approaches to critical quantitative research: Exploring inequities in college financing strategies. *New Directions for Institutional Research, 163*, 59–73.

Mansfield, K. C., & Thachik, S. (2016). A critical policy analysis of Texas' Closing the Gaps 2015. *Education Policy Analysis Archives, 24*(3), 1.

Marshall, C. (1999). Researching the margins: Feminist critical policy analysis. *Educational Policy, 13*(1), 59–76. http://dx.doi.org/10.1177/0895904899131006

Marx, K. (1987). *Capital*. Britannica. (Original work published 1867)

McFarland, J., Hussar, B., Wang, X., Zhang, J., Wang, K., Rathbun, A., Barmer, A., Cataldi, E. F., & Mann, F. B. (2018). *The condition of education 2018* (NCES 2018-144). National Center for Education Statistics.

Milner, H. R., IV. (2012). Beyond a test score: Explaining opportunity gaps in educational practice. *Journal of Black Studies, 43*(6), 693–718.

Milner, H. R. (2010). *Understanding diversity, opportunity gaps, and teaching in today's classrooms: Start where you are, but don't stay there.* Harvard Education Press.

Muller, J. Z. (2018). *The tyranny of metrics*. Princeton University Press.

Stage, F. K. (2007). Answering critical questions using quantitative data. *New Directions for Institutional Research, 133*, 5–16.

Murnane, R. J., & Willett, J. B. (2010). *Methods matter: Improving causal inference in educational and social science research*. Oxford University Press.

Omercajic, K. (2015). *Investigating trans-affirmative education policies and practices in Ontario*. Electronic Thesis and Dissertation Repository (No. 3162). https://ir.lib.uwo.ca/etd/3162

Orfield, G., Ee, J., Frankenberg, E., & Siegel-Hawley, G. (2016). *"Brown" at 62: School segregation by race, poverty and state.* Civil Rights Project-Proyecto Derechos Civiles. https://www.civilrightsproject.ucla.edu/research/k-12-education/integration-and-diversity/brown-at-62-school-segregation-by-race-poverty-and-state

Payne, R. K. (2003). *A framework for understanding poverty*. aha! Process.

Piketty, T. (2014). *Capital in the twenty-first century*. The Belknap Press of Harvard University Press.

Rodriguez, A. J. (2001). From gap gazing to promising cases: Moving toward equity in urban education reform. *Journal of Research in Science Teaching: The Official Journal of the National Association for Research in Science Teaching, 38*(10), 1115–1129.

Rothstein, R. (2004). *Class and schools: Using social, economic, and educational reform to close the Black-White achievement gap*. Economic Policy Institute.

Sablan, J.R. (2019). Can you really measure that? Combining critical race theory and quantitative methods. *American Educational Research Journal, 56*(1), 178–203. http://dx.doi.org/10.3102/0002831218798325

Salinas, C. & Lozano A. (2017). Mapping and recontextualizing the evolution of the term Latinx: an environmental scanning in higher education. *Journal of Latinos and Education, 18*(4), 302–315.

Sensoy, Ö., & DiAngelo, R. (2017). *Is everyone really equal? An introduction to key concepts in social justice education*. Teachers College Press.

Taylor, D. (2006). Critical policy evaluation and the question of values: A psychosocial approach. *Critical Social Policy, 26*(1), 243–267.

Thernstrom, A., & Thernstrom, S. (2003). *No excuses: Closing the racial gap in learning*. Simon & Schuster.

Torgerson, D. (2007). Promoting the policy orientation: Lasswell in context. In F. Fischer, J. M. Gerald, & M. S. Sidney (Eds.), *Handbook of public policy analysis: Theory, politics, and methods* (pp. 15–28). CRC Press.

Vasquez Heilig, J., Khalifa, M., & Tillman, L. C. (2014). High-stakes reforms and urban education. In H. R. Milner IV & K. Lomotey (Eds.), *Handbook of urban education* (pp. 523–537). Routledge.

Wilkinson, R., & Pickett, K. (2010). *The spirit level: Why greater equality makes societies stronger*. Bloomsbury Press.

Yosso, T. J. (2005). Whose culture has capital? A critical race theory discussion of community cultural wealth. *Race Ethnicity and Education, 8*, 69–91. http://dx.doi.org/10.1080/1361332052000341006

Zuberi, T., & Bonilla-Silva E. (2008). *White logic, White methods: Racism and methodology*. Rowman & Littlefield.

NOTES

1. We use Latinx as an attempt to decolonize the Spanish language and neutralize gender (Salinas & Lozano, 2017).
2. The focus on the achievement gap centers the individual and not the system. Gutierrez (2008) describes gap gazing as a "fetish" in research that assists in "maintaining an achievement-gap focus," while "offering little more than a static picture of inequities, supporting deficit thinking ..., perpetuating the myth that the problem (and therefore solution) is a technical one, and promoting a narrow definition of learning and equity."

CHAPTER 11

"DROPPIN' THE MIC"

Framing the Implications of Policy-Relevant Research for Maximum Impact

Casey D. Cobb
University of Connecticut

A colleague once told me that her approach to writing the implications section of an article was like "droppin' the mic." She also gave her doctoral students this advice, encouraging them to send clear and definitive messages to readers about the ramifications of their research. The "research implications" sections of journal articles are far too often given short shrift, unconvincing, or underdeveloped. At other times they can be overreaching or undeserved, as when study findings are based on weak research warrants or inconclusive arguments. But when there is the opportunity to frame implications with elocution, researchers should not shy away. Indeed, helping readers make sense of research is an important and often overlooked responsibility of the researcher.[1]

Researchers seeking to maximize their work's impact should first think about the *utility* of their findings or conclusions. How do the research findings fit within the existing body of literature? Do the findings confirm, challenge, or extend a particular knowledge base? Do they disrupt current

Maximizing the Policy Relevance of Research for School Improvement, pp. 265–281
Copyright © 2021 by Information Age Publishing
All rights of reproduction in any form reserved.

knowledge claims or produce new knowledge altogether? For studies that examine impacts or effects, are they supported by strong evidence? To what degree do the findings generalize or transfer to other people, places, and circumstances?

This chapter is intended to help researchers frame the implications of their work. Because effective framing relies on a deep understanding of policy, I expand on the concept of policy and how it manifests across the policy-praxis continuum. I also examine research utilization in education and discuss a conceptual framework for understanding research use. I describe how framing research implications depends on various contextual factors, including the type of research conducted, intended audience, and dissemination outlet. To facilitate research use, researchers should address important problems of practice, engage end-users in the research process (when possible), and maintain analytic rigor.

MAXIMIZING IMPACT THROUGH EXPANDED NOTIONS OF POLICY AND PRACTICE

In framing their implications, researchers may benefit from expanded notions of policy and practice. A deeper understanding of how policy is conceptualized in the field can help position research findings for use. Here I will describe the many types of "Ps" associated with policy—policy, program, procedure, and practice (Rallis et al., 2008),—and contrast their properties using the example of bilingual education policy.

Policy is the broad expression of values, a desired future state. For example, in the United States, the education of language minority students is guided by The Bilingual Education Act, Title VII of the Elementary and Secondary Education Act (ESEA), which "recognizes the unique educational disadvantages faced by non-English speaking students" (U.S. Department of Education, n.d.) and provides federal funding to serve English language learners. States determine their own means to deliver on these services, which run the gamut from bilingual education to "English-only" policies. California, Arizona, and Massachusetts adopted English-only policies following heavily-funded ballot initiatives (Gort et al., 2008). Other state policies call for students to acquire English proficiency while at the same time maintaining their native language.

State bilingual education policy is translated to action through *programs*, which are more specific than statements of values. At the time, English-only states endorsed "structured English immersion" programs where language minority students are taught subjects predominantly in English. States supporting bilingual education instead promote transitional bilingual education programs, dual language programs, or English as a second language (ESL) programs. Even more specific than programs are the *procedures* school leaders follow in serving English learners. For instance, as was the case in Massachusetts following their Question 2 English-only initiative—English learners were capped at one year of sheltered English instruction (de Jong et al., 2005). After that, they were transitioned into mainstream classes.

Finally, in *practice*—where the rubber hits the road—is where the "lowercase p" policy plays out. For example, some Massachusetts districts did not strictly adhere to the one-year maximum procedure and instead adapted to the specific needs of the student. These lowercase *policies* represent "the way things are done around here"; they underlie the operating culture of an organization. Thus, "[p]olicies and programs articulate the *what*—the preferred directions or state—while procedures and practices represent the *how*—the specific rules or laws and actions that will help us move in those preferred directions" (Rallis et al., p. 4)

Researchers who wish their work to be policy-relevant should attend to both the *what* and *how* when framing implications of their research. A primary function of research—particularly with respect to school improvement—is to influence policy, which, in turn, can have significant and immediate effects on practice. In our field, researchers tend to frame the implications of their scholarship for the ("big P") *Policy* audience. We should continue to aim for *Policy* change with our scholarship. But we should also try to use our research to inform those who have a direct influence on "the way things are done around here"—the "little p" *policies*. In most instances, the audience for ("little p") policy are practitioners—school leaders, educators, local leaders. Levinson et al. (2009) speak to the notion of "informal policy" and contend that "when nonauthorized policy actors—typically teachers and students, but possibly, too, building administrators—appropriate policy, they are in effect making new policy in situated locales and communities of practice" (p. 768). In other words, policy is praxis and praxis is policy.

Elsewhere my colleagues and I have described conditions supporting "high leverage policies" (Cobb et al., 2013). One critical contingency involves the "degree to which a policy's message is accurately transmitted to implementers" (p. 268). Policy that is "framed to promote 'district and local sense-making' … has a better chance of success" (p. 269). Framing is about messaging to an audience. It is about meeting them at the appropriate level of understanding so they can make sense of the information within their existing schemas and world perspectives—but also stretching their thinking. The act of framing plays into users' sensemaking. As Tseng (2012) observes, "Knowledge from research does not remain as distinct pieces of information once it enters people's minds and discourse" (p. 7). Moreover,

> evidence is not merely attached to the user's store of knowledge like barnacles are to clams ... rather [it] is a formative process in which evidence is acted on by the user. It is sorted, sifted, and interpreted; it is transformed into implications and translated into inferences. (Tseng, 2012, p. 7, as cited in Kennedy, 1984, p. 225)

As emphasized above, researchers should frame implications with the end user in mind (more on this later). Research consumers will vary in terms of their understanding of policy and may not think of how research findings apply to big "P" policy, little "p" policy, programs, procedures, and practices. The researcher's role is somewhat analogous to Vygotsky's (Chaiklin, 2003) notion of a teacher meeting students at their "zone of proximal development." Researchers should help the user by scaffolding what their study findings mean in light of these broader conceptions of policy.

RESEARCH-TO-PRACTICE, RESEARCH-TO-POLICY[2] GAPS

Undoubtedly, a larger issue motivating this edited volume is the research-to-practice gap in education (Coburn & Stein, 2010; Levin, 2011). Contributing to the much-lamented gap are a variety of factors, but all center on a misalignment between the worlds of researchers and practitioners. Research studies may be inaccessible or difficult to understand in practical terms (Corcoran et al., 2001; Levin & Cooper, 2011); miss the mark of the immediate needs of educators (Honig & Coburn, 2008); offer inconclusive or contradictory findings (Corcoran et al., 2001); or lack a solid theoretical foundation to advance knowledge development (Orr & Cobb, 2019). The research-to-practice gap has prompted calls for concerted efforts to make research knowledge of utility to practitioners and policymakers, which has given rise to utilization networks such as the Evidence Informed Policy and Practice in Education in Europe (Levin, 2013) and other initiatives worldwide (Burns & Schuller, 2007; Levin, 2013; Nutley, 2013). Collective efforts aside, the researcher's responsibility is to help research users make meaning of their scholarship.

Program evaluation is useful for thinking about the translation of research to practice. Evaluation has a different purpose than basic or applied research in that evaluation calls for judgments of value on behalf of a client's specific interests. Patton (2008) urges program evaluators to embrace "utilization-focused evaluation" to ensure the data collected and analyzed will have a meaningful and direct use to the client. Although evaluations, like research, can be ignored by policymakers and practitioners alike, there is an inherent relationship between consumer (client) and evaluator that sets the expectations for findings to be used.

In the research arena, the relatively recent advancement of research partnerships, such as those encouraged through grant programs from the Institute of Education Sciences (n.d.), networked improvement communities (LeMahieu et al., 2017), and design research models (Anderson & Shattuck, 2012), adhere to an operating principle similar to evaluation. Short of establishing formal partnerships to make research more policy-relevant, attention on the part of researchers on how users make sense of findings is a logical first step toward maximizing research utility. But before getting too far in the discussion on how to frame research implications, it is important to first understand what knowledge is being framed, for what purpose, and for whom.

RESEARCH USE

The deeper purpose of framing research implications is to encourage research use. *Research use* has been studied and written about extensively, captured by a variety of related terms such as knowledge mobilization (Levin, 2013), knowledge utilization (Estabrooks et al., 2008), knowledge transfer (Mitton et al., 2007), and research uptake (Cherney et al., 2012). Researchers intend for their scholarship to have an impact on the field. What that influence looks like takes many forms.

Indeed, research consumption can be viewed along a continuum "ranging from simply raising awareness of research findings, through changing knowledge, attitudes and understanding, to direct changes in policy decisions or service delivery" (Walter et al., 2005, p. 340, as cited in Levin, 2013). Weiss (1979) developed a useful typology for research use, separating it into three distinct categories of *instrumental, conceptual,* and *symbolic* uses. Instrumental use involves the direct application of research knowledge by practitioners or policymakers, and it presumes a rational response among consumers of research. Symbolic use is where research is applied or exploited to support an existing or preferred political position. It pertains to situations where established beliefs about a certain practice or policy are buoyed by research that seems to fit these beliefs. Finally, conceptual use occurs when research causes changes in the user's thinking or understanding or challenges their assumptions. Conceptual use tends not to be immediate. Rather, it results from the incremental accretion of knowledge over time. Conceptual understanding may derive from a single research study or an accumulation of research that alters how the user understands an educational phenomenon, problem, or practice.

Common sense would assume that when most researchers think about their research having "impact," they are likely thinking in terms of its *instrumental use*. They hope findings from their research will be directly applied to policy and practice. Underlying this expectation is that the research consumer responds rationally to "what the research says." However, this is an unrealistic assumption (Levin, 2013). The instrumental impact that a single study can make, no matter how rigorous and convincing that study may be, is dubious at best. Multiple studies on the same topic that draw similar conclusions are more likely to have an impact on policy and practice, but this still rarely results in instrumental use. Instead, conceptual use is more in keeping with an accumulation of research that occurs over time, in multiple studies and in various settings.

As researchers, our primary focus is on producing research. We generate research findings so that others can act upon it. However, our field would benefit from paying more attention to the demand side of the research-to-practice relationship. That is, we would be wise to heed the needs of the practitioner and policymaker or at least engage them in the research process[3]:

> People often describe the need to move "research to practice" or "research to policy." Left there, these approaches can seem like a one-way street, neglecting the equally important need to move an understanding of practice and policy to research. (Tseng, 2012, p. 4)

Understanding how research is currently used, particularly from the perspective of decision makers, can help us maximize our research impact. As researchers, we cannot control the end use of our research—that is, whether it manifests in symbolic, conceptual, or instrumental use. But we can perhaps do better at framing implications to foster enhanced conceptual understanding among end users. Conceptual use is arguably a precondition of instrumental use, which is a direct translation to action. Thus, researchers should consider framing research with users' conceptual understanding in mind.

FRAMING CONTINGENCIES: RESEARCH METHOD, AUDIENCE, AND OUTLET

The framing of implications is contingent upon many factors, including the type of research produced, the intended audience, and the dissemination outlet. I expound on each framing contingency below, highlighting potential strategies researchers can use to maximize impact.

Framing Based on Research Method

The framing of implications is dependent in part on the method on which the research findings are based. Research findings derive from a range of designs and analytic methods that are themselves grounded in particular epistemological and ontological perspectives. Research methods are commonly, if not over-simplistically, sorted into the broad categories of quantitative, qualitative, and mixed methods. Ways of knowing underlying these approaches include post-positivist, interpretivist, post-modern, and critical epistemologies.

However, in the policy arena, post-positivistic quantitative studies have dominated. At the turn of the century, the reauthorization of the Elementary and Secondary Education Act called for educational reforms to be based on "evidence-based" practices. A repurposed U.S. Department of Education privileged evidence that was produced by randomized clinical trials or RCTs (Biesta, 2010; St. Pierre, 2002). The U.S. Department of Education's *What Works Clearinghouse* defined the types of educational research that qualified as evidence-based and is still anchored by the often mentioned "gold standard" of experimental research, as well as a few quasi-experimental designs. In turn, state agencies adopted similar evidence-based criteria for screening educational interventions and reform strategies of acceptable use (U.S. Department of Education, 2016).

Quantifiable evidence supported by statistically significant results can carry greater weight among policymakers, who seem to find research results more interpretable when presented in terms of causal effects. Researchers themselves may find it more readily apparent how impact studies can be framed for implications, especially with policy audiences primed for causal predictions and explanations. Quantitative researchers seeking guidance on how to communicate the implications can look at how their findings stack up against the extant literature. In general, the more consistent their findings are with other studies, the stronger their position to influence policymakers. Conversely, if their findings run counter to other study results, or reveal new or different insights, this shapes how they may frame the utility of their findings. That is, counterclaims or new discoveries could be framed explicitly with a user's conceptual understanding in mind (framed for conceptual use). An important point here is that findings from single studies must be considered alongside the existing body of knowledge; it is a starting point that can begin to help shape the framing of implications.

Current norms surrounding evidence-based research have (improperly) privileged RCTs and quasi-experimental research at the expense of other robust methods of research. For instance, qualitative research paradigms tend to take a constructivist approach to knowledge and adhere to a more inductive form of analysis. By doing so, qualitative approaches offer opportunities to contextualize research findings and engage the researcher (and research user) in deep meaning-making. Qualitative designs, such as phenomenology, grounded theory, and narrative analysis, give voice to participants and allow for the close inspection of phenomena in situ. For example, the seminal ethnography, *The Man in the Principal's Office*

(Wolcott, 2003), offered a detailed and contextualized description of the a principal's daily job. The study revealed insights on how and where the principal spent their time, the unique and varied challenges of the role, and their struggle to accommodate competing priorities. It exposed the nested nature of school leadership, the overwhelming "busy-ness" of the job, and the political milieu in which actions are taken. Wolcott's study expanded understanding of the complex role of school principal and prompted new frameworks for examining their professional worlds. Positivist-oriented quantitative studies are simply ill-equipped to yield such in-depth meaning-making.

Other forms of qualitative research, writ large, are guided by the tenets of postmodernism. Postmodernism encompasses a range of theories—critical, race, queer, postcolonial, or intersections thereof, among others (St. Pierre, 2002). Postmodern analyses have the potential to bring about changes in attitudes and beliefs by putting readers in cognitive dissonance, offering counternarratives, and challenging long-held assumptions. Qualitative research also tends to situate findings "in the field" and is presented in ways that resonate with those who live and work there (Davies, 2000). Researchers who publish qualitative research should take advantage of the opportunity to speak in the language of their audiences when framing research implications. If framed in such a manner, qualitative research findings are uniquely positioned to yield conceptual use.

As an illustration, Fernández and López (2017) applied critical policy analysis (CPA) to study the dynamics of Latin@ parental involvement in schools. They examined "how the role, function, and meaning of involvement are not only prescribed for parents, but well-delimited within school spaces occupied by marginalized parents." The authors commented on the use and role of CPA in understanding education policy, which is informative for researchers framing implications:

> As critical educators and scholars, it is important that we raise fundamental questions about our own taken-for-granted assumptions and shed light on the discourses that shape our world and our understanding of phenomena within it. CPA not only challenges us to see the world differently, but to take critical action to change our practices so that we don't continue to perpetuate inequities in our profession as well as in our daily lives. (p. 127)

Consider a policymaker who reads two widely different studies on parent involvement: one that synthesizes the extant empirical research on the "effects" of parent engagement on student achievement and the other referenced above by Fernández and López (2017). Both have the potential to inform practice and policy. They both have value but bring far different understandings on the topic. Each in their own way, the studies help readers make sense of parent engagement and offer an evidentiary base on which to take action.

Framing Based on Audience

Tseng (2012) urges researchers to think about writing to those actors who have the most influence on policy and practice—the decision makers. She argues

> the simple but convenient categorization of practitioners and policy makers is more nuanced than two camps and includes highly influential intermediaries. Intermediaries are individuals or organizations who translate and package research for use by legislators, agency staff, and nonprofit and private service providers. (p. 5)

Advocacy groups and think tanks play an important role in determining which policy ideas gain ground, which reform efforts fail, and how money gets appropriated. State and local agencies lacking the capacity to draw on research rely on professional associations, technical assistance providers, and consultants for research consumption.

The most common opportunity for scholars to raise implications for their work is at the end of a traditional journal article. Based on my experience as a journal editor, many scholars treat the "implications" section almost as an afterthought. They spend most of their intellectual energy on the analysis and interpretation of results and give short shrift to the recommendations for practice. Not all research falls in this camp, but the reality is that the implications sections of papers are usually relatively brief. There is nothing inherently wrong with brevity, but if the messages are too brief, too broad, too wavering, or too qualified, they run the risk of being ineffectual.

Implication sections are weak when they do not take into account a specific audience or audiences. If implications are written without an audience in mind, there is a good chance no one is listening. There could be many other reasons for weak implications sections, of course: the research findings themselves could be weak, stemming from poor designs, underpowered studies, or unfocused analyses. But assuming researchers have produced something of value, they may fail to make it explicit to their audiences. Researchers may simply shy away from making assertive recommendations because they feel it is not their place. But it absolutely is their place to engage with their audiences, especially if they want research to have an impact. Researchers who consider how consumers *use* research are more effective messengers. For example, writing research implications that aim for direct, instrumental use (e.g., "principal preparation programs should add social justice leadership to their curriculum") may not have as much impact as meeting consumers at the conceptual level first (e.g., "aspiring principals who seek the perspectives among the caregivers of minoritized students fundamentally changes the way principals about schooling"). Researchers looking to maximize impact should consider framing implications in ways that invite readers to challenge and perhaps alter their own assumptions. Knowing your audience is a critical first step when trying to shape conceptual understanding.

Framing Based on Publication Outlet

Framing implications of research for maximum impact depends on the dissemination outlet, which itself is inextricably tied to the audience. Policymakers are more likely to read policy briefs and summaries of research because these formats are more digestible and quicker to read than primary sources. Practitioners may tend to read similar outlets but also actively seek research studies and syntheses that address specific problems of practice. News reporters are an often-overlooked audience and can be highly influential to policymakers and practitioners in their own right, mainly because they have an expanded platform for their work but also because they write in an easy to follow and compelling narrative style. Intermediaries, such as chiefs of staff, often translate research findings for their own audiences. Finally, researchers represent an audience as well, and they tend to consume select journal articles, books, and research papers.

Other dissemination outlets include practitioner-based journals, think tank reports, and conference papers. One of the limitations of traditional academic journal articles is that they are generally written for other academic audiences. The accessibility and utility of academic research for practice and policy come into great question over the years (Biesta, 2007; Levin, 2011; McIntyre, 2005). Research must have influence first on *practitioners* and *policymakers*. As noted above, *people* read research findings and translate that knowledge into changes in practice and policy. Insights into how consumers and users of research make sense of complex information is vital to its ultimate impact. Being clear in framing implications of research makes it possible for consumers to see the possibilities for its utility. Knowing how to connect with an audience is not necessarily about convincing them of the merits of a study—it is more about meeting users where they are conceptually and then leading them to see how it matters to practice and policy.

Finally, social media outlets (e.g., Facebook, Twitter), online academic clearinghouses (e.g., researchgate.net, academia.edu), and even college and university communications websites also play a role. Electronic media outlets reach a wide set of audiences and are far more accessible than traditional academic publications. Research authors can use these outlets to circulate their work and even directly message the implications of their findings. These outlets call for succinct, " 'droppin' the mic-type" language that can garner attention. Authors should choose language that will cut to the core and draw readers to the primary source, whether it be a journal article, policy brief, or report. Another strategy is to hyperlink to the abstract (such as on researchgate.net), making sure the abstract includes a clear delineation of the major research implications for policy, practice, and other research. Abstracts are relatively easy to consume and serve as another source for pointing readers to the original study.

OTHER CONSIDERATIONS IN WRITING FOR MAXIMUM IMPACT

Capstones, with their strong emphasis on policy and practice, can be useful models for educational leadership scholars looking to frame implications of their work. The Carnegie Project on the Education Doctorate (CPED) initiative triggered a wave of reforms within educational leadership doctoral programs, including revamping the doctoral dissertation. CPED was a response to redesigning the educational leadership doctorate and distinguishing it from traditional PhD programs. The traditional dissertation mimics the academic journal article in substance and format, except dissertations are far lengthier and usually without page limits. The emphasis of the empirical dissertation is on producing new knowledge and sharing it with the research community. CPED introduced an alternative final product to the traditional dissertation, referring to it as a capstone.

Capstones can take many different forms, but the common thread is a prioritization on practice. That is, a focus on research that addresses a real problem of practice and often one faced by the student researcher in their professional setting. Dissertations and capstones share many similarities. Their methods of inquiry follow a similar pattern—the identification of a researchable problem, an exhaustive review of the literature that bears upon it, the articulation of a conceptual or analytic framework, and a systematic investigation to address research questions. The largest difference, however, lies in their expected contribution. Traditional dissertations are organized by sections devoted to problem identification, theoretical framework, methods, findings, and discussion. This last section is where authors may raise implications for policy and practice, offer recommendations, or suggest ideas for future research. Attention to these areas is often limited and the narrative is usually brief. In many cases these topics are treated more as a formality than a thoughtful examination of what the research means for advancing the field and knowledge base. It is not that surprising that these final elements of the dissertation are given limited attention. With rare exceptions, dissertations do not produce highly impactful findings; they tend to be academic exercises designed to prepare nascent researchers for the longer term in academia.

Doctoral capstones, on the other hand, are designed for the expressed purpose of directly addressing authentic problems of practice. The problems are usually highly relevant to the student researcher and locally situated. But they also tend to be problems common to the field, and thus are germane to other audiences and settings. Unlike the traditional dissertation, the capstone's primary goal is not necessarily to add to the literature base; rather, it is to offer the field a robust analysis that leads to specific policy or practice recommendations. The emphasis on the final written (and delivered) product is on the *implications* of the study for practice and policy. These are usually specific to a particular (local) context but are also intended to be considered by readers for their applicability in other settings. For instance, a study on how school leaders within a district implement a state bullying policy has ramifications for the case district under study, other districts across the state, as well as the state policymaking body that developed and oversees the policy.

Educational leadership researchers may also benefit from "taking a page" from other disciplines, such as economics. Economists organize their research papers by starting with the punch line first. Instead of telling a story from beginning to end, they summarize key findings and implications upfront, in addition to offering more complete accounts toward the end of their papers. It is really nothing more than an advanced organizer, albeit one that includes a summary of findings (in contrast to merely an outline of what the article will accomplish). Advanced organizers of this sort can be highly effective at grabbing the reader's attention, priming them for what is to follow, and delivering a powerful message. Starting a research paper with a summary of findings and their implications also predisposes the reader to think about implications as they consume the entire article. Plamen Nikolov (2013), an economics professor at Harvard University, offers this rationale:

> Although your writing should not follow a journalistic style, its structure can be organized like a newspaper article.... Notice how newspapers start with the most important part, then fill in background later for the readers who kept going and want more details. A good joke or a mystery novel has a long windup to the final punchline. Don't write papers like that—put the punchline right up front and then slowly explain the joke. Readers don't stick around to find the punchline in Table 12. Many papers get this wrong,

> and many readers never really find out what the contribution of the paper is until the last page. (p. 3)

FINAL THOUGHTS

Researchers wanting their scholarship to have high impact should focus on its potential contributions upfront. Well before engaging in a study, think about your research in terms of its possible use. Although it may sound obvious, ensure your research questions and main topic of study are important to the field.

In 2016, the University Council of Educational Administration (UCEA) devoted resources and a conference session to examining research needs in the field. An initial mapping exercise of research in educational leadership over the past decade revealed gaps in specific areas in our field. The ultimate goal was to identify priorities in the field and articulate a more extensive, possibly *collective* research agenda in educational leadership (UCEA Executive Committee, 2016). By doing so, concentrated efforts, resources, and focus could be brought to bear on those compelling questions. The exercise was a genuine attempt to ensure, up front, that future research would have significant implications for policy and practice. Several others have mapped the field to help identify specific areas of need (e.g., Hallinger, 2014; Heck & Hallinger, 2005; Wang & Bowers, 2016).

In addition to picking worthy study topics, another way to maximize research use is by moving the research closer to practice. Consider the relatively recent emphasis on design-based research (Anderson & Shattuck, 2012; Stoker & John, 2009), improvement science (Bryk, 2015), research partnerships (Penuel et al., 2015), and engaged scholarship (Franz, 2010; Van de Ven, 2007). Such models foster what Delanty (1997) calls a "discursively mediated relationship between social science and society [which] takes place in the public identification and definition of collective problems" (p. 140). Researcher-practitioner-policymaker partnerships increase the likelihood of research being used in the field with/by those who may use the results or who would actively participate in the research design and interpretation of findings. A good example is the longstanding Consortium on Chicago School Research (Roderick et al., 2009). Another is the federal Institute for Education Sciences' (IES) efforts to incentivize research partnerships through a major grant program (Institute of Education Sciences, n.d.). Elmore (2004) implored policymakers and scholars alike to think about reform from the "inside out." Finally, Tseng (2012) found that such partnerships could encourage "process use" (a hybridized form of conceptual use), whereby practitioners come to understand research through their active participation in producing it—in contrast to learning or applying research produced *by others* (Tseng, 2012).

In this chapter, I have issued several contingencies for framing research implications. Effectively framing implications depends on many factors, including the research product, audience, and disseminating outlet. Inherent in that first factor is the production of *high-quality,* rigorous research grounded in strong logic and based on valid and trustworthy research warrants. Quality matters and so too does relevance. Performers need to be suitably in tune with their audience to successfully "drop the mic."

REFERENCES

Anderson, T., & Shattuck, J. (2012). Design-based research: A decade of progress in education research? *Educational Researcher, 41*(1), 16–25.

Biesta, G. J. (2007). Bridging the gap between educational research and educational practice: The need for critical distance. *Educational Research and Evaluation, 13*(3), 295–301.

Biesta, G. J. (2010). Why "what works" still won't work: From evidence-based education to value-based education. *Studies in Philosophy and Education, 29*(5), 491–503.

Bryk, A. S. (2015). 2014 AERA distinguished lecture: Accelerating how we learn to improve. *Educational Researcher, 44*(9), 467–477.

Burns, T., & Schuller, T. (2007). *Evidence in education: Linking research and policy.* Organisation for Economic Co-operation and Development.

Chaiklin, S. (2003). The zone of proximal development in Vygotsky's analysis of learning and instruction. In A. Kozulin, B. Gindis, V. Ageyev, & S. Miller (Eds.) *Vygotsky's educational theory and practice in cultural context* (pp. 39–64). Cambridge University.

Cherney, A., Povey, J., Head, B., Boreham, P., & Ferguson, M. (2012). What influences the utilisation of educational research by policy-makers and practitioners?: The perspectives of academic educational researchers. *International Journal of Educational Research, 56*, 23–34.

Cobb, C. D., Donaldson, M. L., & Mayer, A. P. (2013). Creating high leverage policies: A new framework to support policy development. *Berkeley Review of Education, 4*(2), 265–284.

Coburn, C. E., & Stein, M. K. (2010). *Research and practice in education: Building alliances, bridging the divide.* Rowman & Littlefield.

Corcoran, T., Fuhrman, S. H., & Belcher, C. L. (2001). The district role in instructional improvement. *Phi Delta Kappan, 83*(1), 78–84.

Davies, P. (2000). Contributions from qualitative research. In S. Nutley & J. Webb (Eds.), *What works: Evidence-based policy and practice in public services* (pp. 291–316). The Policy Press.

de Jong, E. J., Gort, M., & Cobb, C. D. (2005). Bilingual education within the context of English-only policies: Three districts' responses to Question 2 in Massachusetts. *Educational Policy, 19*(4), 595–620.

Delanty, G. (1997). *Social science: Beyond constructivism and realism.* Open University Press.

Elmore, R. F. (2004). *School reform from the inside out: Policy, practice, and performance.* Harvard Education Press.

Estabrooks, C., Derksen, L., Winther, C., Lavis, J., Scott, S., Wallin, R., & Profetto-McGrath, J. (2008). The intellectual structure and substance of the knowledge utilization field: A longitudinal author co-citation analysis, 1945 to 2004. *Implementation Science, 3*(49), 1–22. https://doi.org/10.1186/1748-5908-3-49

Fernández, E., & López, G. R. (2017). When parents behave badly: A critical policy analysis of parent involvement in schools. In M. D. Young & S. Diem (Eds.), *Critical approaches to education policy analysis* (pp. 111–129). Springer International.

Franz, N. (2010). A holistic model of engaged scholarship: Telling the story across higher education's missions. *Journal of Higher Education Outreach and Engagement, 13*(4), 31–50.

Gort, M., de Jong, E. J., & Cobb, C. D. (2008). SEeIng through a bilingual lens: Structural and ideological contexts of structured English immersion in three Massachusetts districts. *Journal of Educational Research & Policy Studies, 8*(2), 41–67.

Gunter, H. (2013). Researching and conceptualising the field. *Journal of Educational Administration and History, 45*(2), 201–212.

Hallinger, P. (2014). Reviewing reviews of research in educational leadership: An empirical assessment. *Educational Administration Quarterly, 50*(4), 539–576.

Heck, R. H., & Hallinger, P. (2005). The study of educational leadership and manage-ment: Where does the field stand today? *Educational Management Administration & Leadership, 33*(2), 229–244.

Honig, M. I., & Coburn, C. (2008). Evidence-based decision making in school district central offices: Toward a policy and research agenda. *Educational Policy, 22*(4), 578–608.

Kennedy, M. M. (1984). How evidence alters understanding and decisions. *Educational Evaluation and Policy Analysis, 6*(3), 207–226.

Institute of Education Sciences (n.d.). *Partnerships and collaborations focused on problems of practice or policy, CFDA Number: 84.305H.* https://ies.ed.gov

LeMahieu, P. G., Grunow, A., Baker, L., Nordstrum, L. E., & Gomez, L. M. (2017). Networked improvement communities: The discipline of improvement science meets the power of networks. *Quality Assurance in Education, (25)*1, 5–25.

Levin, B. (2011). Theory, research and practice in mobilizing research knowledge in education. *London Review of Education, 9*(1), 15–26.

Levin, B. (2013). To know is not enough: Research knowledge and its use. *Review of Education, 1*(1), 2–31.

Levin, B., & Cooper, A. (2012). Theory, research and practice in mobilizing research knowledge in education. In T. Fenwick & L. Farrell (Eds.), *Knowledge mobilization and educational research: politics, languages and responsibilities* (pp. 17–29). Routledge.

Levinson, B. A., Sutton, M., & Winstead, T. (2009). Education policy as a practice of power: Theoretical tools, ethnographic methods, democratic options. *Educational Policy, 23*(6), 767–795.

McIntyre, D. (2005). Bridging the gap between research and practice. *Cambridge Journal of Education, 35*(3), 357–382.

Mitton, C., Adair, C. E., McKenzie, E., Patten, S. B., & Perry, B. W. (2007). Knowledge transfer and exchange: Review and synthesis of the literature. *The Milbank Quarterly, 85*(4), 729–768.

Nikolov, P. (2013). *Writing tips for economics research papers*. Harvard University. http://www.people.fas.harvard.edu/~pnikolov/resources/writingtips.pdf

Nutley, S. (2013). Reflections on the mobilisation of education research. In B. Levin & J. Qi (Eds.), *The impact of research in education: An international perspective* (pp. 243–262). Policy Press.

Orr, M., & Cobb, C. D. (2019). Epistemic drift: Theory-building and research in educational leadership. In A. Danzig & W. Black (Eds.), *Who controls the preparation of education administrators?* Information Age Publishing.

Patton, M. Q. (2008). *Utilization-focused evaluation*. SAGE.

Penuel, W. R., Allen, A. R., Coburn, C. E., & Farrell, C. (2015). Conceptualizing research–practice partnerships as joint work at boundaries. *Journal of Education for Students Placed at Risk (JESPAR), 20*(1–2), 182–197.

Rallis, S. F., Rossman, G. B., Cobb, C. D., Reagan, T. G., & Kuntz, A. (2008). *Leading dynamic schools: How to create and implement ethical policies*. Corwin Press.

Roderick, M., Easton, J. Q., & Sebring, P. B. (2009). *The consortium on Chicago School research: A new model for the role of research in supporting urban school reform*. Consortium on Chicago School Research.

St. Pierre, E. A. (2002). Comment: "Science" rejects postmodernism. *Educational Researcher, 31*(8), 25–27.

Stoker, G., & John, P. (2009). Design experiments: Engaging policy makers in the search for evidence about what works. *Political Studies, 57*(2), 356–373.

Tseng, V. (2012). The uses of research in policy and practice and commentaries. *Social Policy Report, 26*(2), 1–24.

UCEA Executive Committee (2016). *Developing a research agenda for the educational leadership community: A review of the gaps and a call for involvement*. Special Session at the Annual Meeting of the University Council for Educational Administration. Detroit, MI.

U.S. Department of Education. (n.d.). *Office of Civil Rights. Developing programs for English language learners: Glossary*. https://www2.ed.gov/about/offices/list/ocr/ell/glossary.html

U.S. Department of Education. (2016). *Non-regulatory guidance: Using evidence to strengthen education investments*.

Van de Ven, A. H. (2007). *Engaged scholarship: A guide for organizational and social research*. Oxford University Press on Demand.

Walter, I., Nutley, S., & Davies, H. (2005). What works to promote evidence-based practice? A cross sectoral review. *Evidence & Policy, 1*(3), 335–363.

Wang, Y., & Bowers, A. J. (2016). Mapping the field of educational administration research: A journal citation network analysis of the discipline. *Journal of Educational Administration, 54*(3), 242–269.

Weiss, C. H. (1979). The many meanings of research utilization. *Public Administration Review, 39*(5), 426–431.

Wolcott, H. F. (2003). *The man in the principal's office: An ethnography*. Altamira Press.

NOTES

1. Tseng (2012) reminds us that, "[r]esearch does not speak for itself, nor does it have definitive implications for particular problems of practice or policy. Research users must always interpret the meaning of research and its implications for their specific problems and decisions" (p. 7).
2. In the interest of brevity, I will hereafter use the single phrase "research-to-practice" to also represent "research-to-policy." Use of the single phrase is also justified because policy can be construed as a type of practice.
3. Gunter (2013) issues an important caution regarding government-based research agendas that result in monopolistic control.

SECTION III

ENGAGING USERS OF RESEARCH TO COMMUNICATE ITS RELEVANCE

CHAPTER 12

COMMUNICATING WITH POLICYMAKERS

Heather E. Price
Marian University

If we want research to work for the public good, it is essential to communicate the research to policymakers. In the following chapters in this book, different types of publications and media outlets explain the high value of converting research language from jargon to plain speech, translating complex theories into metaphors, and turning data points into stories that policymakers can present to the legislators for discussion and consideration. This chapter precedes the others because it takes a step back to discuss the complicated task of how to communicate with policymakers from the start of a study, thereby involving policymakers as collaborators in the research process.

Six stages are outlined in the communication chain that developed over years working with policymakers (see Figure 12.1): form a collaboration, assess the collaboration's needs, design the study, share data, discuss results, and establish a feedback loop. For each stage in this chapter, the purpose is explained, techniques to achieve these collaborative goals are shared, justifications from research are given about why the techniques work, and illustrations are provided on how it executes in practice.

Maximizing the Policy Relevance of Research for School Improvement, pp. 285–314
Copyright © 2021 by Information Age Publishing
All rights of reproduction in any form reserved.

The concepts presented here draw upon foundational, methodological ideas by education researchers such as Anthony Bryk, Cynthia Coburn, John Easton, William Penuel, Catherine Snow, and James Spillane. Human-centered design principles are also central to the procedures described (ideo.org, 2014). As the examples will illustrate, all projects will want to modify these techniques per the context and scope of each project.

Figure 12.1

Communication Chain With Policymakers: Six Stages

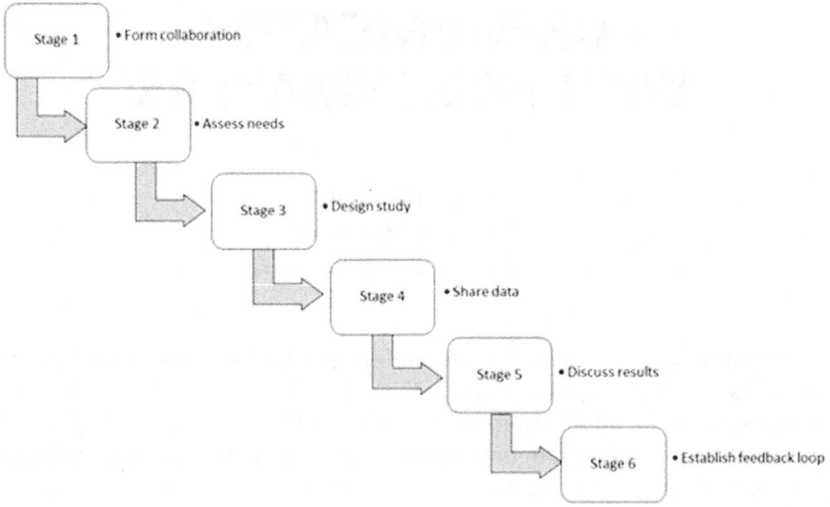

Operational Definitions

For the purposes of this study and the scope of the ideas discussed in this chapter, the following parameters on the definition of policymaker, researcher, and policy are:

Policymakers. Policymakers can be a widely used term to describe people behind the laws, rules, and regulations that define the scope, conditions, and purposes of an action. Policymakers are thought of as those at the top of the power structure occupying the legislative or the cabinet of the executive branches in government. In addition to these formal lawmakers and enforcers, there are policymakers who work further down the hierarchical structure guiding the spirit of the laws and regulations. These policymakers are not quite "on the ground," but they work directly with practitioners on the ground, developing systematic procedures and programs to attain the goals of the legislation.

Superintendents, community leaders, and state agency employees (from the states' departments of education, health, labor, human services, etc.) guide a variety of organizational policies that impact students. These organizational leaders make and implement policies that go beyond the legal obligation to improve the opportunities of student and educator constituencies. They also evaluate whether the implemented policies, procedures, and programs work effectively, efficiently, and fairly across different spaces and contexts. This chapter's techniques aim to engage policymakers by focusing on the importance of collaborative communication with them in effort to maximize the policy relevance of education research for school improvement.

Researchers. Whether at a university, think tank, consulting group, or policy organization, researchers too often work in vacuums publishing their study findings in hope that policymakers will discover and apply them. Other researchers, such as school district institutional research staff, work within an organization. Their research usually addresses specific questions, but the results are rarely generalized, shared externally, or published to build shared knowledge outside the organization.

Policy. Policy refers to procedures followed to implement a law, rule, regulation, or organizational goal. Institutional structures, such as federal, state, and municipal governments as well as organizations like districts, schools, and businesses use policies to standardize practices to achieve goals and/or maintain legal compliance.

The techniques in this chapter work similarly no matter the institutional policy level, as long as the policymakers work directly with the on the ground implementers. The techniques and the researched theory presented here have not been tested with formal lawmakers or enforcement policymakers.

STAGE 1: COMMUNICATING TO FORM A COLLABORATION

Purpose of Stage 1

Empowering policymakers to be part of the research process through research-policy collaborations makes the communication bidirectional. Collaborations that come together for one reason may stay together for another reason. Savvy researchers will focus on building strong relationships with policymakers in the first project in order to preserve productive working relationships for subsequent projects.

Key Points

Such partnerships come in many forms, from one-time collaborations to long-term consortiums (Coburn & Penuel, 2016; Coburn et al., 2013;

Snow, 2015; Warren et al., 2018). These partnerships are less often a dyad of a single-organization policymaker and researcher and more commonly multi-partner collaborations (Bryk et al., 2015; Fishman, Penuel, Allen, & Cheng, 2013). They are not the antiquated, unidirectional collaborations where the researcher is the source of knowledge, and the practitioner is the receiver and implementer (Bryk, 2015; Fishman, Penuel, Allen, & Cheng, 2013). Nor are the collaborations discussed in this chapter the type of "technical assistance" projects where an organization contracts a research firm to produce an internal report or analysis for a specific internal task. Technical assistance consulting does not inform policy inasmuch as it supplements human capital needs to complete an organizational task.

Collaborative partnerships are somewhat new to education (Bryk, 2015). Figure 12.2 shows the evolution from researcher-centric to collaborative partnership projects in schooling research and its impact on developing quality policies.

Collaborations that are common for school improvement are ones that benefit all involved. Popular collaborations are ones such as compacts between traditional districts and area charter schools, area district cooperatives, mayor-headed consortiums, teacher networks, and community-school partnerships. These collaborations often integrate external research

Figure 12.2

Recent Changes in Education Research Partnerships

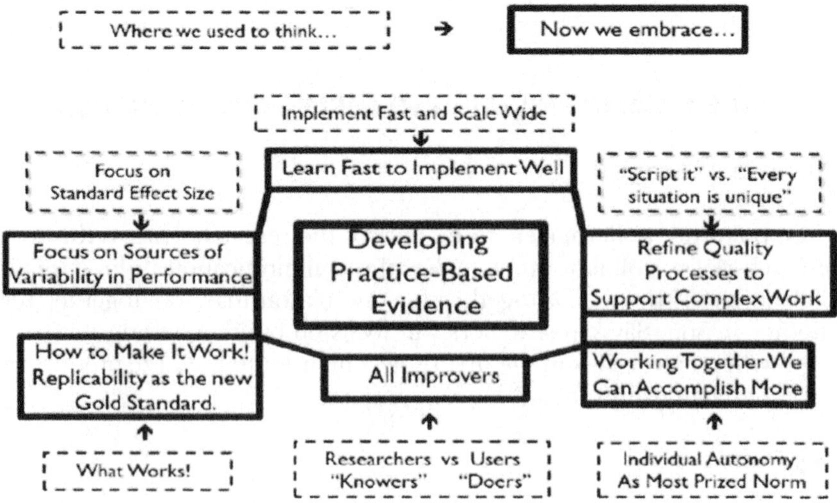

"*Source:* Bryk et al. (2015, p. 186).

experts from area universities, philanthropic, or nonprofit advocacy groups. Established collaborations can be identified by such nomenclature as: consortiums, university-district alliances, district cooperatives, state-level departments of education, research-practice partnerships (Penuel & Gallagher, 2017; Tseng et al., 2017), practice-embedded educational research (Snow, 2015), networked improvement community (Bryk et al., 2015), or even the Regional Educational Laboratories (Institute for Educational Statistics, 2018).

Assembling collaborators requires an honest look at the absorptive capacity of the represented organizations. Absorptive capacity equates the "ability to recognize the value of new information, assimilate it, and apply it in novel ways as part of organizational routines, policies, and practices" (Farrell & Coburn, 2017, p. 136). As Figure 12.3 shows, preconditions of baseline prior knowledge, communication pathways, strategic knowledge leadership, and resources are preconditions needed on the side of the organization to facilitate a productive partnership. Similarly, researchers need to provide clear guidance in the processes, flexibility and adaptability in their thinking, and share work and norms with partners (Farrell & Coburn, 2017, p. 136). The beginnings of a collaboration can work to build absorptive capacity with strategies to engage learning on both sides. Central to building these capacities is trust and legitimacy (Bryk et al., 2010; Bryk, et al., 2015; Coburn et al., 2013; Coburn & Penuel, 2016; Tschannen-Moran & Hoy, 2000).

Why Collaborations Work

The collaborations which facilitate effective communication with policymakers work from the assumption that all the parties involved in the project bring to the table expert knowledge that complements the other's knowledge (Bryk et al., 2010; Fishman, Penuel, Allen, & Cheng, 2013; Snow, 2015). The diversity of expertise and experiences brought to the partnership build strong policies and programs because the unintended consequences can be better imagined and planned for due to the wide range of experiences of those around the table. Moreover, these partnerships offer opportunities for all parties to learn more and expand professionally (Bryk et al., 2015; Snow, 2015).

Trusting that each organization in the partnership has children's best interests as their core mission becomes the foundation to these essential interpersonal relationships (Jones & George, 1998). Small joint tasks early in the partnership can work to build trust with and reliance on each other (Powell, 1996). Asking questions of each other instead of presenting positions builds trust (Bryk et al., 2010; Coburn & Penuel, 2016; Tschannen-Moran & Hoy, 2000). Presenting evidence instead of opinion builds legitimacy (Bryk

Figure 12.3

Absorptive Capacity and Organizational Learning Process

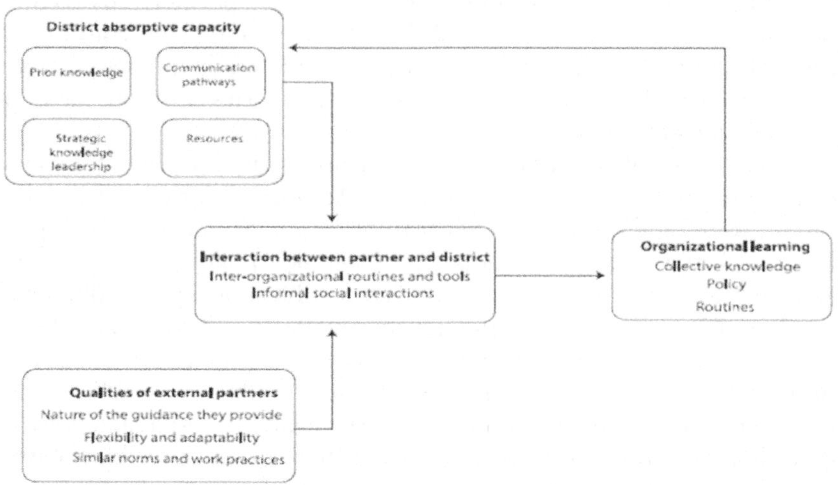

Source: Farrell & Coburn (2017, p. 140)

et al., 2015; Fishman Penuel, Allen, Cheng, & Sabelli, 2013). Listening and integrating each other's professional experiences into the framework legitimizes the work of others as well as builds a stronger frame (Bryk, et al., 2015; Fishman, Penuel, Allen, & Cheng, 2013).

Time-to-completion of the project goals in collaboration is often longer than a single-organization project. That said, collaborative projects often culminate with fewer mistakes, better results, and more promise for wide application because the diversity of stakeholders around the design table is more likely to predict and identify assumptions, biases, and contextual considerations at the onset, rather than discover them during the research phase (Bryk et al., 2010; Fishman, Penuel, Allen, & Cheng, 2013).

Collaborations built on trusted relationships between researchers and policymakers keeps communication lines open and clear of noise (Bryk et al., 2010). Group members may grow, change, or rotate as the collaborations evolve, but many of the researchers and policymakers stay the same. The relational rapport goes a long way to integrate research into education policy.

Successful Techniques at Stage 1

Beginning a collaboration can be daunting, as the task is large and time is precious. For new partnerships, it is important for researchers to have done their homework so that they can start from a general area of interest for policymakers. Attending listening sessions of school board meetings, reading legislative education committee meeting minutes, keeping up on the education section in newspapers, or monitoring social media blogs, group pages, or chat rooms of educators provide researchers an "ear to the ground" to predict the upcoming needs in the education sector. These spaces also inform researchers about which organizations may likely have vested interests in the project. From this information, researchers can sculpt their research interests in relation to these needs and begin to contact policymakers with an idea about a collaborative project.

Helpful approach: Developing a Letter of Intent (LOI) is one way to solicit a diverse set of policymakers with a shared educational research goal. One approach is to contact policymakers directly about the LOI and have them distribute the LOI to other organizations that they think would be good partners in the project. Successful LOIs do not have to have a monetary aspect; researchers organizing the network and working on the "backstage" aspects of the project are labor- and money-saving incentives to attract organizational partners.

Some collaborations are already established for other reasons. In these cases, the task of researchers is less arduous because the ear to the ground homework will point researchers to established relationships and partner collaborations. Researchers can harness these established collaborations to build a partnership with policymakers for their school improvement research.

Examples. Regional Educational Laboratory (REL) collaborations align on a similar theme, such as the Midwest alliances, and involve projects from studying achievement gaps to establishing cross-district student mobility data measures. Consortiums of philanthropic, community, and school districts such as those in Chicago or New York come together to improve an area-wide problem like graduation rates and then grow into coalitions that work with city officials to address additional community needs.

The remainder of this chapter explains procedures related to communication with these collaborators by assessing policymakers' needs, designing studies with policymakers at the table, developing data-sharing structures across organizations, and making results accessible and useful.

STAGE 2: COMMUNICATING TO ASSESS NEEDS

Purpose of Stage 2

Stage 2 involves listening to the nuances of context and the politics contributing to the goals of the study, collection of data, and interpretation of the results. As researchers, you only bring the general topic to the table at

Stage 2 that was established in the ear to the ground research performed in Stage 1.

Key Points

Building relationships with policymaker collaborators requires actively listening to prominent issues in their space and then considering possible studies addressing those concerns. Asking policymakers about the questions they want answered, the needs they find most challenging, or the problems they want to solve shapes the specifics of a partnership study (Bryk, 2015; Penuel et al., 2018). As researchers, we contribute meaningful literature, knowledge, and prior experiences to the partnership in the execution of the study.

Facilitating sessions to assess needs of policymakers follows a familiar structure for researchers: determine the primary issue, drill down into the reasons why this topic is important, and identify the potential policies impacted by the results. Considering this "end game" at the start of the partnership study keeps the study on track, making the data collection and analysis efficient and effective for researchers and valued for the policymakers.

Why needs assessments work. Listening to the needs of the policymakers shapes the bounds of the study specifics, thereby crafting a study that finds answers to questions that resonate with policymakers. The key to active listening is asking questions. The five essential questions to ask are (Ryan, 2017): Wait, what? I wonder …? Could we …? How can I help? What truly matters?

Successful Techniques to Stage 2

Stage 2 works well as an extended all-day meeting where the collaborators put aside other work and concentrate on the idea sharing and brainstorming with each other to build a theoretical framework and articulate the potential impact of the developing study. Steps in co-design methods can facilitate this needs assessment (Coburn et al., 2013; IDEO.org, 2014).

WORKSHOP 1

Rather than a formal meeting or research presentation, workshops work well to assess needs. Researchers are the facilitator at this workshop, not the informant. Researchers work to scaffold the discussion—from wide to narrow, from broad to specific, from disjointed to interlinked—around the general topic identified in Stage 1.

> **Helpful approach:** It may be the case that policymakers are overwhelmed with needs and cannot distill them down into their individual aspects. If this situation arises, facilitate a time where participants share stories from their organizations. Rather than have the owner of the story tell it to the whole session, break the team into small groups of 3–4, have the owner tell the story to the group, and have the group take notes on the story. After everyone tells a story, have the group go around and share their notes. Each group then culminates their notes into one report-out to the larger team. From this activity, begin to draw out themes of needs among the team members (see IDEO.org for more details).

Determining the Primary Issue

A ballot-style activity listing the priorities of policymakers around the table is a non-confrontational approach to determine prominent priorities. Many priorities will be context-specific. To get to the commonalities among the priorities, tally the priorities and group them by broad themes to find the patterns and similarities. Partners around the table may get uncomfortable when the details are not included in the tally—assure these partners that the details will be integrated in the next stage.

Venn or tree diagrams work well in many situations to show how priorities are interrelated. Once the priorities are all represented in clusters, assign names to the patterns and themes. This approach should be familiar to researchers because it is similar to practices used to analyze qualitative data (Miles & Huberman, 1994). Hold another ballot vote on the top 2–3 priorities from these clustered needs on the general topic.

Example. In an inter-district urban regional collaboration, a litany of issues rose to high priority around the general topic of student instability, including school dropout, student mobility, homelessness, and school closures. It became evident to all partners that addressing student mobility (both moving into and out of the district) was top priority because the research needed on dropouts, homelessness, and school closures depended on the student mobility data. Thus, other issues were not abandoned, rather, student mobility was prioritized.

For each of the highest priorities tallied, break the partners into groups to imagine the scope and outcomes related to these top priorities. Distribute representatives from the various organizations across each group (rather than our innate desire to break into work groups with those who we know well) to insure diversity of context. Get groups to come to consensus on the following statements listed in Small Group Activity 1 (adapted from Chen, 2008; Booth et al., 2016):

Small Group Activity 1: Assessing Needs

a. (Topic) We want to study … [name the problem].

    - (Question) Because we want to find out …
    - (Significance) In order to help my organization understand …
    - (Potential Practical Application) So that we as policymakers can then …
    - With this research, we seek to change … practices? norms? public knowledge?

b. What is a researchable question to ask in order to seek out these answers?

    - Research question:
        - o How can you observe the presence or absence of the variables?
    - Define the variables.
        - o Is this question based on fact-based knowledge?
        - o Are these variables able to be observed (measurable) by you?
        - o Are these variables able to be observed by others?

c. Write a series of expected findings.

    - Explain in statements how you expect one variable to affect the other (i.e., hypotheses)
    - Claim why you anticipate the variables to behave in the expected manners

d. State why finding answers matters.

    - In statements, answer the questions: "So what? Why does it matter?"
    - Brainstorm titles for policies that could result from the expected results

Once the Small Group Activity 1 outlines the needs, the groups share out their activity exercise with the others.

At this stage of the process, critiques can dampen the mood in the room and tarnish newly forming and fragile relationships. Instead of critiques, guide the collaborators to take notes on additional expected findings and policies that could result from the proposed project. This brainstorming stage allows possibilities to flourish and relationships to build (ideo.org, 2014).

Explain why this topic is important. Asking people to explain why a topic is important can be daunting. As researchers, we often couch the significance of the study within the bounds of other literature and the gaps of knowledge in the academic sphere. Practitioners often have the opposite angle: the significance of the study is that it will immediately help a few very particular students or educators. For policymakers, how it contributes to the greater academic discussion is too abstract, and how it immediately helps a few names on a list is too concrete. Policymakers need to hear the middle: the significance of the study in the long run and in the short term.

Example. Discussing the ideas around student mobility voiced teachers' concerns about attending to the newly entering students' needs while maintaining coherence in the classroom lessons for the other students. Researchers voiced their interest in the topic regarding the range of operational measures related to student instability. Policymakers voiced their needs around human resource staffing to comply with homelessness mandates and supplying the state with appropriate student population counts.

Outlining expected findings may make you feel like you are getting ahead of yourself, but research shows this type of talk-out helps to reveal patterns of underlying issues and concerns (ideo.org, 2014). Collaborators may not be particularly forthright about sharing certain issues simply because they are so commonplace and normative that there is little conscious awareness around the issue (Lizardo, 2007; Price & Smith, forthcoming; Vaisey, 2009). In statistical terms, these issues and concerns often act as constants. As such, people stop focusing on the issue with no variation because the mind interprets it as a fixed, or static, trait (Lizardo, 2007; Vaisey, 2009). When a group of diverse partners convene, however, the constants in one organization may not be common in other organizations, and thus there is room for variation and change reveals itself. It may not vary in the relative space of one organization, but it is variable in the absolute space of multiple organizations. Talking out helps identify these areas for organizational improvement and policy impact.

Identify potential policies from expected results. Policymakers are looking for the "Goldilocks" explanation: How can putting time, effort, and money toward this topic lead to efficient use of funds to improve a situation that is currently taxing the community, organizations, and/or individuals? Sharing potential policies in small breakout groups will doubly serve to reveal the subjectivity of interpretation of the issue, underscoring the importance of context. Moreover, potential policies will reflect the values bias of collaborators and the scope of service of the organization. Working in small groups brings these implicit notions to the forefront. Sharing out can show that these notions stand seemingly independent of each other or they may meld together.

For the policymaker, diverse notions are not a problem as long as potential policies will not work against each other. Discussing potential policies works to help policymakers consider the extent to which this primary issue can work toward a Goldilocks middle-solution policy.

Example. When discussing the issues around student mobility, policymakers identified a variety of potential policy interventions. They imagined that working toward inter-district measures of student mobility could create comparable measures to share with state officials to request assistance or apply for grant monies. Within their own districts, policymakers imagined the potential to improve systems to track students so as to ensure proper services, such as homelessness or special education services.

Reassess. Once the issues are defined and the aims of the research are established, reassess the partners around the table: Who is not at the table who can offer expert assistance? Who is the target of the solution—is there a representative from that group at the table? If not, how do you recruit them to attend? Identify which partners have the network to access these people. Determine how to invite them to the table.

Example. In the inter-district urban regional collaboration, it became evident that representation from the personnel who interact with the students during enrollment intakes or outtakes would be important contributors to future work since they directly interact with the mobile families. In addition, the district personnel in charge of student enrollment data also became informants in future discussions since the precision of their reporting of student mobility would heavily influence the decision-making for policymakers.

Assessing needs also requires understanding what was implemented in the past, why those policies did or did not work, and the associated unintended consequences (Bryk et al., 2015). After holding the workshop and imagining the research projects and outcomes that could result from the 2–3 priorities, provide some "incubation time" for the partners to go back to their organizations, gather feedback on the different ideas, then convene to reevaluate and choose the key issue for *this* project.

Be transparent. As the partners go to their organizations to share the priorities and gather feedback, questions on details will surface. As the research partner, ensure all collaborators easy access to the summary documents developed during the workshop so they can answer their constituents' questions. These can be formally developed as slides used during a presentation to organizational members or they can be as informal as photos of the whiteboard and handwritten notes from the workshop. The importance of transparency is all-access, not fancy delivery. Trust in the collaboration is tenuous at this early stage—do not fail to deliver the materials just because you want to put finishing touches on a presentation. Instead, keep communication flowing and get the information into collaborators' hands (Bryk et al., 2010; Tschannen-Moran & Hoy, 2000). Including watermarks of "Not for Distribution" is enough to compensate for any informal sharing of information. Remember: It is not your project; it is everyone's.

STAGE 3: COMMUNICATING ON THE STUDY DESIGN

Purpose of Stage 3

As discussed in Section II of this book, the tenants of strong research design are imperative to aligning results and findings to policies and recommendations. Communicating with the policymakers during the design phase of the study will work to keep policymakers engaged in the project, temper outcome expectations within the limits of the study, and, perhaps most importantly, identify challenges in context so that the execution of the data collection and analysis can have fewer surprises and glitches.

Key Points

Be transparent. As a researcher, you may assume that no one cares about the details of designing the study or that the learning curve is worth the time investment, but it is. As a researcher, learning how to articulate technical methods to a policymaker is an important skill for communicating research. If research is to translate into policy, researchers first need to learn how to talk plainly (Gutiérrez, 2011). This does not imply losing details or precision. Instead, it requires translation skills: pulling jargon out of insider-speak and pushing it into communication with others (Billing, 2013). Researchers also need to be cognizant of acronym use—the more partners in the collaboration, the less likely they are all going to share the same frame of reference for acronyms.

Developing the research literacy among collaborators builds organizational learning and absorptive capacity. It provides shared talking points from which to make decisions about the best research design to use with this project, in this context, and with these constituents. Building these skills during the design phase provides a solid foundation to interpret findings and develop policies in relation to the scope and limits of the study.

Why building study designs collaboratively works. Designing studies with policymakers requires a humility on the researchers' end and a learning curve on the policymakers' end (Bryk et al., 2015; Coburn et al., 2013). These two avenues intersect when we as researchers integrate research literacy into the collaboration. Research literacy includes practicing how to sift through research together to read and synthesize it into a literature review, read research with a critical eye, outline potential policies and decisions based on the evidence, transfer other research into a study applicable to the context of this study, and envision how to test the impacts of policies and decisions (Bryk et al., 2015; Coburn & Penuel, 2016; Coburn et al., 2013). Also important is understanding variation, including 'positive deviant' cases (Bryk et al., 2015).

Successful Techniques to Stage 3

Stage 3 works well over a period of time where some background work is done in independent spaces, then collaborators convene a working meeting to share their thoughts and reflections. Researchers absorb these work group results, draft a study design, and then revise it per the collaborators' feedback. Figure 12.4 illustrates the sequential steps within Stage 3.

Background Topic Research

The outline of the independent and dependent variables of interest in Stage 2 (from Small Group Activity #1) provides a roadmap to the literature to be reviewed. It is in the review of the literature where the expertise

Figure 12.4

Ordering of Stage 3

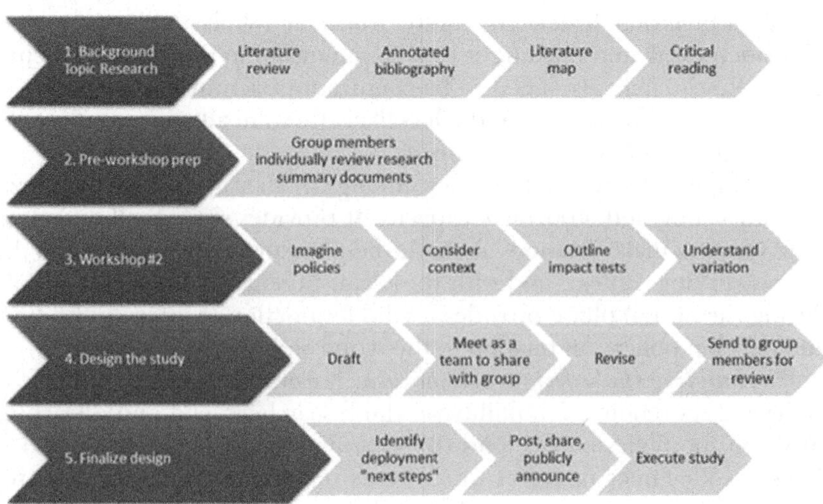

of researchers takes the lead. Policymakers and other partners rarely have the time to overcome the academic jargon or to sift through the extant literature. Researchers deliver this expert knowledge.

The trust built in Stage 1 needs to be upheld, while sharing the knowledge using clear communication to the policymakers about the reviewed literature. Visually mapping the studies to key variables helps to clearly communicate to policymakers why studies were reviewed and allows for generalizations on expected impacts and influences. These depictions often take the form of tree diagrams, such as the one shown in Figure 12.5.

Figure 12.5

Ordering of Stage 3

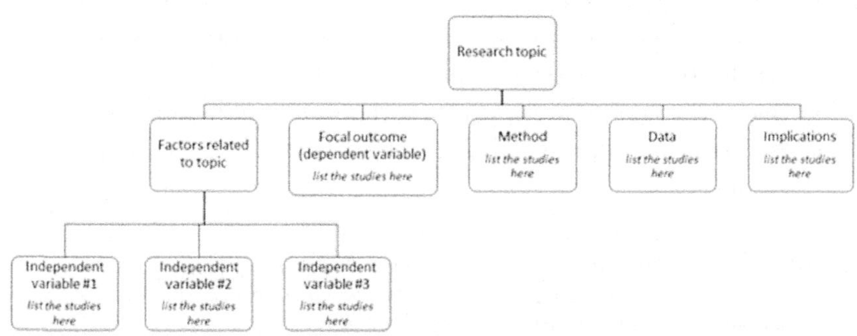

From the review, hypotheses may need revision. At a minimum, policymakers' expectations will need tempering given the preponderance of prior research findings. Keeping a shared file with an annotated bibliography can uphold transparent communication for this portion of the study design. As part of the annotated bibliography, note the critiques and assumptions of reviewed studies.

Example. A citywide collaboration in the Midwest formed around the need for summer programming. The background review of research made clear that most summer programming for urban students works to prevent "summer learning loss" rather than boost students' achievement beyond the school year. This clear and consistent finding in the literature worked to temper the expectations among collaborators from the initial hope that students would gain extra months of academic progress through summer programming to instead expect that summer programming would prevent loss of learning. To be sure, this would still positively impact classroom learning at the start of the school year and likely raise test scores, but this summer programming would not be expected to push the city's students' test scores ahead of its neighboring suburban peers.

Preworkshop Preparation

Before convening another workshop, all collaborators review the background annotated bibliography and literature map. Encourage a critical read of reviewed literature. Providing policymakers with some key questions to ask when reading studies can help to build research literacy and provides a clear set of points to discuss when talking about existing research.

Critical checks to use while reading studies (Warren, 2016):

- Is this the best group of people to study in order to match the research question?
- How are the key concepts measured? What are the strengths and weaknesses of those measures?
- Does the evidence speak directly to the study's questions?
- Does that evidence adequately support the hypotheses, claims, and conclusions summarized in the findings?
- Does the evidence imply cause, and how is that measured?
- If comparing multiple groups, did the evidence compare those groups?

Example. In reviewing the literature on summer programming impacts, some reports implied causation which led the group to a discussion on correlation and causation and the methodological designs needed to test causal claims.

WORKSHOP 2

Transforming general literature to specific ideas for this study works well with facilitation of another workshop. Collaborators will likely have done their own reading on the topic. Encourage the sharing of these studies during the workshop. Review them with the same critical checks listed above.

Imagining evidence-based policies and decisions. Imagining evidence-based policies and decisions helps identify the rationale behind the expected findings. Theoretical frameworks help illustrate the reason's undergirding hypotheses (Miles & Huberman, 1994). Pressing policymakers to brainstorm process models related to their imagined policies and decisions goes a long way to develop shared understanding of the needed study design. These models generate dialogue regarding the rationale of how and why something may work in a particular way and allows the literature findings to be integrated into the context-specific framework.

Example. A theoretical framework collaboration in a citywide collaboration was as simple as showing how summer programming can impact students' school year learning. Figure 12.6 shows that summer programming maintains academic thinking so schools do not have to review prior year learnings; thus, teachers can teach more content in a school year and improve upon prior annual achievement rates

Figure 12.6

Example of a Process Model

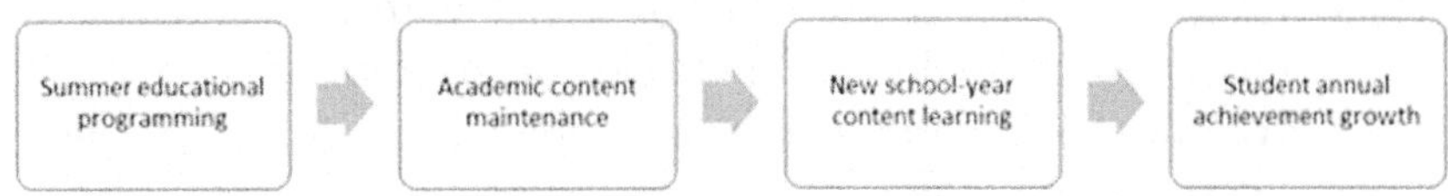

In Stage 3, the researchers are not only facilitating the development of the process model in line with the literature, but also noting the qualitative, context-specific information shared in the group. Information about the nuance of context, the experience of implementation, and the variation among the cases reveals itself during the development of the process model.

Considering context. As part of the study design, it is important to gather information on the possibilities and challenges in gathering appropriate data. Rather than proposing a new data collection effort, which takes time and infrastructure development, use this workshop time to inventory the assets of the organizations using Small Group Activity 2. In this activity, collaborators identify their existing resources available for this study. Simultaneously, collaborators build their research literacy.

Small Group Activity 2: Operationalizing Concepts

a. Why do the study?

What Is the purpose of the study?

- What is it NOT?
- For each key concept in the logic model:

b. What is the working definition of the key concept?

- What are the characteristics of it?

- o Academic (from the literature)
- o Practitioner (from the field)

c. How do other researchers measure the concepts? Are they observable or abstract?

- Which variables align with the concepts?
- Which concepts cannot be measured well?

d. Do the measures capture the conceptual intent?

- If you ask others in this field, how well does this constructed measure align to the concept at face value? (Face validity)
- How do the limitations of the measures narrow the understanding of the concept?

Example. In the citywide collaboration, operationalizing the concepts of learning loss, achievement gains, and academic growth became central. Sketching out what that looked like for the summer instructors at the various nonprofit organizations participating throughout the city helped shape the instructor trainings.

Testing impact. Testing impact does not mandate that the study be quantitative. It does require there to be checkpoints embedded in the study to assess the extent to which the goals of the study are being reached (Bryk et al., 2010; Bryk et al., 2015; ideo.org, 2014). Embedding assessments allows researchers to check assumptions, tweak procedures, and maximize the stability of the end results. Testing impact throughout the life of the study also provides policymakers concrete talking points with which to update their constituents and their superiors, committees, and boards of directors. In addition, tests throughout the study provide fodder for public-facing websites and media outlets to keep up enthusiasm for the project.

Example. Providing parents with progress reports on their students' summer program attendance was a simple report that additionally served to keep computerized attendance records of students. This practice worked to provide researchers with an intersecting "control" variable with which to observe the varying impact of programming across provider organizations.

Understanding variation. Embedding tests for impact inevitably will raise concerns about "How much impact is good?" and "Why doesn't this work the same all the time?" One step to understanding variation is to think together about how to test for impact in different contexts and hypothesize why the impact may differ by context. Many shared ideas will be based on prior personal and professional experiences of the collaborators. These experiences help researchers understand context.

During this share-out, positive deviant cases may surface. There is a lot to learn from these positive outlier stories (Bryk, 2015; ideo.org, 2014). Spend extra time as a whole group to deconstruct the reasons why some cases beat the odds and exceed expectations. Outline the qualities of the case related to the literature to explain the expected outcomes and have the collaborators articulate their insider knowledge of the characteristics that may contribute to exceeding expectations. These characteristics are likely underexplored in the literature and provide researchers with novel ideas to test in this study.

Example. A novel, positive deviant case uncovered among the inter-district urban regional collaboration was that the districts with numerous neighborhood school choice options experienced much higher re-enrollment of students who previously left the district compared to other districts with nearly no choice options. Districts without many school choice options seldom experienced re-enrollment of former students. This uncovered a new datum to capture in understanding the reason why students left their prior school to return to their local public school.

Sharing context encourages collaborators to draw upon variation in the prior research to revise hypotheses. This step in the workshop will communicate the generalizability of this particular study with the policymakers, as well as identify challenges which could arise during the execution of the study.

Design the Study

After holding the workshop, compile and synthesize the information to draft a study design. Key aspects to articulate are the finalized ideas on:

a. The research question(s)

b. Expected findings

   - Hypotheses
   - Rationale of the variables working in the expected manners

c. Variable definitions

   - How can you observe the presence or absence of the variables?

d. Why the answers will matter

   - In statements, answer the questions: "So what?" and "Why does it matter?"

- How does it inform an educational problem?
- How does it contribute to the knowledge in the existing research?
- How could the expected findings be used to develop policy?

e. Data collection details

- How are the data measured?
- Who is the sample? Who does it exclude?
- Where were the data collected?
- When were the data collected?

f. The type of research study (Chen, 2008):

- Descriptive: Understanding what and who
- Exploratory: Understanding reasons why
- Explanatory: Understanding how reasons work (causes and effects)
- Evaluation: Testing solutions and policy effects on the expected outcomes

Distribute the draft to all collaborators and hold a virtual forum to discuss it. Collect critiques and feedback from the forum.

Finalize the Design

Revise the study design per the collaborators' feedback. Keeping a detailed list of the feedback and logging where it was addressed or why it was not addressed keeps communication transparent and maintains trust.

Send the revised plan back to the collaborators for consensus approval. Consensus is important to keep partners involved, but it is also important for policymakers to see the level of support for the project, thus making the outreach messages stronger when delivered to constituents. After consensus, openly store the design plan and identify steps to start the data collection and execution of the study. Policymakers may also be inclined to publicly announce the study to garner enthusiasm in their constituencies.

Example. In the partnership with the inter-district urban regional collaborators, Stage 3 began with analysis and synthesis of nearly 200 articles on student mobility that included identifying different types of mobility, compiling the different formulae used by the districts to measure student mobility, and creating a study to build cohesion in measuring student mobility across partner districts. Only then could there be a study designed to measure student mobility between districts in order to draft policies to reduce it (Price et al., 2015).

STAGE 4: COMMUNICATING ABOUT SHARING DATA

Purpose of Stage 4

Data sharing increases the legitimacy of the research analyses because policymakers know that at any time they can access the data and test their hunches and alternative explanations of the findings. Sharing data provides a venue to allow dialogue among policymakers from different organizations or sectors.

Why sharing data works. Data sharing is a form of communication to policymakers in and of itself. Articulating the data processing strengthens bonds between partners and develops shared understanding. Sharing data can surface system glitches or inefficiencies and thus becomes an indirect point of organizational learning for absorptive capacity. Open access to the data provides a service to policymakers and efficiency to researchers.

Sharing data works as an incentive to participate. The start-up costs of merging, cleaning, and housing data are often beyond the scope of labor hours of participating schools, districts, and other organizations. Researchers performing this data cleaning and management can often attract partners to the study who might only find the project mildly attractive. Sharing data can also attract organizations because it gives them an inside look into the functioning of the other organizations.

Transparency is essential. These data are not yours but are the collaborative team's data. Of course, there may be Institutional Review Board (IRB) stipulations about whom, when, or where data may be directly accessed. Transparency in sharing data does not have to mean a row-by-row sharing of every datum. Transparency in sharing data means that the underlying processes, methods, procedures, and assumptions are made clear to everyone. Mapping the structured query language (SQL) processing order, for example, helped the citywide coalition understand how "just getting the data" is not simply a press of a button, but an extensive and complex process.

Successful Techniques to Stage 4

Data sharing can be as simple as a final, static dataset for all partners to use. Sharing data needs to comply with Family Educational Rights and Privacy Act (FERPA) and thus will likely be de-identified for any individual-level student or teacher data. De-identified IDs can be used in place of contact-specific identification data. In this case, each organization would develop their own source key to link their individual-level identifiable data to the study's sharable de-identified ID.

Vet data processes, methods, procedures, and assumptions with as many partners as possible *before implementation*. This is again where the diverse expertise and experience of the team is essential to efficiency and accuracy. Partners, because they have prior knowledge, can often spot a flaw in logic or a glitch in the data that the researchers do not see.

Data Sharing Agreements

Partnerships expected to last for multiple years on encompass one or more projects run more efficiently with data sharing agreements (DSAs). DSAs articulate the infrastructure of: who manages which datasets; who has access to which data at what times; who distributes data to others outside the partnership; and, how the data are expected to be used. Drawing up DSAs raises questions that serve to clearly communicate roles and responsibilities between collaborators and thus to build trust. The process also provides an entrée into a discussion with everyone about FERPA laws in educational research.

Developing a DSA takes effort and time. It requires consensus and shared governance principles. Operating with a DSA upholds trust between partners. Clear DSA guidelines keep partners from going rogue with data and add a layer of legal protection for all partners. For researchers, a DSA offers a "fast track" approval for analyses of the project. For policymakers, a DSA offers a readily accessible reference document that identifies who to contact about different aspects of the project.

Dashboards

Many years of expected collaboration may benefit from the development of "dashboards," where partners share an electronic platform that pulls data to answer their own internal questions. These platforms are often dynamic and require infrastructure to maintain functionality. Most dashboards require DSAs for clear operations purposes. These platforms also offer incentives to keep partners engaged in longitudinal studies.

Dashboard development often occurs on the sideline of the main project where the lead researcher (principal investigator) and a few of the organizational partners (directors of school research, directors of institutional effectiveness, and the directors of information technology) meet to determine the dashboard architecture and the policies of data access and use. Typically, the organizational partners then assign their internal employees the task of developing the skeleton of the dashboard and use training data to test the functionality. Researchers train the organizational members to maintain the daily functions of the dashboard.

Example. Sharing data with the inter-district urban regional collaboration was basic: we interviewed district officials and synthesized the data into comparative charts where policymakers could easily see how the other districts measured student mobility. Artifacts of exit interview templates and calculations for different types of student mobility were included in the comparative charts. The literature reviewed for this project was uploaded into a shared file space with the annotated bibliography. All policymakers were e-mailed links to these cloud-stored folders.

Example. The coalition among citywide organizations was much larger in scope. DSAs between the coalition organizations were essential to maintain confidentiality of student data. Individual-level student data were secured at each district and the coordination of merging student data with other community data were relegated to aggregate data sets only. Whether aggregated to the church, school, or neighborhood level, student identities were protected outside the source organizations. Given the policy intentions, these meso-level data worked well for the project and there was no need to risk external access to the student-level data.

STAGE 5: COMMUNICATING ABOUT RESULTS

Purpose of Stage 5

Once all partners have had sufficient time to review the final report results, convene a meeting for a discussion of understanding. This meeting should be internal and include some aspect to celebrate the accomplishment of the project goals. The bulk of the meeting should then focus on how to translate these results into policy of practice. *Give this meeting time and space*. This dialogue is critical to translating the project into policy.

Key Points

Individual summary reports may take researchers a week to develop, code, revise, and format, but it is worth the effort because it works to maintain future relationships with policymakers. As these collaborations continue, the individual summary reports format becomes refined and can eventually become semi-automated, programmed syntax.

Results will not be accepted the first time they are presented to the collaborators. There will be revisions. Expect this. Communicating with policymakers during a project means that our researcher blind spots will shine brightly to the diverse group of people around the table. They will call them out. It will be uncomfortable but will improve final results.

Why discussing results works. Becoming familiar with the fact that everyone has blind spots—even education researchers—provides us opportunities to integrate frequent discussions of our results as preliminary drafts and lead with the premise that sharing results better refines interpretations, as well as collects ideas about alternative explanations. This diversity works to refine results to the most solid and error-free conclusions.

Invite critiques. Openly inviting critiques about the results will make researchers feel vulnerable. This vulnerability is honest and has the real effect of building strong and trusted relationships with policymakers (Brockner et al., 1997; Jones & George, 1998; Mayer et al., 1995).

Successful Techniques to Stage 5

Ask policymaker collaborators how they want to receive final results (Coburn & Penuel, 2016; Penuel, et al., 2018). Many schools want to know how they fare in relation to the other schools, so offering schools individual reports where they can see their rank in relation to other participants can improve participation rates and collaboration longevity. Simple accessibility via a shared website, data file, or hardcopy of a report provides the most useable information for partners and policymakers.

Holding a third workshop to bring together all collaborators helps to get everyone on message. It is essential that all collaborators have ample time to review results before the meeting so they can gather their critiques.

WORKSHOP 3

Convening a meeting of everyone involved will reveal how the diversity of represented organizations interprets results differently. Proceed with respect and patience during this conversation to keep the bidirectional communication lines open.

Policymakers may initially react as not liking the results. They may desire different outcomes because the results are not as they expected or are too nuanced to present to their constituencies. This creates a sense of angst. Policymakers may press researchers to go back and run different tests and models or recode different variables. Activate the trust built throughout the project by drawing upon the theoretical framework and variable operationalization rationales in Stage 3 to remind collaborators why this design was deemed—by consensus—to be the most appropriate for this study, and outline why the rerun and recode suggestions were ruled out in earlier meetings.

Example. The results of the citywide collaboration around summer programming were less grand than the collaborators hoped. However, the attendance records provided clear data showing that there were weeks of programming where students attended less regularly, such as around the 4th of July holiday. After that holiday, attendance did not rebound to June levels. This pattern in the data helped all of us to then look at June versus July results separately. But separating the results into two sections did not change the takeaway points. It was at this juncture that the represented organizations also expressed how the initial weeks of the programming were less robust than hoped. This helped all of us to understand the slower-than-expected results in June while the holiday drop-off helped to interpret the July results.

The research literacy developed in Stage 3 and the trusted relationships built throughout the collaboration work to improve the angst (Brockner et al., 1997; Penuel & Gallagher, 2017; Tseng et al., 2017). As a group, facilitate a discussion to identify prior research from the literature review to help explain the project results. The dialogic process will build a repertoire of talking points for policymakers to use when presenting the results to their constituents or proposing policy ideas to their committees. Craft talking points together and build a consensus around these results.

Post Workshop

After the meeting, hold sessions to share results publicly to constituents of the organizations and within organizations.

Public constituent session. A public symposium is not like presenting at a conference. It looks more like organizing a mini political convention. Provide a press release. Hold a public lecture with panelists selected from the team to represent the organizations from the partnered project. Invite key constituents and area leaders and record the event for distribution. Inviting key constituents and the media to the symposium works to garner attention for the policymakers. Policymakers are experienced at navigating this space, even when a naysayer speaks up. Policymakers lead this event, while researchers stay in the backstage and speak up only when invited to respond by the policymakers.

Within organization session. Crafting professional development sessions to train the implementor-practitioners on how to execute the policy is crucial (Penuel & Gallagher, 2017; Snow, 2015; Tseng et al., 2017). This session includes sharing with others the goals with others involved in the project and the process that occurred to shape the policy. Relaying information about the involvement of organizational policymakers and other collaborators not only provides point people for reference and questions, but also increases the legitimacy of the project. Commonly in educational settings, policies come to practitioners lacking the credibility of being informed by those close to the problem. This historical pattern influences many organizational climates to immediately react to policies as ill-informed and destined to fail (Penuel & Gallagher, 2017; Tseng et al., 2017). Thus, sharing with others about the collaboration in the project and who was all involved acts to dispel the knee-jerk organizational reaction to reject the new policy/procedure. This process speaks again to drawing upon the absorptive capacity and organizational learning climate discussed by Farrell and Coburn (2017).

Be transparent within the organizations. Within the bound of IRB stipulations, share the documents with the organizational implementer-practitioners, and log files that contributed to the results. Just as researchers do not collaborate without sharing files to check each other's work, treat the collaborators similarly. This does not mean that there needs to be a formal meeting to walk everyone through every detail, but it does mean to keep track of the evidence of how the results were reached. Simply embedding hyperlinks to files in footnotes of report drafts goes a long way to build research literacy and maintain trust with the collaborator members. (Of course, remove the hyperlinks before sharing as a general public release document, or, alternately, include password protections on the hyperlinks so that drafts are protected from accidental sharing.)

Examples. Sharing results with the urban regional districts was as simple as shared data access and a final report. In the partnership with the citywide coalition, sharing results included neighborhood launch parties, public-facing websites with downloadable reports, and press releases.

STAGE 6: COMMUNICATION FEEDBACK LOOP

Purpose

Providing professional support in Stage 6 maintains trusted relationships with key policymakers and goes a long way to increase the legitimacy of the research and education research in general (ideo.org, 2014).

Key Points

Once the final results are released, it's imperative for policymakers to take ownership of the programs and policies produced (Farrell & Coburn, 2017).

Be transparent. The project continues beyond the initial data collection and analysis. Policymakers and practitioners will have questions and the researchers need to be there to provide assistance. Remember that the reason researchers entered into this partnership was to produce high-impact research with policy influence.

Why feedback loops work. Policies implemented to replicate results from the study will lead to new ideas and revisions. With concerted effort invested is the collaboration, the partnership can continue to build, and this educational research project will continue to impact students (Tschannen-Moran & Hoy, 2000). The channels to policymakers can become an open line of communication as long as they remain bidirectional.

Successful Techniques at Stage 6

The traditional research project ends with the launch of a new policy, but marks the beginning of policy implementation and maintenance, including policy impact testing. Keep communication lines open between the researchers and the policymakers. Regularly check on progress, ask the five essential questions, and gather constituent feedback.

Example. As the citywide summer program project demonstrated, the policies needed adaptation in various contexts (Farrell & Coburn, 2017). Between summers, the coalition met regularly to continue to review the data in detail, discuss constituent feedback collected via surveys, and refine the study design of the most appropriate group with which to compare the participants' progress. In addition, openly storing the resources for this project and the minutes of these meetings became crucial as personnel within participating organizations changed.

DISCUSSION

Partnering with policymakers as collaborators requires us to listen to policymakers, speak plainly and directly, put the key stakeholder (usually the children) at the center of the discussion, attend to the political sensitivity of the study, and keep deadlines (Coburn et al., 2013; Warren et al., 2018). These alterations can sometimes create uncomfortable feelings for researchers who are accustomed to being in full control of every move in their research studies (Coburn et al., 2013). Letting go of ownership and embracing collaborations offers the promise to deliver highly impactful research because the policymaker audience is invested from the start (Warren et al., 2018).

Meetings. There are lots of meetings. In an era where we are overscheduled, another meeting is not what we want. However, involving policymakers in research requires relationship-building, trust development, and integrating diverse perspectives. These goals are better accomplished in face-to-face meetings where non-verbals can be read, multi-tasking can be put aside, and tone can be assessed. Virtual webinar meetings can work as intermediary touchpoints for 1–2 hour meetings, but straight face-to-face encounters cannot be fully substituted. Make these meetings count by scheduling full-day consultations filled with roundtable discussions and use lectures only to transition from one agenda item to another. Eat together, give time to informally talk about the day, note who is not speaking, follow up with him or her, and share reflections.

The first collaboration takes time to build. Pad scheduling so that trust does not get tarnished by missed deadlines. Long-term effort to continue developing research literacy contributes greatly to making future communications more efficient (Bryk et al., 2010).

Lastly, be transparent. Let everyone know the limitations before executing the data collection, and regularly remind stakeholders of those limitations while the project is underway. Loop back to the limitations in the final product or policy by including a "future research" section (common to such publications) or a "next steps" list of improvements to begin working toward. Clearly articulating the limitations may foreshadow the "Phase II" project proposal for further collaboration or the serve as the foundation of the next policy recommendation.

CONCLUSION

Collaborations which facilitate effective partnerships work from the assumption that all the parties involved bring to the table expert knowledge that complements the others' knowledge (Bryk et al., 2010; Fishman, Penuel, Allen, & Cheng, 2013; Snow, 2015). The diversity of experiences brought to collaborations build strong policies because the range of stakeholders around the design table are more likely to predict and identify assumptions, biases, and contextual considerations at the onset rather than discover them during the research phase (Bryk et al., 2010; Fishman, Penuel, Allen, Cheng, & Sabelli, 2013).

Communicating *with* policymakers early and involving them often during the research process could alter the scope of your study, but the end result will be a study that merits immediate use by policymakers (Coburn & Penuel, 2016; Coburn et al., 2013; Snow, 2015) to improve opportunities for children. When researchers and policymakers invest in a collaborative process, it mutually benefits scholarship on the issue and maximizes the chances of educational research being heard by the policymaking community.

There are no silver bullets in education. Whether it is the access to schooling, the regulation of schools, the qualifications of educators, or the educational capital of students, nothing is the one policy that will slay educational inequity. Rather, it is with a host of policies and social changes that researchers and policymakers can collaborate to develop an arsenal to fight for equity. Convening policymakers to the table from the start of the project works to open communication by building relationships steeped in trust and committed to this common good.

REFERENCES

Billing, M. (2013). *Learn to write badly: How to succeed in the social sciences.* Cambridge University Press.

Brockner, J., Siegel, P. A., Daly, J. P., Tyler, T., & Martin, C. (1997). When trust matters: The moderating effect of outcome favorability. *Administrative Science Quarterly, 42*(3), 558–583.

Booth, W. C., Colomb, G. G., Williams, J. M., Bizup, J., & Fitzgerald, W. T. (2016). *The craft of research* (4th ed.). University of Chicago Press.

Bryk, A. S. (2015). 2014 AERA distinguished lecture: Accelerating how we learn to improve. *Educational Researcher, 44*(9), 467–477.

Bryk, A. S., Gomez, L. M., Grunow, A., & LeMahieu, P. G. (2015). *Learning to improve: How America's schools can get better at getting better.* Harvard Education Press.

Bryk, A. S., Sebring, P. B., Allensworth, E., Luppescu, S., & Easton, J. Q. (2010). *Organizing schools for improvement: Lessons from Chicago.* The University of Chicago Press.

Chen, X.-P. (2008). Independent thinking: A path to outstanding scholarship. *Management and Organization Review, 4*(3), 337–348.

Coburn, C. E., & Penuel, W. R. (2016). Research–practice partnerships in education: Outcomes, dynamics, and open questions. *Educational Researcher, 45*(1), 48–54.

Coburn, C. E., Penuel, W. R., & Geil, K. E. (2013). *Practice Partnerships: A strategy for leveraging research for educational improvement in school districts.* William T. Grant Foundation.

Farrell, C. C., & Coburn, C. E. (2017). Absorptive capacity: A conceptual framework for understanding district central office learning. *Journal of Educational Change, 18*(2), 135–159.

Fishman, B. J., Penuel, W. R., Allen, A.-R., & Cheng, B. H. (2013). *Design-based implementation research: Theories, methods, and exemplars.* Teachers College Press.

Fishman, B. J., Penuel, W. R., Allen, A.-R., Cheng, B. H., & Sabelli, N. (2013). Design-based implementation research: An emerging model for transforming the relationship of research and practice. *National Society for the Study of Education, 112*(2), 136–156.

Gutiérrez, K. (2011, April 7). *How to inform policymakers: A strategic approach for academics.* Paper presented at the American Educational Research Association annual conference, New Orleans.

IDEO.org. (2014). *The field guide to human-centered design.* http://www.designkit.org/resources/1

Institute for Educational Statistics. (2018). Regional Educational Laboratory Program. https://ies.ed.gov/ncee/edlabs/projects/topics.asp

Jones, G. R., & George, J. M. (1998). The experience and evolution of trust: Implications for cooperation and teamwork. *Academy of Management Review, 23*(3), 531–546.

Lizardo, O. (2007). "Mirror neurons," collective objects and the problem of transmission: Reconsidering Stephen Turner's critique of practice theory. *Journal for the Theory of Social Behaviour, 37*(3), 319–350.

Mayer, R. C., Davis, J. H., & Schoorman, F. D. (1995). An integrative model of organizational trust. *Academy of Management Review, 20*(3), 709–734.

Miles, M. B., & Huberman, M. (1994). *Qualitative data analysis: An expanded sourcebook*. SAGE.

Penuel, W. R., & Gallagher, D. J. (2017). *Creating research practice partnerships in education*. Harvard Education Press.

Penuel, W. R., Farrell, C. C., Allen, A.-R., Toyama, Y., & Coburn, C. E. (2018). What research district leaders find useful. *Educational Policy, 32*(4), 540–568.

Powell, W. P. (1996). Trust-based forms of governance. In R. M. Kramer & Tom R. Tyler (Eds.), *Trust in Organizations. Frontiers of Theory and Research* (pp. 51–67). SAGE.

Price, H., Scott, L., Stuit, D., Brandt, C., & Shaw, L. (2015). *Measures for examining student mobility*. Midwest Regional Education Laboratory (REL).

Price, H. E. & Smith, C. S. (forthcoming). Procedures for reliable cultural model analysis using semi-structured interviews. *Field Methods*.

Ryan, J. E. (2017). *Wait, what? And life's other essential questions*. HarperCollins.

Snow, C. E. (2015). 2014 Wallace Foundation Distinguished Lecture: Rigor and realism: Doing educational science in the real world. *Educational Researcher, 44*(9), 460–466.

Tschannen-Moran, M., & Hoy, W. K. (2000). A multidisciplinary analysis of the nature, meaning, and measurement of trust. *Review of Educational Research, 70*(4), 547–593.

Tseng, V., Easton, J. Q., & Supplee, L. H. (2017). Research-practice partnerships: Building two-way streets of engagement. *Social Policy Report, 30*(4), 1–17.

Vaisey, S. (2009). Motivation and justification: A dual-process model of culture in action. *American Journal of Sociology, 114*(6), 1675–1715.

Warren, M. R., Calderón, J., Kupscznk, L. A., Squires, G., & Su, C. (2018). Is collaborative, community-engaged scholarship more rigorous than traditional scholarship? On advocacy, bias, and social science research. *Urban Education, 53*(4), 445–472.

Warren, R. (2016, August 3). One thing I learned. *American Sociological Association Newsletter*.

CHAPTER 13

RESEARCH-PRACTICE PARTNERSHIPS

An Innovative Approach to School Improvement

Stephen MacGregor and Amanda Cooper
Queen's University

INTRODUCTION

Research brokering organizations play an important role in the movement of knowledge and the development of connections among different education stakeholders and contexts to improve the use of research. Traditional research brokering organizations (e.g., the American Educational Research Association; the National Academies of Sciences, Engineering, and Medicine; the RAND Corporation) represent just one of the brokering mechanisms that support the policy relevance of research for school improvement. Innovative brokering mechanisms such as research-practice-policy partnerships (RPPs) blur the boundaries of research and policy contexts by positioning brokering as "joint work at boundaries" (Penuel et al., 2015) and by recognizing that research use in policy is a "many

Maximizing the Policy Relevance of Research for School Improvement, pp. 315–335
Copyright © 2021 by Information Age Publishing
All rights of reproduction in any form reserved.

faceted social process involving multiple actors engaged in assembling, interpreting, and debating what evidence is relevant to the policy choice at hand" (National Research Council, 2012). RPPs are long-term, mutualistic collaborations among researchers, practitioners, and policymakers "that are organized to investigate problems of practice and solutions for improving schools and school districts" (Coburn & Penuel, 2016, p. 48). Three main types of RPPs have been recognized in recent years: research alliances, design-based partnerships, and networked improvement communities. Moreover, as interest in these brokering mechanisms grows, hybrids and entirely new types of RPPs continue to develop (Tseng et al., 2017; Henrick et al., 2017). In contrast to "the predominant producer-push dynamic of research to practice [and policy]" (Coburn et al., 2013, p. ii), the integrated, multi-stakeholder approach of RPPs can create opportunities to accelerate the impact of research on school improvement. Coburn et al.'s (2013) definition of RPP is about practice; however, our environmental scan looked for and uncovered many RPPs that also have a policy focus, such as the KNAER network in Ontario, Canada. Similarly, many RPPs were focused and aligned with policy agendas (e.g., increasing math scores); as such, we argue that policy cannot be divorced from our considerations. Consequently, policy relevance of research in our chapter refers to the ways in which evidence is used in RPPs around key policy priorities of the school districts.

The recent and widespread growth of RPPs as a brokering mechanism reflects the mounting calls for research to have greater impact in educational practice and policy. In 2016, for example, the National Network of Education Research-Practice Partnerships was founded to connect the growing professional learning community of researchers, practitioners, and policymakers engaged in RPPs across the United States. Yet, despite early empirical evidence of the promise of RPPs for improving the policy relevance of research (e.g., Biag, 2017; Parr & Timperely, 2015; Tseng et al., 2017; Turley & Stevens, 2015) the evidence base for these partnerships is still emerging (Coburn & Penuel, 2016). Tracing tangible effects of how research affects practice, schools, and policy is notoriously difficult (Honig, 2009; Oliver et al., 2014; Nutley et al., 2007; Sa & Hamlin, 2015), as schools are complex social systems. This chapter will shed light on the following question: What brokering activities are RPPs engaging in to improve the policy relevance of research? To answer this question, we draw on the results of an environmental scan of RPPs from Australia, Canada, the United Kingdom, and the United States. The scan uncovered 79 RPPs, of which we concentrate on a subset of 33 RPPs that exhibited an explicit focus on policy relevance.

Following from the guiding question above, this chapter is organized into two sections. First, we provide an international mapping of the brokering activities RPPs are engaged in, using A. Cooper's (2014) brokering functions: linkage and partnerships, awareness, accessibility, engagement, capacity building, implementation support, organisational development and policy influence. By drawing on these functions and the specific brokering activities that each contains, we respond to the need for "targeted studies of specific strategies that partnerships use" (Coburn & Penuel, 2016, p. 52). Second, taking into consideration the findings from the preceding section, we outline concrete steps in three areas (increasing partnerships, mechanisms to address timeliness and user needs, and evidence tools) that people involved in or around RPPs can take to enhance the visibility and reach of their research on school improvement, particularly in the realm of educational policy and policymaking.

THE INTERNATIONAL PROLIFERATION OF RPPs

In this section we present a broad look at the proliferation and work of RPPs as a mechanism for improving the policy relevance of research. Whereas much of the extant literature has focused on researchers' first-person accounts of their experiences in RPPs (Coburn & Penuel, 2016), this mapping provides an international overview of the work of these partnerships. In particular, we examine one element of the collaborative processes that is central to RPPs: brokering activities. From this mapping we derive key takeaways for how these partnerships provide opportunities to enhance the visibility and reach of research evidence.

An Environmental Scan of RPPs

The findings we present below derive from a broader environmental scan of the international RPP landscape. The purposes of environmental scans are "to learn about events and trends in external environments; establish relationships between them; make sense of the data; [and] extract the main implication[s] for decision-making and strategy development" (Costa & Jorge, 1995, p. 5). Hence, an environmental scan was well suited for understanding the nature and pace of change surrounding RPPs as well as "opportunities, challenges, and likely future developments" (Conway, 2009, p. 2). Our method was one of *conditioned viewing* (Choo, 2001), wherein we examined the routine documents, reports, publications, and information systems of RPPs identified as well-respected sources (Graham et al., 2008).

Between Fall 2017 and Fall 2018, examples of RPPs were identified using a structured search protocol. Similar to other environmental scan studies (e.g., Arain et al., 2017; Ritchie et al., 2016), data collection primarily involved entering keyword search strings into the Google search engine. Each search string contained a sector term (e.g., education or school), a research term (e.g., research or evidence), and a partnership term (e.g., partnership or network). Additional examples of RPPs were identified using the researchers' prior knowledge of the field by scanning for linkages between RPPs (e.g., Australia's Evidence for Learning and the United Kingdom's Education Endowment Foundation) and by examining the work of eminent RPP scholars (e.g., Cynthia Coburn, William Penuel, Caitlin Farrell). As with any recent development, many terms were observed to be in active use to describe what we refer to as RPPs (e.g., university-school partnerships, professional learning communities, communities of practice). Consequently, our scan retained only those examples that exemplified the five characteristics of Coburn et al.'s (2013) widely-cited definition: RPPs are long-term, focus on problems of practice, are committed to mutualism, use intentional strategies to foster partnership dynamics, and produce original analyses. The full scan produced 79 RPP examples; the focused examination here looks at 33 of those RPPs that exhibited an explicit focus on the policy relevance of research (e.g., in a mission statement, vision statement, or strategic planning document).

One of the conceptual frameworks that guided our examination of each RPP was A. Cooper's (2014) brokering functions (Figure 13.1). Constructed from an empirical study of 44 research brokering organizations in the Canadian education sector, A. Cooper's framework enabled classification of the different brokering activities engaged in by the RPPs: linkage and partnerships, awareness, accessibility, engagement, capacity building, implementation support, organisational development, and policy influence. Each brokering function (e.g., capacity building) comprises a variety of specific activities for improving the visibility and reach of research evidence (e.g., online tutorials and training sessions). Below we outline exemplary activities under each brokering function to provide a broad look at how researchers engaged with RPPs are improving the policy relevance of their research.

The International RPP Landscape

The proliferation of RPPs is a relatively recent phenomenon. The University of Chicago Consortium on School Research, founded in 1990, marked one of the first prominent examples of the partnership structure later termed "research-practice partnership." Since then, the ethos and structure of RPPs has spread internationally. In our policy-focused sample alone (Table 13.1), we observed examples of RPPs in various countries:

Figure 13.1

Cooper's (2014) Brokering Functions, Which Identify Eight Major Categories of Research Brokering Activities

LINKAGE & PARTNERSHIPS

Facilitating connections among diverse stakeholders and supporting collaboration
- Event strategies: Talks, Conferences, Workshops
- Network strategies (RSS, E-Bulletins, Directories of researchers, Social media)

AWARENESS

Increasing awareness of empirical evidence on a topic
- Literature review
- Systematic review
- Reference lists/ Annotated bibliographies
- Research reports
- Conceptual papers

ACCESSIBILITY

Increasing accessibility to research by tailoring products to particular audiences
- Research summaries
- Executive summaries of research reports
- Policy briefs
- Fact sheets

POLICY INFLUENCE

Using research to galvanize policy priorities or change
- Advocacy materials,
- Media strategies: press releases, newspaper articles, blogs and online forums, appearances on TV, radio
- Policy briefs, Fact Sheets
- Social media

BROKERING FUNCTIONS

ENGAGEMENT

Increasing engagement with research content through making it appeal to more of our senses
- Multimedia products
- Sound Clips
- Interactive (Prezi)
- YouTube Channels,Videos
- Powerpoint presentation
- Data Visualization

ORGANIZATIONAL DEVELOPMENT

Assisting to build strategic KMb plans and processes or evaluating existing programs and practices
- Annual meetings, awards
- Strategic plans
- Promotional materials
- Annual reports

IMPLEMENTATION SUPPORT

Consulting to provide assistance to implement KMb initiatives
- Toolkits
- Hotlines
- Consultation requests
- Support services

CAPACITY BUILDING

Facilitating professional learning and skill development around KMb
- Terms/ Glossaries
- Research based FAQs
- Online Tutorials
- Workshop/ Training sessions
- Success stories/ Cases

Australia, Canada, the United Kingdom, and the United States. Many of these examples now include education stakeholders in addition to researchers and practitioners, including community groups (n = 14), nonprofits or charities (n = 16), private sector workers (n = 7), and government actors (n = 8). Moreover, the diversity of RPPs was evident in the number that involved multiple of these broader stakeholder configurations (n = 13).

Linkage and partnerships. Central to all RPPs is their ability to build connections and support collaboration among diverse education stakeholders. Earlier empirical work has illustrated the link between positive stakeholder relationships and partners' capacity to positively influence student achievement (Anderson-Butcher et al., 2016; Cooper, 2007), their sense of community (Baumfield & Butterworth, 2007; Bartholomew &

Table 13.1

International Portrait of RPPs With an Explicit Focus on the Policy Relevance of Research

Country	N	Network Name	Other Stakeholders Involved1
Australia	1	Evidence for Learning	C
Canada	3	Alberta Research Network	G
		Knowledge Network for Applied Education Research	C, N, G
		Sustainability and Education Policy Network	C, N
United Kingdom	4	Coalition for Evidence-Based Education	N, P
		Education Endowment Foundation	P, G
		Evidence Based Education	C
		School Improvement Partnership Programme	G
United States	25	Baltimore Education Research Consortium	C, N
		California Collaborative on District Reform	G
		Carnegie Foundation for the Advancement of Teaching	N
		Chicago Alliance For Equity in Computer Science	N
		Cleveland Alliance for Education Research	N
		Collaborative for Academic, Social, and Emotional Learning	N, P, G
		Education Consortium on Research and Evaluation	C, N
		Education Northwest	P
		Education Policy Innovation Collaborative	N, P
		Education Research Alliance for New Orleans	C
		Equity Implemented Partnership	–
		Great Schools Partnership	N, G
		Houston Education Research Consortium	–
		John W. Gardner Center for Youth and Their Communities	C
		Los Angeles Education Research Institute	C
		Madison Education Partnership	N

(Table continued on next page)

Table 13.1

International Portrait of RPPs With an Explicit Focus on the Policy Relevance of Research (Continued)

Country	N	Network Name	Other Stakeholders Involved1
		Metropolitan Educational Research Consortium	–
		NYC Early Childhood Research Network	–
		ODE/OSU English Language Learner Partnership	–
		Partnership for Early Education Research	C, N
		Research Alliance for New York City Schools	C, N
		Tennessee Education Research Alliance	–
		The Network - Wisconsin Collaborative Education Research	C
		UChicago Consortium on School Research	C, N, P, G
		Urban Child Study Center	C, N, P

Note. 1C = Community groups, N = Nonprofit or charity, P = private sector, G = government

Sandholtz, 2009), and their potential to benefit from skill-building exercises (Ndunda et al., 2017; Ralston, Tarasawa, et al., 2016; Ralston, Weitzel, et al., 2016). Relatedly, this policy-focused sample exhibited concerted efforts to build connections between researchers and practitioners as well as with broader stakeholders. The most common activity was the convening of symposia and working groups to promote active learning about policy issues. For example, both the Carnegie Foundation for the Advancement of Teaching and the Sustainability and Education Policy Network, among others, bring together educators, policymakers, researchers, and (in some instances) students to collaborate on solutions to locally relevant issues. The policy learning goal of these collaborative meetings was generally focused on expanding stakeholders' understanding of "the nature of policy problems and the potential of various solutions to address them" (Howlett et al., 2009, p. 180).

We also observed more long-term and issue-specific efforts to build and strengthen connections. For example, the Ontario Knowledge Network for Applied Education Research (KNAER) has partnered with the Ontario Federation of Indigenous Friendship Centres in order to meet the needs of Indigenous students and their families. Titled the Indigenous Education

Knowledge Network, this thematic network of KNAER galvanizes priorities for policy change by working to disrupt the traditional knowledge hierarchy of empirical, theoretical, and experiential ways of knowing (Nutley et al., 2007). Together with the symposia and working groups, these different approaches represent a continuum of linkage and exchange efforts that provide a basis for other brokering activities.

Awareness. A persistent and erroneous assumption in some efforts to strengthen research-to-practice and research-to-policy connections is that awareness of research findings is enough to bring about change (Levin, 2013; Wilson & Sheldon, 2019). In contrast, RPPs foster collective awareness of both which policy issues deserve priority as well as how different types of evidence can speak to those issues. Building awareness thus entails a broader focus on the mutual and targeted learning that occurs among stakeholders (e.g., building awareness about historically underserved communities; Biag, 2017). In our sample we observed a range of activities being used to promote such learning, including the cooperative setting of research agendas, the sharing of works in progress, and the collaborative analysis and contextualization of research findings. Particularly common was the relatively low-cost activity of preparing and distributing working papers and research reports. For example, the Tennessee Education Research Alliance, the Education Policy Innovation Collaborative, and the Research Alliance for New York City Schools have all implemented robust mechanisms for sharing findings from in-progress projects. Although such findings are not typically peer reviewed, this activity enables stakeholders to address a well-documented challenge of research dissemination: "that findings become available only when nobody cares anymore" (Pollard, 2008, p. 14). Further addressing the issue of contributing to ongoing policy conversations, the Education Research Alliance for New Orleans holds a monthly "Policy and Research Brown Bag Series" to share research findings in an off-the-record and comfortable setting. These informal research-to-policy channels enable researchers to build awareness of research findings that would otherwise fail to filter through academic-facing publications or fail to reach relevant stakeholders within the time horizon of the policy issue.

Accessibility. Accessibility of research for target audiences "relates to both the cognitive and physical dimensions of research-based knowledge" (Cherney et al., 2015, p. 176). Even if policymakers are aware of research evidence, they require accessible and high-quality syntheses if that evidence is to have purchase in issues of school improvement. Examples of RPP initiatives aimed at improving the cognitive accessibility of research included abbreviated and plain language reports of current research evidence, policy briefs that fed back into partnership design and implementation challenges, and research and data dialogues. An outstanding example of combining these strategies to improve accessibility is the "Data Talks" series led by the John W. Gardner Center for Youth and Their Communities. Indeed, this series featured in earlier study of the Gardner Center's efforts:

> [These talks] assemble together the community school coordinators and administrators, district officials, service providers, and other partners. During these briefings, researchers present key takeaways of the study, provide relevant handouts (e.g., one-page data analyses for each community school), and pose discussion questions known as Considerations for Practice to stimulate dialogue about how findings may be used for action. (Biag, 2017, p. 15)

RPPs also engaged in efforts to improve the physical accessibility of research, which primarily involved making evidence summaries, policy briefs, and partnership reports (e.g., implementation guides) freely available in online repositories. Just as Coburn et al. (2013) detail that RPPs generate data and produce original analyses, mechanisms for the wider sharing of that data and analyses appear increasingly important (e.g., see Cooper et al., 2019). A leading example is the publication repository of the University of Chicago Consortium on School Research. With a current archive of over 226 resources organized by more than 20 document types (e.g., research brief, frequently asked questions, infographics) and all tagged according to topic area, the temporal and clarity issues of research accessibility are effectively minimized.

Engagement. Research engagement is a fundamental step in research achieving policy relevance and, ultimately, contributing to impacts on policy (Morton, 2015). This principle is evident in that "the primary task of policy makers is to develop and implement public policy rather than to consider research.... [Hence,] a catalyst or prompt occurs to initiate the process of engaging with or using research" (Redman et al., 2015, p. 149). Engagement in this formulation again means viewing research use as a professional learning process (Rickinson, 2017), wherein activities for promoting use improve how research speaks to users' culture and context. Respecting the broader social arrangements of RPPs, we observed activities to bolster research engagement, such as the involvement of target audiences in output production (e.g., key takeaway documents), the creation of multimodal products that respect audiences' changing preferences for consuming information (e.g., podcasts, infographics, interactive findings documents), and the convening of multi-stakeholder meetings to incorporate policymaker and practitioner perspectives. For some RPPs it appeared these engagement efforts were still being trialled; whereas for others, many different mechanisms are used in parallel to maximize reach. An example of an RPP using many engagement activities in parallel is the Collaborative for Academic, Social, and Emotional Learning, with outputs that include traditional peer-reviewed articles, books, implementation guides, infographics, reports, and videos. Many other active RPPs were found to be exploring podcasting as a mechanism to improve engagement (e.g., Evidence Based Education).

Capacity building. Capacity building among partners is a central element in the ability of RPPs to address persistent challenges of education policy and practice (Henrick et al., 2017). As evidenced in studies of district and school data use (e.g., Datnow et al., 2012; Farley-Ripple & Buttram, 2015), capacity building approaches—particularly those that make use of the interactional dynamics enabled by RPPs and that deviate from one-size-fits all approaches—are important for "enhancing [policymakers' and practitioners'] capacity to use research" in addition to "bolstering researchers' capacity to conduct and communicate useful research" (Tseng et al., 2017, p. 5). In our RPP sample, capacity-building efforts included creating accredited professional development programs through the university partner, promoting issue-focused networks and learning cycles, instituting collaborative grant writing workshops and feedback sessions, building online professional learning resources, and establishing mechanisms for ongoing feedback. Two noteworthy examples of capacity building for the use of research evidence were the online glossaries developed by the Carnegie Foundation for the Advancement of Teaching and the Great Schools Partnership. These glossaries provide mechanisms to understand the scientific and technical information underlying specific policy issues, providing the potential for more informed advocacy (Jenkins-Smith et al., 2014).

Implementation support. Implementation support refers to actions undertaken to support the use of research evidence in specific policy issues. Whereas intuition would suggest that the strength and preponderance of evidence on a given issue might speak for themselves, "centuries of experience" (Bauer & Kirchner, 2019, p. 1) and the burgeoning field of implementation science suggest otherwise. Implementation in education is most often found to occur in the form of training and support among partners (Albers & Pattuwage, 2017), and for those actions to be successful, there must be recognition and active managing of barriers and facilitators across multiple levels of policy contexts (Bauer & Kirchner, 2019). Our sample of RPPs exemplified implementation activities, such as: research training through direct partner involvement; the development of best practices for collecting, managing, and reviewing data; the creation of toolkits and cost-benefit guides for weighing potential policy alternatives in relation to the research evidence; and the use of indicators and metrics for assessing the effectiveness of specific policy alternatives. Two RPPs that were exceptional in this work were the United Kingdom's Education Endowment Foundation and Australia's Evidence for Learning.[1] In particular, both RPPs have produced an evidence toolkit that provides cost-evidence strength-impact data on different educational improvement strategies. The intent of these toolkits is to provide policymakers and practitioners with processed evidence summaries that bolster the likelihood of research-informed decision-making.

Organizational development. Decisive to the successes realized by RPPs is how continuous learning feeds into partnership systems and structures. The current landscape is one where it is believed that partner interactions "should be cultivated rather than managed" (Pattinson et al., 2016, p. 516), where a culture of collaboration is an important feature in the philosophy and approaches of leadership (Webb et al., 2009), and where new roles emerge and traditional roles evolve to facilitate the development of strong relationships and flows of resources among partners (Anderson-Butcher et al., 2016; Bosma et al., 2010). Moreover, organizational development includes the development of robust communication and collaboration mechanisms (Tseng et al., 2017) to support "continuous dialogue and responsiveness between the partners" (Ancess et al., 2007, p. 333). In our sample we observed RPPs that had developed strategic roles to support partnership work (e.g., brokers, boundary spanners, and champions), online communication infrastructure, mechanisms to store and share data, and the development of resources for identifying entry points to change. A model of exemplary efforts directed at partner interactions were those of the University of Chicago Consortium on School Research. Not only did this RPP exhibit the greatest variety of stakeholder partners (Table 13.1), it employed an expansive staff with roles dedicated purely to partnership work, such as communication specialists and data archivists. A model of exemplary efforts directed at communication and collaboration mechanisms were those of the New York City Early Childhood Research Network, which instituted a number of activities and services to connect members (e.g., coaching, mentoring, learning communities, and monthly networking meetings).

Policy influence. Although policy influence is the overarching theme of this chapter, its inclusion as a specific function of RPP brokering activities is important. Policy influence as a general concept conceals the different ways research can influence policy; instead, four types of *research use* can categorize the activities of RPPs (Boaz & Nutley, 2019; Farrell et al., 2017; Weiss et al., 2005):

- *Instrumental use*, where research is used directly as the basis for a decision;
- *Conceptual use*, where research contributes to changes in ways of understanding and perceiving an issue;

- *Political/symbolic use*, where research is used to support or justify a decision; and
- *Imposed use*, where a higher level of a system compels research use within a lower level of the system.

Large-scale studies have shown all types of use to be present in RPPs "because they provide opportunities for sustained interactions between researchers and [policymakers and] practitioners around evidence" (Farrell et al., 2017, p. 9). Thus, when considering how activities depicted in the preceding categories of A. Cooper's (2014) framework have influence on policy, it is further necessary to consider the *type* of influence. In our sample, many RPPs were highly active in conceptual use activities such as information exchange, seeking to deepen partners' knowledge of specific issues (e.g., KNAER's resource sharing on Twitter and multi-stakeholder blog). Examples of instrumental use were less overt, yet some RPPs provided promising examples (e.g., the Metropolitan Educational Research Consortium's completed projects portal that includes resultant academic articles, media coverage, and podcasts where partners discuss findings). Conversely, we did not observe any obvious political/symbolic use or imposed use of research evidence, suggesting these uses are not openly documented.

Elements of Effective Brokering in RPPs

Drawing from our landscape map, we highlight three elements of effective brokering that serve as a basis for the strategies and functions RPPs are engaging in to improve the policy relevance of research:

1. **Increased Interaction and Partnerships Among Researchers, Practitioners, and Policymakers:** Developing trusting relationships among stakeholders is a precondition to realizing the potential of RPPs to have influence across multilevel policy contexts "where collaboration, learning, complex information sharing and problem-solving, shared decision-making, and coordinated action are required" (Brown et al., p. 74).
2. **Mechanisms to Address Timeliness and Needs of Users:** To effectively communicate research evidence is to see "a connection be made between the problems of utilization and specific strategies that contribute to their solution at reasonable cost" (Knott & Wildavsky, 1980, p. 574). Within RPPs, these strategies treat the building of evidence awareness as a time-sensitive learning process, respond to the need for evidence to be cognitively and physically

accessible, and maintain engagement through speaking to cultural and social contexts in multimodal formats.

3. **Evidence Tools:** Emphasis is placed on the continuous and mutual learning processes that "focus on enhancing [policymakers'] capacity to use research, bolstering researchers' capacity to conduct and communicate useful research, or shoring up the capacity of the partnership itself through staffing or collaboration tools" (Tseng et al., 2017, p. 5). Moreover, RPPs are building their knowledge of how to support implementation across multiple levels of policy context (e.g., national, provincial, district).

CONCRETE STRATEGIES TO IMPROVE EVIDENCE USE IN POLICYMAKING FOR SCHOOL IMPROVEMENT

There are many strategies that could contribute to improving evidence use in policy and, by doing so, positively contribute to school improvement. Oliver et al.'s (2014) scoping review of barriers and facilitators of the use of evidence in policymaking identified the top five barriers to using evidence in policy as: (1) availability and access to research/improved dissemination, (2) clarity/relevance/reliability of research findings, (3) timing/opportunity, (4) policymaker research skills, and (5) costs. On the facilitator side, Oliver et al. highlight five most prominent facilitators to evidence use in policymaking: (1) availability and access to research/improved dissemination (same as barrier), (2) collaboration, (3) clarity/relevance/reliability of research findings (same as barrier), (4) relationship with policymakers, and 5) relationship with researchers/info staff. We organized strategies that could improve the use of evidence in policy by three areas that emerged as elements of effective brokering and address Oliver et al.'s barriers and facilitators: increasing partnerships (addressing relationships with policymakers and researchers), creating mechanisms to respond to user needs (addressing the availability of research, its relevance, and timing/opportunity to infuse evidence into real-time decision-making), and tools/platforms to improve the availability of research in formats that can be utilized and navigated by policymakers and school leaders based upon specific needs and budgets.

Increasing Interaction and Partnerships Among Researchers, Policymakers, and Practitioners

The literature consistently suggests collaboration and co-production as a potentially powerful mechanism for large-scale school improvement (Coburn et al., 2013; Liou & Daly, 2016; Moolenaaret al., 2011); absent from that discussion are concrete configurations and models to go about this challenging work. Sasse and Haddon (2018) in their recent report, *How Government Can Work with Academia,* list seven concrete avenues to increase the use of evidence in policymaking, including: expert networks, advisory committees, policy reviews, secondments, commissioned research, statements of research needs, and research and evidence centers (p. 27).

Expert networks. Creating expert networks along priority areas is a long-term strategy that can build the necessary trust and relationships to improve education. The first step to establish an expert network is to identify participants across different institutions in the priority area: (a) researchers, (b) relevant intermediary or professional organizations, (c) policymakers from relevant ministries and state education agencies, and (d) practitioners (teachers, educational leaders) to inform the change strategy. Policymakers and educational leaders can build and maintain a stakeholder spreadsheet (Sasse & Haddon, 2018, p. 28) by project, initiative, or policy area. This might be constructed from the practice side or research producers might amass relevant names and intermediaries of experts that could inform different policy areas.

Advisory committees. The utility and impact of advisory committees depends on the frequency and quality of interaction—but used at key decision-making moments, an advisory committee is a relatively inexpensive mechanism to improve the quality of tools, interventions, and implementation strategies. Sasse and Haddon (2018) list four types of committees: advisory nondepartmental public bodies (sponsored by a governmental department to provide advice), expert advisory committees (permanent committees), cross-cutting committees (that work across government departments or school districts), and ad hoc committees and academic panels (that do not have a formal or permanent role, but are used as needed).

Secondments. A secondment is when a full-time professional is moved from their job and embedded into another role in a different area of the system. Sasse and Haddon (2018) discuss secondments of researchers into government to strengthen evidence use in policy:

> When secondments go well they create significant benefits in both directions: academics have knowledge, expertise, skills and modes of thinking that can be invaluable to a department; and secondees can use the knowledge they develop to inform future research and educate other academics and students about the realities of government. Secondment schemes help policy officials to build networks in academia and vice versa. (p. 40)

Beyond Sasse and Haddon's example specifically about academics being seconded to government, there might be other models where practitioners are seconded to policymaking environments, or where policymakers are seconded to research or practice contexts for mutual learning. Secondments are an embedded approach to building partnerships to cross-pollinate between research-practice-policy worlds for school improvement.

Strategies to Address Timeliness and Meet the Needs of End-Users

Much of the literature on the lack of evidence use in education laments that research and its products simply lack relevance for policymakers and practitioners due to their format and lack of actionable implications. However, there are strategies that can mitigate these elements.

Statements of research needs. Sasse and Haddon (2018) suggest that governments can create an explicit list of research needs, so that researchers might focus on areas more relevant to those needs. We expand that thinking to suggest that school districts could similarly create posts on their websites that recommend studies and research areas they would like to have addressed. Having school districts actually create a statement of the different areas for which they need research conducted can contribute to researchers undertaking more relevant studies. Similarly, having policymakers and practitioners co-produce the research questions with researchers can drive practice-informed research (rather than research-informed practice).

Rapid Response Policy Units. An innovative mechanism being used in Canada by Dr. John Lavis and the McMaster Health Forum team are rapid response policy units (https://www.mcmasterforum.org/find-evidence/rapid-response). This rapid response strategy allows the policymaker to reach out for help on a question that has policy implications within a defined number of days (3 days, 10 days, 30 days, or longer). While different levels of work can be turned around in that time (3 days yields a less in-depth report than a 30-day horizon), it still allows policymakers to ask the initial question of researchers. Then a research team amasses the evidence in that area as quickly as possible, focusing on actionable implications. Similar structures exist for school districts (such as Hamilton, Ontario's E-Best Team) in which practitioners and school leaders ask a question that the research unit responds to, called BLAMs (Bottom-Line-Actionable-Messages).

Evidence Tools

Much of the literature on increasing research use lacks concrete tools to go about that work (Nutley et al., 2007; Cooper, 2014). However, tools are arising that provide innovative solutions to the consistent issues that have left policy, research, and school improvement disconnected.

Evidence Toolkits for Teaching and Learning. One group of tools includes interactive platforms that allow educational decision-makers to drive inquiry and results. The Education Endowment Foundation has created interactive interfaces for educational leaders and policymakers summarizing across over 30 areas (e.g., homework, sports participation, arts participation, digital technology), the strength of evidence in a particular area, and the cost of an intervention or strategy, as well as its impact (https://educationendowmentfoundation.org.uk/evidence-summaries/teaching-learning-toolkit). The most innovative part of the platform is that users decide how to search and manipulate the findings. For instance, principals can search by the least expensive strategy if they have a limited budget left to effect change in their school. While most toolkits and products have had limited uptake in education (Edelstein, Shah, & Levin, 2012), models like the Education Endowment Foundation have shown increased potential for uptake by more directly responding to the problems of practice experienced by educators and community partners.

Asset Maps. Practitioners and policymakers often struggle to access the expertise they need to inform a particular area due to a lack of information about which researchers or organizations are active in a particular area (Oliver et al., 2014; Sasse & Haddon, 2018)and assess the state of research in this area, we updated a systematic review.\\n\\nMETHODS: Systematic review. We searched online databases including Medline, Embase, SocSci Abstracts, CDS, DARE, Psychlit, Cochrane Library, NHSEED, HTA, PAIS, IBSS (Search dates: July 2000 - September 2012. However, asset maps that outline different people and organizations—searchable by priority area and geographic location—can allow policymakers and practitioners to find relevant expertise or build expert networks that we discussed in an earlier section. One such example is an asset map created by the Ontario Brain Institute called AxON, the Atlas of Ontario Neuroscience (http://axon.braininstitute.ca/index.html). These types of asset maps could be built for different areas of educational policy and school improvement initiatives.

Other evidence tools. Many other examples exist of tools for increasing the policy relevance of research. For instance, Start and Hovland (2004) created a handbook for researchers entitled *Tools for Policy Impact* that provides tools in four areas: (1) context assessment tools (to understand the system and context where change will happen), (2) research tools, (3) communication tools (such as an organizational readiness assessment), and (4) policy influence tools. Many of these tools could be used to influence school improvement and policymaking in K–12 education sectors.

CONCLUSION

Our chapter has outlined a growing strategy—the use of RPPs in education to improve evidence use for school improvement. The RPPs we summarized are engaged in eight brokering functions: (1) increasing linkage and partnerships, (2) awareness, (3) accessibility, (4) engagement, (5) capacity building, (6) implementation support, (7) organizational development, and (8) policy influence. We have also provided some ideas that policymakers, school districts, and researchers can employ to potentially improve the connections between research-policy and practice in K–12 education systems.

NOTE

1. The classification of these examples as RPPs was initially a topic of disagreement among our research team, yet closer examination of their collaborative processes revealed that much of their work is made possible through RPP-type arrangements.

REFERENCES

Albers, B., & Pattuwage, L. (2017). *Implementation in education: Findings from a scoping review*. Evidence for Learning. https://www.ceiglobal.org/

Ancess, J., Barnett, E., & Allen, D. (2007). Using research to inform the practice of teachers, schools, and school reform organizations. *Theory Into Practice, 46*(4), 325–333. http://doi.org/10.1080/00405840701593915

Anderson-Butcher, D., Iachini, A. L., Ball, A., Barke, S., & Martin, L. D. (2016). A university-school partnership to examine the adoption and implementation of the Ohio Community Collaboration Model in one urban school district: A mixed-method case study. *Journal of Education for Students Placed at Risk, 21*(3), 190–204. http://doi.org/10.1080/10824669.2016.1183429

Arain, M., Suter, E., Mallinson, S., Hepp, S. L., Deutschlander, S., Nanayakkara, S. D., Harrison, E. L., Mickelson, G., Bainbridge, L., & Grymonpre, R. E. (2017). Interprofessional education for internationally educated health professionals: An environmental scan. *Journal of Multidisciplinary Healthcare, 10*, 87–93. https://doi.org/10.2147/JMDH.S126270

Bartholomew, S. S., & Sandholtz, J. H. (2009). Competing views of teaching in a school-university partnership. *Teaching and Teacher Education, 25*(1), 155–165. http://doi.org/10.1016/j.tate.2008.07.001

Bauer, M. S., & Kirchner, J. (2020). Implementation science: What is it and why should I care? *Psychiatry Research, 283*, 1–6. https://doi.org/10.1016/j.psychres.2019.04.025

Baumfield, V., & Butterworth, M. (2007). Creating and translating knowledge about teaching and learning in collaborative school-university research partnerships: An analysis of what is exchanged across the partnerships, by whom and how. *Teachers and Teaching, 13*(4), 411–427. http://doi.org/10.1080/13540600701391960

Biag, M. (2017). Building a village through data: A research–practice partnership to improve youth outcomes. *School Community Journal, 27*(1), 9–27. http://www.schoolcommunitynetwork.org/SCJ.aspx

Boaz, A., & Nutley, S. (2019). Using evidence. In A. Boaz, H. Davies, A. Fraser, & S. Nutley (Eds.), *What works now? Evidence-informed policy and practice*. Policy Press.

Bosma, L. M., Sieving, R. E., Ericson, A., Russ, P., Cavender, L., & Bonine, M. (2010). Elements for successful collaboration between K-8 school, community agency, and university partners: The Lead Peace partnership. *Journal of School Health, 80*(10), 501–507. https://doi.org/10.1111/j.1746-1561.2010.00534.x

Brown, C., Daly, A., & Liou, Y.-H. (2016). Improving trust, improving schools. *Journal of Professional Capital and Community, 1*(1), 69–91. https://doi.org/10.1108/JPCC-09-2015-0004

Cherney, A., Head, B., Povey, J., Ferguson, M., & Boreham, P. (2015). Use of academic social research by public officials: Exploring preferences and constraints that impact on research use. *Evidence & Policy, 11*(2), 169–188. https://doi.org/10.1332/174426514X14138926450067

Choo, C. W. (2001). Environmental scanning as information seeking and organizational learning. *Information Research, 7*(1), 1–37. http://informationr.net/ir/7-1/paper112.html

Coburn, C. E., & Penuel, W. R. (2016). Research-practice partnerships in education: Outcomes, dynamics, and open questions. *Educational Researcher, 45*(1), 48–54. http://doi.org/10.3102/0013189X16631750

Coburn, C. E., Penuel, W. R., & Geil, K. E. (2013). *Research-practice partnerships: A strategy for leveraging research for educational improvement in school districts*. William T. Grant Foundation. http://wtgrantfoundation.org/

Conway, M. (2009). *Environmental scanning: What it is and how to do it*. Thinking Futures. https://thinkingfutures.net/

Cooper, A. (2014). Knowledge mobilisation in education across Canada: A cross-case analysis of 44 research brokering organisations. *Evidence & Policy, 10*(1), 29–59. https://doi.org/10.1332/174426413X662806

Cooper, A., Shewchuk, S., MacGregor, S., Mainhood, L., Beach, P., Shulha, L., & Klinger, D. (2018). *Knowledge mobilization networks in action: A scoping review of research practice partnerships in education*. A report prepared for the Ontario Ministry of Education. Queen's University.

Cooper, L. A. (2007). Why closing the research-practice gap is critical to closing student achievement gaps. *Theory Into Practice, 46*(4), 317–324. http://doi.org/10.1080/00405840701593907

Costa, & Jorge. (1995). An empirically-based review of the concept of environmental scanning. *International Journal of Contemporary Hospitality Management, 7*(7), 4–9. http://doi.org/10.1108/09596119510101877

Datnow, A., Park, V., & Kennedy-Lewis, B. (2012). High school teachers' use of data to inform instruction. *Journal of Education for Students Placed at Risk, 17*(4), 247–265. https://doi.org/10.1080/10824669.2012.718944

Edelstein, H., Shah, S., & Levin, B. (2012). Mining for data: Assessing the use of online research. *International Journal of Humanities and Social Science, 2*(9), 1–12. http://www.ijhssnet.com/

Farley-Ripple, E., & Buttram, J. (2015). The development of capacity for data use: The role of teacher networks in an elementary school. *Teachers College Record, 117*(4), 1–34. https://www.tcrecord.org/

Farrell, C. C., Davidson, K. L., Repko-Erwin, M., Penuel, W. R., Herlihy, C., Potvin, A. S., & Hill, H. C. (2017). *A descriptive study of the IES Researcher–Practitioner Partnerships in Education Research Program: Interim report* (Technical Report No. 2). National Center for Research in Policy and Practice. http://ncrpp.org/assets/documents/RPP-Technical-Report_Feb-2017.pdf

Graham, P., Evitts, T., & Thomas-MacLean, R. (2008). Environmental scans: How useful are they for primary care research? *Canadian Family Physician, 54*(7), 1022–1023. http://www.cfp.ca/

Henrick, E. C., Cobb, P., Penuel, W. R., Jackson, K., & Clark, T. (2017). *Assessing research-practice partnerships: Five dimensions of effectiveness*. William T. Grant Foundation. http://wtgrantfoundation.org/

Honig, M. I. (2009). What works in defining "what works" in educational improvement: Lessons from education policy implementation research, directions for future research. In G. Sykes, B. Schneider, & D. N. Plank (Eds.), *Handbook of education policy research* (pp. 333–347). Routledge.

Howlett, M., Ramesh, M., & Perl, A. (2009). *Studying public policy: Policy cycles & policy subsystems* (3rd ed.). Oxford University Press.

Jenkins-Smith, H. C., Nohrstedt, D., Weible, C. M., & Sabatier, P. A. (2014). The advocacy coalition framework: Foundations, evolution, and ongoing research. In P. A. Sabatier & C. M. Weible (Eds.), *Theories of the policy process* (3rd ed., pp. 183–223). Westview Press.

Knott, J., & Wildavsky, A. (1980). If dissemination is the solution, what is the problem? *Science Communication, 1*(4), 537–578. https://doi.org/10.1177/107554708000100404

Levin, B. (2013). To know is not enough: Research knowledge and its use. *Review of Education, 1*(1), 2–31. https://doi.org/10.1002/rev3.3001

Liou, Y.-H., & Daly, A. J. (2016). Diffusion of innovation: A Social network and organizational learning approach to governance of a districtwide leadership team. *Pedagogía Social: Revista Interuniversitaria, 28*, 41–55. http://doi.org/10.7179/PSRI_2016.28.04

Moolenaar, N. M., Sleegers, P. J. C., & Daly, A. J. (2011). Ties with potential: Social network structure and innovative climate in Dutch schools. *Teachers College Record, 113*(9), 1983–2017. http://www.tcrecord.org/

Morton, S. (2015). Progressing research impact assessment: A "contributions" approach. *Research Evaluation, 24*(4), 405–419. https://doi.org/10.1093/reseval/rvv016

National Research Council. (2012). *Using science as evidence in public policy*. Division of Behavioral and Social Sciences and Education, the National Academies Press. http://www.nap.edu

Ndunda, M., Van Sickle, M., Perry, L., & Capelloni, A. (2017). University-urban high school partnership: Math and science professional learning communities. *School Science and Mathematics, 117*(3–4), 137–145. http://doi.org/10.1111/ssm.12215

Nutley, S. M., Walter, I., & Davies, H. T. O. (2007). *Using evidence: How research can inform public services*. Bristol, United Kingdom: Policy Press.

Oliver, K., Innvar, S., Lorenc, T., Woodman, J., & Thomas, J. (2014). A systematic review of barriers to and facilitators of the use of evidence by policymakers. *BMC Health Services Research, 14*(1), 1–12. https://doi.org/10.1186/1472-6963-14-2

Parr, J. M., & Timperley, H. S. (2015). Exemplifying a continuum of collaborative engagement: Raising literacy achievement of at-risk students in New Zealand. *Journal of Education for Students Placed at Risk, 20*(1–2), 29–41. http://doi.org/10.1080/10824669.2014.983512

Pattinson, S., Preece, D., & Dawson, P. (2016). In search of innovative capabilities of communities of practice: A systematic review and typology for future research. *Management Learning, 47*(5), 506–524. https://doi.org/10.1177/1350507616646698

Penuel, W. R., Allen, A.-R., Coburn, C. E., & Farrell, C. (2015). Conceptualizing research–practice partnerships as joint work at boundaries. *Journal of Education for Students Placed at Risk, 20*(1–2), 182–197. http://doi.org/10.1080/10824669.2014.988334

Pollard, A. (2008). Knowledge transformation and impact: Aspirations and experiences from TLRP. *Cambridge Journal of Education, 38*(1), 5–22. http://doi.org/10.1080/03057640801889949

Ralston, N. C., Tarasawa, B., Waggoner, J. M., Smith, R., & Naegele, Z. (2016). Developing practitioner-scholars through university-school district research partnerships. *Journal of Public Scholarship in Higher Education, 6*, 94–107. https://jpshe.missouristate.edu/

Ralston, N. C., Weitzel, B., Waggoner, J., Naegele, Z., & Smith, R. (2016). The partnership pact: Fulfilling school districts' research needs with university-district partnerships. *AILACTE Journal, 13*, 59–75. http://ailacte.org/content.php?page=AILACTE_Journal

Redman, S., Turner, T., Davies, H., Williamson, A., Haynes, A., Brennan, S., Milat, A., O'Conner, D., Blyth, F., Jorm, L., & Green, S. (2015). The SPIRIT Action Framework: A structured approach to selecting and testing strategies to increase the use of research in policy. *Social Science & Medicine, 136–137*, 147–155. https://doi.org/10.1016/j.socscimed.2015.05.009

Rickinson, M. (2017). Communicating research findings. In D. Wyse, N. Selwyn, E. Smith, & L. E. Suter (Eds.), *The BERA/SAGE Handbook of educational research* (2nd ed., pp. 973–997). SAGE. https://doi.org/10.4135/9781473983953.n49

Ritchie, S. D., Patrick, K., Corbould, G. M., Harper, N. J., & Oddson, B. E. (2016). An environmental scan of adventure therapy in Canada. *Journal of Experiential Education, 39*(3), 303–320. https://doi.org/10.1177/1053825916655443

Sa, C., & Hamlin, D. (2015). Research use capacity in provincial governments. *Canadian Public Administration, 58*(3), 468-486. https://doi.org/10.1111/capa.12125

Sasse, T., & Haddon, C. (2018). *How government can work with academia*. Institute for Government.

Start, D., & Hovland, I. (2004). *Tools for policy impact: A handbook for researchers*. Overseas Development Institute.

Tseng, V., Easton, J. Q., & Supplee, L. H. (2017). *Research-practice partnerships: Building two-way streets of engagement* (30 No. 4). Social Policy Report. Society for Research in Child Development. http://www.epi.umn.edu/mch/resource-research-practice-partnerships-building-two-way-streets-of-engagement/

Turley, R. N. L., & Stevens, C. (2015). Lessons from a school district-university research partnership: The Houston Education Research Consortium. *Educational Evaluation and Policy Analysis, 37*(1S), 6S–15S. http://doi.org/10.3102/0162373715576074

Webb, R., Vulliamy, G., Sarja, A., Hämäläinen, S., & Poikonen, P. L. (2009). Professional learning communities and teacher well-being? A comparative analysis of primary schools in England and Finland. *Oxford Review of Education, 35*(3), 405–422. https://doi.org/10.1080/03054980902935008

Weiss, C. H., Murphy-Graham, E., Birkeland, S. (2005). An alternate route to policy influence: How evaluations affect D.A.R.E. *American Journal of Evaluation, 26*(1),12–30. http://doi.org/10.1177/1098214004273337

Wilson, P., Sheldon, T. A. (2019). Using evidence in health and healthcare. In A. Boaz, H. Davies, A. Fraser, & S. Nutley (Eds.), *What works now? Evidence-informed policy and practice*. Policy Press.

CHAPTER 14

COMMUNITY ACTIVISM AND ADVOCACY

Catharine Biddle
University of Maine

Dana Mitra
Pennsylvania State University

INTRODUCTION

Grassroots activism or advocacy in education can be a powerful way to both shape public opinion and put pressure on educational institutions to ensure that their enactment of policy is aligned with public values. This type of organizing is typically defined as members of a community within a particular field—be it residential, institutional, or virtual—taking sustained action around collectively-defined issues of concern (Christens & Speer, 2015). The focus of these collective efforts is frequently on change, and its strategies may take a variety of forms, including protest or civil disobedience, lobbying, or mobilized engagement in public forums such as school board meetings, traditional or social media, or community hearings (Alinsky, 1970; Ishimaru et al., 2018; Mapp & Warren, 2011; Welton & Freelon, 2018).

Maximizing the Policy Relevance of Research for School Improvement, pp. 337–358
Copyright © 2021 by Information Age Publishing
All rights of reproduction in any form reserved.

The diversity of issues and tactics for stakeholder group mobilization means that researchers must be thoughtful about how they seek to support community activism and advocacy through and with their research. Community groups may be mobilized around a single issue or grow into a long-term advocacy group that tackles multiple issues (Atlas, 2010; Mapp & Warren, 2011). They may be mindful of maintaining equitable power structures that are inclusive of all community voices, or they may represent the interests of a powerful few (Biddle et al., 2018; Fisher et al., 2018). Depending upon their point of origin, they may be strategically linked to intermediary organizations that are able to spark and sustain their capacity building (Christens & Speer, 2015). While this diversity of issues and tactics does create complexities for building meaningful relationships between researchers and community organizing efforts, it also creates many different sites of engagement for research creation and use.

One of the most popular strategies has been to proactively engage communities from the start through participatory action research (PAR) methodologies, changing the researcher-public dynamic through the use of partnership and democratizing knowledge creation (McTaggart, 1997). These strategies are known by many names within the methodological literature, including youth-researcher partnerships (YPAR; Cammarota & Fine, 2010; Christen & Dolans, 2011; Delgado & Staples, 2007; Ginwright et al., 2006), community-based partnerships (CBPAR; Jason & Glenwick, 2016), citizen science (Irwin, 2002; Silvertown, 2009), developmental evaluation (Patton, 2010), research-practice partnerships (Coburn & Penuel, 2016), or activist research (Guajardo et al., 2017). While these approaches differ in their specific protocols, they all share an appreciation for locally-relevant problem formation, de-centering the researcher as the gatekeeper of knowledge creation and putting knowledge to work within communities. Some of these traditions also embrace the use of that knowledge to expose and, coupled with effective organizing, transform local systems of power.

Christens and Speer (2015) argue that community organizing is bound together by several elements that include: (a) assessment/relationship development; (b) participatory research; (c) action or mobilization; and (d) evaluation and/or reflection. In this chapter, we present the work of UP for Learning—an organization dedicated to providing technical assistance to support the expansion of youth-adult partnership—as a case of how community organizing led by youth used educational research to stimulate community dialogue on the purpose of schooling and to influence the implementation of state policy. The theory of action of this grassroots strategy centers on student-facilitated dialogues between community members and peers about the goals of school, grounded in research on personalized learning. At the heart of these conversations is a focus on the need for educational change and a shift from a discourse of school failure to the possibility and agency of schools to shape student-centered learning experiences and to prepare young people for college, career, and civic life.

As the facilitators of these dialogues, students are engaged with research on education and communication strategies to introduce the community to new possibilities for structuring learning while engaging existing mindsets and beliefs about education, personalized learning, and student capacity for driving their own educational decisions. The case highlights the value of student organizers as strategic partners for research dissemination while emphasizing the varied potential sites of engagement for researchers in an organizing effort.

CASE BACKGROUND

In 2013, the Vermont State Legislature passed Act 77, titled, "An Act Relating to Encouraging Flexible Pathways to Secondary School Completion" (S130. U.S.C. § 941, 2013). The opportunity for flexible pathways, or the opportunity for students to engage in learning outside of traditional classroom settings for high school credit, were coupled in the legislation with the mandate that all students from seventh grade through twelfth grade have personalized learning plans (PLPs). These personalized learning plans were designed to support student, teacher, and parent engagement in conversations about how a student would fulfill high school graduation credits in ways that best fit their personal interests (both inside and outside the classroom). The legislation was passed with the goal that by identifying early on which students would benefit from flexible pathways to graduation, schools would both increase secondary school completion rates as well as increase postsecondary readiness among Vermont students.

This two-pronged strategy of competency focused on learning and flexible pathways was a source of excitement in the state, but also confusion. The means for creating "a personalized learning process" (S130. U.S.C. § 941, 2013, p. 2) was left up to districts and school sites to determine, although a statewide working group on personalized learning was convened to help develop recommendations for how to implement such a process. The hope, spelled out in the legislation itself, was that the process would engage students, faculty, and families in personalized learning plan formulation, resulting in both a plan forward and a shared sense of ownership over the plan between all of these stakeholders in a student's learning. The policy was itself developed through such a process of building extensive grassroots support of teachers, administrators, and families. The resulting set of policies were meant to "reflect a student's emerging abilities, aptitude and disposition" and "define the scope and rigor of academic and experiential opportunities necessary for a secondary student to complete secondary school successfully, attain post-secondary readiness, and be prepared to engage actively in civic life" (VS130. U.S.C. § 941, 2013, pp. 5–6).

POINT OF ENGAGEMENT: CREATING A SPACE FOR YOUTH AND TEACHER LEADERS TO ENGAGE WITH PUBLISHED AND COMMUNITY-BASED RESEARCH

One possible site of engagement for researchers looking to support community organizing around their research is through their creation or participation in spaces in which communities are coming together to mobilize. The fundamental shifts in learning and assessment required by Act 77 caused great confusion for how schools should implement the policies. The need to communicate the possibilities elevating student agency inherent in policies like personalized learning and, relatedly, competency-based education created an opportunity for an intermediary organization to partner youth and adults to deepen the work of change. Shaping Our Future Together was the brainchild of Dr. Helen Beattie, executive director of the intermediary organization Unleashing the Power of Partnership for Learning (referred to as UP for Learning). Instead of simply engaging youth in creating "marketing" for the policy, the program trained youth and adult teams to engage their communities in dialogues regarding how their districts would implement the personalized learning mandate.

The Shaping Our Future Together initiative invited student-teacher teams from participating schools to engage with four bodies of research as part of a yearlong class for college or professional development credit: personalized learning, strategic framing, dialogue for change, and youth-adult partnership. By engaging in these bodies of work through monthly readings and discussion groups, both students and teachers in these youth-adult teams deepened their understanding of the following concepts.

Common Narrative

Strategic framing derives from the literature on communication for social change (Benford & Snow, 2000; Johnston & Noakes, 2005). Groups develop a common narrative by reframing stakeholder's mental models of education, teaching and learning by telling a compelling public story starting from a clear statement of values (Park et al., 2013). In the case of Shaping Our Future Together, this common narrative develops from a focus on education as a collective good, seeks equitable outcomes, builds strong communities, and teaches about cognitive development, positive youth development, and progressive teaching and learning practices.

Youth-adult Partnership

Youth-adult partnership is the process of youth and adults working together as equal partners towards a common goal (Wheeler, 2000). Youth participation in youth-adult partnerships in school has been linked to increased engagement in school and civic responsibility, as well as positive youth development and well-being (Mager & Nowak, 2012). For adults, youth-adult partnerships can provide renewed energy for their work as educators and administrators (Mitra, 2005). Creating a space in which youth and adults can contribute equitably to community organizing and change requires careful consideration of how both age and other aspects of identity (such as race, gender, and ability) shape the power dynamics between all members of the group (Conner et al., 2013; Lac & Mansfield, 2018; Taines, 2014). Minoritized youth and girls, for example, often benefit less from youth organizing efforts that do not purposefully center equity as one of their core missions (Bertrand, 2014). There is always a risk that organizing efforts with ill-defined core commitments will merely empower the empowered, rather than providing an opportunity for collective action to further social justice (Mansfield, 2014). This tendency may be particularly powerful in community organizing that engages with schools which have a long history of social sorting and reproduction (Bertrand, 2014; Khan, 2012; Mansfield, 2014).

UP for Learning's training, site-based coaching, and dual-enrollment coursework consciously drew from the research base supporting the power of youth-adult partnership to support student engagement. By meeting in an off-campus location for their dual-enrollment course meetings, students and teachers were able to break out of their institutionally defined roles in ways that supported intergenerational power sharing. Within this class environment, youth, and adult contributions to the process of strategic framing and dialogue for change were valued equally and seen as important for creating a plan of action for school reform that includes the input of youth and adult stakeholders. Groups could receive coaching before returning to their schools to continue their work within institutions that were typically less hospitable to supporting shared leadership between youth and adults in this way.

Dialogue for Change

The Communicating School Redesign (CSR) process saw dialogue as being at the center of meaningful change. Dialogue, rather than discussion or debate, was seen as essential to shifting public understanding (Freire, 1970). The CSR approach positioned students and teachers in a role of leadership for this dialogue, training school-based teams in facilitative leadership and supporting their training of additional youth and adults in facilitation at their schools. The approach relied on field-tested protocols, many from the School Reform Initiative, to focus dialogic encounters in ways that preserve the values of trust, asset-based thinking, and a focus on equity and justice

Offered annually, the course followed a two-semester structure, designed to allow youth-adult teams to focus on first understanding the principles of strategic framing, school redesign research, and the fundamentals of youth-adult partnership before launching into a cycle of participatory action-research with their schools. As part of this cycle, youth-adult teams collected data on stakeholder knowledge of school redesign and Act 77 at their schools. Then, teams analyzed these data and used them to select target stakeholder groups for their communication efforts. Teams then designed communication strategies, many geared toward opening spaces for dialogue, to enhance stakeholder groups understanding of school redesign, as well as Act 77. According to the syllabus, these strategies ideally led to engagement with the school board, the faculty, and the student body, respectively (see Figure 14.1).

An additional tool that informed CSR teams' work was the Public Understanding and Support Assessment Rubric. Developed by the CSR faculty, the rubric was meant to "chart changes in the public's mental models over time." Teams used this rubric to tune the survey and interview protocols created by CSR faculty to collect baseline data on public understanding of Act 77 and school redesign in their communities. The rubric was then used as the framework for analyzing both the survey and interview data that teams used to craft their communication plans.

The CSR program provided a process to share community perspectives on the personalized learning process. Each year, the youth and adult participants in the CSR program began by collecting data on the perceptions of teachers, students, community members and parents regarding the three pillars of personalization as defined in the Vermont context (Bishop et al., 2017): personalized learning plans, flexible pathways, and proficiency-based education. When the program began, mere months after Act 77 was passed, informational interviews with administrators, high school students, and teachers suggested that almost no one knew anything about Act 77 and how it would be implemented, much less why it had been passed.

POINT OF ENGAGEMENT: CRAFTING STRATEGIES TO EFFECTIVELY ENGAGE AND MOBILIZE THEIR COMMUNITIES AROUND KEY ISSUES

Existing and partnered research activities can help community organizing efforts better understand the distribution of power as well as the pressure

Figure 14. 1

The Communicating School Redesign Action Cycle

they will face for institutional change, the communication needs of different audiences, and the narratives that mobilize those audiences. CSR teams drew on a combination of campaign-based tools to raise awareness about Act 77, followed by dialogue-driven strategies that aimed to engage the community in conversations about their beliefs, misgivings, or excitement about personalized learning. Teams engaged their communities through both traditional media—such as op-ed writing, press releases and interviews—and through social media, including creative Instagram campaigns, the creation of YouTube videos, and websites showcasing the flexible pathway options at their schools. For adults, these were often opportunities to engage their apprehension; for students, these dialogues were opportunities to elevate their voices in their communities around teaching and learning. To support teams in using these strategies, CSR instructors amassed examples from each year of the program.

In crafting communication strategies, CSR teams worked to brainstorm and then pilot metaphors for personalized learning that would resonate with students and adults. Harwood Union High School, for example, used the metaphor of high school being like a "Choose Your Own Adventure Story," in which you could make meaningful choices about how you wanted to arrive at graduation. North Country Union chose to represent flexible pathways as a subway map, with students able to arrive at different destinations through different travel routes, but within a bounded system. The Hazen Union High School team favored a cooking metaphor that positioned a high school education as a recipe that could be tweaked to the cook's taste. The purpose of the metaphors was to arrive at a powerful set of images that would do some of the heavy lifting of making tangible and explicit the mindset shift required by personalized learning. By framing personalized learning in new ways, the hope was also to introduce resources for communicating across a variety of different stakeholder groups, including students, teachers, and community members.

The facilitation of dialogue among all these groups was the critical feature of teams' communication action plans. Students, through the CSR course, received training in effective dialogue facilitation strategies, including the use of protocols, how to hold space for competing ideas, and the difference between dialogue and debate. Teams adapted a wide variety of protocol strategies to best meet the needs of their school context. Some chose to lead chalk talks (facilitated silent dialogue) with students in their teaching advisories or homerooms; some coupled these with teacher-student dialogues that were inclusive of the whole school. Other teams chose to engage adult stakeholders separately, facilitating in-services or faculty meetings with teachers, leading reflective dialogues at school board meetings, or hosting conversations and community meals at parents' homes around their towns.

Here, we discuss three cases of teams from various high schools engaging in these strategies. Each of these teams chose to engage their communities in different ways that best met the needs of their schools and broader community as they worked to create a common narrative.

Facilitating All-School Dialogue at Harwood Union High School

At Harwood Union High School, the youth-adult CSR team focused their efforts on articulating a shared meaning of personalized learning between teachers and students, placing an emphasis on the shared values beneath the policy goals. The formation of such shared meaning could then be leveraged through strong counseling and teacher advisory systems in the school. Harwood Union, a mid-size high school enrolling about 600 students in rural Vermont, began their work of translating their data into action with a question. The team, made up of the principal, a personalized learning coordinator, a teacher, and four students, wondered if there was a strong enough shared understanding between Harwood's students and teachers of the Act 77's key components, such as good relationships with students and core understanding of relevance. This shared understanding, they felt, was key due to the way in which counseling for personalized learning plans was going to be provided through the teaching advisory system at the high school. The teacher advisory system paired one teacher with a group of students to mentor, similar to a homeroom system, but with time and curriculum to support close relationship building. As one teacher on the Harwood CSR team put it:

> [Our team] started saying that it was going to be really important to work with the faculty because they're really the core of being responsible for much of making sure that the Act 77 goes forward, particularly if we think about personalized learning plans. If we think about [our school], we're adapting and adjusting [teacher advisory] so that that can happen. There was a lot of thought process in helping the faculty understand that and really thinking about strategies for that, but at the same time, realizing that students weren't aware in that partnership. I think that's when we really started saying, "Boy, this is a place where having a dialogue would be enormously powerful" so that we could talk about the components that are at the heart of this, and we really looked at relevance and relationship because they're really at the heart of the mission of Act 77.

The group collectively decided to center their questions around the components they saw as key to Act 77—relevance and relationships. The team began to work to make an all-school dialogue into a reality. The first step towards planning was for the team to decide what the focusing questions for this dialogue would be. How would youth and adults be engaged in ways that allowed them both to be heard? How would space be held to hear a variety of differing viewpoints about personalized learning and flexible pathways? Careful planning went into the framing of the questions themselves. In the words of one adult team member:

> I think the most challenging piece about that was deciding on the questions. What were we going to talk about? Framing questions so that students would understand them, or faculty for that matter, in the way that we wanted them to.... I think that's always the challenge, is describing

> questions so that people will understand how it was.... Keeping them open-ended enough that people could really have a dialogue versus just getting just a one-shot answer.

A secondary concern was having a sufficient number of facilitators to cover the entire student body and faculty. While students and teachers involved in the CSR team had received training in facilitation, they were only eight people, and it was important to the team that students act as facilitators in order to signal the importance of youth as serious contributors to these dialogues who would be heard. To this end, students were recruited from other leadership groups across the school, including the Youth and Adults Transforming Schools Together (YATST) group (based in another UP for Learning program) and representatives from the student government. The CSR course instructors provided an afternoon of facilitation training one day prior to the schoolwide dialogue. Because of the time constraints, the training was specifically focused around the particular protocol that the students would be facilitating. "It was a huge undertaking," an adult team member observed:

> We used Wagon Wheels and then we used a protocol I'd never used before. It was called the Critical Friends protocol and it was one that Daniel, the CSR instructor, had had from his bag of tricks from many years ago. It was like a cascading dialogue format. It started with looking at the data points that you are discussing and then having everyone have an opportunity to voice. We moved from "Why is this a problem?" to "What can we do about it and what are the actionable steps that we, as a group, would recommend?" Then we did a modified version of affinity mapping at the end where people then took their solutions that were on Post-Its® and we posted them up on a master sheet and then grouped them into categories that made sense. It was pretty cool. (See Figure 14.2)

Afterwards, with the help of other student leadership groups and the CSR team members, students and adults worked together to distill all the suggestions into "master action steps" that were shared with the whole school. In the words of one team member:

> That was made public. They're up on a bulletin board. They were shared in an assembly. We're starting to tick away at many of those action steps. One of them, teacher feedback, was already underway. We're communicating with people that there's a proposal [for teacher feedback forms] in process and this one's going to come to fruition very quickly. The other piece of our communication strategy now is to make sure that we keep that cycle open, that these are the action steps, this is the plan, this is the strategy, this is how you can get involved if you want to, but making sure we're communicating to people that those things are happening.

Figure 14. 2

The Communicating School Redesign Action Cycle

Photo credit: UP for Learning (written permission to use the photo has been provided).

In the view of this CSR team, many of the master action steps, such as implementing a teacher feedback form or having regular student-teacher conferences, were directly related to the groundwork necessary for the successful implementation of personalized learning plans. In the words of one adult team member:

> Teacher-student conferencing—that came up 71 times in the dialogues. That's pretty significant. Some of the action steps were pretty straightforward, like teachers arrange for conferences formally each semester. That really pertains to the personalized learning plan without people really knowing that.

In keeping with the spirit of communication for social change by focusing on community values around relevance and relationships, rather than exclusively on Act 77, this CSR team expanded the scope of their communication strategy to include engaging teachers and student beliefs about teaching and learning more broadly.

Cross-School and Cross-Community Collaboration

Civic dialogue also developed across school districts and communities, which provided an opportunity for stakeholders to articulate their values about education and their hopes and dreams for the young people in the community. It also provided opportunities to learn and value people across differing perspectives and roles. In the spring of 2016, four CSR teams in the Southwestern corner of Vermont—Whitcomb High School, South Royalton High School, Chelsea High School and Rochester High School—decided that their communities were connected enough through geographic proximity that it made sense to organize opportunities for dialogue across these four schools. From this, a student-facilitated convening called "Student Congress" was born around the theme of discussing school redesign, personalized learning, and in particular, Act 77. In the words of one participant, the groups wanted to "keep it alive and not let it be a one-time thing." One participant described the process of coming to agreement about how this collaboration would proceed, supported by the UP for Learning faculty:

> The UP for Learning facilitators put us in a circle, and we sat there until we figured out how to do it. Initially, it was like we were going to do the Congress, and then we figured out we'd do a facilitator training.... We picked a facilitator training date, and the UP for Learning people came down, trained all the kids, and then we had our Student Congress, which was completely student-led.

The CSR youth-adult teams from each school worked together along with instructors of the CSR course to try to put together an agenda and a facilitator training for young people from outside of the CSR teams from each school so that they would be prepared to facilitate activities with large groups of their peers. Thirty freshman, sophomores, and juniors from the four schools attended the facilitators training and, similar to the Harwood Union High School training, were given a one-day crash course in facilitative leadership techniques focused specifically on the protocols that would be used as part of the Student Congress. A student talked about the training as an opportunity to get "authentic exposure to how these dialogue protocols would work," preparing them for the more than 100 students that would join them on the day of the Congress.

A great deal of preparation was needed ahead of time, much of which was coordinated by the adult members of the team. The event was held at the Bethel Town Hall, a place familiar to students from all the various schools. However, the day of, students took the lead in facilitating the day for their peers. As one adult CSR team member described it:

> It was a lot of logistics on [the adults] getting materials ready. [We were] in the town hall for three hours Sunday before. Then when the students got there the morning of, they totally took the reins and it was awesome, I didn't have to say more than three words. It was really neat. That was kind of the play-by-play of all of the planning that went into it.

The day itself was fully facilitated by the student leaders who had participated in training with UP for Learning. The agenda included a variety of dialogue-driven activities around the core ideas behind Act 77 and school redesign that puts students at the center of their learning, including the opportunity to examine documents related to Act 77 and pull out key words representing the central ideas of the legislation and a student panel that featured high schoolers currently taking advantage of flexible pathways in order to showcase the possibilities present in the legislation. The event concluded with a chalk talk, or silent dialogue strategy, centered around prompts related to how the Student Congress, moving forward, could leverage youth voices to support personalized learning in their home schools.

After the Student Congress day, teachers commented on the direct effects of the Student Congress and takeaways from the Student Congress, saying that it was important to continue to allow times for students to get together and articulate their views on issues relating to their education. As one teacher stated:

> That was from the beginning our core CSR team's goal, was to target students just because we were thinking less is more and we didn't want to overstretch ourselves. The students had some takeaways and it definitely increased drastically after the Student Congress. They still talk about that. I think one of the biggest takeaways was, "Stand up and advocate for yourself," which makes me happy on so many levels. Education is only one minor piece of advocacy so I've heard that, kind of, "Don't be afraid to speak out." "Don't be afraid to speak your mind" [is the] takeaway.

The ripple effects of this strategy have been important as many of the schools in this region are grappling with potential consolidation due to another act passed by the legislature seeking fiscal efficiency across Vermont's small school system. One educator discussed how he planned to continue to engage students together in this way by providing more opportunities for them to continue to reflect across schools on these issues:

> try to use student council as a way to keep the longevity of Student Congress going and hopefully shifting more from just that information-based event. We know what all this about. Now, how can we advocate for ourselves, and how can we bring in more opportunities and more resources into this small supervisory union so that we are getting those opportunities that the big schools have?

Changing Community Mindsets and Beliefs Through a Multitargeted Approach

One school exemplified creative ways to leverage existing structures while creating new opportunities for dialogue. A multitude of interactive strategies helped to provide ways that a range of stakeholders could engage in the conversation and led to shifts in practice. This holistic strategy also led to a deepening of student voice in how the school operated, which offered opportunities to examine equity within a broader range of school processes.

Mount Anthony High School is large for Vermont, enrolling over 900 students. The school joined the CSR program with a team consisting of the school's new principal, their school-to-work partnerships coordinator, and two students. While this smaller team attended the official CSR course meetings run by UP for Learning, the full Mount Anthony team consisted of a larger team of teachers and students with whom this smaller team would convene regularly. Over the course of the year, the Mount Anthony CSR team, who branded themselves "The Explorers," engaged in a holistic approach to communicating about personalized learning to students, teachers, parents, and community members in different venues, at different times. In keeping with the CSR approach, these efforts began with gathering information about the state of stakeholders' awareness and knowledge of Act 77 and school redesign, followed by activities design to spark and encourage dialogue about these issues.

The work of the group began with the interviews with key decision makers in the district and a survey that the CSR course has teams administer to their stakeholders. One of the participants in the group discussed how important the survey was given the size of their school:

> As a group, we basically took a look at our survey and chose focus areas, places where we knew there were gaps in maybe differences between what students thought and what teachers thought, or even in just the knowledge that folks had about Act 77, and then just employed some different facilitation strategies that we had learned in our class to then get ideas from our group about what were ways that we could spread information most effectively, because we have a really large school and a large student body.

In a large school, choosing a targeted approach did not feel as effective as using a kaleidoscope of strategies to try to get out the message about Act 77 and school redesign. Some examples of strategies that the team used included:

- developing a logo (through focus group consultation with students and educators)

- Teaching Advisory presentations and protocols with students
- exit conversations with graduating seniors with the principal
- presentations to middle and elementary school students about Act 77
- partnership with a small local liberal arts college to discuss writing PLPs with students
- Teacher Learning Community (TLC) designed to examine the brain science behind Act 77
- five parent meetings to discuss Act 77 and school redesign
- creating a movie about Act 77 to be placed on the school website

Running through all these strategies, however diverse, was the decision to think creatively about existing structures and leverage them to help engage everyone in the community in dialogue. While some of the strategies used by the Mount Anthony team required the creation of new opportunities for stakeholders to speak (such as parent meetings or exit interviews with outgoing seniors), many of their strategies used existing programs/structures to discuss Act 77 with teachers and students. In addition to leveraging teaching advisory time, as Harwood Union did in their all-school dialogue, the team also leveraged adult professional development time, including already existing time for professional learning community meetings, in order to allow teachers space to engage deeply with their own beliefs about student-centered learning and personalization. A member of this CSR team recounted:

> We did some teacher learning communities around constructing (a solid PLP practice) and had teachers work with their peers in co-designing how we are approaching PLP's, how we are approaching the school changes that we need to make in light of Act 77. They are going to make some recommendations for schedule changes. They are going to make some recommendations for how we are going to advise them.

Another team member reflected:

> That became [teachers'] professional work this year. I think that's been very successful. For example, one of the things that I think we need to do is take more brain-based learning, or what we know about the brain, and incorporate it into how we teach. So, there was a group of teachers that was really interested in kind of investigating that and that became their TLC. And a whole bunch of people signed up for that.... There was a group that looked at brain research and began to just really think about how they could work on things like working memory and stuff as part of their classes without

> getting too goofy. And there was a group that sought out to prove that Act 77 was not based on solid brain research.

Incorporating and working with some educators' resistance to the ideas underlying Act 77 is an important foundation of the dialogic principles that strategic framing practice is based on. The Mount Anthony CSR team's ability to allow these diametrically opposed viewpoints to live within their practice differentiates the work that they are doing from traditional public relations campaigns which seek to didactically educate or inform, rather than listen and create opportunities for opposing viewpoints to hear one another. One team member reflected on how their understanding of framing was able to facilitate this dialogue among teachers:

> The metaphors, I would say, we employed more with our teachers because we have an interesting situation at Mount Anthony of having an administration change this year, and so there was a bit of resistance on the part of the teachers to really get behind this act. And so, we, I would say, employed using the metaphor strategy more with our teachers than we did our students because the kids, more often than not, were open to the change, and they see the benefit personally, so that was easier.

These Teacher Learning Community meetings used a variety of strategies to discuss Act 77 and personalized learning plans, specifically. Students were asked to come and speak to the TLC, creating opportunities for teachers not involved in the CSR team to hear student voices as well. As one team member described:

> We had the students come in to that group during that discussion and give us their feedback about the PLP that we're utilizing now, and what types of questions they would like to see on it and how should we help them to answer those questions, and what would be the best format for helping us to fill out a PLP?

Lastly, the team decided to directly engage the concerns of the most vocal naysayers who, they discovered in their key informant interviews, were largely concerned with the negative effect that personalized learning might have on college acceptance for college-bound students. The team thought creatively about partnerships with higher education institutions. The Mount Anthony team asked a small local liberal arts college, where students must do their own personalized learning plans for their higher education, to come and discuss this practice with their students:

> We have a number of different colleges in town, so we've partnered with a local liberal arts college. Part of their graduation requirements were to write their own personalized learning plan. So, they've been coming and

> talking to students at our middle school about what that looks like and what that means, so we've partnered with them.

By using a broad array of strategies bound together through a common narrative informed by clear values around personalized learning, the Mount Anthony CSR team was able to integrate the information that they were getting from the entire school community to allow those experiences to speak to each other and shift practice in some helpful ways around PLPs and assisting students in taking more advantage of available opportunities. For example, hearing from both parents and graduate seniors opened a reexamination of the processes for ninth graders to plan and reflect on what they would like to accomplish in high school. In the words of one CSR team member:

> What I realized during this process is I think the parents are less—I mean the majority of parents are less—concerned about Act 77 and more concerned about their kid having an idea of what's possible, and what we realized kind of early on is that we hadn't been good at getting kids really thinking about where to go. So, I began to shift those meetings to: those are the questions you need to be asking in ninth and tenth grade to get to your senior year when this can be happening. And these are the things—like if you discover in ninth grade that you really love art—these are the things that you can keep taking every year. And that was based on work I was doing with parents but also on talking to this year's seniors whose big regret was all the things they didn't realize in ninth grade.

Another way in which the CSR work has had ripple effects within school practice is the practice of student senate. The Mount Anthony student senate is now working on creating a student-teacher feedback tool that can be used across classrooms within the high school to promote youth-adult dialogue on teaching and learning. A team member described how this happened, saying:

> I mean there are kids in the youth-adult partnerships that are on student senate. One of the adults that advises student senate is the other adult taking the course. So, there is some crossover, for sure, but I think what student senate is now starting to talk about is how they can construct a tool to allow students to give feedback to teachers about their courses. I don't want that to be an evaluation tool but definitely this is what I've taken from this course. These are the experiences I loved. This is what is working so great. And I think that is really fascinating—that in a year we've moved it that far, that students have the idea that is there a way we can give teachers feedback.

The school is interested in deepening and continuing this work through the possible introduction of another UP for Learning program, called Youth and Adults Transforming Schools Together. The program partners youth with school-based adults to assess the school's practice around the four Rs: rigor, relevance, relationships, and shared responsibility.

The Mount Anthony CSR team leveraged existing structures, as well as creating new opportunities for dialogue with a variety of stakeholders, in order to further awareness and understanding of Act 77 in their community. The power of a holistic strategy was the incredible opportunities it provided for empowering stakeholders with different methods to speak to each other and thus create actual shifts in practice that could address multiple stakeholder needs at one time, such as those of both parents and students, or both students and teachers. This holistic work has also opened to the door to new ongoing engagement with student voice in SVHS's school culture. All the members of the team talked about the incredible time commitment and dedication that facilitating these many strategies took. It was also clear that having the principal as a member of the team was critical in opening the institutional doors that allowed this team to accomplish so much in one year.

POINT OF ENGAGEMENT: EVALUATING THE OUTCOMES OF THEIR ORGANIZING EFFORTS

Another potential site of engagement for researchers in community organizing efforts is in working with groups to evaluate the reach and impact of their organizing efforts. As time went on, more people were aware of the areas of middle and high school education that would be technically affected by the policy. To understand changes in stakeholder awareness and beliefs over time, Dr. Beattie and the co-instructors of the CSR program worked to develop a survey that assessed the mindsets and beliefs of stakeholders on these issues, based on their Public Awareness and Support Assessment Rubric, which broke stakeholders down into three categories:

- Pre-awareness suggested that stakeholders were unaware of the policy changes and held traditional beliefs about school design.
- Awareness suggested that stakeholders had some awareness of school redesign.
- Understanding suggested that stakeholders were aware and supportive of mindsets and beliefs underpinning school redesign.

School-based teams were able to use the survey data to target their communication strategies to the areas of greatest need; in the long-term, the data was aggregated to get a picture of how mindsets and beliefs on these issues may or may not be changing across the state. Overall, over 3,500 youth and adults took the survey between 2014 and 2017.

Survey data from the first year suggested that stakeholders demonstrating an understanding of Act 77 were in the minority, even among teachers and administrators. However, as the policy progressed towards implementation, understanding of Act 77 itself increased, particularly as dialogue about the policy remained a focus of the media and public sphere (Olofson, 2017). Fifty percent of educators, for example, reported in 2016 that they fully understood Act 77, as to 21% in 2014. However, the survey data also indicated that one-quarter of all educators still reported that they had little to no understanding of Act 77 in 2016, demonstrating the need for the broad-based communication work done by CSR teams, even after the full implementation of the act.

CONCLUSION

The case of the Communicating School Redesign initiative demonstrates the myriad of ways that community organizing, particularly involving youth, can assist in research dissemination around local policy implementation. For researchers, the strategic importance of coordinating with intermediary organizations or community groups that support organizing and local capacity building should not be overlooked.

CSR provided space for voice, dialogue, and deliberation at the community level on what personalized learning can mean for a broad range of children. CSR showed the value of a process of youth-led community dialogues and widespread participation in making sense of data related to educational change. The perspectives and leadership of young people allowed a greater sensing mechanism regarding how the policy was landing. Additionally, the case demonstrates how involving youth in policymaking and implementation may open up opportunities for conversation about difficult issues, such as equity, since young people offer perspectives and insights that others cannot provide. In order to do this, however, it is critical that efforts at youth recruitment on the front end of the work involve diverse groups of youth and establish equitable group dynamics that go beyond balancing youth and adult voices to respecting all aspects of youth and adult identity (Mansfield, 2014).

CSR also showed the strength of designing student-led change processes suited to local contexts. CSR provided a process to deepen understanding across stakeholders and to create a vision and agency for how schools and communities wanted personalized learning to proceed. Schools used student-led processes to engage their communities around personalized learning through messages that were locally meaningful and informed by the specific communication needs of the school and community context. Student-led change processes aimed at deepening the goals of the initiative, aiding in implementation, and identifying the spaces in which schools and communities might want to push toward a clearer view of the policy that aligns with the needs of young people in that region.

Intermediary organizations can assist in building the capacity for grassroots organizing that engages meaningfully with research. The support of UP for Learning as a capacity-building organization to support this action by CSR teams in schools was critical to their success in continuing to focus on building local meaning from research on personalized learning over the course of a year in a sustained way. As with other types of counter-normative work happening around teaching and learning activities in schools (Mitra, 2007), it can be difficult to hold a vision of change as well as a vision of youth or community members as partners. UP for Learning provided ongoing support for and reinforcement of these goals throughout the process. Additionally, for both students and educators, the work of planning the events and strategies for engaging their schools around these issues was on top of their normal workload and extracurricular activities. These initiatives would likely have been easily disrupted if not for UP for Learning's holding time for planning and capacity-building training. These findings suggest that for researchers interested in engaging in community organizing to both create new knowledge and operationalize key findings from research, partnership with an intermediary organization may be a key feature of success to help stabilize the work and expand its reach.

REFERENCES

Alinksy, S. (1971). *Rules for radicals: A practical primer for realistic radicals.* Vintage.

Atlas, J. (2010). *Seeds of change: The story of ACORN, America's most controversial antipoverty community organizing group*. Vanderbilt University Press.

Benford, R. D., & Snow, D. A. (2000). Framing processes and social movements: An overview and assessment. *Annual Review of Sociology, 26*(1), 611–639.

Bertrand, M. (2014). Reciprocal dialogue between educational decision makers and students of color: Opportunities and obstacles. *Educational Administration Quarterly, 50*(5), 812–843.

Biddle, C., Mette, I., & Mercado, A. (2018). Partnering with schools for community development: Power imbalances in rural community collaboratives addressing childhood adversity. *Community Development, 49*(2), 191–210.

Bishop, P., Downes, J., & Nagle, J. (2017). How personal learning is working in Vermont. *Educational Leadership, 74*(6). http://www.ascd.org/publications/educational-leadership/mar17/vol74/num06/How-Personal-Learning-Is-Working-in-Vermont.aspx

Cammarota, J., & Fine, M. (Eds.). (2010). *Revolutionizing education: Youth participatory action research in motion*. Routledge.

Coburn, C. E., & Penuel, W. R. (2016). Research–practice partnerships in education: Outcomes, dynamics, and open questions. *Educational Researcher, 45*(1), 48–54.

Conner, J., Zaino, K., & Scarola, E. (2013). "Very Powerful Voices" The Influence of youth organizing on educational policy in Philadelphia. *Educational Policy, 27*(3), 560–588.

Christens, B. D., & Dolan, T. (2011). Interweaving youth development, community development, and social change through youth organizing. *Youth & Society, 43*(2), 528–548.

Christens, B. D., & Speer, P. W. (2015). Community organizing: Practice, research, and policy implications. *Social Issues and Policy Review, 9*(1), 193–222.

Delgado, M., & Staples, L. (2007). *Youth-led community organizing: Theory and action*. Oxford University Press.

Fisher, R., DeFilippis, J., & Shragge, E. (2018). Contested community: A selected and critical history of community organizing. In R. Cnaan & C. Milofsky (Eds.), *Handbook of community movements and local organizations in the 21st century* (pp. 281–297). Springer.

Freire, P. (1970). *Pedagogy of the oppressed*. Bloomsbury.

Guajardo, M. A., Guajardo, F. J., & Locke, L. (2017). An introduction to ecologies of engaged scholarship: Stories from activist-academics. *International Journal of Qualitative Studies in Education, 30*(1), 1–5.

Ginwright, S., Cammarota, J., & Noguera, P. (2006). *Beyond resistance!: Youth activism and community change: New democratic possibilities for practice and policy for America's youth*. Routledge.

Irwin, A. (2002). *Citizen science: A study of people, expertise and sustainable development*. Routledge.

Ishimaru, A. M., Rajendran, A., Nolan, C. M., & Bang, M. (2018). Community design circles: Co-designing justice and wellbeing in family-community-research partnerships. *Journal of Family Diversity in Education, 3*(2), 38–63.

Jason, L., & Glenwick, D. (2016). *Handbook of methodological approaches to community-based research: Qualitative, quantitative, and mixed methods*. Oxford University Press.

Khan, S. (2012). *Privilege: The making of an adolescent elite at St. Paul's school*. Princeton University Press.

Lac, V. T., & Cumings Mansfield, K. (2018). What do students have to do with educational leadership? Making a case for centering student voice. *Journal of Research on Leadership Education, 13*(1), 38–58.

Mager, U., & Nowak, P. (2012). Effects of student participation in decision making at school. A systematic review and synthesis of empirical research. *Educational Research Review, 7*(1), 38–61.

Mansfield, K. C. (2014). How listening to student voices informs and strengthens social justice research and practice. *Educational Administration Quarterly, 50*(3), 392–430.

McTaggart, R. (Ed.). (1997). *Participatory action research: International contexts and consequences*. Suny Press.

Mitra, D. L. (2005). Adults advising youth: Leading while getting out of the way. *Educational Administration Quarterly, 41*(3), 520–553.

Mitra, D. L. (2007). The role of administrators in enabling youth-adult partnerships in schools. *NASSP Bulletin, 91*(3), 237–256.

Noakes, J. A., & Johnston, H. (2005). *Frames of protest: Social movements and the framing perspective.* Rowman & Littlefield.

Olofson, M. (2017). *The Communicating School Redesign mental models questionnaire: 2016-17 and aggregate results.* UP for Learning. www.vtcla.org/wp-content/uploads/2014/09/CSR-UFL-2017-Report-Final-2.0.docx

Park, V., Daly, A. J., & Guerra, A. W. (2013). Strategic framing: How leaders craft the meaning of data use for equity and learning. *Educational Policy, 27*(4), 645–675.

Patton, M. Q. (2010). *Developmental evaluation: Applying complexity concepts to enhance innovation and use.* Guilford Press.

Silvertown, J. (2009). A new dawn for citizen science. *Trends in Ecology & Evolution, 24*(9), 467–471.

Taines, C. (2014). Educators and youth activists: A negotiation over enhancing students' role in school life. *Journal of Educational Change, 15*(2), 153–178.

Warren, M. R., & Mapp, K. L. (2011). *A match on dry grass: Community organizing as a catalyst for school reform.* Oxford University Press.

Welton, A. D., & Freelon, R. (2018). Community organizing as educational leadership: Lessons from Chicago on the politics of racial justice. *Journal of Research on Leadership Education, 13*(1), 79–104.

Wheeler, W. (2000). Emerging organizational theory and the youth development organization. *Applied Developmental Science, 4*(S1), 47–54.

CHAPTER 15

SPEAKING UP AND SPEAKING OUT

Editorials as a Means to Shape Public Perceptions and Educational Policy

David DeMatthews, Richard J. Reddick, and Lebon James III
University of Texas at Austin

INTRODUCTION

This edited book is dedicated to how researchers can maximize the impact of their research for changes in policy to support school improvement. The underlying assumption of the book is that well-designed research with strategic approaches to communication can reach and inform policymakers, which in turn can contribute to policies that support school improvement. We strongly believe in the merit of attending to how researchers can be more strategic in their efforts to design and implement research that is relevant and can be translated for policymakers' decision-making and legislative agendas. However, a focus on research design and dissemination to policymakers may not be sufficient. Knowledge generated through research is not always widely available or accessible to policymakers (Reimers & McGinn, 1997).

Maximizing the Policy Relevance of Research for School Improvement, pp. 359–373
Copyright © 2021 by Information Age Publishing
All rights of reproduction in any form reserved.

Most knowledge produced by researchers is locked away behind peer-reviewed journals with paywalls. Even if policymakers could access these journals, they and members of the public would find themselves lost and disinterested in the dense format and academic jargon. In other instances, given that most policymakers are elected officials, policy decisions can also be based on perceptions of public opinion. Indeed, our democracy depends on some degree of public input in the policymaking process (Fishkin et al., 2000). Consequently, researchers who are knowledgeable about school improvement and have generated research with important implications for policy will often have to look to other methods to communicate with policymakers and those who elect and appoint policymakers.

Editorials and other opinion-oriented writings have been used to impact policymakers as well as the general public. Editorials are often made widely available through media outlets, unlike most peer-reviewed research. They are also written in accessible language. Persuasive, opinion-oriented writings have a long history of impacting policymakers and the general public. Between 1776 and 1983, Thomas Paine wrote pamphlets that would eventually be published as *Common Sense*. Paine used accessible but persuasive language to make a case for independence from Great Britain. Readers from varied socioeconomic classes considered Paine's arguments and many were moved to action, which had a major impact on American history. More recently, journalists and members of the general public have relied on editorials in newspapers to inform and persuade the general public on critical social issues or to get the attention of policymakers. For example, Ta-Nehisi Coates (2014) wrote "The Case for Reparations" in *The Atlantic*, where he powerfully described how the legacies of slavery, Jim Crow, and racist housing policies have created a compounding debt that needs to be addressed. While Paine argued a case for revolution and Coates made a case for reparations, many local and regional newspapers publish editorials that speak to critical issues in public education, such as bonds and school finance, critical decisions of state education agencies, testing policies, school closures, charter schools and competition, and school district governance ethics and accountability.

Policymakers can be impacted by reading editorials themselves, or through voters who become persuaded and informed by editorials. Coates's (2014) case for reparation has been raised in presidential debates and discussed on major media outlets, which can inform voters' decisions at the ballot box. Public opinion can have a significant impact on public education. Elected school board members hire, evaluate, and terminate superintendents and advance policy agendas for improving schools. Governors appoint commissioners of education while state legislatures create mandates and provide funding for programs they deem necessary and important. As most researchers already know, many of these policy and program decisions are not guided by educational research to any large degree, if at all. Editorials published in local, state, and national newspapers and publications are one important way of providing policymakers and the general public with critical information that can inform their decisions. Editorials are also a way for researchers within universities to find connect with the general public, among whom their relevance has been in decline for decades.

Editorials can be powerful tools if researchers are willing and able to use them to disseminate critical information. In this chapter, we begin by defining what we mean by editorials and calling for more scholarship that engages the general public and policymakers. Next, we describe how two educational researchers working in higher education utilize editorials to influence policymakers and the general public. We include examples of how researchers can draw from their areas of expertise and scholarship to impact public perceptions and discourse in local, state, and national media outlets. We conclude with practical steps and recommendations for writing editorials.

EDITORIALS AND SCHOLARSHIP OF ENGAGEMENT

Editorials are typically short 500–1,000 word essays on a timely topic published primarily in newspapers and other publications. Editorials can be submitted to editorial boards or they can be solicited from editors through contacts with different organizations. Often, editorials explain a critical topic, challenge, or critique a set of actions, persuade readers to take a specific position or action, or praise individuals or organizations for an accomplishment. Many editorials provide some initial explanation of a timely issue and include objective information about the issue. Writers frequently avoid personal attacks and instead offer a coherent framing of a problem with potential solutions or constructive criticism. While editorials are short and cannot fully delve into the complex social, political, cultural, or economic issues they consider, they should provide a thoughtful summary of key facts and a powerful or thought-inducing set of conclusions that readers will remember.

Education researchers can make valuable contributions when they consider editorials as tools for disseminating and translating their research and discipline-related knowledge. Not every research study or theory will be useful or impactful as an editorial. However, researchers can certainly find opportunities to explain a critical topic, challenge a set of policy decisions, advocate for action, or praise an organization. Unfortunately, few researchers have engaged in such writing. To some degree, researchers working in institutions of higher education have avoided these outlets because they are not fully recognized for promotion and tenure. In addition, untenured faculty may be fearful of writing editorials that may anger colleagues, university administrators, or policymakers. Senior faculty mentors often advise junior faculty to "keep their heads down" as they traverse the tenure process and engage post-tenure in such writings. Unfortunately, even after six or seven years on the tenure track, few newly tenured professors change their behaviors and begin writing for different venues.

Faculty-researchers' focus on publishing in obscure peer-reviewed research journals is one of many factors that have contributed to the loss of confidence in higher education. In the mid-1990s, president of the Carnegie Foundation for the Advancement of Teaching Ernest L. Boyer identified this decline in public confidence as a critical problem confronting higher education. Boyer (1996) noted that:

> being an intellectual has come to mean being in the university and holding a faculty appointment (preferably a tenured one), writing in a certain style understood only by one's peers, and conforming to an academic rewards system that encourages disengagement and even penalizes professors whose work becomes useful to nonacademics. (pp. 22–23)

In response to this form of scholarship, Boyer called for colleges and universities to also value a "scholarship of engagement" which extended beyond presenting to "colleagues at the Hyatt in Chicago" (p. 27). Scholarship of engagement included intellectual work in the civic space where researchers and others continuously communicate to creatively understand and address pressing social problems. Boyer's emphasis on a scholarship of engagement was not writing off traditional forms of research that advance knowledge within specific domains or interdisciplinary research that cuts across disciplines within higher education. Rather, the scholarship of engagement was about leveraging the great resources and assets of universities to address the urgent social issues in education and health.

Decades after Boyer's remarks on the scholarship of engagement, a 2018 Gallup survey revealed that less than half of American adults reported having a "great deal" or "quite a lot" of confidence in higher education (Newport & Busteed, 2017). Just 33% of Republicans had confidence in higher education. Last year, the new Harvard University president Lawrence S. Bacow expressed his concern that Americans are doubting whether "colleges and universities are even good for the nation" and forcing academia to ask the question: "What does higher education really contribute to the national life?" (Jaschik, 2018). A similar concern emerged from *New York Times* columnist Nicholas Kristof (2014), who stated that "some of the greatest thinkers on problems at home and around the world are university professors, but most of them just don't matter in today's great debates" (para. 1). Such questions about higher education's contributions and public confidence need to be taken seriously by education researchers and should raise concern. While many factors unfairly impact public confidence, such as attacks on higher education by politicians for political gain, other criticisms are valid and should not be avoided.

Editorials represent a critical opportunity for faculty to make a larger impact while also rebuilding trust and confidence in higher education. The authors of this chapter have come to recognize that editorials are critical to disseminating research and informing the general public and policymakers. The authors also recognize that university faculty must engage more broadly in dialogue that extends beyond obscure journals buried behind paywalls and academic conferences. In the next section, the authors detail why writing editorials has become a critical part of their identity as researchers and university faculty.

WRITING EDITORIALS AS TENURE-TRACK FACULTY

A new generation of faculty are entering institutions of higher education. Many of these professionals recognize that higher education is increasingly detached from solving society's most pressing problems and they have a sincere desire to see that their research and scholarship have a positive impact. However, untenured faculty find themselves in a conservative system that rewards certain types of scholarship that does not necessarily have to benefit society. Specifically, the tenure and promotion process often provides little or no reward for informing policymakers or the general public. Many untenured faculty are given the advice to keep their heads down, avoid controversy, and do the work that gets them promoted—publish in top-tier academic research journals. Few junior faculty members can immediately and effectively produce in top-tier research journals and engage policymakers and the public. Consequently, most junior faculty are not being mentored and encouraged to translate their research and use other forms of writing to advance their ideas in the public sphere.

As tenured faculty (lead authors), we recognize that we have tremendous privilege and understand that untenured faculty must focus attention on meeting the criteria for tenure. However, we also feel it is important that all faculty and graduate students (third author) are mentored and supported in ways that promote a scholarship of engagement and a commitment to informing policymakers and the public on critical issues. In what follows, we provide additional detail on why we write editorials, when we started, what topics we have covered, and why we feel this work is critical. We also note some of the different publications that have published our work to highlight the importance of fit between a topic and media outlet. We begin with Richard Reddick's experiences writing editorials given his senior status in the field and consistent record of editorial publications in local, regional, and national venues. Next, David DeMatthews shares his experiences writing editorials beginning as an assistant professor and newly-tenured associate professor. Finally, Lebon James III shares his experiences writing editorials as a former assistant principal and doctoral student in educational policy and planning.

Why I Write Editorials: Richard Reddick

I have always seen myself as a community-engaged scholar, deeply involved in problems of practice that impact the constituencies I represent—first generation, low income, communities of color. With a research focus centered on the lived experiences of Black faculty in predominantly White institutions, mentoring in the cross-race and cross-gender contexts, and the social adaptation of Black families, there are many opportunities for me to share my research findings and interests with the public.

I will admit to not quite understanding or endorsing the belief that impactful scholarship is only sharing ideas with the small colloquy of academics who are in the same area of inquiry. Perhaps as a condition of my research, work, and service being embedded in the community in which I grew up, it always seemed exploitative—even disrespectful—to speak to only the peer-review community, but ignore the people who shared their experiences, perspectives, and time that enabled my work to reach the academy. I also found myself greatly enjoying the experience of conversing with neighbors and local leaders and having my assumptions challenged by folks doing the work of supporting children and families and improving institutions on the ground.

My initial forays into public scholarship were co-authored perspectives with trusted colleagues who saw a convergence of their research or practitioner work and mine. I strongly advocate entering the editorial world in this manner. An experienced mentor can contribute both the confidence and authority that comes from engaging in public scholarship which can be helpful to the newcomer. At the same time, the emergent coauthor can provide the needed critical or scholarly contribution. For these two initial pieces, I wrote with my colleagues Julian Vasquez Heilig ("Perspectives: Black Males in the Educational Pipeline," *Diverse Issues in Higher Education,* August 13, 2008) and Gregory Vincent ("Black Youth Should be Nurtured, not Targeted," *Austin American-Statesman,* August 25, 2014).

As a higher education scholar with a practitioner identity that spans the P–20 range, I found myself eager to engage with the public on issues, but the traditional means of scholarly inquiry meant that articles and chapters were not timely enough. Fortunately, another colleague of mine connected me with my institution's communications staff, and I established a relationship with the office and one staffer in particular. Initially, I was invited to write pieces and Matt, my colleague in the Communications department, would send out an "all call" for anyone to respond. Over time, Matt started to understand my unique "lane"—critical examinations of structural inequity in higher education, with a focus on faculty of color. But perhaps the most significant early editorial I wrote was immediately after the *Fisher v. University of Texas* Supreme Court decision in 2016. My friend and colleague Stella Flores, a professor at NYU, shared my name with the staff at The Conversation, a national editorial platform. Their call came minutes after the decision as I was walking out of a hotel to a flight. By the time the plane landed, I had a 400-word response, published that afternoon ("Eliminating Inequalities Needs Affirmative Action," *TheConversation.com,* June 24, 2016).

The most important aspect of writing editorials, in my opinion, is being able to write briefly and directly in a very tight window of time. While some ideas—such as a "back to school" column—are those one can plan for, a legal decision, policy outcome, and in some cases, traumatic events, can happen at any time. I have found that opinion editors are eager to hear from scholars who can quickly introduce research and data to a controversial issue. Those editors have occasionally reached out to me asking if I would be willing to write on educational issues and those that relate to equity. I should note that my relationship with our communications staff is strong, and they share very direct feedback about the focus and quality of my initial drafts. As with any skill, the more one writes, the more proficient and efficient one becomes. Strong editorial writing requires an ability to focus intently on an issue and turn around a piece in a very short window of time. Fortunately, I stay abreast of policy news in the field and I look for opportunities to share my perspectives when the higher education world intersects with popular culture. I have written for *Fortune, CNN Business, The Hill, Psychology Today,* and *USA Today* on the national level and for most of the Texas major dailies, including the *Houston Chronicle, Dallas Morning News, Austin American-Statesman, San Antonio Express-News,* and the *Corpus Christi Caller Times.* I also have written for major venues that bridge research and practice, such as the *Chronicle of Higher Education.*

I still marvel at how an editorial can draw interest from people in many walks of life and the unique opportunity it provides to share ideas with folks in other professions and parts of the world. While there is an issue and concern about "trolls" in the online context (which colleagues, particularly women of color, have shared as major reasons why they choose note to write editorials), most of the interactions I have are positive, and when time allows I engage with people who have taken time to respond. It is important to remark that engaging in discourse in the public marketplace does mean that one can attract a following—some of whom are supportive, and some of whom are quite critical. For both constituencies, social media ensures that the ideas are circulated rapidly, and I feel a responsibility to introduce perspectives that many folks in my personal, professional, and academic community share. I am also cognizant that I have the protection of tenure and hold some social privileges that make this form of public engagement less risky for my colleagues who hold multiple marginalized identities. For those who find the need to engage in a more inclusive space than the academy, editorials are an ideal form of engagement that immerses the writer in the equally rewarding and daunting marketplace of ideas beyond the ivory tower.

Why I Write Editorials: David DeMatthews

I entered academia after spending about a decade working in urban public schools, partly because I wanted to elevate the voices of my colleagues and students. As an administrator seeking to improve a middle school in the District of Columbia Public Schools (DCPS), I rarely felt that I was able to openly and fully communicate with important constituencies. While DCPS staff worked tirelessly to improve student outcomes, I witnessed how educator, family, and student voices were excluded from important decision-making processes. I began writing editorials in my third year as an assistant professor at the University of Texas at El Paso (UTEP). Prior to my arrival to the El Paso region, the El Paso Independent School District (EPISD) engaged in unethical practices a few years earlier that marginalized English language learners (ELLs). After the district's superintendent and several others were sent to federal prison, EPISD began to advance a school improvement agenda that would view ELLs culture and language as an asset. This meant making a shift from a transitional bilingual education model and a district culture that did not adequately value the cultural and linguistic assets of Mexican American students to a dual-language model that emphasized biliteracy and biculturalism. Several colleagues and I have conducted research (DeMatthews, 2014; DeMatthews et al., 2017) and provided professional development in the district in support of teachers and principals.

The findings from our research highlighted the positive impact dual language was having on achievement, but also how teachers view Mexican American ELLs. Teachers were valuing students' cultural and linguistic assets rather than viewing them as a testing liability. Many families were pleased with what they saw, although like any reform, dual language had its setbacks and challenges. My colleague and I took the opportunity to share some of our findings in an editorial in the *El Paso Times* (DeMatthews & Izquierdo, 2015, October 25). The editorial praised the district, teachers, and principals for their efforts. After my initial editorial, I have written editorials for local (e.g., *El Paso Times, Austin American-Statesman, San Antonio Express-News*), state and regional (e.g., *Texas Tribune, Houston Chronicle, Baltimore Sun*), and national newspapers and magazines (e.g., *USA Today, Education Week, The Hill*). My editorials have covered a broad array of education-related topics that impact principals, teachers, and students.

In each editorial, I do my best to rely on my research experience as well as past practitioner experiences I have from working as a teacher, assistant principal, and district administrator. I want to highlight two additional topics where my research was directly related to editorials I wrote to engage the public. First, I wrote about police violence in Baltimore. My research has been primarily focused on how principals create more inclusive and inequitable urban schools. My scholarship is partly informed by my experiences as a teacher and administrator in Baltimore, MD and Washington, DC. After the murder of Freddie Gray and the Baltimore Riots, I decided to conduct a study on how high school principals and Social Studies teachers responded when school restarted (DeMatthews & Tarlau, 2019). Proceeding a U.S. Department of Justice report on the Baltimore Police Department, I wrote in support of Black Lives Matter and how schools can and should work to address issues of police brutality. I drew from my own professional experiences, a small study I was conducting in Baltimore, and publicly available documents to write "The Principal as Community Advocate" in *Education Week* (DeMatthews, 2016, August 29) and "Understanding Black Lives Matter Through the Eyes of a Teacher" in the *Baltimore Sun* (DeMatthews, 2016, August 25).

Second, I have written about special education policies in Texas. My research has focused on how principals and districts support the inclusion of students with disabilities. In Texas, between 2004 and 2016, a problematic high-stakes accountability policy led to the delay or denial of special education for eligible students with disabilities. Using publicly available data, I worked with a colleague to show that special education identification rates dropped throughout the state (DeMatthews & Knight, 2019). Next, we wrote several editorials, including "In Light of Texas' Failures on Special Education, Parents Must Protect their Children's Rights" in the *Houston Chronicle*. (DeMatthews & Knight, 2018, February 10). In the editorial, we made the case that the state department of education has failed to implement and monitor the nation's special education law and should take several specific steps as a consequence. I have personally and professionally found this form of scholarship rewarding. In some cases, I have received dozens or even hundreds of e-mails in response to editorials that have led to new relationships with legislatures, philanthropists, advocacy groups, and faculty in the region and across the United States.

Why I Write Editorials: Lebon James III

My passion for education research began years before graduate school. I have served in several capacities, including as a secondary teacher, instructional coach, and assistant principal. These experiences informed my perspective on education reform and provided me with some insider knowledge that I use to navigate my research interests. My practitioner's expertise was supplemented with on-the-job training, professional learning, and mentorship. My professional experiences in education created a yearning to learn more about the experiences of school practitioners in varying contexts. As a doctoral student, my desire to engage in public scholarship is rooted in my understanding that the public should be informed about research conducted in academia and how this research can provide insight into public education in their state, region, or municipality.

Editorials are fundamental for researchers because they allow us to inform many audiences about trends in education, advocacy work, political climates, and much more. Recently, I co-authored my first editorial, which was featured in the *San Antonio Express-News, Laredo Morning Times, Amarillo Globe News,* and *UT News* (DeMatthews & James, 2019). Our article considered teacher strikes, teacher shortages, and teacher pay in Texas and across the United States. This editorial was informed by the literature on teacher labor markets, conversations with educators, and our former roles in education. In my experience, I have witnessed how teacher turnover impacts student learning, the organizational structures of schools, and work-life balance for educators who take on additional roles and duties. In some respects, our editorial functioned as a relatable voice for teachers who experience these situations. However, our editorial was also aimed at increasing public sphere awareness for policy change.

Writing my first editorial was both an informational and reflective experience. By no means did I see it as an easy task. It required being intentional to the audience and communicating in a way that was receptive to the reader. I soon learned that how I position myself as a writer for a research journal can be vastly dissimilar from that in an editorial, due to the different audience, word count limitations, conciseness of the topic, and timeliness of the editorial piece. As I prepare for upcoming manuscript submissions, I reflect on what those submissions will look like as an editorial and the impact they will have on the audience who reads them. Additionally, I speak to the advice of individuals such as Dr. Reddick and Dr. DeMatthews, who have experience in this field. Their knowledge and mentorship is critical to my growth because they provide perspectives in writing that may differ from mine or provide an added layer to how I approach editorial work.

Editorials will continue to be a part of my work as a researcher and scholar because they serve as a mechanism to inform the public about research practice. My often difficult days as a practitioner made it challenging to consume the dense literature in the field of education. Editorials were one way I could stay informed in an efficient manner, while also creating spaces for discussion. Additionally, they can provide timely insight for policymakers and district leaders on local issues that may not receive national attention. My research interests encompass a range of topics, including K–12 educational leadership preparation programs, teacher labor markets, and the relationship between housing markets and schools. I seek to inform the public about my research in a relative yet critical way. I am excited to grow as a researcher while also utilizing editorials to inform various audiences.

TIPS FOR WRITING EDITORIALS

The authors of this chapter have collectively written several dozen editorials in local, regional, and national media outlets. We have talked with editors and solicited feedback on our writing. Based on these experiences, we have generated a small list of advice for researchers seeking to write an editorial. This is not a comprehensive list or a step-by-step guide, but rather a few critical points we think will help guide researchers engaging in this new style of writing.

Be Timely

In academia, researchers often publish their work in obscure, paywalled journals. The peer-review process often takes several years, from the first draft to the journal article being accepted and printed. Editorials that are submitted early in a week could potentially be printed in Sunday's paper. This raises the standard for writers to address critical and timely issues. Excellent research that is well-written but not timely or connected to a current issue or event may not be published. Thus, researchers need to pay close attention to the news cycle and current events in politics and policymaking. At the local level, researchers might take note of contentious school board meetings, superintendent turnover, or new curricular policies. At the state level, researchers might want to pay heed to the agendas of state education agencies, school finance bills in the state legislature, and shifts in statewide accountability systems. At the national level, researchers might consider federal legislation, executive action taken by the President or Secretary of Education, or other key policy actors, such as teachers unions and think tanks. Lastly, researchers should focus attention on the critical issues that families, communities, teachers, and administrators are struggling with or remain unresolved by policymakers, such as school shootings, issues related to mental health, and bathroom usage policies.

Be Creative

Editorial opportunities can arise when popular culture intersects with the research and policy world. Sometimes the connections are obvious—a social movement like #MeToo, or the omission of marginalized communities at an awards show, for instance, can inspire a thoughtful editorial linking research and practice. In other circumstances, it might require more thought—one of our colleagues wrote an editorial grounded in a character's depiction in a popular movie. Not all the creative angles will resonate with editors and the public, so be prepared to hear that feedback as well.

Know Your Audience

Writing for academic peer-reviewed journals requires researchers to know their audience and the type of journal for which they are writing. Researchers often familiarize themselves with the journal's editor and those serving on the editorial board. They may also consider the journal's intended audience and any affiliation with professional organizations. Researchers writing editorials must also consider the audience of a newspaper or media outlet. If the editorial is unsolicited, the author may want to first reach out to the editor. Most publication's websites list contact information for opinion editors. If the author has already written the editorial, they might want to read previous editorials from the newspaper to get a sense of the topics that have been published earlier. The author needs to consider whether their topic is relevant to a given outlet's reader. For example, sending an editorial focused narrowly on a New Jersey policy to the *USA Today* or *Education Week* may not be sufficiently relevant to national readers of those newspapers. Similarly, an editorial focused on a national policy issue may be less suitable for a local newspaper or media outlet. When writing editorials, it is essential that authors consider the newspaper's audience and help readers understand when a topic is critically important within a given context or locale.

Not an Academic Manuscript

Peer-reviewed academic journals often require a comprehensive literature review, which helps the reader situate the article within the current literature. Often, the first 5–8 pages of a journal article are filled with an introduction and literature review, before meaningfully discussing a research study's methodology. Editorials are between 500–1,000 words, which means there is not space for lengthy explanations. When writing an editorial, the author must provide relevant details, but cannot spend too much time on background information. A second difference between an editorial and an academic article is the position taken by the author. Most researchers conduct studies using methodologies designed to limit or reduce bias. However, editorials are persuasive opinion pieces that may require the author to reject their researcher neutrality and take a stance on an issue.

Accept Early Rejections and Feedback

New and emerging scholars often have to deal with rejection when submitting their first manuscripts to peer-reviewed research journals. The peer-review process and mentoring help researchers develop their writing skills. Similarly, writing editorials requires time, practice, and mentoring. Researchers who begin writing editorials should expect rejections and seek to learn from their mistakes, especially if they are submitting editorials without first discussing the topic with the newspaper's editor or editorial team. It is also possible that the particular idea or topic you wish to write about is oversaturated or that the venue you have in mind has already solicited an editorial on the topic before you even started to write. Many editors and journalists will offer assistance to researchers, especially if the researcher communicates a desire to publish an editorial on a critical issue. Researchers should seek out partnerships with journalists and editors and recognize that writing editorials will require learning and an investment of time. As many prolific senior scholars have discovered, practice makes perfect in academic writing. Practice also makes perfect for writing editorials—the more you write, the more successful you are likely to become in the future.

CONCLUSIONS

Researchers have historically published their research in peer-reviewed research journals, but oftentimes policymakers do not have access to these outlets or are turned off by academic writing. Editorials offer an additional way of connecting policymakers and the general public with important research findings that can be used to drive policy decisions or inform local, state, and national elections. A secondary outcome of this form of public scholarship is service to communities and the opportunity to rebuild confidence in institutions of higher education. We argue that writing editorials should not replace the important work of educational researchers publishing in peer-reviewed journals. Rather, we believe editorials offer an important, supplemental venue for sharing research and informing policymakers and the general public. We recognize there are some risks that accompany the editorial writing process—such as immersing oneself into politically charged debates—and that for those without the protections of tenure and those who hold marginalized identities, this can be a fraught and hazardous experience. We have provided additional reasons why we have written editorials and some tips and insights we learned along the way. We hope this chapter is helpful for researchers seeking to generate more impact and that it prompts a new aspect of their scholarship.

REFERENCES

Boyer, E. L. (1996). The scholarship of engagement. *Bulletin of the American Academy of Arts and Sciences*, *49*(7), 18–33.

Coates, T. (2014, June). The case for reparations. *The Atlantic*. https://www.theatlantic.com/magazine/archive/2014/06/the-case-for-reparations/361631/

DeMatthews, D. E. (2014). Looks like ten miles of bad road: Cheating, gaming, mistrust, and an interim principal in an urban Texas high school. *Journal of Cases in Educational Leadership*, *17*(4), 19–33.

DeMatthews, D. E. (2016, August 29). The principal as community advocate. *Education Week*, *36*(2), 20–24. http://www.edweek.org/ew/articles/2016/08/31/the-principal-as-community-advocate.html

DeMatthews, D. E. (2016, August 25). Understanding Black Lives Matter through the eyes of a teacher. *Baltimore Sun*. http://www.baltimoresun.com/news/opinion/oped/bs-ed-teachers-blm-20160825-story.html

DeMatthews, D. E., & Izquierdo, E. (2015, October 25). EPISD leads with dual language learning. *El Paso Times*. http://www.elpasotimes.com/story/opinion/columnists/2015/10/25/column-episd-leads-dual-language-learning/74541508/

DeMatthews, D. E., Izquierdo, E., & Knight, D. (2017). Righting past wrongs: A superintendent's social justice leadership for dual language education along the U.S.-Mexico border. *Education Policy Analysis Archives*, *25*(1), 1–28.

DeMatthews, D. E., & James III, L. D. (2019, October 24). Address teacher pay before crises hit. *San Antonio Express-News*. https://www.mysanantonio.com/opinion/commentary/article/Opinion-Address-teacher-pay-before-crises-hit-14560306.php

DeMatthews, D. E., & Knight, D. S. (2018, February 10). In light of Texas' failures on special education, parents must protect their children's rights. *Houston Chronicle*. https://www.houstonchronicle.com/opinion/outlook/article/Pollard-In-light-of-Texas-failures-on-special-12597381.php

DeMatthews, D. E., & Knight, D. (2019). The Texas special education cap: An investigation into the statewide delay and denial of support to students with disabilities. *Education Policy Analysis Archives, 27*(2), 1–34.

DeMatthews, D. E. & Tarlau, R. (2019). Activist principals: Leading for social justice in Ciudad Juarez, Baltimore, and Brazil. *Teachers College Record, 121*(4), 1–36.

Fishkin, J. S., Luskin, R. C., & Jowell, R. (2000). Deliberative polling and public consultation. *Parliamentary Affairs, 53*(4), 657–666.

Jaschik, S. (2018, October 9). Falling confidence in higher ed. *Inside Higher Education*. https://www.insidehighered.com/news/2018/10/09/gallup-survey-finds-falling-confidence-higher-education

Kristof, N. (2014, February 15). Professors, we need you! *New York Times Sunday Review*. http://www.nytimes.com/2014/02/16/opinion/sunday/kristof-professors-we-need-you.html

Newport, F., & Busteed, B. (2017, August 16). *Why are Republicans down on higher ed?* Gallup. https://news.gallup.com/poll/216278/why-republicansdownhigher.aspx?g_source=Education&g_medium=newsfeed&g_campaign=tiles

Reddick, R. J. (2016, June 24). Eliminating inequalities needs affirmative action: How else do you eliminate inequality? *The Conversation*. https://theconversation.com/eliminating-inequalities-needs-affirmative-action-61559

Reddick, R. J., & Vincent, G. J. (2014, August 25). Commentary: Black youth should be nurtured, not targeted. *Austin American-Statesman*. http://www.mystatesman.com/news/news/opinion/commentary-black-youth-should-be-nurtured-not-targ/ng8Zs/

Reimers, F. & McGinn, N. F. (1997). *Informed dialogue: Using research to shape education policy around the world*. Praeger.

Vasquez Heilig, J., & Reddick, R. J. (2008, August 13). Perspectives: Black males in the educational pipeline. *Diverse Issues in Higher Education*. http://diverseeducation.com/article/11550/

CHAPTER 16

WHY WE'RE BLOGGERS

Utilizing Blogs and Social Media to Influence Education Policy Conversations and Decisions

Diane Ravitch
New York University

Julian Vasquez Helig
University of Kentucky

T. Jameson Brewer
University of North Georgia

The lack of innovative knowledge mobilization has limited the impact of educational researchers, faculty, and graduate students in the public discourse (Vasquez Heilig & Brewer, 2019). For example, research on peer review has found that one-third of social science and more than 80% of humanities articles are never cited (Remler, 2014). Furthermore, while the number of academic books rose by 45%—from 43,000 to 63,000—between 2005 and 2014, the average sales per title fell from 100 to 60 (Jubb, 2017). Considering these dismal findings, it's incumbent for scholars to find ways to mobilize knowledge beyond peer-reviewed journals and books to make knowledge more readily available to the public.

Maximizing the Policy Relevance of Research for School Improvement, pp. 375–386
Copyright © 2021 by Information Age Publishing
All rights of reproduction in any form reserved.

The purposeful engagement of scholarly work and insight in social media to disseminate knowledge into the public discourse is a potential evolution of academia's mores. Faculty can immediately create a larger impact of scholarly work in the public space by exploring blogging. Blogging increases the impact and usability of scholarly insights by means of multidimensional, interactive media that target a wide range of stakeholders. In this chapter, we profile how three educational researchers utilize blogs and social media in varying frequency (prolific, occasional, sporadic) to have a larger influence on policy conversations and decisions. The chapter is a guide for educational researchers, faculty, and graduate students to improve the visibility and impact of their research. We provide examples of how prolific, occasional, and sporadic bloggers can better situate their scholarship so that it has a greater impact in the public discourse.

Why I Am a Prolific Blogger: Diane Ravitch

When I began thinking about why I blog, and why I blog prolifically, I turned to one of my favorite essays, George Orwell's *Why I Write*. Orwell listed four reasons to write: (1) "sheer egoism. Desire to seem clever, to be talked about, to be remembered after death;" (2) "aesthetic enthusiasm," that is, "perception of beauty in the external world, or, on the other hand, in words and their right arrangement.;" (3) "historical impulse," that is, "the desire to see things as they are, to find out true facts and store them up for the use of posterity;" and 4) "political purpose," that is, "using the word 'political' in the widest possible sense. Desire to push the world in a certain direction, to alter other peoples' idea of the kind of society that they should strive after" (Orwell, 1946).

One of those four motives I can exclude at once, and that is aesthetic enthusiasm. I love words, but I don't have to blog to find an outlet for them. I also write books, and my purpose there is not purely aesthetic. I think every writer has a touch, more or less, of "sheer egoism." We write as a way of proving we are alive. I think here of Edna St. Vincent Millay's poem "The Poet and Her Book," where she says that so long as her books are alive, she is alive too. I definitely have the "historical impulse," to find out the truth and spread it. But, like Orwell, my primary purpose is political, to push the world in a certain direction. If you agree with me, you will find my posts encourage you; if you don't, you won't read them or you will ignore them.

I began blogging in 2007, after Deborah Meier and I wrote a joint article explaining why we disliked the test-centric reforms of the Bloomberg-Klein regime and published it in *Education Week*. An editor liked our article and invited us to start a blog called "Bridging Differences." Deborah wrote a post and I responded to it; I wrote a post and she responded to it. The assumption was that she was the liberal, I was the conservative, and we would try to find common ground. It was fun but also very time-consuming. I spent many hours on each of my posts. Deborah kept me on my toes, and each of us explored the issues where we agreed and disagreed.

Then, in the spring of 2013, I finished a new book called *Reign of Error: The Hoax of the Privatization Movement and the Danger to America's Public Schools* (Ravitch, 2013). At that time, I decided that a weekly or biweekly blog did not give me as much space as I wanted. I decided to start my own blog, which I called simply "Diane Ravitch's Blog." I thought I might post something once a day. But being a voracious reader and also being the recipient of dozens of emails every day from teachers and parents, I soon found that once a day was not enough to say what I wanted to say. So, I began posting as often as I felt like it, which might be five, seven, or ten times a day. Most of the posts were links to articles that appeared somewhere else first, and they covered the news from coast to coast. Or they were links to other bloggers whose work I admired. I realized very quickly that I could use the blog not only to express my views, but to give the space to other bloggers, usually because they knew far more than I did, and I wanted to give them a platform.

I use the blog to comment on news events that are important to educators but not to the mass media and to report or critique new research and studies. I also used my personal experience and my knowledge of the history of education to put events and studies into perspective. Sometimes I thought of myself as the editor of a small newspaper with an audience of educators, parents, and journalists. For a while I watched the page views and was amazed to see the growing numbers of people reading the blog. I remember when I hit the first one million views and then regularly reported each new milestone. Then I stopped caring about the numbers. I don't report them anymore.

Blogging has made me a better writer, or so I believe. It used to be, when I wrote strictly as a scholar, that I never spoke in my own voice, that I spoke as if from afar (the detached voice of authority), and that I hid my views. Having been a blogger for more than a decade, I now write more easily. I don't ponder every word. I connect my brain and my heart as I write. I reach inside to find the words and they flow. That's the way I blog, and I think it has changed the way I write books as well.

What matters most to me is that my blog is a platform with which to inform others, encourage those who are demoralized, and take a stand on important issues. Deborah once asked me why I blog, and I said that what was happening to teachers and to public schools made me angry. That anger turned into a passion to tell the truth as I saw it and to defend students, public schools, and hardworking teachers. As a historian, I have always tried to be scrupulous about not "taking a stand," not being merely a polemicist. I realize that no one is without opinions, but I tried not to take sides in histories like *The Great School Wars* (Ravitch, 2000a) or *The Troubled Crusade* (Ravitch, 1985) or *Left Back* (Ravitch, 2000b). When I realized that I was wrong about testing, accountability, and choice, I knew I had to take sides. *The Death and Life of the Great American School System* (Ravitch, 2010) takes a strong stand against testing and choice, backed with data. *Reign of Error* (Ravitch, 2013) takes a strong stand against privatization of public schools, with data.

With blogging, one takes sides; that's the point of blogging. I have used my blog to push against the abuse and misuse of standardized testing. I draw upon my experience as a member of the National Assessment Governing Board, which oversees the National Assessment of Educational Progress (NAEP), to comment on testing. I have used the blog to push against the privatization of public schools, not only because I am a graduate of the Houston public schools, but because I have become convinced that privatization does not improve education and turns it into a consumer good rather than a civic responsibility that belongs to all of us. I have criticized the small but powerful network of billionaires who have used their vast resources to micromanage teachers and the public schools, about which most are ill-informed.

I am not a detached bystander. I am in the arena, fighting for ideas. I have tried, to put the matter in Orwell's words, "to push the world in a certain direction" (Orwell, 1946, para. 9) that is, to support democracy and the right of citizens to decide what matters most in their public schools. I have tried "to alter other peoples' idea of the kind of society that they should strive after" (para. 9) meaning, a democratic society where everyone's voice has equal weight in deciding matters of public policy. My fundamental belief is that we, as Americans, should pursue equality of educational opportunity, not consumer choice or data-driven decision-making. What I desire is a world in which every child attends the same kind of school that Bill Gates wants for his own children, with small classes, expert teachers, ample facilities, and the resources it needs for the children it enrolls. I want a society with a vibrant and creative middle class, where poverty has been banished. I know how far we are from that world, but that is my ideal.

I also believe that teachers deserve the respect of society. I have never been a classroom teacher, except in higher education, and I respect those who do every day what I cannot do at all. I believe that teachers should be certified professionals and that their experience should be respected. I believe that students need well-educated, well-prepared, experienced teachers in their classrooms. I believe that principals should have been exemplary teachers who can rightly be called the "head teacher" of their school. I believe that superintendents should be experienced educators who know the needs of the classrooms and the schools.

I blog daily, many times a day, because I want to make a difference and I believe that I can make a difference. I hear from journalists, state school board members, state superintendents, classroom teachers, and parents, who read the blog and pay attention. Whether they agree with me or not, they consider what I have to say. If they did not read what I write, they would have only the press releases of think tanks and interest groups with their own political agenda, paid for by their patrons. Of course, I have a political agenda. But no one pays me to have a political agenda. I do not accept advertising on my blog. My agenda is based on my life experience, my knowledge of the history of American education, my observations of schools, and my reading. People trust me, I think, because no one pays me for my views. They are my own.

Surely there are readers of my blog who wish I didn't post something new so often. They have the choice not to read what I write. I am a prolific blogger because I love to communicate, I want a better world, I want better schools, I want to support the teachers who devote their lives to their work, I want to encourage a love of learning, and I want to make a difference.

Why I Am an Occasional Blogger: Julian Vasquez Heilig

Is there a better place than a blog from which to excerpt contributions to a book chapter about blogging? Back in 2014, two years after I began my blog "Cloaking Inequity," Gustavo Fischman and Adai Tefera inquired if I would be willing to get involved with their public scholarship and knowledge mobilization efforts. Fischman asked if I would join the advisory board of the Arizona State University (ASU) Fulton Teachers College knowledge mobilization initiative. Tefara requested a post for the ASU "Equity Alliance" blog. I agreed to both. So, 13,500 blog clicks later, I will excerpt sections from Vasquez Heilig (2014) to discuss why I blog occasionally.

For a scholar, focusing on book contracts and peer-reviewed research articles placed behind journal paywalls is safety—as comfortable and warm as cuddling up with a blanket and a book in front a fireplace on a cool fall evening. Should faculty only focus on these traditional notions of scholarly activity in 2019? In 2006, I arrived at the University of Texas at Austin (UT-Austin) as a junior faculty member. The department was in a period of transition at the time, as the previous generation of baby boomer scholars was heading into retirement. One of the aspects of this transition that caused me to ponder the future role of my research was the stacks and stacks of out-of-date journals and books in the hallways that the departing faculty had left behind. I pondered what should and would become of my scholarly activity in the short-term and the long-term.

Inherently in politics and education, there are positions staked out in any given topic under study. Early in my career, I published a peer-reviewed paper based on my dissertation that was critical of No Child Left Behind (NCLB) and high-stakes testing in *Educational Evaluation and Policy Analysis* (Vasquez Heilig & Darling-Hammond, 2008). The paper didn't sit well with the dean of the College of Education at UT-Austin, and I learned this in a meeting with my department chair and a vice president. Then, in 2009, that same paper competed university-wide and won the Hamilton Award as UT-Austin's best research paper—a first for the College of Education, a person of color, and a junior faculty member. Despite the award, the admonishment that I received served as a stern warning that my scholarship focusing on equity and educational policy was going to attract adversaries. So, I laid low for six years.

In 2012, I emerged from my tenure process chrysalis. In the fall, after attending a social media professional development seminar for faculty at the UT-Austin John L. Warfield Center for African and African American studies, I decided that I was going to undertake a post-tenure blog project. I was initially inspired to begin the blog because of a media release authored by the Knowledge Is Power Program (KIPP) charter schools in response to a peer-reviewed paper we had published examining charter school attrition in the *Berkeley Review of Education* (Vasquez Heilig et al., 2011). Discussing data from this same paper caused Jonathan Alter, former editor of *Newsweek*, to attack and accuse me of "dissing" charters when I discussed the research on MSNBC's Melissa Harris-Perry Show, my first appearance on national TV.

Facing criticism from KIPP and on national TV, I had no recourse to discuss the merits of the scholarship in the public space. So, I began my blog in July of 2012. I named it *Cloaking Inequity* as homage to the concept of camouflage from critical race theory (CRT). What is camouflage and CRT? Solórzano (1998) related that CRT in education challenges the traditional claims of the educational system such as "objectivity, meritocracy, color-blindness, race neutrality, and equal opportunity" (p. 122). CRT theorists argue that these traditional claims act as a camouflage for the self-interest, power, and privilege of dominant groups in U.S. society (Calmore, 1992; Solórzano, 1997).

Once I began the blog, I realized that there were unlimited avenues in social media—from LinkedIn to Facebook to Twitter—by which to share blog posts with the public. I surmised that my scholarship could extend from the proverbial ivory tower to the public space in ways that I had never imagined. For example, when testifying at the Texas Senate, several legislators stopped me in the hallway to remark that they had read one of the recent posts on *Cloaking Inequity*.

Cloaking Inequity is scholarly. It provides a public platform to release recent book chapters, peer-reviewed articles, and policy reports. Furthermore, instead of waiting a year to publish in the traditional journal format, I can provide rapid scholarship to the public via statistical analyses that are relevant for the discourse surrounding hot education reform topics. The blog is also a tool by which I invite colleagues across the nation to contribute critical perspectives in posts examining various timely educational policy issues. I am also able to provide voice to teachers and others who have important educational reform counter-narratives to share.

Since 2012, the blog's more than 800 posts have been read in 192 countries by more than a million readers. *Cloaking Inequity* has been ranked by Teach100 as one of the top 50 education blogs in the world and has won four blogging awards over the years. In 2013, it was also named by the readers of *Education Policy Analysis Archives* journal as one of the top education policy blogs in the nation.

Via my roles in various organization and sources that contact me on e-mail, I have broken stories on *Cloaking Inequity*. For example, in 2016 I broke the news about the NAACP's national charter moratorium resolution in a post that drew 25,000 readers in 24 hours (Vasquez Heilig, 2016). A few years ago, I also broke a story on the NCAA's decision to no longer allow online charter credits to count towards eligibility for student athletes (see Vasquez Heilig, 2014).

However, there is critique, ad hominem, and "trolling" that accompanies your scholarship entering the public space. The ad hominem has been particularly noteworthy. Here are a few examples in response to research published on *Cloaking Inequity*:

> You have done a disservice for prostituting your services.... You are a joke. Hope you don't ever set your face in our community.

> Look, I'm going to guess that, in spite of the glamour-shot pose on your blog, you really don't have a lot of street in you.... You do your colleagues no favors by dragging your credentials and their name through this particular trailer park.

> It's actually a little painful for me to see a ... totally distorted view... It should be painful, too, for taxpayers covering their professors' salaries.

My mother always told me, "If you can't take the heat, get out of the kitchen." It's true that scholars have their squabbles, but when your scholarship enters the public space the venom rises to new levels of potency. There are other costs that result from making your scholarship more accessible to the public. I have experienced and noted that it can cause you to be disinvited from events, affect your ability to receive grants from some organizations, and can impact your colleagues that must interact with individuals in the public space who are antagonistic towards your scholarship.

However, I believe that benefits of public scholarship and knowledge mobilization via blogging outweigh the costs. Fish (2013) described his perceived role of scholars in *The New York Times*, stating "Academic work proceeds within the confines of that world, within, that is, a professional, not a public, space, although its performance may be, and often is, public" (p. 2). Kristof (2014) wrote, "Some of the smartest thinkers on problems at home and around the world are university professors, but most of them just don't matter in today's great debates" because of "an [academic] culture that glorifies arcane unintelligibility while disdaining impact and audience" (p. 6). Kristof concluded by challenging, "There are, I think, fewer public intellectuals on American university campuses today than a generation ago.... So, professors, don't cloister yourselves like medieval monks—we need you!" (p. 18).

This new era of media has enabled scholars to make their scholarly activities more accessible to the public. However, the traditional measurement of success, tenure, and promotion in the academy do not typically value these types of public engagement. As a result, I don't have the luxury of blogging every day or even every week. While I am now a fully-tenured professor, I have a deanship role and continue to feel intrinsic pressure from the traditional metrics of success in academia. Notably, some metrics—such as those designed by *EducationNext* and *Education Week* to rank faculty influence and public impact—are only considered for public relations purposes rather than for tenure, promotion, and merit review. Ultimately, institutions of higher education desire that their faculty are impactful in the field, yet pre- and post-tenure evaluation processes only measure traditional notions of that impact (i.e., awards, grants, selectivity of journal and book publishers, etc.).

Regardless, I proffer it is incumbent upon scholars to make their work more accessible to the public and allow their research and data to be more available to the public's "great debates." Scholars should seek to integrate their scholarship into society in new ways via social and traditional media. Blogging and social media are the technological canvas by which scholars can empower citizens as critical consumers of emerging knowledge and leave a lasting legacy beyond a pile of discarded books and journals forgotten in a hallway post-retirement.

Why I Am a Sporadic Blogger: Jameson Brewer

My very first publication was a blog post on Anthony Cody's *Living in Dialogue* blog at *Education Week*. I had recently completed my master's thesis exploring the ideologies and dispositions of Teach For America

(TFA) and how those realities fostered unrealistic expectations and hyper-accountability and caused a culture of burnout and shame. I had plans to refine my thesis into a manuscript to be submitted to a peer-reviewed journal—later it was (Brewer, 2014)—but having never published a peer-reviewed article at that time, the process and possibility seemed daunting and slim as it often does to graduate students and junior faculty members. I knew that the findings of my thesis could not be shelved in an unpublished manuscript nor could the data wait through a long and arduous peer-review process. Philip Kovacs, a professor at the time, encouraged me to translate the points of my nearly 100-page thesis into 500—1,000 words. I did, and Philip submitted the blog to Anthony who posted it that very day (Brewer, 2012a).

As noted above, public scholarship often elicits responses from critics at a rate significantly higher—and often more personal—than scholarship printed exclusively behind paywalls. As was the case, my first blog post garnered comments from TFA supporters. My responses to, and the subsequent conversation with, one individual were pulled by Anthony and turned into their own blog posts given the length and depth of the conversation (Brewer, 2012b, 2012c). While I suspect that little progress was made in conveying my points—bolstered by empirical evidence—with the individual I was in a public conversation with, what I can be sure of is that the civil back-and-forth was, by its public nature, useful. In short, I regularly receive e-mails from TFA corps members and alumni expressing their thanks for sharing my views and the data in a public forum, as TFA works tirelessly to silence dissenting voices. Those who have reached out to me have expressed that they feel alone, as if in a silo, carrying the weight of a culture of silence and sycophancy that TFA fosters. With little doubt, had I simply published my master's thesis in a peer-reviewed journal it would have been out of reach to the majority of those who read the series of blog posts and found some comfort in them.

While I do not blog as frequently as Diane or Julian, that initial foray into publishing research that found a foundation in a blog post cemented for me the importance of breaking down the barriers of the ivory tower and sharing our work in public spaces. Information is vital in democratic engagements. As a researcher, I feel a unique obligation to bring my work into the public sphere as much as possible despite a growing resistance directed towards expertise (Nichols, 2017). Working at a state university, that obligation, in my view, is compounded by the public nature of my institution. I'm also a member of the Scholars Strategy Network (SSN), an organization that seeks to bridge the gap between researchers and policy-makers. We author policy briefs that, in many ways, are similar to a blog post in that they must be no more than two pages and must be completely jargon-free. The point here is to make scholarship not only accessible in its language and accessible in terms of price (open-access), but to find ways for academics to actually inform policy decisions.

As an untenured professor I am keenly cognizant of the risks associated with public scholarship, as public comments beget public attention that is not always flattering. There are, in fact, concerted efforts to wield unflattering public perceptions in order to silence and threaten professors both with their jobs (see, for example, Turning Point USA, n.d.) and their lives (Cuevas, 2018; Howey, 2018). I am also aware that the traditional promotion and tenure guidelines at many universities minimize the value of blogs, op-eds, and policy briefs compared to peer-reviewed articles, books, and book chapters. As noted below, it doesn't have to be one or the other. Working with a commitment to publish in peer-reviewed journals *and* publishing in public platforms not only expands the audience of our work considerably, but it satisfies our calling to provide insight and analysis to the broader public and, as a result, respects the obligation that researchers have to the common good.

CONCLUSION

Blogging is a medium that most scholars resist because of perceived time limitations, but it is actually a conduit by which they can bridge distance and place. In some cases, publishing work that does not carry a traditional understanding of academic work can also seemingly present obstacles for faculty members—particularly junior faculty who may worry about navigating a tenure landscape if they perceive there are political components to such reviews. What we recommend is that blogging and op-eds should be grounded in the academic work and the academic data. When this is done appropriately, the work—while written free of jargon—should still be understood as an extension of traditional academic work. Moreover, if the work is grounded in data and theory, this type of public and forward-facing work bolsters, in our view, a faculty member's application for tenure as the work can be seen as grounded in data, not politics, but provides a valuable contribution to society beyond academic journals.

Blogging can create national and international connections in a free and readily available public discourse that has never been possible in history before the current technological and information age. Vasquez Heilig and Brewer (2019) argued that this approach is not a this-*or*-that proposition, but instead is a this-*and*-that proposition. Scholars should continue the traditional ways of approaching research, scholarship, and service (i.e., peer-reviewed journal articles and books). However, with blogs, scholarly insight enhances purposeful knowledge mobilization in the public discourse. The role of the scholar no longer needs to be limited to the oft echo chambers of the ivory tower's peer-reviewed journals and books that are on average not widely read or used. A commitment to blogging and public scholarship is an important endeavor to address the persisting lack of scholarly influence and relevance of the vast majority of academics in the public discourse.

REFERENCES

Brewer, T. J. (2012a). Hyper-accountability, burnout and blame: A TFA corps member speaks out. *Education Week: Living in Dialogue*. http://blogs.edweek.org/teachers/living-in-dialogue/2012/02/hyper-accountability_burnout_a.html

Brewer, T. J. (2012b). Teach for America corps members in dialogue: Can this model work? *Education Week: Living in Dialogue*. http://blogs.edweek.org/teachers/living-in-dialogue/2012/02/teach_for_america_corps_member.html

Brewer, T. J. (2012c). Teach for America members debate: The leadership pipeline. *Education Week: Living in Dialogue*. http://blogs.edweek.org/teachers/living-in-dialogue/2012/02/teach_for_america_corps_member_1.html

Brewer, T. J. (2014). Accelerated burnout: How Teach For America's academic impact model and theoretical framework can foster disillusionment among its corps members. *Educational Studies, 50*(3), 246–263.

Calmore, J. (1992). Critical race theory, Archie Shepp, and fire music: Securing an authentic intellectual life in a multicultural world. *Southern California Law Review, 65*(5), 2129–2231

Cuevas, J. (2018). *A new reality? The far right's use of cyberharassment against academics: A firsthand account by a targeted faculty member.* https://www.aaup.org/article/new-reality-far-rights-use-cyberharassment-against-academics#.W2metC2ZNTY

Fish, S. (2013, December 9). Scholarship and politics: The case of Noam Chomsky. *New York Times*. https://www.nytimes.com/2013/12/10/opinion/fish-scholarship-and-politics-the-case-of-noam-chomsky.html?_r=0

Howey, B. (2018). *Right-wing groups are recruiting students to target teachers.* https://www.revealnews.org/article/right-wing-groups-are-recruiting-students-to-target-teachers/

Jubb, M. (2017). *Academic Books and their Futures: A Report to the AHRC and the British Library.*

Kristof, N. (2014, February 15). Professors, we need you! *New York Times.* http://www.nytimes.com/2014/02/16/opinion/sunday/kristof-professors-we-need-you.html?_r=0

Nichols, T. (2017). *The death of expertise: The campaign against established knowledge and why it matters*. Oxford University Press.

Orwell, G. (1946). *Why I write.* Retrieved September 19, 2019 from https://www.orwellfoundation.com/the-orwell-foundation/orwell/essays-and-other-works/why-i-write/

Ravitch, D. (1985). *The troubled crusade: American education 1945–1980*. Basic Books.

Ravitch, D. (2000a). *The great school wars: A history of the New York city public schools*. Johns Hopkins University Press.

Ravitch, D. (2000b). *Left back: A century of failed school reforms*. Simon & Schuster.

Ravitch, D. (2010). *The death and life of the great American school system: How testing and choice are undermining education*. Basic Books.

Ravitch, D. (2013). *Reign of error: The hoax of the privatization movement and the danger to America's public schools*. Knopf.

Remler, D. (2014). *Are 90% of academic papers really never cited? Reviewing the literature on academic citations*. http://blogs.lse.ac.uk/impactofsocialsciences/2014/04/23/academic-papers-citation-rates-remler/

Solórzano, D. G. (1997). Images and words that wound: Critical race theory, racial stereo-typing, and teacher education. *Teacher Education Quarterly, 24*(3), 5–19

Solórzano, D. G. (1998). Critical race theory, race and gender microaggressions, and the experience of Chicana and Chicano scholars. *Qualitative Studies in Education, 11*(1), 121–136

Turning Point USA. (n.d.). *About turning point USA*. https://www.tpusa.com/aboutus/

Vasquez Heilig, J. (2014, February 28). Pile of old books vs. inspiring citizens as critical consumers of knowledge for the great debates. *Cloaking Inequity*. http://qwww.niusileadscape.org/bl/pile-of-old-books-vs-inspiring-citizens-as-critical-consumers-of-knowledge-for-the-great-debates-by-julian-vasquez-heilig/#more-1515

Vasquez Heilig, J. (2016, July 29). Breaking News: @NAACP calls for national moratorium on charters. *Cloaking Inequity*. https://cloakinginequity.com/tag/naacp-charter-resolution-2016/

Vasquez Heilig, J. (2014, April 22). NCAA bans 12 Inc. online charters: No Rose Bowl, no Final Four. *Cloaking Inequity*. https://cloakinginequity.com/?s=ncaa+final+four

Vasquez Heilig. J., & Brewer, J (2019). Making the case for academia's engagement in knowledge: Mobilization and purposeful public scholarship in social media. *Critical Questions in Education, 10*(2), 81–91.

Vasquez Heilig, J., & Darling-Hammond, L. (2008). Accountability Texas-style: The progress and learning of urban minority students in a high-stakes testing context. *Educational Evaluation and Policy Analysis. 30*(2), 75-110.

Vasquez Heilig, J., Williams, A., McNeil, L., & Lee, C. (2011). Is choice a panacea? An analysis of black secondary student attrition from KIPP, other private charters and urban districts. *Berkeley Review of Education, 2*(2), 153–178.

COMMENTARY

CHAPTER 17

REFRAMING RELEVANCE

Strategies for Closing the Gap

Elizabeth Farley-Ripple, Katherine Tilley, Samantha Shewchuk, and Scott Sheridan
University of Delaware

As researchers, many of us aspire to have an impact on policy and practice—that is, to positively contribute to the students, families, schools, and communities across the nation by producing evidence that is useful for decision making. To do so requires us to be in many ways responsive to the needs of those stakeholders and to ensure the relevance of our work to those needs. In this endeavor, we must first ask what we mean by relevance and what the sources of possible "irrelevance" are; and, second, we need a framework to guide efforts to become more relevant. Practically speaking, relevance is the extent to which our research is connected and applicable to the challenges that face our education system—essentially a precondition for use. Yet that connection it is often elusive, both because of and leading to gaps between research and practice. At the Center for Research Use in Education (CRUE), we are guided by a framework driven by early knowledge utilization literature in which research and practice (alternatively, policy) are distinct communities, with separate institutional and professional contexts and cultures (Bogenschneider & Corbett, 2011),

Maximizing the Policy Relevance of Research for School Improvement, pp. 387–403
Copyright © 2021 by Information Age Publishing
All rights of reproduction in any form reserved.

and that the gap between them may be understood in multiple ways. We have written about the larger framework elsewhere (Farley-Ripple & et al. 2018) but in this commentary, we use these "gaps" as an analytical tool with which to consider relevance and argue that we can make headway on the relevance issue if our work meaningfully attends to those gaps. We begin by explaining the application of our framework as an analytical tool, then offer examples for each gap, then conclude with some next steps for our collective work as a field.

Before we begin, it is important to lay out some caveats for this discussion. First, as we have articulated elsewhere, a core principle for the work of the Center is that linking research and practice is a *bidirectional* process, and, therefore, a problem unlikely to be solved by either demanding uptake of research by practitioners or by demanding changes in how researchers produce or disseminate research. Rather, we believe that efforts to strengthen ties between research and practice need to reduce barriers and leverage existing mechanisms that may enable stronger ties. However, in keeping with the purpose of this book, we focus our comments on considerations for researchers specifically.

Second, we recognize that policy and practice communities are not the same, and may differ in terms of goals, language, and time frames (Tseng & Nutley, 2014) as well as differ in their perspectives on key issues (simply ask a teacher). In the Center's work, we focus exclusively on the role of research in school-based decision making and our data support claims about the implementation or practice level of the educational system. Nonetheless, much of the literature on which our conceptual foundations are built come from the broader field of knowledge utilization and research use, including the role of research in policy within and outside of education as well as at higher levels of the education system (e.g., district, state). Further, as Rickinson and colleagues (2017) argue, policymakers and practitioners both experience challenges negotiating a wide range of evidence, struggle with the issue of what is available versus appropriate, and may use evidence in many ways. We therefore believe that the ideas generated here are instructive for relevance to various parts of the educational system, though we still approach this with caution.

Lastly, throughout this commentary, we use data from the Survey of Evidence in Education (SEE-S) and from complementary qualitative data analyses to illustrate opportunities for improving the relevance of research to practice, specifically school improvement practice. These data include interviews with dozens of educators, researchers, and intermediary organizations, as well as responses from more than 2,500 educators in 94 schools across the country sampled by urbanicity, population served, and governance. These data allow for a large-scale portrait of school-based decision making. However, at the time of this publication, these data represent about half of our intended sample, so we would like to point out that these findings are not yet nationally representative and should be considered preliminary evidence.

RELEVANCE AS GAP-CLOSING

Dunn's (1980) analysis of case studies of knowledge utilization offered five models or frames for theorizing about the problem of knowledge utilization: product-, inquiry-, problem-, structural-, and process-contingent models. These models were intended to provide greater detail to the larger "two-communities" metaphor applied to the gap between research and policy, the weakness of which, he argued, is its generality. In his analysis, these five models are used to generate hypotheses about the conditions in which research knowledge would be used. We take up these ideas in our work as a Center, hypothesizing that observable gaps between research and practice communities in schools may be attributable to disconnected perspectives. In the specific context of education and practice, we interpret Dunn's models as gaps in assumptions and perspectives about the usefulness of research products; the nature and quality of research; problems that research addresses; the structures, processes, and incentives surrounding research production and use; and the relationships between communities.

These gaps also serve as a way of evaluating the relevance of research to practice. That is, research designed and produced in ways that address these gaps will be more relevant, and subsequently, more likely to be used, than research that is not responsive to these gaps. While the expectation in our work is not that the burden of gap-closing falls on researchers, a deeper understanding of these disconnects point to opportunities to rethink our collective work.

Relevance Through Products

There is evidence from previous studies that research is not "useable" without additional development (Havelock et al., 1969; Lindblom & Cohen, 1979; Louis & Dentler, 1988) and that the characteristics of research evidence may present challenges for uptake (Birkeland et al., 2005; Corcoran et al., 2001; Gross et al., 2005; Hannaway, 1989; March, 1994; West & Rhoton, 1994). Huber (1991) calls attention to two particularly relevant factors, media richness and information overload, pointing to empirical research which suggests that the features of the medium used to convey information influence interpretation and that interpretation is "less effective if the information to be interpreted exceeds the capacity to process information" (p. 103). From this perspective, researchers have traditionally failed to disseminate research products tailored to meet the needs and communication approaches that resonate with school-based practitioners (Cook et al., 2013). Researchers, for instance, tend to disseminate research in traditional academic formats (e.g., peer-reviewed journal articles and conference presentations). However, emerging evidence on the information-seeking habits of educators reveals that research-related sources, such as online databases and research journals, are used much less often (Shipman et al., 2015).

Prior evidence suggests that format matters (Corcoran et al., 2001; Gross et al., 2005; Reichardt, 2000; West & Rhoton, 1994), and that information needs to be presented in a way that practitioners can interpret, adapt to their contexts, and implement with fidelity. Emerging findings from our Center suggest several features of products that may be instructive for researchers. We asked school-based practitioners to provide us with open-ended answers about specific research-based resources that were influential in a recent organizational decision. Of the 367 resources identified, nearly half (46%) were books, far more than any other format, especially materials in academic formats such as journal articles or research summaries (16%). More broadly, when asked about preferred formats for consuming research, early analyses of our survey data clearly point to professional development materials as the most valued, followed by conference presentations, news outlets, and multimedia products.

Underlying format preferences are likely features of content and presentation that may better meet the needs of educators than traditional research products. For example, books may be popular because they better match the needs and communication approaches that resonate with educators. School-based practitioners who participated in interviews explained that the books they used to inform organizational decisions offered clear and consumable content and provided sound, realistic, and actionable strategies to use within the complexity of everyday practice. Early analyses of survey data confirm that educators prioritize information that is understandable, is easy and free to access, is concise, is actionable, models strategies, and is available online (as indicated by mean ratings of importance).

Not surprisingly, even thoughtfully constructed implications for policy and practice in traditional research products do not meet these needs, offering directions for researchers in terms of product development and dissemination—directions which may not fit their current practices (see Tilley et al., 2019). In this sense, one dimension of relevance can be achieved by rethinking how we as researchers share our work.

Relevance Through Problems

Research may be made more relevant to practice by addressing a gap in the perspectives of researchers and practitioners surrounding problems of practice. The ways in which the two communities identify, understand, and experience problems may be different for a variety of reasons. Education researchers and practitioners are operating in vastly different contexts (Coburn & Talbert, 2006; Honig, 2003; Huberman, 1994). In the research community, problems are often studied using rigorous scientific methods, following a specific, planned research design which attempts to control for all possible variables. Often researchers attempt to address problems and produce findings that will impact a wide-ranging audience, nationally or even globally, with priority placed on thoroughness, rigor, and generalizability.

In contrast, for practitioners, problems are localized, intertwined, and immediate (Leithwood & Steinbach, 1995; Supovitz & Klein, 2003). School-based practitioners face a wide variety of problems across their districts, schools, and classrooms, often simultaneously. Preliminary analysis of open-ended survey data that asked practitioners to identify a problem their school faced in the last year revealed a dozen or more initiatives *per school*. These initiatives ranged from restructuring the school day to adopting curriculum to designing policies and practices. For practitioners, problems are always localized. That is, they take place within the district, school, and classroom. Moreover, for practitioners, these problems are real, daily occurrences with consequences that affect real people. Problems for practitioners are not only their problems; they are also the problems of their constituencies, parents, and students, adding pressure for timely action. Furthermore, political expediency means that it may be beneficial to give the appearance to be combatting a problem, when realistically, the research shows that such problems may take a longer time to fix. This is necessary because students will be out of the schools by the time any research-based efforts bear fruit, and constituents are looking to benefit themselves as well as those who come after them.

Relevance, then, may represent the extent to which the questions researchers ask match the problems educators face. Practitioners in our survey have described a wide range of challenges and decisions, from curriculum alignment to engaging non-English speaking families to how to organize the master schedule. The empirical literature base regarding the types of problems school-based practitioners face is lacking, as is a standardized mechanism for how information about needs can flow from practice to research. So how do researchers decide which problems to study? Emerging results from a pilot administration of the *Survey of Evidence in Education-Research (SEE-R)*, conducted with 78 education researchers across the United States, found that half said that input from educators was "not at all" or only "a little" important in shaping their research questions, in spite of responding that their research was intended to influence problems of practice. Conversely, 80% of researchers indicated that previous literature was "moderately" or "very" important in shaping the research questions.

Moving forward, researchers seeking to ensure the relevance of their work to policy and school improvement efforts should consider attending much more specifically to the needs of practitioners. Too often, though for a range of reasons, researchers are driven by other factors (see discussion of structures, processes, and incentives, below). Changing researchers' practice demands that we not merely assume the needs based on anecdote or impression, but deeply understand the nature of educators' work and how it is situated in the system. We advocate researchers spend a good deal more time in the field, not merely for data collection, but to develop a better knowledge base to inform their work. Further, we also argue that partnerships with professional associations, which already possess this deep understanding, may help the research community achieve relevance at a greater scale.

Relevance Through Methods

As noted throughout this volume, the *how* of research is also consequential. Previous studies suggest that school-based decision-makers often prefer evidence from organizations or contexts (e.g., demographics, location, performance) similar to their own, regardless of study design (Corcoran et al., 2001; Finnegan et al., 2013; Prendergast & Rickinson, 2019) and value other characteristics that make research compatible with their interests, goals, and needs (see Neal et al., 2018 for a discussion). In contrast, efforts to push evidence-based practices in schools tend to emphasize "what works." For example, the What Works Clearinghouse employs standards that place great weight on internal validity for drawing causal inference (i.e., randomized experiments), yet in our data half of respondents assigned slight to no importance to these features. Further, only 40% of respondents indicated that having adequate methodological detail in a research product was a very important feature.

These preferences raise questions about how practitioners value traditional research methods (Broekkamp & van Hout-Walters, 2007) or, alternatively, they suggest limited capacity to critically interpret research (Reichardt, 2000; Supovitz & Klein, 2003; West & Rhoton, 1994). However, the gap may be deeper than a mere disconnect in methodological preferences.

The scientific community, including those of us in the social sciences, has long embraced principles of logical empiricism as the dominant mode of inquiry (Pallas, 2001; Paul & Marfo, 2001; Tebes, 2005). In other words, the foundations of science as we practice it today have deep roots in ideas about objectivity, rationality, and logic. Alternative epistemological perspectives, however, value different forms of knowledge, including knowledge in action (Amin & Roberts, 2008; Schön, 1995) or knowledge in practice (Billet, 2001; Gherardi, 2009; Pols, 2014). These forms of knowledge are often tacit, embedded in the work of educators and education decision makers, and are valued in policy and practice far more than the ostensibly objective, rational knowledge offered by science.

These epistemological differences necessarily manifest themselves in debates about research methods (e.g., the qualitative versus quantitative debate). As a result, much of the work we hope to be policy- or practice-relevant may have poor fit with worldviews derived from experience and practice-based knowledge (see Smeyers & Depaepe, 2006). Most often we find that implications for practice and policy are considered at the end of a project—when seeking to understand implications for practice—rather than considering ways in which other forms of knowledge may be incorporated into *how* we conduct the research.

However, there are many (often marginalized) modes of research which embrace principles more closely aligned with epistemologies of knowledge in action and practice, most notably participatory approaches to research (sometimes referred to as coproduction). As Kemmis et al. (2014) summarize, participatory research can *uniquely* create conditions for practitioners to understand and develop practice "from within" practice traditions, to participate in and develop forms of action and interaction in which practice is conducted, and to individually and collectively transform the conduct and consequences of their practice. Variations on participatory research—such as participatory action research, youth participatory research, and community-based participatory research—have extensive traditions in education research, though less in the policy space, and have long been called for in addressing the research-practice divide (Cousins & Earl, 1992; Meyer et al., 1998). Many more examples are available in the field of evaluation, in which participatory models, including developmental, empowerment, and horizontal evaluations, are less peripheral to the scholarly community and have established a theoretical and empirical link to evaluation use (Cousins & Chouinard, 2012; Daigneault, 2014).

Recent efforts to improve the role of research in education policy and practice have adopted similar principles, increasing engagement across the boundaries of research, policy, and practice communities. For example, research-practice partnerships (RPPs) have been shown to be promising for engaging policy or practice partners early in the research process, and, as a result, have fostered learning across boundaries that are believed to lead to both better research and better practice. However, as acknowledged by Nolan and colleagues (2007), approaches under this umbrella vary dramatically in the nature of engagement, from research conducted entirely by outsiders to truly participatory and emancipatory models. Therefore, while increased calls for participatory models of research are certainly a step toward bridging this epistemological divide, we caution against overreliance on engagement as a resolution to a fundamental rethinking of what knowledge "counts" in our work.

Relevance Through Relationships

Central to our work at CRUE is the fact that the research and practice communities are often distinct entities, something akin to ships passing in the night. This conceptualization (and often reality) of two communities is problematic for achieving relevance, as ties between the two are often weak. At the same time, many studies have found that the use of research evidence is a function of that relationship (Backer et al., 1986; Coburn & Stein, 2010; Cousins & Simon, 1996; Honig & Venkateswaran, 2012; Huberman, 1990; Landry et al., 2001; Laviset al., 2003).

Further, that relationship is often understood and enacted in different ways, some of which promote relevance more than others. For example, Lavis et al. (2003) categorizes relations as producer-pushed (e.g., dissemination), user-pulled (e.g., active search by users), and exchange (e.g., interaction between users and producers during key processes). An extensive review by Langer et al. (2016) finds that interventions focused on push or pull were likely to have no effects on strengthening evidence use. Relationship-focused interventions, however, may have promise, as they provide opportunity for interaction. Relationships based on interaction promote trust, transparency, exchange of ideas, and shared understanding, which enable researchers to be more responsive to the needs of practitioners (Harrison et al., 2017). In short, such relationships can support relevance.

We point to RPPs as a potentially effective structure that surmounts typical barriers to research use, including relevance, timeliness, access, and actionability (Henrick Cobb et al., 2017; Farrell et al., 2017; Snow, 2014). RPPs have been supported with federal funds as well as funds from local and foundation sources. As they have become more widespread, some evidence suggests that research resulting from this work is useful and has had an impact on local decision making, though significant additional research on outcomes of RPPs is needed (Coburn & Penuel, 2016). Unfortunately, RPPs are relatively rare, leaving relationship-building among researchers and practitioners to individual or institutional efforts, rather than systematic engagement. Early analyses of our survey data found minimal evidence of relationships among researchers and practitioners, with low reports of RPP participation (1%), participation in research in *any* way (19%), reaching out to a researcher about a school-related issue (10%), or being contacted by a researcher (15%).

On the other hand, our work does show that there are other ways to build relationships directly with educators. For example, educators do report using and seeking research-based information from professors in their pre- and in-service preparation programs. Additionally, both researchers and educators report having attended practice- or research-focused conferences respectively. In fact, in one of our forthcoming case studies, we document the adoption of a handwriting intervention resulting directly from joint conference attendance. Although these are infrequent in our data, it is worth acknowledging that multiple opportunities exist for building relationships. Furthermore, benefits can and should flow in both directions (Colbeck, 2000)—teaching and advising in preparation programs as well as attendance at practitioner conferences benefits not only educators but researchers, expanding opportunities to learn about and from practice.

As a last point on relevance through relationships, we point out that relationships need not always be direct. For most educators, including those in our sample, access to research is mediated by external organizations such as professional developments providers, professional associations, and other educational intermediaries who serve as research brokers (Malin et al., 2018; Neal et al., 2019). Malin and colleagues' work on Edutopia, the Marshall Memo, and Harvard's Usable Knowledge offer cases in point. In our own work, we find local, state, and national associations—teacher unions in particular—important resources for educators seeking research-based information to inform decisions. These brokers are already trusted, providing information relevant to practice, so building stronger ties to these organizations may be a highly productive step in improving the relevance of research.

Relevance Through Structures, Processes, and Incentives

Our last approach to relevance represents a shift in thinking. Whereas the prior gaps—in products, problems, methods, and relationships—are about the work of researchers, the gaps in structures, processes, and incentives shape research processes. In this case, achieving relevance is about creating the conditions that support research production and use, and is more likely the purview of leadership in the research community, whether funders, institutions of higher education, or publishers.

Our argument here is that the aforementioned gaps did not come from thin air, but rather from systemic responses to the larger ecosystems of school improvement and research (Nelson & Campbell, 2019; Shepherd, 2007, 2014). Researchers, for example, are subject to the demands of their institutions for promotion and tenure, to expectations of funders that are increasingly relied upon to make research possible, to publishers and editors that can serve as gatekeepers, and to the normative expectations of being a scholar into which we are socialized from the start of doctoral preparation (Bogenschneider et al., 2000; Colbeck, 2000; Huberman, 1983, 1990; Jacobson et al., 2004; Naidorf, 2014; Sá et al., 2011; Snow, 2014). In our preliminary work leading up to survey development, CRUE scholars interviewed researchers about their work and its connection to practice. Common themes emerged across these conversations, highlighting the disconnect between the incentive structure of research production, gaps in training and preparation, and their goals as scholars.

With respect to incentive structures, researchers we spoke with expressed concern about the time it takes to do impactful work and the demands of the expectation to conduct and publish work. One scholar noted:

> It's not enough to just get the word out and convince people; you've got to provide ongoing support too. I think most educational interventions—and certainly strategy instruction—are not something that you can just read about or hear about in a brief workshop and then be able to do well.

Other examples pointed to well-documented challenges with traditional values in promotion and tenure systems in higher education:

> Sometimes it's a hard balance when you're in a tenure-track position at a university and part of your goal has to be to publish your results in peer-reviewed journals that are of good quality.... And so, I think that is a tension that sort of goes up against my real goal, my ultimate goal, that those findings find their way to teachers and practitioners.

Efforts to promote conditions that address these issues, which, in turn, promote relevance, are found globally and across sectors other than education and may be instructive. Institutional structural supports, such as translation centers, positions for knowledge brokers, and outreach centers provide support for making research relevant to practice (Jacobson et al., 2004). Within the academy there are efforts to rethink the role of engagement and broaden what "counts" in promotion and tenure (Boyer, 1990; see Doberneck, 2016 for discussion) and calls for shifts in doctoral training (Austin & McDaniels, 2006; Paul & Marfo, 2001; Snow, 2014).

In the larger ecosystem, there has also been visible progress in conditions that support relevance. Several high profile philanthropic and federal funding sources have established agendas to promote more engaged scholarship (e.g., the Spencer Foundation and the William T. Grant Foundation), including providing funds for developing partnerships over time. Additional efforts include emphasizing more extensive and engaged dissemination plans, for example, in changes in the Institute for Education Sciences' request for applications. A more emergent set of efforts that promote relevance are found in global examples of research support or accountability for impact (e.g., ARC "Engagement and Impact" consultation (Australia), REF process (U.K.) and organizations of institutions seeking to maximize impact (e.g., Research Impact Canada). While we acknowledge accountability for impact is controversial in many ways, it does represent a shift in structures, processes, and incentives *toward* relevance.

These examples are not intended as recommendations but rather to point to a growing acknowledgement that research relevance is in fact shaped by the conditions in this larger ecosystem of research production and use, and that as researchers or leaders in the research community, we can influence those conditions in ways that help us achieve our goals as scholars.

ACHIEVING RELEVANCE TOGETHER

In this chapter we have sought to reframe relevance as attending to one of several gaps between the research and practice communities. Through this framework we identify sources of irrelevance and opportunities to address them, with the ultimate goal of supporting the use of research evidence. Our discussions invoke prior literature and current data, all of which point to the multifaceted nature of the disconnects that we are likely all too familiar with in our own experience. In this light, the path ahead may feel daunting at best, and insurmountable at worst.

However, no single researcher can address the longstanding barriers to research use in education. Our earlier caveat is worth restating: the problem of research use is bidirectional (perhaps multidirectional), and we have specifically focused on considerations for the researcher. In fact, a review of opportunities and challenges across our five gaps points unequivocally to a need to revisit research production *systemically*, to change not individual behavior but actions and conditions throughout the evidence ecosystem.

So, the path ahead is one demanding both individual and collective action. As a reader of this volume, you are likely one of myriad educational researchers frustrated with the disconnect between research and practice, seeking new ideas and strategies to be part of the solution. As an individual, we hope that the reframing of gaps is useful in informing the choices you make about your next research project, whether in topic, method, or dissemination. Through these choices, we can improve the relevance of research, but also generate knowledge and practices about research production that are valuable beyond our own work. Further, in our other roles as a teachers, leaders, collaborators, and advocates, we are positioned to be change agents, and we are in the company of many others, including the authors in this book. Together, we can mobilize newfound knowledge and practice to transform the evidence ecosystem and, ultimately, more meaningfully support educational policy for school improvement.

ABOUT THE CENTER AND ITS GOALS

The Center for Research Use in Education (CRUE) is an IES-funded knowledge utilization center charged with the measurement and description of research use in schools. Our mission is to expand the study of research use and produce a more holistic picture of what drives it, from the production of knowledge by researchers to the application of research in schools. We also seek to identify strategies that can make research more meaningful to classroom practice. At our center, we believe that education research is an important part of the educational process. We further believe that rigorous evidence, whether qualitative or quantitative, can foster better opportunities and outcomes for children by empowering educators, families, and communities with additional knowledge to inform better decision making. For this reason, we seek to support strong ties between research and practice.

ACKNOWLEDGMENTS

The research reported here was supported by the Institute of Education Sciences, U.S. Department of Education, through Grant R305C150017 to the University of Delaware.

REFERENCES

Amin, A., & Roberts, J. (2008). Knowing in action: Beyond communities of practice. *Research Policy, 37*(2), 353–369. https://doi.org/10.1016/j.respol.2007.11.003

Austin, A. E., & McDaniels, M. (2006). Using doctoral education to prepare faculty to work within Boyer's four domains of scholarship. *New Directions for Institutional Research, 2006*(129), 51–65.

Backer, T. E., Liberman, R. P., & Kuehnel, T. G. (1986). Dissemination and adoption of innovative psychosocial interventions. *Journal of Consulting and Clinical Psychology, 54*(1), 111–118. https://doi.org/10.1037/0022-006X.54.1.111

Billett, S. (2001). Knowing in practice: Re-conceptualising vocational expertise. *Learning and Instruction, 11*(6), 431–452. https://doi.org/10.1016/S0959-4752(00)00040-2

Birkeland, S., Murphy-Graham, E., & Weiss, C. (2005). Good reasons for ignoring good evaluation: The case of the drug abuse resistance education (DARE) program. *Evaluation and Program Planning, 28*(3), 247–256. https://doi.org/10.1016/j.evalprogplan.2005.04.001

Bogenschneider, K., & Corbett, T. J. (2011). *Evidence-based policymaking: Insights from policy-minded researchers and research-minded policymakers.* Routledge.

Bogenschneider, K., Olson, J. R., Linney, K. D., & Mills, J. (2000). Connecting research and policy: Implications for theory and practice from the Family Impact Seminars. *Family Relations 49*(3), 327–339. https://doi.org/10.1111/j.1741-3729.2000.00327.x

Boyer, E. L. (1990). *Scholarship reconsidered: Priorities of the professoriate*. Lawrenceville, NJ: Princeton University Press.

Broekkamp, H., & van Hout-Wolters, B. (2007). The gap between educational research and practice: A literature review, symposium, and questionnaire. *Educational Research and Evaluation, 13*(3), 203–220. https://doi.org/10.1080/13803610701626127

Coburn, C. E., & Penuel, W. R. (2016). Research–practice partnerships in education: Outcomes, dynamics, and open questions. *Educational Researcher, 45*(1), 48–54. https://doi.org/10.3102/0013189X16631750

Coburn, C. E., & Stein, M. K. (2010). Key lessons about the relationship between research and practice. In C. E. Coburn, M. K. Stein, J. Baxter, L. D'Amico, & A. Datnow (Eds.) *Research and practice in education: Building alliances, bridging the divide* (pp. 201–226). Rowman & Littlefield.

Coburn, C. E., & Talbert, J. E. (2006). Conceptions of evidence use in school districts: Mapping the terrain. *American Journal of Education, 112*(4), 469–495. https://doi.org/10.1086/505056

Colbeck, C. L. (2000). Reshaping the forces that perpetuate the research-practice gap: Focus on new faculty. *New Directions for Higher Education, 2000*(110), 35–47. https://doi.org/10.1002/he.11003

Cook, B. G., Cook, L., & Landrum, T. J. (2013). Moving research into practice: Can we make dissemination stick? *Exceptional Children, 79*(3), 163–180. https://doi.org/10.1177/001440291307900203

Corcoran, T., Fuhrman, S. H., & Belcher, C. L. (2001). The district role in instructional improvement. *Phi Delta Kappan, 83*(1), 78–84. https://doi.org/10.1177/003172170108300116

Cousins, J. B., & Earl, L. M. (1992). The case for participatory evaluation. *Educational Evaluation and Policy Analysis, 14*(4), 397–418. https://doi.org/10.3102/01623737014004397

Cousins, J. B., & Simon, M. (1996). The nature and impact of policy-induced partnerships between research and practice communities. *Educational Evaluation and Policy Analysis, 18*(3), 199–218. https://doi.org/10.3102/01623737018003199

Cousins, J., & Chouinard, J. (2012). *Participatory evaluation up close: An integration of research-based knowledge (Evaluation and society).* Information Age Publishing.

Daigneault, P. M. (2014). Taking stock of four decades of quantitative research on stakeholder participation and evaluation use: A systematic map. *Evaluation and Program Planning, 45*, 171–181. https://doi.org/10.1016/j.evalprogplan.2014.04.003

Doberneck, D. M. (2016). Are we there yet?: Outreach and engagement in the consortium for institutional cooperation promotion and tenure policies. *Journal of Community Engagement & Scholarship, 9*(1), 8–18. https://digitalcommons.northgeorgia.edu/jces/vol9/iss1/3

Dunn, W. N. (1980). The two-communities metaphor and models of knowledge use: An exploratory case study. *Knowledge: Creation, Diffusion, Utilization, 4*(1), 515–536. https://doi.org/10.1177/107554708000100403

Farley-Ripple, E., May, H., Karpyn, A., Tilley, K., & McDonough, K. (2018). Rethinking connections between research and practice in education: A conceptual framework. *Educational Researcher, 47*(4), 235–245.

Farrell, C. C., Davidson, K. L., Repko-Erwin, M., Penuel, W. R., Quantz, M., Wong, H., Riedy, R., & Brink, Z. (2018). *A descriptive study of the IES researcher–practitioner partnerships in education research program: Final report.* University of Colorado, Boulder, National Center for Research, Policy, and Practice. www.ncrpp.org.

Gherardi, S. (2009). Knowing and learning in practice-based studies: An introduction. *The Learning Organization, 16*(5), 352–359. https://doi.org/10.1108/09696470910974144

Gross, B., Kirst, M., Holland, D., & Luschei, T. (2005). Got you under my spell? How accountability policy is changing and not changing decision making in high schools. In B. Gross & M. Goertz (Eds.), *Holding high hopes: How high schools respond to state accountability policies* (pp. 43–80). Consortium for Policy Research in Education.

Hannaway, J. (1989). *Managers managing: The workings of an administrative system.* Oxford University Press.

Harrison, C., Davidson, K., & Farrell, C. (2017). Building productive relationships: District leaders' advice to researchers. *International Journal of Education Policy and Leadership, 12*(4).

Havelock, R.G., Guskin, A., Frohman, M., Havelock, M., Hill, M., & Huber, J. (1969). *A comparative study of the literature on the dissemination and utilization of scientific knowledge.* Center for Research on Utilization of Scientific Knowledge, Michigan University. https://files.eric.ed.gov/fulltext/ED029171.pdf

Henrick, E. C., Cobb, P., Penuel, W. R., Jackson, K., & Clark, T. (2017). *Assessing research-practice partnerships: Five dimensions of effectiveness.* William T. Grant Foundation. http://wtgrantfoundation.org/

Honig, M. I. (2003). Building policy from practice: District central office administrators' roles and capacity for implementing collaborative education policy. *Educational Administration Quarterly, 39*(3), 292–338. https://doi.org/10.1177/0013161X03253414

Honig, M. I., & Venkateswaran, N. (2012). School–central office relationships in evidence use: Understanding evidence use as a systems problem. *American Journal of Education, 118*(2), 199–222. https://doi.org/10.1086/663282

Huber, G. P. (1991). Organizational learning: The contributing processes and the literatures. *Organization Science, 2*(1), 88–115. https://doi.org/10.1287/orsc.2.1.88

Huberman, A. M. (1983). Improving social practice through the utilization of university-based knowledge. *Higher Education,12*(3), 257–272. https://doi.org/10.1007/BF00154422

Huberman, A. M. (1990). Linkage between researchers and practitioners: A qualitative study. *American Educational Research Journal, 27*(2), 363–391. https://doi.org/10.3102/00028312027002363

Huberman, M. (1994). Research utilization: The state of the art. *Knowledge and Policy, 7*(4), 13–33. https://doi.org/10.1007/BF02696290

Jacobson, N., Butterill, D., & Goering, P. (2004). Organizational factors that influence university-based researchers' engagement in knowledge transfer activities. *Science Communication, 25*(3), 246–259. https://doi.org/10.1177/1075547003262038

Kemmis, S., McTaggart, R., & Nixon, R. (2014). Introducing critical participatory action research. In Kemmis, S., McTaggart, R., & Nixon, R. (Eds.) *The action research planner* (pp. 1–31). Springer. https://doi.org/10.1007/978-981-4560-67-2

Landry, R., Amara, N., & Lamari, M. (2001). Utilization of social science research knowledge in Canada. *Research Policy, 30*(2), 333–349. https://doi.org/10.1016/S0048-7333(00)00081-0

Langer, L., Tripney, J., & Gough, D. A. (2016). *The science of using science: Researching the use of research evidence in decision-making.* EPPI-Centre, Social Science Research Unit, UCL Institute of Education, University College London. https://www.alliance4usefulevidence.org/

Lavis, J. N., Robertson, D., Woodside, J. M., McLeod, C. B., & Abelson, J. (2003). How can research organizations more effectively transfer research knowledge to decision makers? *The Milbank Quarterly, 81*(2), 221–248. https://doi.org/10.1111/1468-0009.t01-1-00052

Leithwood, K., & Steinbach, R. (1995). *Expert problem solving: Evidence from school and district leaders.* State University of New York Press.

Lindblom, C. E., & Cohen, D. K. (1979). *Usable knowledge: Social science and social problem solving.* Yale University Press.

Louis, K. S., & Dentler, R. A. (1988). Knowledge use and school improvement. *Curriculum Inquiry, 18*(1), 33–62. https://doi.org/10.1080/03626784.1988.11076025

Malin, J. R., Brown, C., & Trubceac, A. S. (2018). Going for broke: A multiple-case study of brokerage in education. *AERA Open, 4*(2), 1–14. https://doi.org/10.1177/2332858418769297

March, J. G. (1994). *A primer on decision making.* The Free Press.

Meyer, L. H., Park, H. S., Grenot-Scheyer, M., Schwartz, I., & Harry, B. (1998). Participatory research: New approaches to the research to practice dilemma. *Journal of the Association for Persons with Severe Handicaps, 23*(3), 165–177. https://doi.org/10.2511/rpsd.23.3.165

Naidorf, J. C. (2014). Knowledge utility: From social relevance to knowledge mobilization. *Education Policy Analysis Archives, 22*(89), 1–31. http://dx.doi.org/10.14507/epaa.v22n89.2014

Neal, J. W., Neal, Z. P., Lawlor, J. A., Mills, K. J., & McAlindon, K. (2018). What makes research useful for public school educators? *Administration and Policy in Mental Health and Mental Health Services Research, 45*(3), 432–446. https://doi.org/10.1007/s10488-017-0834-x

Neal, J. W., Neal, Z. P., Mills, K. J., Lawlor, J. A., & McAlindon, K. (2019). What types of brokerage bridge the research-practice gap? The case of public school educators. *Social Networks, 59*(2019), 41–49. https://doi.org/10.1016/j.socnet.2019.05.006

Nelson, J., & Campbell, C. (2019). Using evidence in education. In A. Boaz, H. Davies, A. Fraser, & S. Nutley (Eds.), *What works now?: Evidence-informed policy and practice* (pp. 131–150). Policy Press.

Nolan, M., Hanson, E., Grant, G., Keady, J., & Magnusson, L. (2007). Introduction: What counts as knowledge, whose knowledge counts? Towards authentic participatory enquiry. In M. Nolan, E. Hanson, G. Grant, & J. Keady (Eds.), *User participation in health and social care research* (pp. 1–13). Open University Press.

Pallas, A. M. (2001). Preparing education doctoral students for epistemological diversity. *Educational Researcher, 30*(5), 6–11. https://doi.org/10.3102/0013189X030005006

Paul, J. L., & Marfo, K. (2001). Preparation of educational researchers in philosophical foundations of inquiry. *Review of Educational Research, 71*(4), 525–547. https://doi.org/10.3102/00346543071004525

Pols, J. (2014). Knowing patients: Turning patient knowledge into science. *Science, Technology, & Human Values, 39*(1), 73–97. https://doi.org/10.1177/0162243913504306

Prendergast, S., & Rickinson, M. (2019). Understanding school engagement in and with research. *The Australian Educational Researcher, 46*(1), 17–39. https://doi.org/10.1007/s13384-018-0292-9

Reichardt, R. (2000). *The state's role in supporting data-driven decision-making: A view of Wyoming.* Mid-Continent Research for Education and Learning. https://eric.ed.gov/?id=ED449186

Rickinson, M., De Bruin, K., Walsh, L., & Hall, M. (2017). What can evidence-use in practice learn from evidence-use in policy? *Educational Research, 59*(2), 173-189.

Sá, C. M., Li, S. X., & Faubert, B. (2011). Faculties of education and institutional strategies for knowledge mobilization: An exploratory study. *Higher Education, 61*(5), 501–512. https://doi.org/10.1007/s10734-010-9344-4

Schön, D. A. (1995). Knowing-in-action: The new scholarship requires a new epistemology. *Change: The Magazine of Higher Learning, 27*(6), 27–34.

Shepherd, J. P. (2007). The production and management of evidence for public service reform. *Evidence and Policy, 3*(2), 231–251. https://doi.org/10.1332/174426407781172225

Shepherd, J. P. (2014). How to achieve more effective services: The evidence ecosystem. Cardiff University, What Works Network, Cardiff University. http://orca.cf.ac.uk/id/eprint/69077

Shipman, T., Bannon, S. H., & Nunes-Bufford, K. (2015). The information-seeking habits of in-service educators. *College & Research Libraries, 76*(2), 120–135. https://doi.org/10.5860/crl.76.2.120

Smeyers, P., & Depaepe, M. (Eds.). (2006). *Educational research: Why" what works" doesn't work.* Springer.

Snow, C. E. (2015). 2014 Wallace Foundation distinguished lecture: Rigor and realism: Doing educational science in the real world. *Educational Researcher, 44*(9), 460-466.

Supovitz, J. A., & Klein, V. (2003). *Mapping a course for improved student learning: How innovative schools systematically use student performance data to guide improvement.* Consortium for Policy Research in Education. https://repository.upenn.edu/cpre_researchreports/39

Tebes, J. (2005). Community science, philosophy of science, and the practice of research. *American Journal of Community Psychology, 35*(3-4), 213–230. https://doi.org/10.1007/s10464-005-3399-x

Tseng, V., & Nutley, S. (2014). Building the infrastructure to improve the use and usefulness of research in education. In K. S. Finnigan & A. J. Daly (Eds.), *Using research evidence in education* (pp. 163–175). Springer.

Tilley, K., Wang, R., & Blackman, H. (2019, April). *A (mis)match? Evaluating the preferences of characteristics of research products among research-users and producers.* Paper presented at the annual meeting of the American Education Research Association, Toronto, Canada.

West, R. F., & Rhoton, C. (1994). School district administrators' perceptions of educational research and barriers to research utilization. *ERS Spectrum, 12*(1), 23–30.

ABOUT THE EDITORS AND AUTHORS

EDITORS

Angela Urick is an associate professor in the Department of Educational Leadership in the School of Education at Baylor University. In her academic program, she trains aspiring district leaders as well as education administrators in state level organizations. She specializes in leadership for school improvement for more equitable student opportunities. Through her work on academic climate and the relationship between principals and teachers, she uses innovative applications of theory and advanced quantitative techniques to understand the broader complexities of how leadership and policy decisions may influence school progress. From 2015–2017, Dr. Urick served as PI on a faculty research grant from the American Educational Research Association (AERA) sponsored by the National Science Foundation to study the extent that instructional leadership may mediate the effects of student economic disadvantage on opportunity to learn. Her work has been published in *Leadership and Policy in Schools, Educational Administration Quarterly, Journal of Educational Administration, Journal of Education Finance,* among others.

David DeMatthews is an associate professor in the Department of Educational Leadership and Policy at the University of Texas at Austin. He has worked with urban districts as a high school teacher, middle school administrator, and district administrator. His research interests include K–12 school leadership, dual-language education, urban education, and social justice. His work has appeared in top-tier peer-reviewed research journals such as *Educational Administration Quarterly, Teachers College Record, Urban Education, Journal of School Leadership*, and *Leadership and Policy in Schools*, as well as in the mainstream media in *Education Week, USA Today, The Hill, The Baltimore Sun, The Texas Tribune, Houston Chronicle*, and the *Dallas Morning News*. David has recently authored a book, *Community Engaged Leadership for Social Justice: A Critical Approach in Urban Schools*, with Routledge.

Timothy G. Ford is an associate professor of Educational Leadership and Policy Studies and Senior Research Scientist for the Oklahoma Center for Education Policy at the University of Oklahoma. His research agenda is focused on improving working conditions for school professionals, which constitute a significant barrier to the effective functioning of schools as social organizations and contribute substantially to employee dissatisfaction, burnout, and turnover. He current serves on the editorial boards of both the *American Educational Research Journal* and the *International Journal of Educational Policy and Leadership*. His work has been published in prominent journals in leadership and educational policy such as *Review of Educational Research, Education Policy, Educational Administration Quarterly, Journal of Educational Administration*, and *Leadership and Policy in Schools*.

AUTHORS

Catharine Biddle is an assistant professor of Educational Leadership at the University of Maine. Her research focuses on how schools can more effectively leverage partnerships with external organizations or groups to address issues of social inequality and how nontraditional leaders—such as youth, parents and other community members—may lead or serve as partners in these efforts. Her interests are driven by her professional background in community development that leverages schools. Prior to joining the faculty at UMaine, Dr. Biddle also served as the executive director of the Nanubhai Education Foundation, an international education nonprofit working in rural India, and as an out of school time educator for the national nonprofit organization Citizen Schools. Her research has been featured in the *Peabody Journal of Education*, the *Review of Research in Education*, and the *American Journal of Education*.

T. Jameson Brewer is an assistant professor of Social Foundations of Education at the University of North Georgia. Broadly conceptualized, his research focuses on the impact of privatization and marketization of public education by way of school vouchers, charter schools, alternative teacher certification, and homeschooling. Follow him on Twitter: @ tjamesonbrewer

Casey D. Cobb is the Raymond Neag Professor of Educational Policy at the Neag School of Education at the University of Connecticut. Dr. Cobb is a National Education Policy Center Fellow and a member of the Research Advisory Panel for the National Coalition on School Diversity. His current research interests include policies on school choice, accountability, and school reform, where he examines the implications for equity and educational opportunity. He is coauthor of *Fundamentals of Statistical Reasoning in Education* (Wiley/Jossey Bass, 4th ed.) and *Leading Dynamic Schools* (Corwin Press). Dr. Cobb is a former member of Connecticut's Region 19 School Board. He holds an AB from Harvard University, an MS from the University of Maine, and a PhD from Arizona State University.

Amanda Cooper, associate professor in Educational Leadership and Policy at Queen's University, is the founder of RIPPLE (Research Informing Policy, Practice and Leadership in Education): a program of research, training and knowledge mobilization aimed at learning more about how knowledge brokering can increase research use and impact in education by facilitating collaboration between multi-stakeholder networks (www.ripplenetwork.ca).

Kendrick Davis is the Vice President of Policy Research for the Campaign for College Opportunity in Los Angeles, California. Kendrick served as an education policy fellow for U.S. Senator Kamala Harris where he was selected as an American Education Research Association (AERA)/American Academy for the Advancement of Science (AAAS) Science and Engineering Congressional Fellow. Prior to his work in D.C., Kendrick served in the mayoral administrations of Michael Nutter and Jim Kenney as the director of science, technology, engineering, and mathematics (STEM) initiatives for the City of Philadelphia. Kendrick earned his PhD in higher education and his master's degrees in law and robotics engineering from the University of Pennsylvania. His bachelor's in mechanical engineering is from Temple University.

David DeMatthews is an associate professor in the Department of Educational Leadership and Policy at the University of Texas at Austin. He has worked with urban districts as a high school teacher, middle school administrator, and district administrator. His research interests include K–12 school leadership, dual-language education, urban education, and social justice. His work has appeared in top-tier peer-reviewed research journals such as *Educational Administration Quarterly, Teachers College Record, Urban Education, Journal of School Leadership*, and *Leadership and Policy in Schools*, as well as in the mainstream media in *Education Week, USA Today, The Hill, The Baltimore Sun, The Texas Tribune, Houston Chronicle*, and the *Dallas Morning News*. David has recently authored a book, *Community Engaged Leadership for Social Justice: A Critical Approach in Urban Schools*, with Routledge.

Elizabeth Farley-Ripple is an associate professor of Education and Public Policy in the School of Education at the University of Delaware. Her research expertise is in policy analysis and evidence-based decision-making, and she has worked on a range of educational and social policy issues, including research use in at all levels of the system, administrator mobility, and school and teachers' use of data. Currently, Dr. Farley-Ripple serves as the Director for the University of Delaware Partnership for Public Education and coleads the IES-funded Center for Research Use in Education.

Carly Feldman served as a 2018–2019 AERA/AAAS Congressional Science & Engineering Fellow where she focused on education and disability policy. She is interested educational policy as a lever to support all children. Her research explores schools' organizational responses to federal and local policy initiatives, and how these organizational structures influence teachers' work. She completed a postdoctoral fellowship with the National Center for Research in Policy and Practice at Northwestern University, earned her doctorate from the University of Wisconsin-Madison in educational policy studies, and her BA in mathematics from Wellesley College. A product of the Vermont public education system, Rachel formerly taught middle and high school math.

Julian Vasquez Heilig is the Dean and a Professor of Educational Policy Studies and Evaluation at the University of Kentucky College of Education. He has held a variety of practitioner and research positions in organizations from Boston to Beijing. His leadership experiences have provided formative professional perspectives to bridge research, theory, and practice. Julian obtained his Ph.D. in Education Administration and Policy Analysis and a Masters in Sociology from Stanford University. He also holds a Master's of Higher Education and a Bachelor's of History and Psychology from the University of Michigan Ann Arbor. He blogs at Cloaking Inequity, consistently rated one of the top 50 education websites in the world by Teach100. Follow him on Twitter @ProfessorJVH.

Kimberly Kappler Hewitt serves as director for the Principal Preparation for Excellence and Equity in Rural Schools (PPEERS) program, which involves a partnership with 10 rural districts. She received the 2016 UNCG School of Education Distinguished Researcher Award and was a 2015 UNCG Faculty Excellence in Research and Creative Activity Honoree. Dr. Hewitt teaches instructional leadership, data use, qualitative methods, and internship classes, and her research focuses on leadership preparation; instructional leadership, equity and social justice, and sustaining reform.

Derek A. Houston is an assistant professor of Educational Leadership and Policy Studies at the University of Oklahoma. Using multilevel and quasi-experimental methods and broadly grounded in critical theory, his research centers issues of equity and justice in an exploration of how resource inequality impacts post-secondary preparation, access, and matriculation for marginalized populations. Follow him on Twitter: @DA_Houston

William Kyle Ingle is an associate professor and assistant chair in the Department of Educational Leadership, Evaluation, and Organizational Development at the University of Louisville. His research interests include human resource functions in education, the politics of education, and economic evaluations of education programs.

Lebon Daniel James III is a PhD student in the Educational Policy and Planning program in the College of Education's Department of Educational Leadership and Policy at the University of Texas at Austin. His research focuses on K–12 educational leadership preparation, the role of principals, and school improvement.

Sarah Winchell Lenhoff is an assistant professor of educational leadership and policy studies at Wayne State University. Lenhoff began her career as a New York City public school teacher. Her research focuses on education policy implementation and equity, analyzed through the lenses of social and organizational psychology. Her recent research has examined district and school infrastructure to support school improvement; the effects of school choice policy on equitable opportunities for students; and the causes and interventions to address student absenteeism. She co-directs the Detroit Education Research Partnership, a research partnership with Detroit Public Schools Community District and the Every School Day Counts Detroit coalition.

Sarah Lilly is a PhD student in the Department of Curriculum, Instruction and Special Education at the University of Virginia. Her research centers on STEM education, particularly focusing on the integration of math and science concepts with computational modeling and engineering design practices in technology-enhanced learning environments. Prior to beginning doctoral work, she taught secondary mathematics for four years as well as created and implemented an interdisciplinary, project-based mathematics, science, and principles-of-technology curriculum for freshmen and sophomore high school students in Albemarle County, Virginia.

Stephen MacGregor is a PhD candidate at the Faculty of Education, Queen's University. His research focuses on how education stakeholders, particularly higher education institutions, can build their capacity in knowledge mobilization to enhance and accelerate research impact. His research draws from the traditions of mixed methods and social network theory in order to model and describe the flows of information and resources in multi-stakeholder networks.

Joel R. Malin is an assistant professor of Educational Leadership at Miami University. Malin's research focuses on research-practice-policy connections, and upon the leadership and organization of complex, cross-sector collaborations. His research in the latter area has primarily addressed college and career readiness reforms, occurring at the intersection of secondary and higher education. In the former area, Joel has been especially focused on: (1) understanding the nature of educators' research use and engagement; (2) understanding the nature and influence of educational intermediaries/brokers that seek to support the use of research and professional ideas in practice; and (3) considering how to leverage existing networks to enhance research engagement. His book, *The Role of Knowledge Brokers in Education* (edited with Chris Brown), was published by Routledge in 2019. Joel, a member of the Scholars Strategy Network, has served as the Treasurer of the American Educational Research Association's (AERA) Research Use Special Interest Group, and was recently honored with the University of Illinois at Urbana-Champaign's Young Alumni Award.

Katherine Cumings Mansfield is an associate professor at University of North Carolina Greensboro. After completing her PhD in Educational Policy and Planning, entered academe fulltime at Virginia Commonwealth University in Richmond. In 2012, Dr. Mansfield was awarded the "Leadership for Social Justice Dissertation Award" and the "Selma Greenberg Outstanding Dissertation Award" sponsored by the American Educational Research Association for her dissertation titled, "Troubling Social Justice in a Single-sex Public School: An Ethnography of an Emerging School Culture." In 2014, graduate students nominated and selected Mansfield to receive the *Charles P. Ruch Award for Excellence in Teaching*. In 2016, fellow colleagues nominated and selected Mansfield to receive the *VCU School of Education Distinguished Junior Faculty Award* presented annually to one junior faculty member who has demonstrated excellence in the areas of teaching, research, and service.

Dana L. Mitra has conducted research on voice and leadership as a Professor of Education Policy Studies at the Pennsylvania State University for the past 15 years. In her work as a professor, she was named as a Students at the Center "Distinguished Fellow" with Jobs For the Future/the Nellie Mae Foundation in 2016. She is founding editor of the *International Journal of Student Voice* and coeditor of *The American Journal of Education*. Dana has published over 30 papers and two books on the topics of student voice and civic engagement. Her books include *Civic Education in the Elementary Grades: Promoting Engagement in an Era of Accountability*, *Student Voice in School Reform: Building Youth-Adult Partnerships that Empower Youth*, and a textbook entitled *Educational Change and the Political Process*.

Ben Pogodzinski is an associate professor of educational leadership and policy studies at Wayne State University. His current research interests focus on how state and district policies, school organizational context, and community factors influence student enrollment and attendance patterns. His additional research focuses on the organization and sustainability of Catholic schools.

Amanda U. Potterton is an assistant professor in the Department of Educational Leadership Studies in the College of Education at the University of Kentucky. Her research and teaching interests include the politics of school choice, charter schools, privatization and public education, and the justice-related implications of these policies for students living in poverty, for students with special education needs, and for students who are English language learners. Amanda's current research agenda focuses on how public-school stakeholders, including parents, students, teachers, school leaders, and other community members, interpret and experience school choice policies and practices in local settings. Prior to pursuing her PhD, she was a New York City Teaching Fellow and taught special education in New York City, and she was a teacher and school leader in the United Kingdom. Amanda holds a PhD in Educational Policy and Evaluation from the Mary Lou Fulton Teachers College, Arizona State University.

Heather E. Price is assistant professor in the Leadership Studies doctoral program at Marian University with a joint appointment in the Social, Behavioral, and Justice Sciences Department. Her research focuses on sociology, school climate, school networks, teacher commitment, and educational policy. Her research is published in peer-reviewed journals of the *American Educational Research Journal, Education Administration Quarterly,*

Educational Policy, Journal of Educational Administration, and *Social Science Research* as well as numerous book chapters. Price serves as a consultant for the Organization for Economic Cooperation and Development (OECD) for the Teaching and *Learning International Survey (TALIS)*. Price actively participates and presents in professional organizations of the American Educational Research Association (AERA), American Sociological Association, and the Sociology of Education Association where she regularly reviews for flagship journals and annual conference submissions. Price has been involved in service to the AERA SESI and other SIGs. Prior to Marian, Price worked years as a senior analyst at the University of Notre Dame and in the private educational policy sector and taught for years in the Milwaukee Public Schools district.

Alexa Quinn is a PhD student in the Department of Curriculum, Instruction and Special Education at the University of Virginia. Her research interests are centered on elementary teacher preparation with a focus on reading and writing across content areas and working with culturally and linguistically diverse students. Prior to beginning doctoral study, she was a fourth grade teacher, instructional coach, and assistant principal in New York City and later worked as a curriculum specialist supporting teachers and students in New York, New Jersey, Washington D.C., and Louisiana.

Diane Ravitch is a historian of education. She earned her PhD in the history of American education from the Columbia University Graduate School of Arts and Sciences in 1975. She has received 10 honorary doctorate awards. She received the Daniel Patrick Moynihan Award from the American Academy of Political and Social Sciences in 2011 and the Grawemeyer Award in 2014. Her most recent book is *Slaying Goliath: The Passionate Resistance to Privatization and the Fight to Save America's Public Schools* (Knopf, 2020).

Richard J. Reddick is a fellow in the W. K. Kellogg Professorship in Community College Leadership and professor of Higher Education Leadership and African and African Diaspora Studies at The University of Texas at Austin. His research focuses on the phenomenological exploration of Black faculty experiences at predominantly White institutions and developmental relationships in higher education.

Pedro Reyes is the Ashbel Smith Professor of Education Leadership & Policy, College of Education, The University of Texas at Austin, Fellow of the H.E. Hartfelder/Southland Corp Regents Chair; Research Scientist at the Population Research Center; and Executive Director and Principal Investigator, Texas Education Research Center. His research focuses on

Education and Opportunity, particularly on student success for children of poverty. His current work is centered at the intersection of school leadership, policy, and student success.

Michael R. Scott is a PhD candidate in educational policy and planning at The University of Texas at Austin. His research emphasizes the geographic principles of place and scale to explore the mechanisms of education and social policy, particularly as they affect students of historically marginalized backgrounds.

Scott Sheridan is a student at the University of Delaware pursuing his PhD in Education. Scott's many research interests include designing effective professional development for technology integration in schools and how research affects the decision-making process in schools. At present, Scott is working on his dissertation studying the effects of Computer Science Professional Development on teachers' classroom practice while volunteering on research initiatives through the Center for Research Use in Education at UD.

Samantha Shewchuk specializes in knowledge mobilization efforts to address the research-policy-practice gaps across public service sectors. Currently, Samantha is a postdoctoral researcher at the Center for Research Use in Education at the University of Delaware where she is managing a project that seeks to map the network of actors, relationships, and processes in the 'third space' between education research and practice.

Jeremy Singer is a doctoral student of educational leadership and policy studies at Wayne State University in Detroit, MI. He serves as a research assistant for the Detroit Education Research Partnership. He formerly taught in the Detroit Public Schools.

Katherine Tilley is a Ph.D. candidate in Education at the University of Delaware and a project associate at the Center for Research Use in Education. She is an applied education researcher with expertise in qualitative and mixed methods evaluation. Her research interests include equity, intergroup relations, sociocultural approaches, diversity, and inclusion, and she is currently completing a dissertation examining the relationship between problem framing and evidence use in school decision making.

Yinying Wang is an assistant professor of Educational Leadership in the Department of Educational Policy Studies at College of Education and Human Development in Georgia State University. Her research interest intersects technology, decision making, emotions, neuroscience, social network analysis, text mining in educational leadership and policy. In addition to teaching educational leadership courses, she also teaches social network analysis. Her background includes medical doctor, classroom teacher, and school administrator.

R. Aaron Wisman is an assistant professor in the Department of Advanced Educational Studies at California State University, Bakersfield. His research interests include school diversity and academic achievement of marginalized students, diversity and equity policies, leadership in high-minority/high-poverty contexts, and school turnaround.

Tyler Woodward is a PhD student in the Department of Curriculum, Instruction, and Special Education at the Curry School of Education and Human Development, University of Virginia. His research interests largely focus on social studies education topics, including the facilitation of controversial issue discussions in secondary history classrooms and teacher development. Before beginning doctoral study, he worked as a sixth and seventh grade history teacher in rural Virginia.

Meredith Wronowski is an assistant professor in the Educational Administration department at the University of Dayton. Her research interests are focused on issues of equity in schooling including the unintended effects of accountability policies on teachers and leaders, opportunity to learn, community-based school improvement, and resegregation of U.S. schools.

Peter Youngs is a professor in the Department of Curriculum, Instruction and Special Education at the University of Virginia. He has published extensively on teacher quality, educational leadership, and school reform and has pioneered the use of innovative research methods, including social network analysis and the experience sampling method, in the area of beginning teacher induction. Dr. Youngs has served as principal investigator for large-scale, mixed-methods studies funded by the Carnegie Corporation of New York, the Institute of Education Sciences, the National Science Foundation, the Spencer Foundation, and the William T. Grant Foundation. These studies have examined (a) beginning teacher commitment and retention, (b) factors that influence elementary mathematics instruction, and (c) principal evaluation. Recent publications have appeared in *Elementary School Journal, Teachers College Record,* and *Teaching and Teacher Education.* He currently serves as coeditor of *American Educational Research Journal.*